The Love of Mountains
Is Best

Robert H. Bates

The Love of Mountains Is Best

CLIMBS AND TRAVELS FROM K2 TO KATHMANDU

Robert H. Bates

PETER E. RANDALL PUBLISHER
Portsmouth, New Hampshire

Peter E. Randall Publisher
Box 4726
Portsmouth, NH 03802-4726

Designed by Tom Allen/Pear Graphic Design

Front endpaper: Mts. Lucania (left) and Steele. Bates and Bradford Washburn descended the ridge at right, 1937. Photograph by Bradford Washburn.

Read endpaper: Steele Glacier, Mt. Steele. Bates and Bradford Washburn descended the ridge at right and followed the glacier to the Donjek River, 1937 (compare to front end leaf). Photograph by Bradford Washburn.

Library of Congress Cataloging-in-Publication data
Bates, Robert H. (Robert Hicks)
  The love of mountains is best : climbs and travels from K2 to Kathmandu / Robert H. Bates.
    p. cm.
  Includes index.
  ISBN 0-914339-50-8
  1. Bates, Robert H. (Robert Hicks). 2. Mountaineers--United States-- Biography. I. Title.
GV199.92.B38A3 1994
796.5'22'092--dc20
[B]   94-25975
                                                                          CIP

To

Gail Oberlin Bates

a grand partner and companion
both at home
and while traveling in regions
from Mt. Ararat to Phoksumdo Tal.

CONTENTS

Foreword IX

Introduction XI

Acknowledgments XIII

BATES CHRONOLOGY XIV

I   Beginnings 1

II   From the White Mountains to Alaska 7

III   Harvard and Mt. Crillon 22

IV   The National Geographic Society Yukon Expedition 39

V   At the University of Pennsylvania, Oxford
and Chamonix 67

VI   Mt. Lucania 71

VII   K2 99

VIII Overland from Peshawar to Istanbul 143

IX   *Five Miles High*, the Alps, and Exeter 159

X   The Wood Yukon Expedition 167

XI   World War II: The OQMG and Mt. McKinley 183

XII   Italy 216

XIII Body Armor and the End of the War 231

XIV After the War 242

XV   The Saint Elias Mountains Again 245

XVI K2 Once More 257

XVII Marriage 291

XVIII The Ojos del Salado 299

XIX Mt. Koven and Glacier Peak 310

XX   The Peace Corps and Kathmandu 314

XXI	Iceland and the Matterhorn Centennial	333
XXII	Outward Bound and Mt. Russell	337
XXIII	Phoksumdo Tal and Sikkim.	343
XXIV	Southern India, Kenya, and the Ruwenzori	351
XXV	Shah Dev.	358
XXVI	Mexico, Tsering, Eastern Europe, and Mt. Ararat	361
XXVII	The Mesahib Expedition and the Coronation	371
XXVIII	Manzoor's Wedding, Tigers, and the Triple Expedition	377
XXIX	Afghanistan and the Minaret of Jam.	383
XXX	China	393
XXXI	Botswana.	403
XXXII	Efforts to Reach the Great Ice Mountain.	409
XXXIII	The White House	414
XXXIV	Egypt.	417
XXXV	India, Nepal, and Bhutan	421
XXXVI	The Great Ice Mountain at Last	433
XXXVII	In Retrospect	473

Index 474

Who Is This Man?

ALTHOUGH THE AUTHOR has been my close friend for more than 60 years, I never think of him as Bob because of an episode in his second year as a student at Exeter. One day while translating the Anabasis in Greek class, he stumbled over the words ". . . bustards and ostriches"—which came out "bistriches." Since then, for me and many of his friends he has always been Bistrich, a special name for a very special person.

This is a remarkable man, and he has written a wonderful collection of tales. Bistrich—but I must call him Bob—has four special characteristics.

He is endlessly enthusiastic and cheerful. When the weather has soured, the tent has burned, the food bags are empty, Bistrich can still sing one of his many ballads, and get others to join. I don't believe I've ever seen him downcast, but I did see him furious once in 1932. We were walking beside a swift stream in Alaska when a treasured hunting gun fell into the rapids, obviously gone forever. Bistrich stormed off, raging; in a futile gesture I reached into the rushing water and my hand grasped the gun. Later he almost collapsed with relief.

He is the warmest most outgoing person I know, making friends around the world—and keeping them for life. He and Gail have opened their home to a stream of former students, Peace Corps Volunteers, and mountaineers from anywhere. He is embarrassed if you ask about his friends and mumbles, "Oh, a few, I guess." But he knows everyone, from kings and princes to Sherpa mountaineers. Ask if he knows anyone in, say, Uganda, and he'll come up with a name.

He, and later he and Gail together have been everywhere worth going! You may be astounded and disbelieving about the details in this record of travels, covering 70 years all over the world. But Bistrich kept a journal on his travels, no matter how difficult, and this book is really a condensation of these journals. I've challenged him once or twice about facts: He has always had them right. But even though we have been close for all these decades, I did not appreciate how much he and Gail had done, how far they had ranged, how varied their experiences have been.

Finally, he is unfailingly generous. He gives himself as no one I have ever known—essential for a good teacher, which he is. He will accept any inconvenience or discomfort to help a friend—or a casual acquaintance. I don't remember ever hearing him say an unkind word, even about someone I know he dislikes (very few) or distrusts. Like one of the Seven Dwarfs, if he can't say something nice, he says nothing at all. The most obstructive bureaucrat, the laziest or most delinquent companion is excused or unmentioned. One might think his world inhabited only by good guys. Fortunately there's a tiny sour side, revealed rarely and only in private. He does not tolerate fools gladly.

Pervading the book are two sentiments: his interest in and affection for people, and his love of mountains, any mountain or hill, without regard to height, or difficulty, or notoriety. For Bistrich high mountains are a feeling, felt in the heart and felt along the blood. And this book is not a book; who touches this, touches a man.

—Charles S. Houston, MD

ACKNOWLEDGMENTS

ONE REASON MOUNTAINS HAVE BEEN BEST for me is because they have brought me my mountain friends, friends who mean more to me than anyone except Gail and members of my immediate family. Most of these friends have been climbing companions on expeditions, and, as you will see, have helped with every part of this book. My only regret is that I cannot show adequately here how much they all mean to me.

Charlie Houston has read the manuscript, written the foreword, and provided pictures from our expeditions to K2 in 1938 and 1953. Brad Washburn has provided many beautiful photographs from our five expeditions to Alaska and the Yukon, and has used his diary to check the details of our long walk from Mt. Lucania in 1937. Bill House, who has also read the manuscript, has contributed his pictures of our 1938 K2 expedition and subsequent travels through Afghanistan, as well as pictures taken in the Tetons in 1940. Adams and Ann Carter have given photographs from the Ojos del Salado and Mt. Russell, and our Memsahib Expedition to K2 in 1974; while Dee Molenaar is responsible for the fine drawings of K2 and the many maps of regions of travel. Nick Clinch, Jeff Foott, and others on our 1985 Chinese-American expedition to the Great Ice Mountain on the Tibet-Xinjiang frontier have also provided much-appreciated photographs.

I thank too Andy Bakewell and Peter Wood for pictures taken on our Yukon expeditions of 1941 and 1951, and George Bell for his pictures taken on K2 in 1953. Thanks to David Robertson, I can show a view of us in the Alps in 1936. My thanks also to Ruth Holcombe for the use of her diary on our crossing of central Afghanistan in 1979, and to Brian Okonek for his view of Mt. Russell in the Alaska Range. Jolene Unsoeld, member of the House of Representatives from the state of Washington's third district, lent the picture of her bearded husband.

In particular, I want to thank George and Jane Russell, with whom Gail and I trekked in Nepal and Bhutan in 1985, for their pictures, encouragement, and the financial support that made this book possible. (George and I have been good friends since before he was president of the Exeter Mountaineering Club in the late 1940s.) Thanks also go to all the devoted members of the Frank Russell Company who helped to decipher and type the manuscript. Also my thanks to Sharon Cloud Hogan for her careful editing, to Tom Allen for his efforts with the design, to Kathleen Brandes for her extraordinary work on the index and accuracy of details, and to Peter Randall, our publisher, with whom I greatly enjoyed working.

Most of all my thanks go to Gail, who took many of the pictures of our travels, gave wise counsel, and month after month put up with a flood of letters, diaries, slides, photographs, and maps that like the Mississippi-Missouri flood burst out of the restraining areas and threatened to engulf our home.

INTRODUCTION

THIS IS NEITHER A BIOGRAPHY nor a book about teaching, though I have been a teacher for more than 40 years, mainly at Phillips Exeter Academy, a fine old boarding school in New Hampshire. During vacations and leaves of absence, mountains and travels have given me experiences very different from those in my academic work. Fortunately, I began climbing when none of the highest mountains had been climbed and jet travel was unknown. Mountains also have brought friends who mean more to me than any mountain, and indirectly my wife, Gail, dear and constant companion for 40 years.

Experiences described here include three visits to K2 (two of them serious attempts to make the first ascent); winter exploration by dog team of the Saint Elias Mountains in Yukon Territory for the National Geographic Society; the third ascent of Denali (Mt. McKinley) for the U.S. Army; testing army clothing and equipment during combat at Anzio in World War II; directing the first Peace Corps group in Nepal; and traveling to the mysterious Great Ice Mountain on the Xinjiang (Sinkiang)-Tibetan border as part of the first China-U.S. mountaineering expedition.

I like people, have had a happy life, and love my family. My extended family includes relatives, former students, former Peace Corps volunteers, and many mountaineering companions. Among the latter are, or have been, for some are now deceased, Charlie Houston, Brad Washburn, Adams Carter, Bill House, John Case, Nick Clinch, Tom Hornbein, Pete Schoening, Terris Moore, Bob Craig, Dee Molenaar, George Bell, Walter Wood, Andy Bakewell, Al Jackman, Willi Unsoeld, and Dave Robertson. Life with Gail and our travels together have been great fun. We have investigated the Ruwenzori, the Kanjirobi Himal, the Atacama Desert, and the Okavango Delta—and we aren't finished yet!

BATES CHRONOLOGY

1911   Born in Philadelphia.

1916   Climbs Flying Mountain.

1918-19   Climbs in White Mountains of New Hampshire.

1920   Summer home at Ogunquit, Maine.

1925   Death of mother.

1927-29   Student at Phillips Exeter Academy.

1929   Enters Harvard College.

1930-31   Meets Bradford Washburn. Winter climbs in White Mountains.

1932   Expedition to Mt. Crillon in the Fairweather Range, Alaska.

1933   Graduates from Harvard. Returns to Mt. Crillon with Washburn, Charlie Houston, and Adams Carter.

1934   Attends Harvard Graduate School.

1935-36   National Geographic Society Yukon Expedition. Begins teaching at University of Pennsylvania.

1937   Climbs Mt. Lucania.

1938   First American expedition to K2. Team climbs 4,000 feet higher on K2 than anyone before, setting American altitude record. Returns overland across Afghanistan.

1939   Begins teaching at Phillips Exeter Academy. *Five Miles High* published.

1940   Climbs in Canadian Rockies and Grand Tetons.

1941   Wood Yukon Expedition. Testing for the army. Climbs Mt. Wood and Mt. Walsh. Leave of absence to work at War Department.

1942   Commissioned captain. Alaskan Test Expedition. Makes third ascent of Denali (Mt. McKinley).

1943   Tests U.S. clothing and equipment. Hudson Bay.

1944   Task force commander. Major clothing and equipment test in combat at Anzio.

1945   Helps to develop body armor. War ends.

1946-47   Receives Ph.D. Thesis: "The Literature of the Mountains."

1951 Saint Elias Mountains, crevasse, missing plane.

1953 K2

1954-55 Marriage and honeymoon.

1956 Chile and the Ojos del Salado.

1957 Wind River Range.

1958 President of the American Alpine Club. Switzerland.

1959 Mexico.

1960 Norway.

1962-63 The Peace Corps and Kathmandu.

1964 Iceland, the Hebrides, and the Matterhorn centennial.

1966 Outward Bound and Mt. Russell.

1967 Phoksumdo Tal, Sikkim, and Ruwenzori.

1968 Shah Dev.

1969 Eastern Europe.

1970 Tsering Yangdon and Mt. Ararat.

1971 Eastern Europe again.

1974 Memsahib Expedition to K2.

1975 Coronation of the King of Nepal.

1976 Retirement. Manzoor's wedding. The Triple Expedition.

1978 Afghanistan and the Minaret of Jam.

1979 China.

1980 Negotiates with the Chinese Mountaineering Association. Botswana.

1981-83 Urumchi. The Great Ice Mountain still off limits. The White House.

1984 Egypt.

1985 India, Nepal, and Bhutan. The Great Ice Mountain at last.

The Love of Mountains
Is Best

Robert H. Bates—with Jackie

CHAPTER I

Beginnings

1911–1929

I N 1558 BENOIT MARTI OF BERNE ascended the Niesen, a Swiss peak, and discovered that an earlier climber had carved in Greek on the summit rock, words which translated, "The love of mountains is best." I wish I had met that unknown visitor, for I agree.

About three and a half centuries later, on a pleasant summer day when I was five, my father, mother and brother, took me on my first climb. Flying Mountain rises 284 feet above sea level at Southwest Harbor on the Maine coast. That day its broad granite ledges were loaded with ripe blueberries and the air was fresh, with a slight breeze off the ocean, the salt air blending with the fragrance of sweet fern and spruce. From the summit the world stretched away and away. The ocean seemed to spread out forever, so different from the way it looked at the shoreline. Even Cranberry Island was clearly visible. That was the start for me, the discovery of what that unknown carver had felt so deeply that he had to incise it at the summit of the Niesen. A deep love of mountains has been with me ever since.

I was born in Philadelphia on January 14, 1911, and named Robert Hicks Bates. Robert was for Robert Fuller, my mother's cousin, and my middle name came from my great-great grandfather, John Hicks, a minuteman killed by the British during their return march to Boston after the battles of Lexington and Concord, on April 19, 1775.

My mother, Edith Newell Richardson, and my father, William Nickerson Bates, met in Philadelphia and were married in 1905. Some time later, they discovered that my mother's Richardson ancestor and John Hicks were buried in the same grave—two of the eight men from

William Nickerson Bates   *Edith Richardson Bates*

Cambridge, Massachusetts, to fall that tragic day. Naturally, the American Revolution has always seemed to be a family matter.

Our home had high ceilings, and pictures on the walls of foreign countries and ancient Greek statues. My family consisted of my father, a professor at the University of Pennsylvania, my mother, once a teacher too, and my brother Bill, four years older. I have early memories of the colorful Greek curtains in my father's study, with its walls of bookcases containing scholarly works in several languages, ancient books, including incunabula, and great tomes concerning Egyptian papyrus fragments.

Our home at 220 St. Mark's Square in West Philadelphia was part of a row of brick houses on a street with many shade trees. Each house had its porch and tiny garden, separated from the street by ornamental iron fencing. It was an easy walk from there to the University of Pennsylvania, where my father taught Greek and gave courses in classical archaeology, his hobby. Our neighbors were mostly university professors, and Margaret Mead lived across the street.

What I remember best about our house was the constant fire of cannel coal burning in the little fireplace with its fringe of Dutch tiles in my father's study, which gave the room a slightly smoky smell. The mantel over the fireplace held a carved redheaded woodpecker, a plaster cast of a fine head of Hercules discovered by a neighboring scholar, and a framed photograph of the Pyramids, with the smooth limestone cap at the top of the Second Pyramid showing clearly. Much later, I learned that my father had climbed this cap, from which, in 1932, Rand Heron, an American climber returning from Nanga Parbat, fell to his death. The whole house expressed an interest in travel, and a special interest in classical archaeology; but also in literature and in the out-of-doors, much of which I absorbed unconsciously as I was growing up.

When I was eight years old, the terrible influenza epidemic of 1919 struck Philadelphia. I became very ill and would not eat. Apparently, I was considered unlikely to survive until one evening my brother came to my bedroom with a piece of chicken from the dinner table and ordered me to eat it. I did, and from then on I improved. I have rarely been ill since.

In the summers we left hot Philadelphia for the cooler air of New England, where my father wrote books and scholarly papers or edited *The American Journal of Archaeology*. He loved both the seashore and the mountains, and when I was five, as already mentioned, he and my mother took me on my first climb: Flying Mountain, on Mt. Desert, a good place to begin. In 1918 and 1919 we rented a cabin on Randolph Hill in New Hampshire, across a valley from Mts. Adams and Madison (5,798 and 5,363 feet), two of the higher peaks of the White Mountains. To be allowed to climb these mountains was presented to me as a privilege, a true sign of growing up.

Those two summers were delightful, most of my days being spent in the woods where a mossy brook could be used for boat races with chips of wood, and explorations could be made along paths and game trails, always with the wild possibility of meeting a bear, though I never did.

The most exciting moment of these summers came the first night I was allowed to spend at a mountain hut, the Madison Hut of the Appalachian Mountain Club on the upper slopes of the mountain. That night I went to sleep in a corner of a large bunk bed and was soon dreaming. I was awakened by terrible screams outside the cabin. I sat bolt upright, terrified. It was completely dark in the bunk room, with many other sleepers now there too. Flashlights went on as the screams subsided. I was too tired from the climb, despite the excitement, to stay awake long, and it wasn't until morning that I learned what had happened. A German professor, or a professor who taught German, I never knew which, had gone to the outhouse in the dark, where he made contact with a porcupine who was chewing the seat. Whether the professor actually sat on the porcupine we were never sure, but I always speculated that he had.

At Randolph my imagination was stirred by stories old-timers told about bears, hikers lost, and the depth of the snow in winter. In addition, the cabin's bookshelf happened to have an old book called *Scrambles in the*

Alps, whose pictures were exciting, to be viewed again and again. Those two summers in Randolph (at ages seven and eight) did more than give me membership in the Randolph Mountain Club; they gave me a love of woods and a lasting exhilaration at being in the mountains.

From then on I saw much less of the White Mountains, though I did occasionally spend weekends with friends there, weekends that I loved. My father built a small summer cottage on land he had long owned at Ogunquit, Maine, a place familiar to him from childhood. With the changed environment, tennis and the beach became more important, and much closer were the rocks and ledges along the shore and the tidal pools, which I considered my own aquaria. I loved the rocks, found routes on small cliffs, and gave names to some of them. Stormy weather was exciting, for the thundering surf added to the thrill of running between waves to outlying rocks and climbing them just before the next big wave surged. Experience taught me to be careful of wet rock, loose rocks, and slippery seaweed. Bald Head Cliff, where layers of sedimentary rock stand on end, also was a great attraction. It is 90 feet high, almost overhanging, and lapped by waves at high tide. It was several years before I dared climb the steeper parts of the cliff.

In the winter, the family frequently took me to lectures at the University of Pennsylvania Museum. Here I saw slides and movies about all sorts of explorations and travel; nomads in Persia making their annual trek to find grass; pygmies in the Ituri Forest; zoologists searching for the okapi; and on one occasion a slender young Englishman, George Leigh Mallory, telling of his experiences on Mt. Everest and his hopes of climbing it in 1924. Pretty dangerous, I thought, but exciting, too.

A year later, the loss of Mallory and Irvine confirmed my impression of the dangers of climbing the world's biggest mountains, but as succeeding years brought new expeditions, my father and I read about them eagerly. Of course, I had no thought of ever taking part in such efforts.

In 1925, when I was just 14, my mother developed pneumonia and, after a short illness, died. I was shocked and my father was utterly devastated. She was the most important thing in the world to him. She was a Radcliffe graduate, very knowledgeable and good-natured, with lots of good friends, and she was 43 when I was born. I had constantly depended on her in ways I did not realize, and then suddenly she wasn't there. She had always run the household quietly and efficiently, and been more fond of social gatherings than my father, who enjoyed people but rarely took the initiative. Her loss changed many things and brought my father and me closer together, while her interest in literature, wildflowers, and the out-of-doors stayed with me.

In the fall of 1927, I left Philadelphia to go to Phillips Exeter Academy, a school my brother had attended before going on to Harvard College. For me, the change was considerable and not just because I was away from home for the first time. Although I had been taught at Penn Charter, a good school in Philadelphia, I had not studied very hard. At Exeter I had to. I did not distinguish myself but made good friends, learned how to study, and did well enough to enter Harvard in the fall of 1929.

That summer, before my freshman year at college, I slightly broadened my climbing experience. Don Tucker, my brother's college roommate, whom I had met on weekends from Exeter, wanted someone to come with him in his secondhand Model-T Ford for a two-week vacation before he began a permanent job. Don had a small tent, and we were to use sleeping bags, catch fish, pick strawberries, climb Mt. Katahdin, and visit Canada. All of these we did. The first day out we caught three bass and had them for breakfast the next morning. Two nights later we made a bough bed on the saddle of Mt. Katahdin, and slept, or tried to sleep, under a tarp, but rain poured down. My Sears, Roebuck cotton sleeping bag with its blue interior became soaked, and in the morning when I struggled out, Don began to laugh. My face was blue, though not from the cold, for the color had come off the wet lining and I was blue all over—blue as an ancient Briton painted with woad. After a wet breakfast, we climbed to the top of the mountain. There was no view, but we agreed we were glad we had stayed and not gone down when the weather looked uncertain.

The previous summer Don had worked for a family who this summer had rented a house on Campobello Island off the Maine coast. They had invited us to visit them. We took the small ferry and were warmly welcomed by the family, who had moved in two days before and were still getting used to the house. They were full of stories about the owners, whom they had never met, but whose possessions and notes to the new tenants were spread around. One said, "Please don't throw away the old hat in the hall. It's Franklin's fishing hat." There were similar notes from Mrs. Roosevelt, the owner, and family pictures of the children and of "Franklin" as undersecretary of the navy. Our hosts told us how Franklin's "promising career" had been ended by polio, and what a pity. Of course none of us then had any idea of FDR's future.

Bradford Washburn

CHAPTER II

From the White Mountains to Alaska

1929-1932

MY FRESHMAN YEAR AT HARVARD went very well, aided by sage advice from my brother Bill. An A in English at midyear helped me to take an advanced course with Professor Bliss Perry, who was about to retire. Throughout most of the year, I also attended without credit a course he gave surveying English literature. He was marvelous. At the end of each class, as he put his books into the green bag he carried, the students clapped enthusiastically as he walked up the aisle from the stage until he left the room.

When June came, I traveled with an Exeter and Harvard classmate, Dick Wells, who had access to an old but recently overhauled family car. The plan was to drive out West, preferably going north of Lake Superior, and on our return to visit a classmate, John Fetcher, in Traverse City, Michigan. Dick also was eager to look up a pretty Wellesley girl who lived in Ohio. We were to camp out and cook most of our own food. Of course things didn't work out as planned, partly because the old Peerless developed an asthmatic radiator, followed by bad gas in the feed line and the need of a new head gasket, which we had to put in at Duluth. We there learned that no auto road yet existed around Lake Superior. This, and the suggestion that the Peerless would soon need more expensive repairs, turned us back east.

On our return to college that fall, something happened that changed my life permanently, for Walt Everett, an Exeter and Harvard classmate and good friend, introduced me to Bradford Washburn, another classmate. I knew Washburn by sight and was aware that before he came to college, he had written a book on mountain climbing, a book so popular that it had been translated into many foreign languages. At the time Dick Wells and I had been struggling with the Peerless in the Midwest, Brad had been leading an expedition to attempt the first ascent of Mt. Fairweather in Alaska. Enough said.

Washburn was fond of the White Mountains, as was Everett, and soon the three of us were making frequent weekend trips to Pinkham Notch in Brad's Model-A Ford Roadster, named Niobe, and purchased with the money from his book. *Among the Alps with Bradford* told of many major climbs Brad and his younger brother, Sherry, had made with guides in the French Alps. These were ascents of the Grépon and other aiguilles in Chamonix, as well as a very sporting new route on the Aiguille Verte. For many years, Brad was the youngest American Groupe de Haute Montagne member of the Club Alpin Français. What he knew about climbing seemed endless. He was excellent company, too, with boundless energy and a good sense of humor. No wonder I didn't mind the five-hour drives to Mt. Washington, alternating in the rumble seat with Walt.

When winter came, we found plenty of reasons for snow camping, usually at Pinkham Notch at the base of the Tuckerman Ravine Trail to Mt. Washington. Here we would stop at the Appalachian Mountain Club hut to see the tough talking, sardonic hut keeper, Joe Dodge, later to be known as "the mayor of Porky Gulch." Usually we brought one of Brad's tents and pitched it near Joe's woodpile, tossing logs off it to serve as deadmen for the tent guys. Joe didn't mind so long as we put the logs back when we left, but once we didn't and next time there was hell to pay. On the rare occasions we slept in the few bunks inside, we heard plenty of stories about the stupid "goofers," who were constantly doing foolish things in the mountains and having to be rescued. Few visitors ever made the long drive to Pinkham in the winter and so we considered ourselves somewhat superior to the normal, summer-only climbers. The only ski "trail" in the White Mountains had been the Mt. Washington carriage road, but a fire trail had been built the summer before, starting at Pinkham, and this we used to climb to Hermit Lake, from where we scouted out areas where Brad hoped to build a Harvard cabin.

Brad was constantly testing equipment or techniques that would be useful the following summer. Burton Holmes, a well-known travel lecturer, was to pay him to make a film of climbing Mont Blanc, the highest peak in the Alps. Walt Everett was to go with him and they were to camp high on the mountain for a couple of weeks, possibly spending a night on top. Walt and Brad wanted me to go with them to France also, but I didn't have the money.

That summer I shared their adventures by mail, and on their return immediately joined Brad for a climb of Mt. Washington. He suggested that we try to do the 4,000-foot climb in an hour and a half from Pinkham Notch: half an hour to Hermit Lake, another half to the top of the headwall, and the final 30 minutes to the top. My summer at the shore had not toughened my climbing muscles, though I had done a good bit of running. I stayed with Brad to the top of the headwall, which we reached in an hour, then sat down and waved him on. I didn't stay long, however, and was only a few minutes behind when he reached the summit in less than the proposed time.

The following fall we were frequently on Mt. Washington, and during Christmas week the Washburns and friends had a skiing and climbing party at the Glen House, an old inn at the base of the Mt. Washington carriage road. Despite bad weather, we made a winter climb of Mt. Washington, going straight up the headwall instead of following the trail at the side. More exciting was an attempt the next day to climb the Pinnacle Gully, a long and difficult ice climb. Sherry Washburn led, cutting steps, and we surmounted the lower bulges before running out of time and descending. It was the steepest ice I had ever climbed.

During Christmas vacation, we talked constantly of plans for an expedition the following summer to climb 15,300-foot Mt. Fairweather on the coast of Alaska, a peak Brad had tried unsuccessfully to climb two years earlier. He was to be the major contributor to the expense, having taken out a big life insurance policy and, using it as collateral, borrowed most of what we needed. He hoped to recoup later through lectures illustrated by slides and movies. During the next months this expedition gradually formed: there were to be the three of us and our classmate Dick Riley, plus Harald Paumgarten, a member of the Austrian 1932 Olympic Ski Team who had stayed on after the Olympics; and Bob Monahan, a forester, one of three men who in September were to set up a weather station on top of Mt. Washington and spend the winter there. Wintering on top of Mt. Washington was not a light assignment, for the mountain has frequent sub-zero temperatures and high winds. The world-record wind velocity of 231 miles per hour was set on Mt. Washington in 1934.

College was going well for me, and the planning for the forthcoming expedition added zest. We each had some special assignment; I was to be

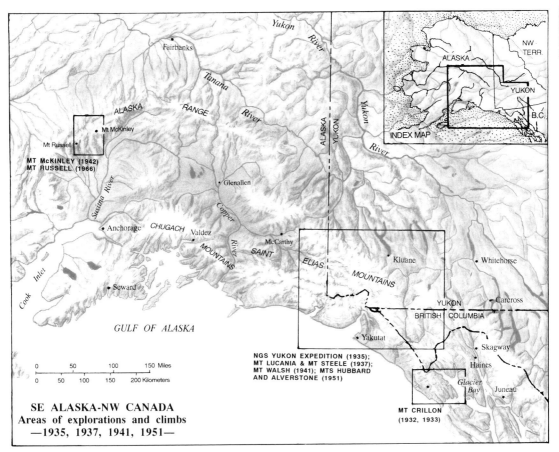

the expedition botanist. Though I had never taken a course in botany, that did not bother the curator of the Gray Herbarium at Harvard, who gave me a plant press and instructions on how to use it. In addition, since at the time there was considerable interest in finding new sources of uranium, I found a friend who made me a primitive, nonelectric sort of Geiger counter with which to screen rocks.

Shortly after our last college examinations, all of us but Bob Monahan were at the station in Boston ready for our nearly two-week trip to Alaska by rail and boat. (We would meet Bob in Alaska.) My father and brother saw me off, and I'm sure they sensed my excitement.

What a grand trip lay ahead! First the train took us through the White Mountains to Montreal, where Brad somehow received permission to use the colonist car on the East-West Express. The colonist car, attached to the day coaches, had seats that could be turned together to form beds, with lots of storage space overhead and a stove and refrigerator. The car was closed to normal passengers, for it was supposed to be used by migrants settling in the western provinces or going across Canada on the way between Asia and Europe. 1932 was a year of the Great Depression all over North America, and since no immigrants or Chinese were traveling, we had our own private coach. We made couches of the seats, put out our air mattresses and sleeping bags, and lived in luxury as the train sped westward.

At Montreal we hastily bought food for the journey, including bread, jam, cereal, milk, and lettuce, which added to the delicious sandwiches and cookies brought from home. As we contentedly lounged in our private dining car, sandwiches in hand, we passed through the devastation of the nickel mines in Sudbury, and sped along the curving, roadless shore of Lake Superior, where Dick Wells and I had tried to go the year before. We were to take five days to cross the continent to Vancouver, with a change to a different colonist car in Winnipeg. It was there that Dick Riley and I became so busy eating plate-size pancakes at five cents apiece that we nearly missed the train.

Frequently the train would stop for half an hour to give the crews a chance to eat and to check for hot boxes. We never missed an opportunity to get off, look for a bakery, grocery, or lunchroom, and bring fresh supplies to our private car. Once we stopped and had a splendid dinner of soup, steak, salad, dessert, and milk. The price was 35 cents. Among our pleasures were visits from brakemen or conductors, good-natured men who didn't mind our freewheeling ways and would stop to tell local stories of hunting and fishing, or, better, bear stories, usually told with what I suspect Mark Twain would call "a few stretchers." As yet we had no bear stories of our own and we loved these. Finally, on our fourth day from Boston, we awoke with cinders pattering against the glass, to see ahead what we had long been awaiting, a distant blue line marked with what seemed to be little white clouds. We had reached the Rockies.

From Calgary on, we stayed in the observation car, rushing from side to side as we passed Banff, Lake Louise, and the Yoho Valley. As we wound on through the Selkirks, we tried to locate the best climbing routes on Mt. Sir Donald, and later watched for Revelstoke with its world-record ski jump. The next morning we pulled into Vancouver station and looked out on the gray, fogbound Pacific.

Taxi competition to take passengers from the station to the Canadian National boat was intense, and we joyfully accepted the offer of a young man who said he could take us all and our baggage in one load. He did. Five of us were inside the cab and 19 pieces of baggage were draped and tied on the roof and body. We and the springs both groaned before we got there but we did. Our bags went on board and we went off to see the town. It was raining hard, and after visiting the museum and library we went to the movies, which showed four films for 20 cents. We also bought some delicious strawberries: two quarts, 15 cents. After a trolley ride we checked in at the boat, where we couldn't believe the luxury of our cabins, and had a good laugh at the sign saying Ring for Berth Ladder. That night, at exactly 10:00 p.m., amidst breaking paper streamers and hoots from the steamer, our ship moved out into the fog.

The weather the next morning continued to be cloudy or rainy, but we thoroughly enjoyed our luxurious life in Georgia Strait, with sea air, surf breaking along the shorelines, and great flocks of sea birds crossing our bow, as well as 17 items on the menu for dinner. In a day and a half, we were in Prince Rupert, where we noted the 18-foot tide and visited the 16-degree Fahrenheit cold-storage plant. Here a toothless old Scot proudly showed us a frozen 300-pound halibut, a 77-pound salmon, and other oddities. The next day, at Juneau, we met Tom Smith, an old-timer who had just taken Bob Monahan and our supplies to Lituya Bay in his gas boat.

The following day we met our pilot, Ansel Eckmann, a short, dapper fellow, who told us to put our gear in his float plane. If he had realized how much weight we put in, he would have refused to fly, he told us later, but he didn't know. He told Dick, Harald, and me to get as far forward as possible and then began to taxi. A very long run finally made us airborne and we flew under the 1,000-foot cloud ceiling the whole way. We passed Admiralty Island and Icy Strait, saw the sunny Fairweather peaks ahead, flew close along the face of the La Pérouse Glacier, washed by the sea, rounded the entrance to Lituya Bay, and ahead was Cenotaph Island with Jim Huscroft's cabin. Eckmann landed close to the cabin and taxied in to the dock, where Bob Monahan and a stocky man in bib overalls were awaiting us.

The bay we had come to is an indentation in the Fairweather Peninsula about 150 miles west of Juneau. This incredible mass of high mountains and glaciers, nearly 80 miles long and 40 miles at its widest, separates Glacier Bay from the Pacific Ocean to the southwest. Glacier-carved Lituya Bay extends nine miles into the interior. It is about three miles wide, with extensions east and west at its inmost point, like the flukes of a whale. Each of these flukes leads to a great glacier that constantly calves off towering pinnacles of bluish ice 200 feet high. The crashes from this falling ice resound throughout the region, and at times the whole interior end of the bay is filled with floating icebergs.

Beyond the bay, west, north, and east, stand big peaks, including 15,300-foot Mt. Fairweather, sometimes considered the highest coastal mountain in the world, and 12,726-foot Mt. Crillon, 25 miles to the east. There are many others. The grandeur of these snowy peaks, the deep forests lining the shores, the silent water, and the abundant wild life, make this a place of compelling beauty. Our base was the cabin of Jim Huscroft, the only inhabitant of this 4,400-square-mile area.

Lituya Bay has an unusual history. On July 4, 1786, the great French voyageur Jean-François de Galaup, Comte de La Pérouse, entered the bay, which he named Port des Français, bought the island in the center from the Indians living there, and decided that here would be the headquarters of a French trading company to rival the British Hudson Bay Company. A few days later, while measuring the bay, two of his boats caught in the outrunning tide were wrecked. He named the island Cenotaph Island to commemorate the drowned men, and left a plaque as a memorial to them.

Jim Huscroft, the stocky, baldheaded man who met us at the dock, had often searched unsuccessfully for the plaque during the 17 years he had lived alone on the island, but the Indians had probably destroyed it long ago. Jim was a true hermit, the only permanent resident of a 150-mile stretch of the Alaskan coast. Occasionally, Ernie Rognan, a Norwegian fisherman, owner of the gas boat *Ya Sure*, would stay with him, but he was almost always alone, except for his yearly trip to Juneau to sell the skins of blue foxes that ran wild on the island, and to buy his year's supplies.

The first thing he did each year on getting to Juneau was to buy a tub of salt mackerel and eat one or two. (He had the finest sockeye salmon in the world at his doorstep but tired of the rich meat.) Then, after buying a supply of snuff, which he loved, he would stop at the post office to pick up a bill or two before gathering his supplies and finally heading for the Elks Club, where they saved the past year's newspapers for him. He always read the latest, then put the others away to read one each day over his morning coffee and sourdough hotcakes.

When I knew him better, I once asked him about reading such old news. "It's a year late," I said.

"Don't make no difference what year. It's all the same."

"Don't you ever look ahead to see what happened?"

"Course not. It'd take away all the fun."

Jim was a powerful man, with arms the size of a normal man's legs. The way he could saw a pine tree into chunks for his stove was awe inspiring.

His cooking was always imaginative, and Christmas was his big day. He planned the momentous affair months in advance, and when he sat down to his solitary Christmas dinner, he had roast goose and, as he said, 14 kinds of pie. (The latter, I suspect, probably lasted him well into February.)

During our occasional stays at Jim's cabin during the summer, I found him to be the kindest man I had ever known. He would give away anything he had and was always thinking of other people's problems. He was born in Steubenville, Ohio, had made three fortunes and lost them all, and after the third—some kind of lumber business—had retired to Cenotaph Island. Some hermits may be unfriendly, but Jim was the opposite. On the rare occasions when a stranger arrived at the island by plane or boat, Jim would be standing on his little dock, bald head gleaming dully, watch in hand, to greet him.

"I make it 11:20," he would say with a little shy smile. "What do you make it?" Then he would reset his watch.

Our expedition plan was to have Ansel Eckmann fly his plane from Cenotaph Island to a lake near Mt. Fairweather, from where we hoped to make the second ascent of the mountain, for the summit had been reached by Terris Moore and Allen Carpé in 1931. Four of us climbed out of the plane at the island, put in supplies Bob Monahan had brought in by boat, and Brad and Eckmann were off again, but not for long. The plane was soon back, with Brad yelling from the cockpit, "The lake's frozen and we've landed the stuff at 16-mile crick." That landing proved an error, for after some discussion we decided that the "crick" was too far from the mountain. In five minutes we changed our plans and decided to try to climb Mt. Crillon, the second highest peak in the range, one never attempted before.

There was time now to look around Jim's cabin more carefully. It was large for a cabin, simply built, but it had character. Prominent was the big stove, the chunks of wood beside it and the blue-gray glacier bear skin we occasionally slept on. A mug on a shelf usually held Jim's false teeth. The kitchen table, made from a broad slab of red cedar, held a pile of plates, while hanging on the wall behind it was Jim's pack, made from an old pair of blue jeans. The crossed legs served as straps, the top was sewed tight, and the only opening was through the fly. Nearby were Jim's dearest possessions: his hand-cranked "washing machine," his radio (which sometimes worked), and his Victrola with piles of records. These he played over and over for us. Many were sentimental, such as "Barbara Allen" and "Little Cabin in the Cascade Mountains." There was also "Oh Bury Me Not on the Lone Prairie," "The Wreck of C & O Number Five," and "Get Away

Old Man Get Away." When the Victrola spring broke, Jim played the records anyway, using his index finger to turn the disc 'round and 'round.

What a wonderful region to be in for one's first mountain expedition! There was a strong element of exploration, too, because no map showed details of what lay between the bay and the cliffs that surround the Crillon Plateau, 25 miles away. Everything was wilderness, marked only by trails worn deep into the forest floor by generations of bears, or the white cliffs of Cenotaph Island, painted by years of use by the kittiwakes and tufted puffins. Seals, sea lions, and eagles seemed perfectly at home. Except for the cries of sea birds, and the soft sound of meltwater flowing out of the bay, there was absolute silence, broken only by enormous crashes when towering pinnacles of ice from the advancing glaciers at the end of the bay struck the water.

How to get to Mt. Crillon was our main problem. We knew that at the part of the bay farthest from the entrance there were two calving glaciers, one entering from the west, one from the east. Each of these had carved a big valley trough running through the mountains and parallel to a line of coastal hills that rimmed the beaches. We believed that the big glacier entering the bay to the east came directly or indirectly from Mt. Crillon, and so exploring that ice route was our first objective.

On the day after our arrival, following a breakfast of Jim's huge sourdough hotcakes with watered huckleberry jam for syrup, we borrowed Jim's dory and rowed down the bay. It didn't matter that the rowboat leaked a bit and couldn't hold much weight, that our mountain was 25 miles away across unmapped country that nobody had penetrated before, and that 1,800 pounds of food and equipment would need to be transported down the bay before we could start to climb above sea level. We had that wonderful feeling of youth that whatever happens we can deal with it.

To reach the glacier, we rowed and sailed nearly four miles, closely observed by seals, threading our way through fantastic blue-white icebergs coming from the two glaciers at the end of the bay. It didn't matter that big waves, set in motion by the thundering glaciers, set the big icebergs with seals on them to bobbing, but the smaller bergs that rubbed and smashed together sometimes were alarmingly near the boat. On the way we joked about climbing mountains the right way, starting out in a rowboat at sea level. The Crillon Glacier was a mile across, with half of its terminal ice towers resting in seawater. The rest of the snout was on land, but advancing and pushing a moraine ahead. Here we landed, pulling the boat up the beach to keep it safe from the frequent big waves formed by the crashes of ice towers into the bay.

Higher still we pitched our two large tents, copies of a design the Mt. Logan Expedition had used. Each had a single pole, was seven feet square, and had a 12-inch wall around the sides. At last we felt that our climb had begun. We still could only guess at the route to Mt. Crillon, but for the next two days we backpacked loads up the glacier, with occasional probing climbs of ridges to our north, from which we caught glimpses of a large snowfield beyond. As we struggled along the ice, which was heavily crevassed but basically clear of winter snow, we began packing 55 pounds apiece. Later we even carried 90 pounds, though 70 became the average. This was a new sport for me, especially since we were constantly moving along a heavily crevassed glacier with occasional forays on loose moraines. Our packboards weighed six pounds apiece, our wet duffel bags were heavy, and our food had commercial packing far heavier than it would be in the freeze-dried era to come. Our only weight saving came in the vegetables, for in waxed cloth bags we had placed dried vegetables specially prepared for us by a Mrs. Kelly in Pittsfield, Massachusetts, known to us as Mrs. Dried Kelly. We used a food bag system, with one day's food for six men in a bag, not counting a few group supplies like butter and sugar, which went with the kitchen. We cooked on Primus stoves, using unleaded gas.

Though it rained much of the time, we had some grand views from our reconnaissances, even if they never showed us a route through the lesser peaks to Mt. Crillon. Gradually we became skillful at packing along ice ridges with surface crevasses on either side, but there were scary moments. One came when Bob Monahan began to slide toward a crevasse. He checked his slide so strongly that his pack overbalanced him and he fell backward headfirst into another sizable crevasse full of meltwater. We stared horrified, but in a moment his head emerged, he found footing, and he crawled out the end of the crevasse, soaked but otherwise unharmed.

A more exciting moment came very early the next morning, when we were in our sleeping bags. It was Harald Paumgarten's turn to cook breakfast for an early departure, but while starting the Primus deep inside the tent, he spilled gasoline and set the whole stove aflame. Tongues of fire leapt five feet against the side of the tent, which fortunately was wet. Harald picked up the stove and started to carry it across the five men still in their sleeping bags to the door, but the stove was blazing hot and it spun out of his hands directly toward my head. Instinct saved me, but the stove bounced onto Dick's bag, where Brad, who was now up, swept the stove aside and smothered it with a bedroll. Everything was damp with moisture or the tent would have burned, and a lot more. As it was, nothing was harmed.

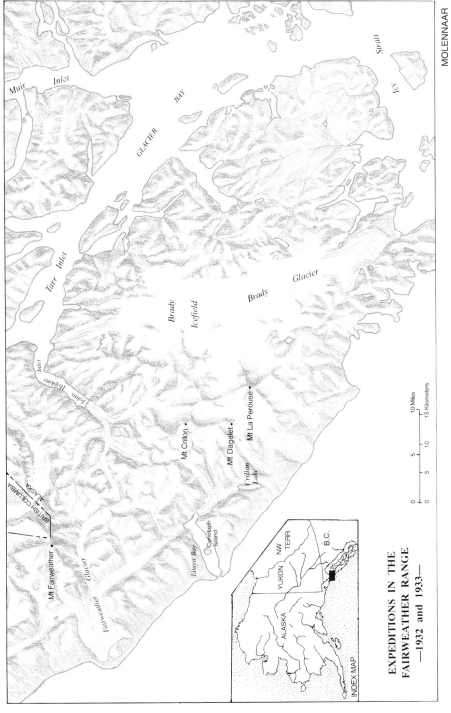

MOLENNAAR

INDEX MAP

EXPEDITIONS IN THE
FAIRWEATHER RANGE
—1932 and 1933—

We were anxious to get a view of Crillon and possible routes to it, but mountains north of the glacier blocked our view. Accordingly, we decided to climb one of these mountains, about 7,000 feet high, which we called Mt. Lookout, for we felt it would show us a direct route to our destination.

To try to avoid soft snow, we arose early and were away by daylight at 2:30 in the morning. We climbed steadily until about 8:00, by which time the dew had ceased sparkling on the lupine and the snow was becoming mushy. Ahead of us was a gendarme of dangerously crumbly rock, which we wanted to go around, but the snow had become so soft that we were soon nearly waist-deep. When Bob fell into a crevasse, his shoulders held him and we pulled him out. Above us a steep, crumbly gully of rotten rock ran to the top of the gendarme ridge, which we had to reach if we were to continue. Brad worked his way up 30 feet, a shower of rocks recording his every move until he reached a small depression, where he stopped precariously and called to me to come on. He was not well placed and could not belay me. Below the gully a snow slope descended, crossed by a nasty blue crevasse about 50 yards below us, then continued down, down, 1,200 feet into the mists below.

I started up the right side of the gully, with Bob standing on steep snow to my left and below. A crack on the right wall above me looked solid and I reached up and pulled. To my horror, I dislodged a huge block of rock, weighing at least a ton, which toppled toward me. Instinctively I pushed away from the block and out into space as it grazed my cheek. I landed on steep snow just above Bob, who grabbed me. Under his arm I could see a cloud of rock dust as the huge chunk split into a shatter of fragments and flying snow. They started an avalanche of wet snow that began hissing and thundering down, filling the crevasse, crossing it, spreading out, and finally disappearing noisily into the mist far, far below. The sounds and the smell of the rock dust are etched in my memory. I have never forgotten to avoid rotten rock whenever possible, and when unavoidable to test each hold carefully.

Climbing with great care, we kept going, and by 12:00 reached what from below had appeared to be the summit. It was not; the true summit, from which we would have our first clear view of Mt. Crillon, was about a quarter-mile ahead. The ridge rose gradually, covered by a foot of snow, with a wind-built cornice on our left projecting out as much as 20 feet over empty space. Again below us steep snow slopes dropped away, crossed by big crevasses.

Once more Brad led, this time along a straight line just to the right of where we believed the cornice began. Occasionally the snow around us

The 1933 Mt. Crillon Expedition at the South Col: Houston (left), R.H.B.,
Child, Washburn, Everett, and Carter

would settle with a heart-stopping thump, and small pieces of snow, dislodged by our steps, would start little avalanches, which would soon roar
down, starting more and more snow slides. We were all relieved when we
finally worked our way across to the highest rock, which, as we had hoped,
turned out to be a glorious viewpoint. It was our first ascent and an exciting
one. We could faintly hear surf breaking on the shore, see Lituya Bay and
the island, and far beyond, 150 miles to the west, the great pyramid of
Mt. Saint Elias (18,008 feet). Much closer and more to the point, we could
also see a potential route to Mt. Crillon, but a very long and roundabout
one, for the cliffs surrounding the mountain seemed impenetrable.

The day was cloudless and the hot sun sent avalanches roaring in every
direction! We ate our cheese, crackers, and chocolate slowly, waiting for the
snow to firm before our descent. The discussion turned to famous
avalanches and how various climbers had been saved by slipping out of
their packs and making swimming motions. Finally the temperature
dropped and we climbed down on safer snow, looking intently at places
where our earlier tracks had cut the snow slope, causing everything below
to slide. Walking where the snow had avalanched was now perfectly safe.
We still had the rotten rock gully ahead, but we found a somewhat safer

descent line down the nose of the gendarme. Not two minutes after we were safely down, however, rockfalls came bounding across our route.

The long descent from our 6,800-foot summit continued, and when the sun disappeared and the glorious red and orange clouds had darkened, a moon helped us. Half an hour before midnight, we reached camp. Our first ascent had taken about 20 hours, and, as I noted in my diary, 22 and one-half hours between sleeps.

That climb was the high point of the summer. We had overcome serious obstacles and our very moderate success inspired us. From our summit vantage point, we had learned that part of the Crillon Glacier flowed southwest to a lake, from which one could probably climb to a peak lower than Lookout. This, in turn, apparently would give access to the huge, crevassed snowfield that extended seven miles, leading gradually upward to the base of the great cliffs that surround Mt. Crillon. Whether these could be climbed was doubtful but we were determined to find out.

Eckmann was almost due to bring us more supplies at Cenotaph Island, and so we returned there and were able to meet him and persuade him to fly everything to Crillon Lake. That seven-minute flight from the island saved us weeks of heavy backpacking, and we began immediately to reconnoiter the new route. This followed bear trails along the lake, then climbed through slide alder and loose rock to beautiful fields of white heather and cyclamen, where there were pools of meltwater, goat tracks, and frequent calls of large marmots, which Jim Huscroft had referred to as "whistle pigs."

From here, during the next week, we established a camp near the top of the ridge at a point where we could descend to the huge snowfield beyond. Pushing on, and marking our route with black-tipped dowels as trail markers, we wound through crevasses until we finally reached a position near the Crillon cliffs, where we put up another camp.

At this point the cliffs were unclimbable, but farther along the line of cliffs there seemed to be a possible very steep rock route to the plateau above, though there was no time to try. We returned to our tents to bring up more supplies, but now the weather turned, playing havoc with the snow bridges on our snowfield route. Finally, soaked and dripping, we returned to Crillon Lake, and then in continuous rain retreated to the bay and Jim Huscroft's cabin. A couple of days later Tom Smith arrived in his gas boat, we said good-bye to Jim, and were off to Juneau and the beginning of the long journey home. We had not climbed Crillon, but we now knew how to get to the mountain and felt it could be climbed.

On the way back to Juneau we stopped at Lemesurier Island, where a prospector and trapper named Joe Ibachs lived. He was a friend of Tom Smith, who had mail for him. Joe welcomed us with great enthusiasm and introduced us to the only other occupant of the island, a man employed by the government to radio weather reports to Juneau. Recently there had been another weatherman, but he had been killed while hunting a bear on the island. The weatherman had hunted with army ammunition, and had actually shot the bear through the heart at close range—too close range—for the bear had been near enough to kill him before dying himself. Afterward Joe and the remaining weatherman had killed a second bear, whom they considered to be a danger.

I had a strange connection with this second bear for, while we were talking, Joe made some coffee. He said he didn't have much there to feed us but he had some blueberries. "You're not giving them those blueberries, are you?" asked the weatherman.

"Sure. They're fine," said Joe. He put a dish before me and I tried them. They were excellent and I quickly ate them.

"What bothered you?" I asked the weatherman.

"Nothing. Only they were picked by the bear."

When we were on the boat leaving Juneau for Vancouver, I began to realize how much had been crammed into that summer. I had loved it all. What fun to be where nobody had been before, to share with companions who trusted you with their lives as you trusted them. I felt I had pulled my weight, and that meant a lot to me.

Probably I should have been pessimistic, for on September 9, 1932, the day we left Juneau for the East, headlines in the Juneau paper read, "Eleven Million Out of Work." The article below read, "President of A.F.L. says number will be increased to 13,000,000 before spring. . . . Jobs must be created by the millions if we are to avoid an unparalleled catastrophe." Not an optimistic forecast as we were beginning our final year at college.

CHAPTER III

Harvard and Mt. Crillon

1929-1934

THANKS TO MY BROTHER'S WISE COUNSEL, I was able to enter good courses at Harvard with excellent professors, and I felt extraordinarily fortunate to be there.

For three years I lived in Dunster House, one of two large dormitories built in 1930. We had our own library, squash courts, and dining hall, like the residents of Lowell House, the only other House at the time. It was fun playing in the first athletic contest between the Harvard Houses, when the Dunster football team beat the team from Lowell by throwing a pass to the center (a trick but legal play) to score the only touchdown.

In Dunster House, I met Waldo Holcombe, and it wasn't long before we decided to room together. Waldo was a big, handsome member of the Harvard crew, a physics major with delightful qualities of curiosity and readiness to join outdoor adventures. Once we made a climb at dawn on Memorial Hall, the huge Harvard Civil War Memorial, the tallest building at the university. Afterward we were to have an early breakfast and then drive to New Haven to see the Harvard-Yale football game, but at breakfast Waldo found that his wallet was gone. It had probably fallen out when his trouser pocket had caught on a projection on the roof. In his wallet was his ticket to the game. Breakfast was forgotten, and an immediate second ascent was carried out, this time much faster because more people were about.

Waldo's father was Professor Arthur Holcombe, a wise and very distinguished professor of government, with a family of three boys and two girls.

The Holcombes were very hospitable and I frequently had Sunday dinner with them. One Sunday Professor Holcombe had just carved the roast and at last was about to eat when someone knocked on the front door, which was just out of sight from where we sat. Professor Holcombe went to the door and we heard scraps of interesting conversation, but we had all finished our plates before he returned to the table.

Mrs. Holcombe was very stern with him. "Arthur, why didn't you tell that young man to come back later or bring him in here?" she declared.

The answer I remember well. "I'm sorry, my dear. That was Joe Kennedy's boy. He couldn't stay. He's just come back from England and he's written something he wants me to read. He's quite a fellow. I think we'll be hearing more of him in the future." What JFK wanted him to read was *While England Slept*. At President Kennedy's inauguration some years later, as I expected, Professor Holcombe had a seat in the front row.

There were parties, of course, and a winter weekend when we won a bet by taking a girl to the top of Mt. Washington, but the joke was on us for she climbed almost as strongly as we did and didn't think it strange. We also did some good ice climbing in the Pinnacle Gully on Mt. Washington, with Brad cutting a long series of steps in the hard ice. I played 150-pound football in the fall and in the spring rugby, which was great fun, while in the winter we climbed and skied. Since there were no rope tows or ski lifts in New England in those days, the narrow fire trail on Mt. Washington was our main practice ground.

My final year at college passed quickly. I was busy with my honors thesis on a manuscript, supposedly by Shelley, that had been found in a museum in Athens. There were also written and oral final examinations for honors in English. When the academic year ended, I was graduated magna cum laude.

At commencement, as Brad and I sat beneath an elm, Harvard President A. Lawrence Lowell spoke briefly to the class of 1933. "You go forth," he said, "into a world uneasy and distressed, but for that very reason needing sound thinking, broad sympathies and above all courage . . .with hope and confidence I bid you good-bye." Brad and I were fond of Lowell, who had shown real interest in our climbing expeditions, and two years later we named the great Lowell Glacier in Canada's Yukon Territory for him.

At commencement we learned that practically none of our fellow graduates had jobs. I knew one fellow slightly who on graduation became vice-president of his father's shoe company, but he was the exception.

There was considerable excitement when somebody announced that Al
Nickerson had a job.

"What's he doing?" we all asked.

"He's turning the handle on a gas pump."

I heard a couple of derisive remarks, but none some years later when he
became president of Mobil Corporation.

Like many of our friends, Brad and I would be starting graduate work
in the fall. All through senior year, we had talked of returning to
Mt. Crillon, landing on Crillon Lake, following the route we had found to
the Crillon cliffs, forcing a route up them, and going on to the summit.
Long before commencement we had weighed out food and placed it in
waxed bags and boxes to take with us. Then, before we knew it, we were at
the station ready to leave for Montreal and Alaska.

The train trip to Montreal was now familiar and Brad, Walt Everett
and I settled down quickly. At Woodsville, New Hampshire, we picked up
Dick Goldthwait, our Dartmouth 1933 geologist friend (a fine skier, head
of the Dartmouth Outing Club, and later a famous geologist), who was
going with us to seek new information about glaciers. At Montreal we
moved quickly into the colonist car as if we were home again. It was not so
exciting as the first time but we saw new scenery, since this time we
changed trains at Jasper and went northwest to Prince Rupert, which we
reached at 10:00 p.m. on the fifth day of our travels.

The next day we continued on by boat and were very amused when the
boat captain reached the Taku Glacier and spent half an hour of whistle-
blowing trying to get ice to fall off. Finally, when a small piece fell, the passengers nearly swooned with delight.

At Juneau, we found that Eckmann had been grounded for drinking.
Instead, Bob Ellis, much younger, was to fly us in. We spent the night in
his hangar and the next day bought dynamite and caps to use with the
device that the Harvard Geology Department had lent Dick to measure the
depth of glacial ice at various points. Finally, on July 1, weather was good
enough to fly to Crillon Lake under a 3,000-foot cloud ceiling.

The other five members of the expedition had preceded us, using Tom
Smith's gas boat to take them and 2,400 pounds of supplies to Jim's cabin
in Lituya Bay. They had brought a canoe too big to be flown in, and their
main assignment was to get the canoe to Crillon Lake. This they had
already accomplished by Herculean efforts, carrying the canoe over three
miles of crevassed glacier and moraine in a tremendous 48 hours of all-out
effort. Halfway up the glacier they had met a big glacial lake, impassable on

Walt Everett cooking

either side, where they sat down in despair. Then a light dawned. In went the canoe and they paddled across, a new method of glacial travel.

Of the five men in this contingent, three were to become my lifelong friends. Bill Child I had known since we were 10. He was now a lanky, good-natured, hard-working fellow who grew a beard that made him look like Abraham Lincoln. His previous climbing had been limited but he was always good fun and did more than his share of the work. Charlie Houston and Adams Carter, then Harvard students, together with Bradford Washburn, have been my closest friends ever since this expedition. All have had outstanding careers. Our lives have been linked by many joint enterprises, frequently connected with mountains.

Howard Platts (nicknamed Hugo) and Russ Dow had read about the expedition as Brad was forming it and came to him to offer their services. Since their fathers both worked for the Boston & Maine Railroad, they had rail passes that took them all the way to Prince Rupert, British Columbia, and back. Both were good workers and fine fellows.

The five already at Crillon Lake were delighted to see us and couldn't wait to begin our climb. Unlike the year before, we now knew where to fol-

Looking NE to Mt. Crillon. We reached our high point at the crest to the right of the summit.

low bear trails through the forest until we reached a rotten rock and snow ridge leading about 6,000 feet to a huge snowfield. Beyond lay a crevassed region, three or four miles in extent, culminating in thousand-foot cliffs that surrounded a plateau leading to the summit. After we forced a route through the barrier cliffs that made the plateau above seem to be a northern Lost World, the route would lie across the windswept plateau for three miles to the southern slopes of Mt. Crillon, which might or might not be buried in powder snow.

It didn't take long to establish a comfortable base camp, and we were soon backpacking up the rotten rock ridges and gullies leading to small snowfields and eventually to the edge of the great snowfield. Our camp at Crillon Lake was only 300 feet above sea level, and Camp I, as we called it, was more than 5,000 feet higher, so it made our up-and-down trips with 60 or 70 pounds of food or equipment a 10,000-foot challenge.

Weather was a problem, for after each heavy snowfall we had to wait for the snow to settle and then remake our tracks, but 11 days after our arrival at the lake we were well established in a snow camp at about 6,000 feet.

I am sure Adams Carter still remembers skiing down a steep, tricky slope carrying dynamite to measure glacier thickness, not realizing that easily detonated dynamite caps also had been placed in his load by mistake.

On the evening of July 11, Brad, Charlie Houston, and I climbed a rock knob from which we had a clear view of the Crillon cliffs in a strong evening light. At what point to attack the thousand-foot cliffs that ringed the Crillon Plateau was a difficult decision, for they were steep everywhere. As we studied the line of cliffs, we determined to try a specific rocky section, though it was clearly very steep and probably dangerous.

After making that decision, we looked in the opposite direction and saw a huge brocken with a figure in the center of it. The small, circular rainbow called "the specter of the brocken" is well known to climbers, at least through the picture of it in Whymper's famous *Scrambles in the Alps*. There Whymper tells of the accident on the Matterhorn when the rope broke and four men fell to their deaths. Immediately afterward, a specter of the brocken appeared to the three survivors. The two Swiss guides swore they saw a cross in the middle of it, claiming that it was a symbol of danger and death. We each thought of that story as we waved at the figure in the center of our brocken. It waved, too. (Each of us, of course, was seeing his own shadow.) Silently, we hoped our brocken was not a foreboding.

We were away at 5:30 the next morning and had not gone far before Charlie disappeared into a crevasse up to his shoulders and got out with difficulty. The snowfield crevasses were worse than we had expected. Four miles later we climbed up a short, steep slope to have a bite to eat and further examine the cliff. A big bergschrund crevasse that marked the separation of the slope above from the glacier floor checked us, and crossing this gulf was our initial problem. Brad, with my help, climbed on Charlie's shoulders, planted his axe in the snow above, and was up; Charlie managed to do the same. For a bit it looked as if I couldn't join them, but finally I came up the rope hand over hand while they belayed.

We were on snow at first, but above rose 1,000 feet of steep, broken rock at a 60-degree angle or steeper. It was too steep for snow to lie, and the rock was so fragmented that every step was likely to dislodge something. The tip of the cliff was overhanging, and as we climbed the sun began to melt the snow there, so that small stones began to fall with a frightening zing-zing. Stones dislodged by Brad above, despite his best efforts, would bound down, too, so that Charlie and I felt under bombardment from two directions. We felt better when we were high enough to be under the overhang, so that the stones shrieking down from the top fell away from us.

The climbing was very delicate with few belays until we traversed across a steep and very slippery snow slope with a deep avalanche groove in it. An hour later, we reached rock again. Here Charlie and I were each struck by pieces Brad had dislodged, but fortunately they were not big enough to knock us off the wall.

When we were about 800 feet above our skis, at about 9,000 feet, we could look across part of the Crillon Plateau. From here we could also see what looked to be a far better route some distance along the cliff, a 50- to 60-degree snow slope. Though we were two-thirds of the way up the cliff, we felt sure that the route we were making was too dangerous for men carrying loads. Having located something better, we started down. For three and a quarter hours we had been bombarded by falling rocks and there was no use staying longer.

The descent was nearly as bad as the ascent. Loose rock was everywhere and there were no secure belays. It took two more hours to get off the cliff, with the whine of falling stones pushing us on. At the top of the schrund we rappelled from an avalanche chute 50 feet to a pile of snow below it—my first rappel, and through a waterfall at that. At the bottom we moved out of danger, ate, and watched rocks and small avalanches pour across parts of our route. It was one of the least pleasant climbs I would ever make.

Two days later we were at the base of the cliff again, but this time at the place we had seen from our high point on the rock cliff. We had started at 9:00 in the evening, carrying trail markers, to try again to force a route to the Crillon Plateau. We were a ghostly band crossing the huge snowfields in a half light, with no sounds but the scraping of the skis on the crust and no light but the vague reflection in the sky of the midnight sun that was never in sight. The North Star loomed cold and distant at a 60-degree angle. We broke trail up the steep slope leading to the area we called the South Col, each man breaking 30 steps and then stepping aside. Beyond the col we had a long descent and a wild ride on skis in the semidarkness to reach the part of the cliff we were about to try. It was now about 2:30 in the morning and we waited till 4:00 to start up the ice cliff. We went in two ropes of three, Brad leading.

Again there was trouble getting the last man over the bergschrund, but a much greater problem was the position of the second rope directly below the first on this 1,000-foot, 50- to 60-degree slope. Those above were being as careful as they could, but once a piece of ice they knocked off struck Charlie in the face and nearly hurled him off. He was partially stunned but held on. Finally Brad, standing on a 60- to 65-degree slope with 1,000 feet of open space below him, cut through a cornice, plunged his axe into the plateau surface, and pulled himself up. We soon followed. After two years of effort, we had finally attained the mysterious plateau. It was 8:00 a.m.

The top of Crillon was cloud covered and looked many miles away, but the view of Mt. La Pérouse and out across the plateau to the Pacific, with Icy Point and Lemesurier Island in the distance, was superb. No better route to the plateau was visible before snow began to fall, making our position vulnerable. We had learned that to climb Crillon a stretch of clear weather was necessary, as was a certain amount of food and shelter on the plateau, for where we had reached the plateau was a long way from the summit of the mountain. With the help of a fixed hand line, we started down, knowing that a snowslide could strip us all off the cliff, but all went well and we reached the bottom safely. As we rested and ate sardines and biscuits, we could see the first small avalanches of the afternoon flowing out across our route. By 8:15 in the evening we were asleep at base camp, where we did not come to until 5:30 the following afternoon. Our 24-hour reconnaissance had been exhausting.

The only casualty was Brad, who had taken off his fogged goggles to see the route more clearly on our descent. He became painfully snow-blind and had difficulty reaching camp. For the next three days he felt as if he

WASHBURN

R.H.B. and Houston reconnoitering the route up the 1,000-foot ice cliff

had gravel in his eyes. We put hot tea bags on them, hoping that the tannic acid would help, but complete rest and absence of light seemed the main solution. In less than a week he was back to normal.

While Brad was snow-blind, we continued to move loads in preparation for the next attack, sometimes carrying more than 100 pounds at a time. By July 26, we were back again at the cliffs. We could see that a high wind was whirling snow off the plateau, but the weather was clear, and so we decided to place fixed ropes up the cliff wall. At the bergschrund we climbed a pile of avalanche debris and I leaned across it. Charlie, wearing his crampons, climbed onto my shoulders (padded with a jacket), and drove two axes into the snow above the schrund, but the ice I was leaning against broke off and I fell headfirst onto the trough of the schrund. I wasn't hurt, but Charlie was left clinging to the axes, his cramponed feet dangling 15 feet directly above me. He held, I scrambled out, and I immediately thrust Ad Carter's axe under his right foot. With this purchase, he was able to move up. The snow was badly crevassed below the schrund, and first Ad and then Bill Child went shoulder deep into hidden crevasses. Bill said he could see down at least 75 feet. We worked our way up 100 feet above the schrund, but met waist-deep powder snow and again had to descend.

Two days later we attacked the cliff once more, in what became 44 hours of effort to reach the summit of Mt. Crillon. This time the snow was firmer, the cornice bigger, and all went well except for a biting north wind.

Crossing the bergschrund: Houston (left), R.H.B., and Carter

WASHBURN

Everett and R.H.B. at about 11,000 feet on the Crillon Plateau;
Mt. Dagelet with the Pacific Ocean in the background

We had brought to the plateau a small seven-by-seven-foot bivouac tent, and crowded into it to escape the wind. When it dropped, we started to cross the plateau toward Crillon. The clear weather didn't last long, however, and soon we were traveling blind, with Brad at the end of the ropes to keep us from swerving. When I led I felt I was walking in a great void of nothing, for the snow was white, both in the air and on the surface, and when I moved my foot forward I never knew whether it might drop three feet or bump into a wall of snow. As we reached the east side of the plateau, the weather cleared briefly and the wind began blowing in furious gusts that occasionally knocked us out of our steps. It was 8:00 p.m., the aneroid read 11,800 feet, and our feet were freezing. We turned back.

An hour later we were in the lee of a serac, where we discussed staying for a bivouac, but the weather looked worse and we descended to our little tent, where at midnight we had a bite to eat and then tried to sleep. When Brad looked out and reported improved weather at 2 a.m., we decided to make another attempt. In 10 minutes he, Walt, and I were off, while the others prepared for an attempt on Mt. Dagelet, a backup team if we got into trouble.

We made good time to the serac where we had considered bivouacking, but the wind was ferocious. We waited until it dropped and then continued across the plateau and started up the long ridge toward Crillon's summit. A gust ripped two trail markers from my hands and jabbed them deep into the snow like darts. Ahead rose a 45-degree bump on the ridge with frost feathers covering blue ice. There was a crevasse at the base but we passed over it and went on. On our right the ridge dropped at least 4,000 feet to the Brady Glacier. Clouds, formed at the edge of the plateau, whipped over us, obscuring the view ahead. Once more we found ourselves in patches of waist-deep snow, but the ridge went on. Suddenly Brad cried, "There's the summit." Ahead of us a peak appeared dimly through the mist, then disappeared.

One hundred and fifty yards ahead, we climbed a steep ice pitch with frost feathers over it. We couldn't see 50 feet, but everything beyond went *down*. We shook hands. The aneroid read 13,080 feet, 254 feet higher than the top of Crillon. Brad tied the American flag to a trail marker and was taking a picture when Walt asked, "What peak is that?" Clouds kept blocking the view, but we could glimpse a peak ahead. At first we thought it was Fairweather, but in a few minutes we had a better view. It was the summit of Crillon and still a long way off. We were on the high point of the ridge, but not on the summit.

We started toward it at once, dropping downhill for 200 yards, but beyond lay a large expanse of waist-deep powder. That was too much for us. We had shot our bolt. We rested, ate some corned beef and chocolate, and began the long trek back to the bivouac tent, where we arrived, deeply disappointed, about three in the afternoon. There was a note. The others had climbed Dagelet. At least that was a success.

All that afternoon avalanches poured down the ice cliff. At 7:30 p.m., we took down the tent, put it in a duffel bag, and tossed it off the plateau. It disappeared for a few seconds but finally appeared hundreds of feet down, below the bergschrund. We started down after it, but more slowly. When I was 50 feet below the plateau edge, a piece of the cornice adjoining ours came off and started a booming avalanche, but no harm was done and it cleared away loose snow. At the cache we found that the others had left a canteen of water for us. Bless them! In an hour we were all united at camp.

That was the end of our attempt on Crillon that summer, for we had used all the food packed in from Crillon Lake. Before our departure for home, there was time to follow a stream to the coast, where sockeye salmon were coming up to spawn and we could come up behind a six-pound fish, grab him in front of his tail, and swing him ashore. Charlie once simultaneously caught one in each hand. There were also miles of big strawberries growing on the inland edge of the beaches along the coast. Brown bears were often at the best berry places, but we would run at them yelling and waving our arms. They always ran away and we would have delicious plunder.

Dick Goldthwait had just finished his very successful glacial measurements for the year, having studied the speed and times of movement of the South Crillon Glacier, as well as the depth of ice, which near our camp was 850 feet. Ice depth he had measured by exploding sticks of dynamite and timing the echoes with an elementary sounding device. Simultaneously carrying dynamite caps and sticks had quickened his pulse on frequent crossings of slippery glacier ice, but his greatest thrill was a radio message from Admiral Byrd in the Antarctic, asking Dick to make radio contact on his return to tell him how to make the device work.

A couple of days before Tom Smith's gas boat was to meet us at Lituya Bay, three of us walked along the shore to an old prospector's cabin, which was supposed to have cooking equipment, though all we found to cook in was an old gold pan and a tobacco can half full of Epsom salts. A stream by the shack had salmon in it, but the water was deep, and we had to shoot one to get it. Cooked on a flat rock, it was delicious. We tried panning some black sand without visible success and were about to turn in when somebody said, "I don't remember seeing those rocks down the beach." None of us did, and in a moment we knew why the "rocks" were moving. They were bears.

Charlie had been lighting a Coleman lantern, and with this in his hand, he joined Russ and me as we ran down the beach to see the "rocks" more closely. It was beginning to get dark and visibility was poor. Suddenly somebody shouted, "Look out! They're coming this way." They were, and fast, too. Without another word, we sprinted toward the ocean's edge. The bears we thought were at our heels, but when we stopped we could hear behind us a crashing and thrashing as the bears tore through the underbrush into the woods in the opposite direction!

The next morning we looked at the bear tracks. They showed the bears rushing toward us, probably curious about the moving light. Most likely at our shout, they had stopped short, tearing up the sand just as we did, then rushed for the woods just as we had rushed for the water.

During the expedition I had collected plants and flowers in a flower press loaned by the Gray Herbarium at Harvard. Unfortunately I am not a botanist and since I could not distinguish rare plants from common ones, I collected samples of everything I could find. All had gone well with my plant collection until our final pack to Jim Huscroft's cabin from Crillon Lake. In pouring rain, I was unable to keep the press dry, and so the collection became very moldy. I was shamefaced later when I turned in the messy pages and the plant press, but a month afterward, an excited call came from a man at the herbarium who announced proudly, "You've brought back a brand new mold. We want to name it after you."

My unscientific reaction must have shocked him. To have a mold named for me, with the result that friends would probably always call me "Old Moldy," didn't seem good at all. "I don't want it," I told the man. "Name it for yourself, but whatever you do don't name it for me."

There were no new, unrecorded species among the plants I had collected, but there were very large range extensions of some of the known plants. That pleased the herbarium and made my unscientific efforts seem worthwhile.

Soon after our return from Crillon, I was back at Harvard again, this time in the graduate school, working to get an M.A. in English. I had greatly enjoyed majoring in English; now I would approach my studies in greater depth and learn whether or not I should try to become a scholar. Instead of living in a dormitory, I joined Ralph Emerson, a classmate, who lived with his brother and wife in a rented house on Shepherd Street across from a Radcliffe dormitory. One day we noticed the shades in one of the dormitory rooms rising and falling in a peculiar manner. Sometimes they went all the way down and sometimes only halfway, but always as if with a purpose. It didn't take long to figure that a message was being sent, and since Ralph knew a little Morse code, we worked out the repeated message. It read, "Can you tango?"

We answered no to that, but we did make a date to meet the girls. They were delightful but we never did learn to tango.

By June I needed only one more course to complete the M.A. degree. I was eager to acquire it, for I had been offered a position teaching English at the University of Pennsylvania in the fall.

The course I took independently in the summer was a study of the works of John Aubrey, the first English biographer, called by a contemporary "maggoty-headed John Aubrey" because of the variety and fertility of his thoughts. I became fascinated by the miscellaneous ideas of this delightful antiquarian dilettante with his penetrating comments. I knew I had done the right thing in refusing to join either of two expeditions I very much wanted to go with that summer: one was to join Charlie Houston to make the first ascent of Mt. Foraker, an important climb; the other was to return to Crillon with Brad, Ad Carter, and Waldo Holcombe, and this time climb Mt. Crillon.

In September, when I arrived at the dean's office of the University of Pennsylvania, I had a shock. The number of students at the university was way down, and there was no place for me or others who would normally be teaching. I had never dreamed of such a thing. The head of the English Department was especially apologetic; he strongly suggested that I sign up to take some graduate courses leading to the Ph.D., with the proviso that as soon as enough students appeared I would have a job.

I agreed, and began to take some useful courses, but to get a feel for teaching and to learn whether it would be something I wanted to do as a career, I also did some practice teaching at Penn Charter, my old school. This was a busy life, but it didn't last long. One evening in late November a phone call came from Brad Washburn in Cambridge, Massachusetts, where he was working at Harvard's School of Geography. His voice was excited. I knew something was up.

"Bob," he said, "the National Geographic Society wants us to map those mountains we saw north of Mt. Saint Elias. We'll leave after Christmas and travel on the glaciers with dog teams. They'll pay all expenses. Can you come?"

Could I come! The hand of fortune had swung my way again. If I had had a job teaching, I couldn't have done it, but I was free—free to help chart the last large blank space on the map of North America! I was ecstatic. All I had to do before departure was to write papers for the courses I was taking. There were no final exams.

Exploring (May 10, 1935): Tents at 8,000 feet, nearly two miles from a peak towering almost 6,000 feet above them. An avalanche from the peak, later named Mt. Kennedy, dusted the tents.

CHAPTER IV

The National Geographic Society Yukon Expedition

1935

FOR A LONG TIME AFTER ALASKA was purchased from Russia, some of the boundaries between Canada and Alaska were vague and disputed; but in the years 1903 to 1920, the International Boundary Commission established the border. After the commission was finished, there were still nearly 5,000 square miles of unknown, unmapped mountainous country to the south and west of Kluane Lake in Yukon Territory. The area is heavily glaciated. As we now know, there is probably more water locked up in the ice of the Saint Elias Mountains than in all the lakes, rivers, and streams in the rest of North America.

The best routes through these mountains are along the glaciers, great ice rivers where in the winter crevasses are buried under snow and travel is far safer than in the summer, when dangerous melting occurs. No airplanes had been flown over this area, for there was no commercial reason to do so, and we realized that a forced landing on wheels anywhere in the region would probably be fatal.

Brad Washburn had put together a party of seven. Andy Taylor, a small, wiry man in his early sixties, with a great scar on his neck where a horse had kicked him, was the oldest. He had been in the Yukon most of the time since the great Gold Rush days at Dawson in 1898. While freighting supplies from Fort Yukon to Point Barrow he had learned from

Eskimos how to handle dog teams. Once, when he broke his leg while alone, he had tied his leg to a tree and pulled away from it until the bones were in position for him to splint. Later he had been the hero of the Mt. Logan Expedition in 1925, when the members were in serious danger in a storm on the Logan Plateau. Andy had hunted, trapped, and prospected all over the Yukon, and his experience was to prove very valuable. An avid reader, every year he carefully read the latest *World Almanac* from cover to cover, and would often come out with unusual bits of information.

Adams Carter had been my old companion on Mt. Crillon in 1933. He was imaginative and absolutely dependable. He and Washburn had made the first ascent of that mountain the past summer. Ome Daiber, from Seattle, was an experienced outdoorsman with professional skill in clothing and equipment, while rugged Hartness (Harty) Beardsley, from Vermont, was best known as a skier of unusual endurance.

The final member of the party was John Haydon, from Kluane Lake, where his father, an Englishman, had settled down with his Indian wife to hunt and trap. Johnny had his father's great energy and also skills he had learned from the Indians with whom he grew up. Six of his dogs and his Yukon sled were of vital importance to the expedition. As usual with our early expeditions, there was to be no radio to send messages, and no doctor.

Since we were expecting very low temperatures and severe weather conditions, we made careful preparations for clothing and footwear, although what we finally wore would seem archaic today. We had specially made dry tan boots for skiing, with high toes so that two pairs of thick, felt insoles could fit inside and still not cramp the foot. We also had dry tan moccasins, which I wore with four pairs of socks and double insoles. Our parkas had protruding wolverine hoods for wind protection, and our big Wood Company sleeping bags—with alpaca wool liners—weighed about 20 pounds each.

Our departure had been delayed to miss the coldest weather, but on February 19, Ad Carter and I left Boston by train, picking up Harty Beardsley on the way. Again we took over the colonist car in Montreal, and adjusted ourselves to five days of travel to Prince Rupert, British Columbia, where we were to buy warm clothing from Bryant's Store, which we knew. On the way the train stopped at Winnipeg, where we wanted to buy some food. We asked the conductor when the train would leave. "When the whistle blows," he answered. Then we asked when the train would reach Prince Rupert. "Right after the engine arrives," was his reply. He was right on both counts, for train travel had many uncertainties.

During our last day on the train, it was obvious that we were running many hours late and would not arrive in time to buy our winter clothing at Bryant's Store, since our boat to Skagway was scheduled to leave early in the morning before the store would open. The conductor, however, knew Bryant and telegraphed a request to him to stay open.

Our train became later and later, and we did not get to Prince Rupert and the store until 2:00 a.m. Bryant and Walter, his assistant, had been drinking Demerara rum while waiting for us, and Bryant at least was feeling happy. He kept offering tremendous bargains, while Walter mainly just clung to the counter, hung his head and swayed from side to side as if in a boat on a high sea. By 3:30, we were loaded with packages, sure we were the only sober people in Prince Rupert.

The boat was late, but we reached Skagway on February 26. Since the weather was sunny, Ad and I had a very cold swim, afterward cooking dinner on the stove of the railroad waiting room before bedding down there in our sleeping bags. The National Geographic Society had told us to save all money possible, and we took this charge literally.

The next morning the Skagway customs man came into the station to charge us duty on the cameras and film we were bringing in for the expedition. We refused to pay, saying we had been extended "the courtesy of the port." He refused to believe us at first, considering us bums. When we produced the official Canadian government document freeing all expedition materials from duty, he looked very chagrined and went off shaking his head. Later we took the narrow gauge White Pass and Yukon Railroad to Carcross (short for Caribou Crossing) at the north end of Lake Bennett, the source of the Yukon River.

Brad, Andy Taylor, and Ome Daiber were there already, and Brad and Andy had made a flight over some of the regions we were going to survey. They had found huge, unknown glaciers and unknown peaks, and located a place where a plane could probably land us.

To say we were intrigued by the Yukon is understatement. Everywhere Indians were mushing dog teams and nobody walked. At the little roadhouse where we were staying, the menu for lunch and dinner was always the same: heart, liver, or steak—all coming from a big moose hung up in the back room. In the main hotel room there was a ping-pong table, and a parrot that rang a little bell, screeched, "Goddamn it," and imitated everybody. The only people staying there were old-time prospectors, an itinerant dentist called Dr. Herkenrath, and a Dr. Henderson, who bought gold claims and was probably a con man. The conversation was almost entirely about claims, mines, and future strikes. Dr. Herkenrath kept talking as he pulled the teeth of glum local Indians, who were lined up to have their teeth pulled so they could get false teeth. He loved ping-pong, and when the only ball was damaged soldered it with silver. We went on playing despite the odd bounces.

The original plan for flights over the unmapped area was to use a new, radio-equipped Pan American Airways plane with a pilot attached to us for that purpose, but the Canadian government eventually ruled that any plane for our purpose had to be Canadian. This was a major blow and a source of considerable added danger, because the youngest of the two available single-engine Canadian planes was seven and one-half years old. Neither had radios, and each was serviced out-of-doors in weather as low as 40 below.

Without a radio, we knew that there would be little chance of finding a grounded plane in a 10,000-square-mile wilderness. Bob Randall, our pilot, once joked, "If we have to make a forced landing out west of the Alsek, I might just as well nose her straight down; it would be much more simple."

Brad was the heart and soul of the expedition. His first flight with Andy had taken them 150 miles to the Alsek River and beyond, into the edge of the vast unmapped mountain area we were to survey. That first flight had shown two new glaciers as long as any previously known in North America, and one even longer. It also had shown a potential landing place about 20 miles up a big unnamed glacier that flowed toward the Alsek. To be established here would put us in the heart of the unknown ranges, but to Brad's great disappointment, Wasson, the chief pilot, would not land there. He was scared he would land too high to take off. How and where to get into the range was now our problem.

After the flight, Brad developed the film in an icy cellar and made a discovery. There seemed to be another flat area without crevasses near the Alsek River on the same ice mass, which we later named the Lowell Glacier.

Wasson said he would land at the lower end of the glacier, at the place shown on the photographs, and he did. He landed Andy Taylor and Ome with a thousand pounds of food and equipment, and then flew 80 miles to Kluane Lake. From there he brought back Johnny Haydon, a Yukon dog sled, six dogs, 50 gallons of gasoline, and 250 pounds of dog food. The dogs were essential to our mobility. All was now ready for occupation, and the next day Andy, Ad, and Harty Beardsley were landed on the glacier with the temperature at −45 degrees Fahrenheit. The temperature stayed cold. For the next 10 days there, it varied from -40 degrees to -5 degrees, never warmer.

MOLENAAR

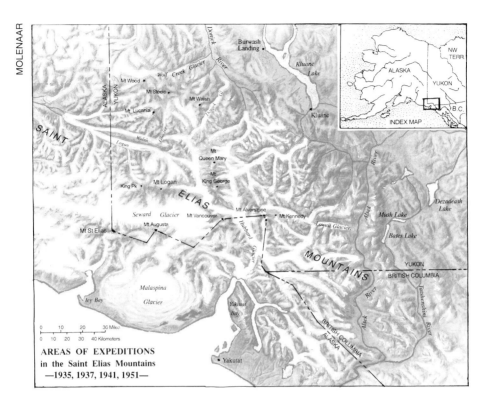

AREAS OF EXPEDITIONS
in the Saint Elias Mountains
—1935, 1937, 1941, 1951—

We had drawn lots to see who would go to the glacier and who would make the great survey flight with Brad, and I was to be his companion. Nobody had ever flown over much of the area and to our knowledge nobody had been in it on the ground. On March 7, we were up early to help with takeoff procedures. Bob Randall was to be the pilot. Our airplane had been in the open all night, with its only protection a tarp over the engine. The skis had been previously jacked up onto blocks so they would not freeze to the snow, but frost had to be brushed off the wings, and the oil for the engine heated on a huge firepot until it was almost boiling and then poured into the crankcase for a quick departure. Before this moment, everything to be taken in the plane had to be aboard, so that once the heated oil was poured in, the propeller needed to be spun and run only briefly preparatory to take off. All this was bitterly cold work at -40 degrees with a light wind.

It was good to be off. I was wearing woolen underwear, a heavy wool shirt with a moosehide shirt over it, and caribou skin pants with warm ski pants over them. I had wristlets, gauntlets with two pairs of heavy wool fillers, and shoepacs with two pairs of felt insoles and three pairs of heavy socks inside. Down clothing was a thing of the future. Brad wore a very

*Bob Randall, pilot for the long
exploration flights*

warm flying suit. Nobody around the plane envied us and the cold ride we were beginning.

We flew for 150 miles over low mountains and heavily wooded valleys dotted with lakes to reach the Alsek River. Just beyond was a big unnamed glacier, and some three miles from the end of it was the tiny camp of our companions. We landed, found them doing well despite the -45 degree temperature, and quickly had the *door off* for the photographic flight to come. For the next three and three-quarters hours, we were flying over unmapped, unexplored country. We realized that any landing where we could not take off again would probably be deadly, for the area was so big, so wide, that the valleys so wild, that it was not possible to file a coherent flight plan. We had no radio—and no map at all.

Most of the flying in our single-engine Fairchild FC-2W2 (a high-wing monoplane) was done at 15,000 to 18,000 feet, where the temperature was 20 degrees *warmer* than on the ground, but the air from the open door was terribly chilling. Brad made a series of pictures of new glaciers, boundary peaks like Alverstone, Vancouver, and Augusta, and unnamed 12,000 and 13,000-foot peaks, plus many lesser summits. Making the first flight around huge Mt. Logan was exciting. We were astonished by the bulk of it, the cliffs of Mt. Hubbard, and the eye-popping immensity of the Seward and Hubbard Glaciers, but even as I watched an avalanche falling thousands of feet, I kept pounding my hands and feet to keep them from freezing in that bone-chilling cold.

Back at Carcross, we both slept for 12 hours. Bob Randall had frozen a knee on the flight, but he had a lot more confidence than our other pilot, Everett Wasson. Bob made an agreement with Brad that if Brad gave him his flying boots after our last flight in the area, he would land at 5,000 feet, 20 miles up-glacier from the present camp, the area where Wasson had refused to go. This he did the next day without difficulty, but bad weather was coming in and he had no time to move the entire camp.

For the next few days Brad and I were marooned in Whitehorse, unable to join the rest of the party. First the plane had an oil leak, then bad weather, next a takeoff on rough ice that shattered a piece of the motor mount; but at last, on March 22, we had our flight. Up at 4:00 a.m., we brushed unusually heavy hoarfrost off the wings and fuselage, and crammed the cabin with frozen salmon for the dogs. (For the last four days they had been eating our rice and cereal at camp on the glacier because they had finished their dog food.) The weather was not too good, but we reached the glacier and landed 20 miles up it, where Bob had left a cache. The wind was so strong that we landed at about 20 miles an hour, with a 40-mile wind whipping powder snow in great gusts. The others, who had moved their camp to a less windy place, came out by dog team, and I went back with them to the camp, where I had to give Harty the bad news that his father had died. His mother wanted him to stay and he said he would think it over. Eventually he stayed.

When I returned to the plane, we left at once, for little clear sky was showing. We had to corkscrew up to get out, and once on top of the clouds there were only a few holes. The air was very rough. Several times we dropped suddenly a thousand feet or more, just as if some giant had swatted us; we were experiencing what is now known as wind shear. When we came through a hole and landed at Carcross, Bob Randall announced that his hair was going gray. He said he would not fly under similar conditions again for a million dollars. Bob must have had a real scare. A furious wind was whipping in and we tied the planes especially strongly to gas drums. Wasson said it was the worst Yukon storm he had ever seen.

After the storm abated, we were grounded for six days. Brad wrote to the National Geographic Society, told of our flight, and announced that we were naming the two largest unnamed peaks for King George and Queen Mary to celebrate their Silver Jubilee. We had eaten the last of the moose heart and liver and seemed doomed to live on moose steak for lunch and dinner, but one evening we had a surprise—moose sausages. A far better surprise came when Officer Kingston of the Royal Canadian Mounted Police brought us to his home for homemade pineapple pie and ice cream. Breakfast was always the same: ancient eggs that Dr. Herkenrath anointed with six kinds of sauce every morning. We took walks or went rabbit hunting with an Indian boy when the weather allowed, but our hearts were with the men on the glacier, and we wanted to be there, too.

Finally, on March 28, we were off on the last exploration and photographic flight. When we dropped off supplies at the upper camp and headed south toward Yakutat, clouds were already forming on Mt. Logan and Mt. Saint Elias. Yakutat Bay looked cold, with blue-green water and large icebergs. We were over Russell Fiord, flying at 15,000 feet without additional oxygen and with no possible landings near, when the motor suddenly stopped. Brad and I looked at one another and then at the cold water and jagged ridges below. Nobody spoke. Bob primed the single motor furiously and dove it several thousand feet. That started it. Sudden relief, but we all had the hidden thought, "Would it stop again?"

We flew down a big glacier we called the Grosvenor (for the president of the National Geographic Society), reached the Alsek River valley, named another huge glacier after Lord Tweedsmuir (Governor General of Canada), and followed it up from the coast to near our home glacier, where we landed. We had discovered a new river, several new glaciers, and an entirely new route for the Alsek; but the motor was missing badly and Bob refused to pick up a load at the lower cache. He was very worried about getting back to Carcross. It was our final planned flight together for at least a month, and our thoughts were with him as he taxied for takeoff.

Base camp consisted of five tents pitched near the base of a huge icefall more than two miles across and 800 to 1,000 feet high. Great peaks spread out in all directions. At camp, we began immediately to put up the knocked-down, beaverboard, five-by-six-by-nine-foot shack that we had made in Carcross during our wait. It was to become Brad's survey office. We were thawing all canned goods in hot water before opening them, for everything was frozen solid.

That night in the tent, I took off my parka and changed my socks, but kept on two pairs of trousers and warm shirts. I was sharing a tent with Andy Taylor and when we crawled into our heavy sleeping bags we had matches and the Primus stove within easy reach, primed and ready to light. Whoever woke first would reach out a hand to light the stove. When it was going well, we would sleep a little more or talk until the upper part of the tent had warmed enough, determined by sitting up to see where the breath line had reached (where breath did not freeze). When I saw Andy holding his glasses over the Primus to get the frost off, I knew it was time to get up. Afterward we all took turns cooking in the big mess tent which warmed up more slowly.

Andy was full of stories. He told, for instance, of the time when he was running a trap line on White River. When there was clear overflow ice on the river, after he had gone 12 miles up it setting his traps or collecting his quarry, he would take off his snowshoes, put on skates, and skate back to his lean-to. One day as he was skinning a marten, five Indians appeared, men in front with guns ready to shoot and two squaws behind holding knives. The men advanced slowly but very menacingly and demanded, "Where you gottum animal? Where you gottum animal?"

Andy was very surprised. He had never seen menacing Indians in the area before, and he said he did not have any animals except a lynx and the marten he was skinning. They kept repeating, "Where you gottum animal?" They had followed very strange animal tracks for several miles right to his door. They would not believe him about the tracks until he put on his skates and skated for them.

We were busy for the next few days measuring by tape a 4,500-foot baseline, using the theodolite to get timed star shots (in a pit dug in the snow to keep out the wind) and setting up survey markers. Ad also introduced Andy to skis. At first he had a frustrating time, but by the end of the day he stated, "Gee, these things have snowshoes skinned a mile."

Working between storms, one lasting 62 hours, we now put in long days setting up survey markers on some of the lower peaks or prominent points, and climbing the icefall to prepare for a move 20 miles north to the eastern cliffs of Mt. Hubbard. Every day we saw magnificent rock and snow peaks, unnamed and new to everyone. Frequently, Ad and I made ski journeys and climbs of small mountains to set up the markers (usually empty gasoline cans on poles). There was continuing excitement in being where nobody had been before, and almost every day we discovered a new mountain or a new side glacier. In clear weather the snowy summits stood out magnificently against the blue sky, and even on cloudy days the blue-green ice gleamed.

Most of the time it was very cold, but temperatures had been lower when the first landings were made. Ad Carter and I spent one very stormy day alternately reading Shakespeare out loud in the tent. We were in our sleeping bags wearing wool hats and mittens. Even when wearing mittens we found that our hands became so cold holding the book that we read only a single page before passing the book to the other fellow to read the next.

Our dogs always slept in the open in small depressions quickly shoveled from the snow, and with only a burlap sack apiece for a bed. Each slept curled up with his tail over his nose, and if snow fell or drifted at night, there was no apparent sign of dogs in the morning. Of course each had a breath hole. When the dog food was cooked (usually a five-gallon can of cornmeal with tallow on top) and the can banged, the snow would erupt with a great chorus of joyful barks. Then each portion of dog food would be swallowed in seconds in great gulps.

Toward the end of April, when snowbirds began to appear, we were worrying about our supply of dog food. We had seen goat, wolf, and wolverine tracks, but no animals; and Brad suggested that Johnny, Andy, and I take the team, with 10 days of food, and descend an unnamed glacier, now named the Dusty, to where we might shoot a sheep or goat to increase our supplies. We left on April 20 and found good going on the big glacier, which had three glaciers flowing into it on the right and a dozen on the left. Nine or 10 miles down-glacier, where we stopped for lunch, Johnny scanned the mountainside with his field glasses and said, "There are two bears up there, one about 50 feet long. Let's go after him." We had seen no mountain sheep or goats, and so I soon had my packboard on and we were off.

We rushed to cut off the big bear, which was headed for a ridge. Once over the ridge, which the other bear had crossed, he probably would be gone forever. Panting and gasping, we finally reached a rock that hid us, scaring a wolverine on the way. As the bear crossed a snow slope about 150 yards above us, I held my breath and fired with our 30.06. He flopped over and began to slide down the slope toward us. Johnny was yelling, "Hell of a good shot. What a hell of a good shot."

I took more shots at him as he slid, and then he was out of sight for a few moments, but he reappeared 50 feet away, lumbering downhill, growling ferociously, and looking big as an elephant. I took two more shots as he disappeared into bushes at the edge of a snow slope. "See his ear wiggle," said Johnny. "Shoot him in the ear." I saw something move and shot it. It turned out to be his tail. We threw snowballs at him, but he did not move. Finally, we walked up to him. The old bear was dead.

He was really old, for his teeth were worn down to the gums. The fur was in prime condition, with not a scratch on it. He was a huge grizzly with just a touch of silver. There was another snow slope just below where he lay, and our idea was to move him down to a flatter area where it would be easier to skin him. I put my pack rope about his neck and with my back to the snow slope, pulled, but the rope broke and I somersaulted down the slope, getting snow into all my clothes. I thought Johnny would die he laughed so hard. Together we rolled the bear to the edge of the slope. Then, as he started to slide, I climbed on top and rode him down to a flat area where we could skin him. Johnny did most of it. He had shot and skinned many bears, but never a bigger one. This skin was nearly eight feet.

We packed the skin to camp, where the dogs came out to meet us, but the smell of bear scared them so that their hair stood on end. They growled at us as if they had never seen us before. That night the bear liver and bear heart were very tasty. The bear, however, had his revenge. To save weight, the three of us had been sleeping spoon-fashion between two opened wool sleeping bags, and the night before we had felt the cold below us. This night we decided to sleep luxuriously, with the bearskin below us. We spread the thick fur under our bottom sleeping bag and turned in early, but not for a good rest as it turned out, for that old bear was full of fleas that quickly moved from his hide to ours.

The next morning Andy cut up the bear and we loaded the sled with meat. We also set up a survey marker for Brad before turning in. The weather was becoming warmer, and I slept without my trousers for the first time since Carcross.

The next day we traveled down the glacier toward the Alsek and finally reached timber. Tracks were everywhere, but the only game we saw was too far away. This did not bother us, however, because we had enough meat now. We cut survey poles, put up other markers, and headed back. Before we left, Johnny blazed a tree, writing our names on it and the date. We were sure that nobody had ever been there before. It made me feel a little like Daniel Boone, who would blaze a tree to announce that he had shot a "bar."

All that night as we slept without fleas on our now luxurious bearskin, snow and wind buffeted the tent, and the next day there was hard travel up the glacier. At times furious gusts stopped us in our tracks and hid us from one another, then it would clear for a moment while plumes of snow a hundred feet high would blow for miles. Finally, with snow well over a foot deep, the old sled bogged down and we had to pitch the tent—a tough job in soft snow with a high wind. We had made only seven miles for the day. In the morning the dogs were frosted up and drifted over.

The gale continued all night and the next day. We cut the load on the dog sled in half, and even so did not get very far. By now we had finished our tea and coffee, jam, and bacon, and were low on gas for the stove, though we had been husbanding it. High winds continued, but an exhausting day finally brought us back to camp, where we hid the meat in our snow cave. That night we did not tell our friends what kind of meat we had brought back, but put some of it through a meat grinder. Only after everyone had declared it excellent did we tell them they were eating bear meat.

Johnny was still partially snow-blind on our arrival. He had lost his snow glasses in our mad rush for the bear and afterward had been using mosquito netting to shield his eyes from the snow glare, but that screen had not been completely successful. Otherwise, we were all in good shape.

During our absence the plane had come in and Brad had made his last photographic flight. We learned also of a communist uprising in China, but just then that didn't concern us. For the next 10 days we worked long hours, sledging our way to the cliffs on the north side of East Hubbard, a

Mt. Kennedy (13,906 feet)

handsome mountain we called Pointed Peak (but now officially renamed by the Canadian government as Mt. Kennedy). Round trips often were 16 miles or more. Brad surveyed as we went, weather permitting, and finally he, Harty, and Johnny occupied a 12,000-foot point on Mt. Alverstone, after crossing a dangerous slope where there had been heavy avalanching. This was our northernmost survey point. Now we could return to our base camp and plan our moves to the south.

On May 3 we had a close call. Four of us were in a tent in our sleeping bags when someone suddenly entered. He accidentally knocked over the lighted stove, which was between us and the door. Flames shot up against the roof of the tent and burning gasoline poured over three sleeping bags and along the floor. The whole tent was about to go, but Brad and I jumped out of our bags and doused the flames with a duffel bag and my sleeping bag, then threw the stove out into the snow.

Three days later half of our dog team disappeared down a tremendous crevasse. The dogs at the time were not hitched to the sled but had been following our steps in single file going up through the icefall above camp. Fanny, one of the youngest dogs, suddenly left the trail and rushed over to investigate a black hole, where surface snow covering a huge crevasse had partially melted. Fanny dropped out of sight with a bark, and before we could stop them two more dogs had bounded over to see what had happened. They disappeared too. In a second, Johnny grabbed two of the other dogs and Harty the last one. Half the team was safe, but we needed them all, and we loved those dogs too.

We roped together immediately and peered down. The crevasse seemed bottomless, and we could see no trace of the dogs. Nevertheless, we set up a belay, and Brad rappelled cautiously into the chasm. Trying not to dislodge ice and snow at the edge of the crevasse, he went down a long way before we heard muffled shouts that he could see them. All three were on an ice ledge 80 feet down. If they had missed the ledge, they would have fallen at least 100 feet farther. Brad never saw the bottom of the crevasse. The dogs were absolutely still but alive when he tied a rope to their harnesses before we hauled him up. As we pulled up the dogs, halfway up we felt a loss of weight, and were not surprised to see only two very scared and whimpering dogs emerge. They seemed unhurt, but where was Monkey, who must have fallen a second time? Ad Carter was on the rope in a moment and rappelled down. He reported that Monkey's harness had broken, but he had landed again on the shelf. This time we pulled him carefully to the surface. Monkey had lost a toenail and had a cut over one eye, but we could find no other obvious injury to the three dogs. The next day, they insisted on working as usual, howling lugubriously when we decided to give them a rest day, and showing no ill effects from their very near miss.

In the next 10 days we not only finished our survey to the south but crossed the main divide of the Saint Elias Mountains that separated the interior from the coast. Across from us rose Mt. Jette, a boundary peak. We were a mile or so from the point where Yukon Territory, British Columbia, and Alaska meet, and to our knowledge were the first people to make this crossing, which had been a major objective of the expedition. More than once we made round trips of 24 miles to get there.

Here we had our last camp together, for the next day Brad, Andy Taylor, Carter, and Beardsley were to begin their move to seawater at Nunatak Fiord. There, if floating ice permitted, Brad and Andy were to continue on in an eight-foot rubber boat another 70 miles down Yakutat Bay to Yakutat. We were not at all sure they could get out that way, and as a safeguard it was decided that Johnny, Ome, and I should go down our original glacier, now named the Lowell, to the Alsek River, cross the river somehow, and reach Bates Lake, about 30 miles beyond, in time for a plane to meet us there on June 1, a date agreed on previously. We could then be flown out, and I could learn whether the others had reached Yakutat safely. If they had not, I would begin rescue activities. Each group knew exactly where the other was going, but nobody else knew our plans, for they were developed during the course of the expedition. Ome, Johnny, and I had 80 or 90 miles to go to the lake, while the others had about 80, partly by rubber boat, to Yakutat.

Our last night together was not a normal one. Our two Logan tents had been pitched side by side, with a snow cave where one could cook dog food out of the wind and away from all the duffel in the tents. Since it was Andy's turn to get dinner, the rest of us had gone off to do the last survey work before our parties separated. As we returned to camp, I could see only one tent and noticed that Andy was cooking in the snow cave outdoors. When we finally reached him and saw a black square of canvas where one tent had stood, Andy remarked casually, "Hi, Bob. You missed all the fun." I stared at him. His eyebrows were burned off and much of his hair, while his wool jacket and trousers showed gaping black burn holes. A blackened five-gallon gasoline can lay on its side in the snow with a half-burned sleeping bag.

A vicious, gusty wind had been blowing while Andy was cooking dog food in the shelter of the snow cave. When a noise caught his attention, he turned to see our tent in flames. He said he never saw anything go up so fast. The tent fabric had had plenty of strains, and a gust of wind apparently had pushed the center pole up through the roof, letting the canvas settle onto a hot stove. Andy went through the flames at once, trying to save something. The gasoline and sleeping bags were the most essential. The gasoline must have been about to explode when he threw out the can, for the paint on it was blistered all over. He snatched what he could and threw it into the snow but the flames burned the hat off his head, burned off his eyebrows, and singed his hair. The important losses were the tent, Brad's sleeping bag, and some of his and Andy's clothing. Andy, however, had saved us from a major disaster. If everything in the tent had gone, we would have been in a bad way. If the blackened five-gallon can of gasoline had exploded, there would have been no more Andy or the other tent either. How we would have survived that, I don't know.

That night seven of us slept in the Logan tent we normally thought tight for four, but we felt lucky to have it. Ad and I slept in an old spare two-man sleeping bag, though not very successfully. We both rolled over once in different directions and then we had two bags, neither too good. Early the next morning, we were up early to face a raw wind. We all had a stirrup cup from the medicine chest, a toast to the success of the other party; then Ome and I were off, headed back up to the divide and on to our main camp, 30 miles to the northeast. On our way, we found the tracks of a big bear that had come for miles straight up what we called the Fisher Glacier to investigate a survey marker, a gasoline can on a pole. The bear was at least 25 miles from timber, and, after leaving the pole, his tracks showed him wandering on in the general direction of Mt. Hubbard. Why? We couldn't guess. Maybe he just came "to see what he could see."

After a hard 16-mile haul, Ome and I reached a small tent. There were no cooking utensils, but we were now back across the height of land and felt that we could reach our main camp the next day in anything but a major storm. We cooked in an old jam can that night and ate some crackers, but, as we quickly found out, gasoline had been spilled on some of the crackers, and we kept burping gasoline fumes.

At eight the next morning as we were leaving Johnny joined us. He had done 22 miles already, for he feared a big storm. Since the dogs were tired, Ome and I increased our loads. We had another 14 or 15 miles to go to camp, with clouds showing bad weather moving in. Spring was coming, too. On the way we found that our snow surface was deteriorating, with cracks hundreds of feet deep opening up. The snow was softening so much that we had heavy going reaching camp through drifting snow.

The next two days we were all three holed up in the little beaverboard office, while a furious storm howled outside. We were very glad we had been able to get all the way here before the storm, but we were anxious to be on our way to Bates Lake. The storm was a big one, with snow piling up outside the little shack while we waited. The beaverboard walls bore strange red and black marks inside, signs of two incidents from the weeks before. One had occurred when Brad was thawing a large frozen bottle of India ink on the stove. He was wearing a white caribou jacket, and when the stopper in the bottle blew off in a shower of ink, his face and his jacket instantly turned half-black and half-white like a harlequin. Later a can of frozen beets, which had not been ventilated enough, erupted too, adding deep red markings to the walls and turning Brad's beautiful jacket into a coat of many colors.

In the crowded little office, with the storm pounding outside, Ome began kidding Johnny good-naturedly about his dogs and his sled and his gun. These were matters of vital importance to Johnny; he was not used to being kidded and I could see that Ome's remarks bothered him. Johnny spent most of that day sharpening his knife on a boot and slicing pieces of toilet paper into strips. I could see that he was becoming very angry, and I also knew there was a strain of violence in his family. (He had seen his mother shoot and kill his father, who at the time was drunk and attacking her.) Ome was only kidding, and since he did not realize the depth of Johnny's annoyance, I had some tense moments before I could decoy Ome outside and tell him to lay off.

The storm finally weakened, and on May 22 we were up at 2:30 a.m. to pack the dog sled and a sled Ome made out of two pairs of skis. The sun now was giving us daylight all night. We piled on nearly 300 pounds of duffel, including my bearskin, which I was eager to bring home. In our cache we were leaving good clothing and enough food to keep three men going for a month, but canned food is heavy, and there was a limit to what we could take in addition to dog food. The night before we left camp, Johnny set out all kinds of food for his dogs: butter, bacon, plum pudding, even pecans. The dogs gorged; in fact, they ate so much that none of them lay down to sleep that night. As we packed the sled they just stood there, legs apart, looking completely stuffed and undoubtedly feeling so.

The crust was splendid when we started, and we made 10 miles before a lunch break. When slush developed, we decided to camp right there. At nine in the evening there was still some slush, but we went on until we found ourselves in a nest of big and little crevasses. When a blanket of clouds interfered with visibility, we camped again. That night no crust formed, and when we went on, the crevasses became more and more dangerous. I was leading when I heard a yell from Johnny behind. The dog sled was jammed in a crack. Two dogs had fallen through, but the momentum of the others had pulled them clear before the sled nosed in.

I rushed back, but the three of us and the dogs could not move the sled. As I hacked away at the ice, trying to free the sled, I had a bad scare. Under my feet there was a sudden noise of snow or ice dropping into empty space. Apparently I was standing over a big crevasse. I quickly stepped away, but it was hard to tell where to move. The whole area was a nest of big cracks. By careful cutting and probing, we found that I had been at the point where a large crevasse met the one where the sled was jammed. Everything felt unstable, as if at any moment we might all go down together. It was no place to camp. Cautiously we unloaded the sled, and, belaying carefully, carried the loads to where Ome and I had left our ski-sled. Here we put up the tent, though there were cracks all around us there, too. All we could do was wait for clear weather and a crust. The dogs hated the place, and Monkey whined so much we had to move him. When Ome went a few feet outside the tent a few hours later, he stepped into a crack nearly four feet wide.

Starting at 2:00 a.m. on May 23, we skied, roped together, some five miles, looking for a route out of the crevasses. Cracks ran in every direc-

DAIBER

Pulling a ski sled toward the Alsek River

tion. Sometimes all of us were over different cracks at the same time, but we kept a taut rope. I remember testing one place with a ski pole and finding a completely hidden crevasse nearly 10 feet wide. Finally, we came across our old trail and had better going. With a wind springing up, the surface was beginning to freeze solid again.

Back at the tent, we repacked our two sleds and were away shortly after 4:30, pulling a big load on our ski-sled. We crossed several hidden cracks. In one Ome went in to his waist, but we found better going soon, reached our original campsite, and soon after came to a boulder-strewn section of the glacier. The traveling here was wretched, but the crevasses were no longer hidden, and we could see that ahead of us, about three miles away, a lake lay at the foot of the glacier snout. Since no more sledging was possible, we took our ski-sled apart and began backpacking. For half a mile there were slippery ice ridges, once with 60-foot drops on either side, but we managed, and by 7:30 that night we were camped on the shore of the lake. It had been an 18-hour day. The dogs were tired, too, but their joyous barks at getting off the glacier expressed our feelings exactly.

The next day we had heavy packing to move our food and duffel off the ice. I wanted to get my bearskin out and began carrying more than 100 pounds at a time, a high load hard to carry over slippery ice. I fell a number of times and had great difficulty each time in rolling over on one knee and getting up.

After supper we carried the dog sled to the top of a big rock, where some day someone might find it. Then Johnny and I, with Tex, his lead dog, walked to the Alsek River about two and one-half miles away, and strolled along the shore looking for the best crossing place. The current was very swift, with pieces of ice floating down it, but in places the river was only 100 yards wide. Elsewhere it was much wider. The shore showed no driftwood, which we had hoped to use in building a raft, but we saw two pintail ducks, and John shot one.

We were back at the tent at 10:00 and up early the next morning, ready to move everything to the river. We did it in relays. That night I figured I had packed that day five trips to the Alsek, a total of 25 miles, with 14 miles of it carrying 75 to 100 pounds, yet this had been an easier day than the preceding two. That night we camped on sand beside the Alsek with pintail duck and dumplings for supper. Across the river we saw a bear, and higher up Dall sheep. We had come only 20 miles from camp, but the going had been tough.

The next day, May 27, we gave up looking for driftwood and Ome lashed our two air mattresses onto a framework of skis, two above and two below, making a tippy raft. Johnny stood on this ingenious creation, using his ski for a paddle, and managed to angle across the river. On the other side he found much driftwood. Using climbing rope, he lashed various pieces to our ski framework and gained greater stability. He then had to drag the contraption upriver, because the strength of the current had moved him a long way downstream. On the way across, when Johnny called the dogs, three of them swam after him. All were swept a long way downstream, and Monkey tried to climb on Cracker's back for a rest on the way over, but the three made it.

Ome and I took the next load over, but when I took the empty raft back across I did not go far enough upstream, so I was swept down past quiet water to a fast current and went half a mile before I could get ashore. Dragging the raft back against that current took all the strength I had, and I had to wade nearly waist deep to do it. I took practically all the duffel over the next time. It was a heavy load and the whole raft was awash. Ome then returned to get Johnny and the other dogs. When the raft was two-thirds of the way over on what was to be the final crossing, Johnny threw the three remaining dogs in the water to teach them to swim, but that fool dog Brownie came to the surface and saw only the far shore. Despite our shouts to turn him, he eventually swam back to the side we had left, landing way downstream. Going back for him took a couple of hours, and considerable swearing, but eventually all dogs and the duffel were finally across the Alsek.

DAIBER

Rafting the Alsek River on a raft made of skis, driftwood, and air mattresses

Wolf, bear, and wolverine tracks lined the river bank. It was too early to camp and so we poured the water out of our boots, wrung out our socks, and Ome and I began to line the raft downstream. It kept grounding on bars and more than once we went in over our knees in sticky mud. When a guide rope snagged, floating ice began to pile up around the raft and the current nearly swamped it. We both got soaked, Ome up to his armpits. Finally we were forced to give up, unpack the raft, and backpack to a gully that looked like a way to begin our climb over a mountain in the direction of Bates Lake. Johnny tried to ride the empty raft down to this gully, which we had seen from across the river, but the raft got into rapids where he literally flew along until a rock punctured a mattress. Luckily he was able to beach the raft near the gully.

The next day was pure hell. Carrying heavy loads, we went up to our knees in mud, slipped on mossy rocks, and fell into pools as we waded up the creek. At times we were up to our middles, wallowing in wet snow, which would suddenly collapse, dropping us into the stream. Alders caught our packs and their roots tripped our feet, but finally we had everything at a place where we could begin to pull a ski-sled. On the way I saw a cross-fox and a number of ptarmigan. Johnny and I shot three of the birds through the head and we each had one for a late supper.

Including my bearskin, we still had three big loads left at the river, and carrying them was wicked. I started again with more than 100 pounds, but finally exchanged some weight with Ome, who gave me his skis. Ptarmigan were everywhere, but we were getting low on ammunition and decided to try to get them with rocks. After pitching the tent, Johnny and I reconnoitered, looking for a good route over the ridge still above us. We climbed a couple of thousand feet, but saw no lake. A valley extended beyond the ridge and then another line of peaks. We dropped down 500 feet or more into the valley, crossed it, and climbed up the other side. After four or five miles, we still had seen no lake. Thankful for the long hours of daylight, we pushed on another three or four miles, and finally saw a lake frozen solid some 20 to 25 miles away. I did not see how we could get ourselves and our duffel that far before June 1. My heart sank as I estimated our food supply and the distances involved.

Then for some reason I looked westward back at the area where we had been, and remarked, "Look at that big mountain over there. I wonder what it is?" Johnny looked and was amazed too; then I recognized it, Mt. Hubbard! Our glacier had curved and the gully we had climbed from the Alsek had wandered so much that we had lost our sense of direction. Now we realized that the lake we were seeing was Mush Lake; Bates Lake must be much closer, where we had already noticed a large white area. What a relief!

We were back at camp at 1:30 in the morning, having been on the go since 7:15 a.m. the day before and having climbed to over 6,000 feet. It was broad daylight when we reached camp and the ptarmigan were cackling. Moments later we were asleep.

At 5:00 a.m. we were up again to get the crust. We made two sleds of skis: one for Johnny and the dogs, the other for Ome and me. Johnny took most of the weight, but Ome and I had 250 pounds as we headed up the slope leading to the ridge. We were barely able to make it. At the top, as we rested, a thrush sat beside me and trilled a lovely song. All the world seemed beautiful again. Then down we went to the valley floor, steering the unwieldy sled, which at the bottom fell apart. Johnny went ahead with the dogs and a couple of hours later, on a patch of heather, we saw the tent. Flowers were blooming and birds were singing. After five cups of tea apiece and some melted cheese on crackers, we fell asleep. The worst must be over.

The next morning we spied a large lake dead ahead of us and some six or eight miles away. For a while all went well, and then again we were in an area of deep, soft snow, with junipers and alders. We crossed and recrossed a creek on slippery stones and fell in several times. The alders would catch on our packs, slash us in the face, or trip us into the creek. What curse on earth is worse to the packer than alders? We staggered down to a canyon, then had to climb 250 feet when the creek went into a narrow gorge. The lake looked miles away, but a final push through windfalls and thick Sitka spruce eventually brought us to it. It was *our* lake, Bates Lake, *the promised land!* And we had reached it the afternoon before the plane was due to arrive! What did it matter that most of the lake was frozen? We were there.

We had emerged at a beautiful little bay, a perfect camping place. A strip of ice at the edge of the lake had melted and the scene of blue water, green trees, white ice, and splendid snowy mountains at the south end of the lake raised our spirits too. At last we were off the ice and snow we had lived on so long. From a distance the lake had seemed to be frozen solid, but where we had emerged from the woods there was some open water, almost enough for a plane to land. As Johnny and I walked along the shore to see how much of the lake was open, two whistler ducks dropped into the water 50 feet from us. We squatted, and as one bird swam past the other, Johnny fired his 30-30 and killed both birds at once with a shot through the head. Since earlier we had hit a ptarmigan with a stone, we now had a bird apiece for supper. On the way back to our camping place, we came across a large porcupine in a small tree. "That's one porky my dogs won't find," said Johnny as we knocked him out. It was then that I learned the Indian method of packing a porcupine home without being stuck by quills (holding the front paws of the porcupine over your shoulders, with his stomach against your back). He would be good for another meal.

A great relief to me was having my bearskin finally at the lake. It had caused much extra packing. In fact, Johnny remarked, "That bear's gone farther by on your back than he ever went on his four legs."

The next morning we had boiled porcupine and applesauce for break-fast, a dish with a sprucy flavor but much to my taste. Ome had sprained his leg and needed to rest in camp while I went back for the last loads. We put hot compresses on his leg, but it remained sore. We felt lucky he had not done it earlier.

The last pack was no better than the one before it. The major differ-ence was that I saw a big bear about 75 yards away. We both stopped and he stood up on his hind legs to get a better look. We stared for several moments, then my skis made a metallic sound and he was off. I was back at camp at 9:45 p.m. and immediately stripped for a quick swim. After that, with tea ready and a ptarmigan cooking, I felt supremely content, even though no plane had appeared.

By June 3, we were carefully checking what rations remained. There were plenty of fish in the lake, but without hooks we couldn't catch them. (I tried unsuccessfully with a bent safety pin.) There was also much game about, but we were low on ammunition and would need to use every shell wisely. During breakfast, Fanny drew our attention to a porcupine in a tree 70 yards from camp and we soon added him to the larder. At lunchtime we feasted on him. The day before, Johnny had shown me a sort of root eaten by bears and also by Indians. We had dug out a number of these bear roots to eat if the need arose.

By 4:00 p.m. no plane had appeared, despite good weather, and so Johnny and I went hunting. About 5:00 p.m. we heard a plane; it was the Fokker. We ran, waved, and shouted as it circled overhead. We rushed madly toward camp, slipping and falling in the mud and splashing through creeks. At last it circled lower and a hand appeared from the cabin door accompanied by a yell that sounded strangely like Brad. Again it circled us, then disappeared in the direction of camp, where our prepared signal fire was sending up smoke. When we finally got back to camp, we could see no plane.

Ome turned to us with a sad face. He handed me a note from Brad explaining that the main party had reached Yakutat on May 29 after a rough trip, then flown to Juneau. He had returned to Carcross, where he learned that our lake was probably still frozen. The note said that a plane would be in for us in 10 days or so.

The plane had thrown out three bundles. The first one, with oatmeal, sugar, cheese, beans, rice, butter, and coffee, had landed smack on a rock, and so the coffee, rice, and beans impregnated the butter in an unusual mixture. The second bundle contained ammunition and crackers. It struck in the top of a big spruce. The ammunition fell to the ground all right, but the cracker boxes exploded; around the tree for many yards pieces of cracker had rained down, with few pieces larger than a quarter. The third package, which held mail, came down right beside the tent unharmed. We were not interested in the food so much as the mail at this point, and I started right in to read my 17 letters. What pleasure! There were notes from Ad and Harty, too.

The food was much appreciated, but it needed supplements, and the following day we added a spruce grouse, a canvasback duck, and another porcupine. Our main success, however, came a day later, when Johnny noticed a big bull moose striding downhill through light alders. My first shot stopped him, and we soon finished him off.

Johnny estimated that he weighed 1,700 pounds; his horns were already 38 to 40 inches and would probably have been 60 inches if he had lived until fall. It took all of our combined strength to move his head and his legs around. We bent down a strong sapling and tied it to a leg to help pull him into position for skinning. When we skinned him, we found 60 or 70 pounds of greenery in his stomach, which was so large it could have contained a curled-up man. We took out the heart, liver, tongue, and sweetbreads, a piece of tenderloin, and a shoulder for the dogs, but it was too heavy. The heart and half the liver alone must have weighed 25 pounds. Finally, we took off our belts, and cut holes in pieces of rawhide to make packs to hold the meat we were taking back. Using our belts as straps, we carried the loads as if they were normal backpacks. What luck, a moose at 100 yards! Our food worries were over. Back at camp, Ome had a big stew of porcupine and soup vegetables ready on our arrival and we ate it all.

The next day we brought in more moose meat. Since ice on the lake had been moved by the wind and now was jammed up against our shore, it was with some surprise that on the following afternoon we heard a plane. This time it was a small seaplane that landed on a patch of open water three-quarters of a mile away. Barr was the pilot and he didn't have much gas. Brad was with him. Barr could carry only 350 pounds besides himself, and since Ome was desperate to get back to his business, I said he should go back with Brad. Barr said he could fly Johnny and me and the dogs to a lake near an Indian village, from which Johnny could walk to Kluane and I could somehow get a ride or walk to Whitehorse.

There was no time to bargain, for the ice was shifting. I left my duffel and climbed into the plane with three dogs. We were off after a short run, skimmed over Bates Lake, then Mush Lake, and landed at the end of Dezdeash Lake. From here, Barr told me, there should be a trail that would lead to Champagne 35 miles or so away. I got the dogs ashore, tied them, and then went back to Barr. Monkey had upchucked on the way and the plane was beginning to smell a bit ripe. Barr was furious! "That will cost you boys five dollars more," he stormed as he started his taxi down the lake.

There had been no time to plan what Johnny and I would need on the way to Champagne, but I had my sleeping bag and packboard and the food bag that had been tossed into the plane before we left. In it there were tea bags, a piece of cheese, and the moose tongue, along with a stove and a frying pan. By the time Barr was back with Johnny, I was frying moose tongue and having a tasty lunch. This time Tip, the lead dog, had added to Barr's unhappiness, but the pilot didn't stay long to complain. My only worry now

R.H.B. and Haydon with moose shot near Bates Lake (the lake was named many years earlier).

was for my skis, my winter boots, and my bearskin, which I had dou-blepacked so far and left in camp. Would I ever see them again?

All of Johnny's stuff was with us, and so we each had a 60-pound load, which we carried along a faint trail until 9:30 p.m., when we turned in, sleeping on our packboards as we had since crossing the Alsek. I had hurt an ankle the day I shot the moose, and so found some of the going, espe-cially through windfalls, a problem.

The next day it rained as we went through a region of small trees with many squirrels. We carried no dog food with us, and each time a squirrel went up a tree, the hungry dogs gathered around it with a chorus of barks. A shake of the tree would send a squirrel flying and a dog would usually grab each end. In a second the squirrel would disappear, except for the tail, hanging from the mouth of one very disappointed dog. Farther along, the dogs caught two big swamp rabbits and I shot two bluebills for lunch. I also found a duck's nest with seven broken eggs where a weasel had sucked

DAIBER

The three who crossed the Alsek and went on to Bates Lake:
Daiber (left), R.H.B., Haydon.

them. There was one unbroken egg and I put it in my pocket. Later we had it and another egg for lunch.

We didn't know how far we had to go, but hoped to reach Champagne that night. At 7:00 p.m. we stopped for tea, and three hours later reached a road. We could smell wood smoke, and a mile farther we reached cabins where dogs barked and young and old Indians in beaded moccasins and buckskin shirts came out to smile, stare, or ask questions. Less than a mile farther, a larger group of cabins told us we were in the center of Champagne.

We slumped down, released our packs, and tied up the dogs. A baseball game, with a stick bat and a moosehide ball, was in progress, with the local mountie pitching. Indians made up the two teams. They had trouble catching the ball but were great throwers. George Chambers, the postmaster, came over to join us and we had a grand supper later at George's Roadhouse, where we swapped stories with George and the mountie until two in the morning. Washing in hot water and sitting in a chair again seemed like heaven.

At Champagne Johnny was not far from Kluane Lake, but I was a good way from Whitehorse. I was told, however, that a police inspector was due shortly and I could get a ride back with him.

After a long sleep and breakfast, we saw George and the Indians trying to break some wild ponies they had just driven in from the hills. Johnny rode a wild one, but he was told it was too easy and they gave him a stallion, who promptly jumped the gate and two fences, then hurtled off into the woods with Johnny still on him. We heard much crashing, but some minutes later Johnny returned leading the stallion. He had earned his food and shelter.

Two days later I said good-bye to Johnny and the dogs. He had become a close friend. That afternoon "Old Jock," the police inspector, arrived with a younger policeman, and we left early the next morning. The first part of the road out was very bumpy; in the back I banged around like a pea in a whistle. Thirty-seven miles from Champagne we reached the mudhole where the inspector had been stuck the day before, and here, fortunately, many spruce poles were lying around. We had already put 10 or 12 poles in the mudhole when the inspector noticed that the car had a flat tire. There was no jack and we needed to cut down a spruce to use as a lever to raise the end of the car.

In the afternoon we reached Whitehorse. Bob Randall, who was at the Whitehorse Inn, told me Brad had just left for Juneau, where Ome supposedly had my gear with him. At the inn I met Walter and Foresta Wood, who were to become close friends, and their guide Hans Fuhrer, whom I liked very much. They were going to Mt. Steele and Mt. Lucania, with the hope to climb each. They urged me to come with them, insisting that they had plenty of food and equipment, but I was now on the home trail and refused.

The next day I took the train to Skagway, and shared a seat with a man who had mining claims in Carmacks. He strongly suggested that I should go there to buy mining claims, too. Carmacks, he said, would beat the old days in Dawson, but prospecting wasn't my thing. At Skagway I boarded a small boat to get to Juneau, where I hoped to find Ome and retrieve my duffelbag.

In Juneau the following day a haircut made me look slightly less jungly. I finally found Ome, who looked different too, and learned that my bearskin and skis had been left behind because Barr couldn't take so much weight in his small plane. Win some, lose some. I wasn't happy about it. Someone was supposed to bring my suitcase of dirty clothes, left in Carcross, to the boat, but it did not reach me. On board I felt out of place in my ski pants, heavy gray shirt, and shoepacs. It was fun to be with Ome again but he was headed for Seattle. At Prince Rupert, where I departed, he stayed on board. We had been through a lot together.

As I headed east from Prince Rupert, I thought of what the expedition had done. Thanks largely to Brad's foresight, we had successfully mapped by dog team nearly 5,000 square miles of mountains and glaciers, eliminating the last large blank on the map of North America. We had made the first crossing of the Saint Elias Range; the first flight around Mt. Logan, Canada's highest mountain, and traced the route of the Alsek River to the sea. We had found some of the subarctic's largest glaciers and named two outstanding peaks for King George and Queen Mary. All this had been done without serious injury of any kind.

Two days later I was on a train headed east by day coach, and five days later I reached our summer cottage in Maine.

Memories of bone-chilling cold and falling into crevasses were already blurring. Perhaps sometime I would be ready to do it again, but right now it felt good to be home.

David A. Robertson and R.H.B. at Chamonix

CHAPTER V

At the University of Pennsylvania, Oxford, and Chamonix

1936

S HORTLY AFTER OUR RETURN from the Yukon, Gilbert Grosvenor, president of the National Geographic Society, offered me a job. It was tempting, but I refused. I had not yet started teaching and wanted to try. In September I was back at the University of Pennsylvania. Sure enough, this time they had a job for me as assistant instructor in English, teaching courses in freshman composition and expository writing; but more students had come at the last minute than were expected, and after two days I was promoted to full instructor with a full teaching schedule. The promotion doubled my salary from $750 a year to $1,500. I enjoyed both the salary and the increased prestige.

Since I was also signed up for graduate work, that meant heavy demands on my time, but all went well. The graduate courses didn't seem too hard, the teaching went easily, and I greatly enjoyed the camaraderie of colleagues in the department. The teachers at the university were a hard-working lot, some very serious and others lighthearted, but my greatest pleasure came from finding among my colleagues Bill Child, my oldest friend and companion on Mt. Crillon, and also Howard Lee, my former Exeter roommate.

During that year (1935-36), I decided that teaching was what I wanted to do. I enjoyed both my students and the thought of eventually having courses of my own when I had a Ph.D. The subject of the thesis would be important, perhaps indicating the area of my future professional expertise. What that would be I had no idea, but at Harvard I had become interested in John Aubrey, the eccentric 17th-century antiquarian and founding member of the Royal Society who was England's first real biographer. At the Harvard library, I had read all I could find about Aubrey, and learned that a miscellaneous collection of his letters, books, and partially completed manuscripts was at Oxford, in either the Ashmolean or the Bodleian Library. I felt that Aubrey might be a good subject for a thesis, and therefore at the end of the college year, armed with a formal letter of introduction from the provost at the University of Pennsylvania, I went to Oxford University, where I was formally accepted as a visiting scholar.

That was a different summer for me, starting with a voyage to Europe on the *Statendam*, a ship beloved by college students. Among those I met were two Princeton undergraduates who wanted to climb in the Alps in the latter part of the summer. One of them, David Robertson, later professor of English at Barnard College, was to become a friend for life.

I had not been to Europe before and loved being in England. Attached to Merton College at Oxford, I worked diligently on Aubrey's fragile papers. His notes were scrawled every which way, sometimes in English, sometimes in Latin, with a mixture of Greek quotations or tombstone readings. Some seemed impossible to decipher. Of much greater interest was a collection of letters to him from prominent people. Aubrey thought that if one could find the date of birth of a number of prominent people, learn from them the approximate dates of the most important happenings in their lives, and put these against a grid showing the positions of the planets at the times of these events, patterns would appear helping to foretell the future. He never got his heavenly grid together, but his idea produced scores of letters from people as different as Isaac Newton, William Penn, Thomas Hobbes, Réné Descartes, and Edmund Halley. Aubrey was also interested in demonology, witchcraft, gossip of all kinds, and anything antiquarian or dealing with the unknown.

I had discovered a rich lode, but one obviously requiring a great deal of selective effort. A basic problem was how best to develop this rich material; another was how to get the time for what would need to be an extremely scholarly enterprise.

On weekends I took advantage of special railroad fares to see various parts of England, including the great cathedrals, and in doing so met interesting people, some of whom became longtime friends. In August, I finally left the dusty Aubrey materials for Zermatt, where David Robertson, Al Edwards, and I made some climbs, including one of Monte Rosa. After the climb, it was so beautiful at the Monte Rosa hut that Robertson and I decided to spend the night there, though we had little money with us. We showed our total wealth to the hutkeeper, who was intrigued by a Baltimore streetcar token in David's possession. He said if he could have the token and I would sing a song, he would take us at half price and call it even. I doubt that he understood the words of "The Strawberry Roan"; however, after a few verses, he indicated that we had paid our debt and there was no need to go on to the end.

A few days later we were in Chamonix. This time we took a guide to climb the Dent du Requin, the shark's tooth, one of the Chamonix Aiguilles. It turned out to be a fun climb on the firmest rock I had so far encountered. For many reasons we hated having to leave the Alps to return home to the United States.

R.H.B. backpacking to Camp III on Mt. Lucania

CHAPTER VI

Mt. Lucania

1937

M T. LUCANIA IN 1937 was the highest unclimbed mountain in North America and one of the least accessible. It had been seen first, as far as we know, in 1897 by the Duke of the Abruzzi, who had just made the first ascent of Mt. Saint Elias. He named Mt. Lucania for the Cunard liner that took him to America. Later surveyed as 17,150 feet high, the mountain was then considered too remote to reach. In fact in 1936 *Life* magazine showed a distant photograph of it with the caption, "Mt. Lucania seems virtually impregnable."

The only climbing party Brad and I knew to have had Mt. Lucania as an objective was Walter Wood's team in 1935. As mentioned, I had met Walter and his wife, Foresta, in Whitehorse that June, and been asked to join his party.

That summer Walter took horses from Burwash Landing on Kluane Lake 30 miles across bush and tundra to the Donjek River, crossed it, and urged the horses on as far as they could go along the edge of the Wolf Creek Glacier (now named Steele Glacier). His team then backpacked to the base of Mt. Steele (16,650 feet), which is linked to Mt. Lucania by a small plateau at about 14,000 feet, the two summits being eight miles apart. Wood had found no access to Lucania except by climbing Mt. Steele first, and the only route up Steele appeared to be by the 9,000-foot east ridge—too steep for campsites. Late that season Walter, his brother, and two companions, having good snow conditions, with a magnificent final push, climbed the great east ridge to the top of Mt. Steele and returned to their base the same day. Lacking tents and supplies, there was no way they could descend to the plateau beyond and reach Mt. Lucania, so many miles

WASHBURN

The Lucania Expedition in front of Reeve's ski-equipped Fairchild 51:
Dow (left), Washburn, R.H.B., Reeve, Bright

farther. Wood and the climbing world in general now had written off
Mt. Lucania as impossible to reach; but that attitude, of course, made it
seem an even greater prize.

Brad had good airplane pictures of Mt. Lucania that he had taken in
1935, and others Russell Dow took in the winter of 1936-37. On them we
noticed a potential route through Lucania's guarding cliffs at the upper end
of the Walsh Glacier, but how could one get there? Even if it were possible
to land a plane on the glacier, who would do it? Also, since our teaching
jobs permitted our coming to Alaska only in the summer, how could we
find a place to take off and land on skis when there was no snow at the airports? There seemed no answer to these problems. Then suddenly two
secret weapons appeared: one was an old cocktail bar, the other a steely-
eyed pilot named Bob Reeve.

Bob Reeve was a character. Before coming to Alaska in 1932, he had
been flying the mail from Lima, Peru, to Santiago, Chile, much of the time
serving as his own mechanic. After several fellow pilots, one by one, had
been killed in crashes caused by engine failure, he left South America and

Valdez in 1937. Note the mudflats.

came to Alaska nearly flat broke. Soon he had his own plane, however, partly because he solved a problem for some Chinese and others who had small gold mines in the mountains, but no easy way of getting to them. In the winter Reeve flew in men and supplies on skis, landing on snow near the mines and flying out rich ore, but when winter snow had melted from the airports, he was stuck. A problem solver, par excellence, Reeve bought an old cocktail bar and hammered it into a strong sheath for his wooden skis. He had noticed how slippery the mudflats were at Valdez when the 20-foot tide went out, and by using these skis on his Fairchild 51 at low tide, he was back in business. Since he could land and take off at Valdez only at low tide, however, his wife always kept an up-to-date tide table in the shirt he was wearing and in his leather jacket.

In January 1937, Brad sent Bob Reeve a photograph and asked him if he could fly a team into the Walsh Glacier at 8,500 feet the following June. This altitude was more than 2,000 feet higher than any of Reeve's ski landings with a load, but he wired immediately, "Anywhere you'll ride, I'll fly. Bob Reeve." That winter our old friend Russ Dow brought the clothing, food, and equipment for our four-man party to Valdez, and Reeve flew it to an airfield near McCarthy, 100 miles from the Walsh Glacier. From here he could fly to the mountain and back without refueling; flying from Valdez, he could not.

On his first flight, a violent wind prevented a glacier landing, but on the next flight he landed with 600 pounds of gear at 8,750 feet. In the following days he and Dow made two more landings, the highest freight landings yet made on skis. The landing strip was so steep and hemmed by crevasses that before takeoff they had to lift the tail and pull the plane around with ropes, but they completed the cache. With our climbing gear and food now in place, Bob was ready to fly our party of four to it in June, and later fly us out.

Brad was already in Valdez when Norman Bright and I arrived on June 11. Norman, one of America's best two-milers, was giving up a trip to Japan with the American track team to join the party. We met in Seattle and went to Valdez by boat. I found him rugged, outgoing, and a fine companion. En route we helped the crew unload freight at small ports and were rewarded by the cook.

Russ Dow, the fourth member of the team, had spent part of the winter in Valdez. He took us to Bob Reeve at the Reeve Airways office, then a small wooden shack with a big skull and crossbones painted beside the Reeve Airways sign. Over the door was the sign, "Opportunity makes damn rascals of us all, but opportunity is *not* knocking here." Then "HANDS OFF OUR TOOLS." On the side of the shack was a painted advertisement in large letters: "Always Use Reeve Airways." Below, larger letters read, "Slow, Unreliable, Unfair, and Crooked." Reeve, lean, in dungarees and a black rain hat, stood in the doorway, a cigarette drooping from his mouth. Bob was his own mechanic and the best flyer I have known.

The weather was bad when the four of us met for the first time on June 11, but Brad had been able to rent a small house where we could stay and keep our gear until we were able to fly in to the mountain. The rent was only $5.00 a month, not a bad bargain, since the bad weather held on. Reeve's plan was to fly two of us at a time direct to the glacier, not via McCarthy. We would need to carry cans of gasoline inside the plane to refill the tank at the glacier, otherwise he would not have enough fuel for the round trip. He warned us that there would be very few places on the way where a forced landing would be possible.

On June 18, a week after our arrival, the weather suddenly cleared as we were starting to eat lunch. There was no time to eat. We all drove to the

Reeve's plane on the Walsh Glacier after the landing. Note left ski and tail.

airport and quickly put in the heavy cans of gas needed for the return trip. A broad expanse of mud, left by the receding tide, lay in front of the plane. Bob sloshed water over some of it, spun the prop, and we were off, sliding and slithering 600 feet across the mud and goose grass before being airborne.

At the airport the weather had looked good, but as we approached the mountain the sky darkened. Bob said, "That stuff ahead is too low. We have 10 minutes more before we will have too little gas to get home."

Brad looked at me, then turned to Reeve and said, "Anywhere you'll fly, I'll ride."

As the weather became worse, Reeve began smoking one cigarette after another. Clouds covered the peaks and they were beginning to creep over the valleys as we reached the Walsh Glacier and began to fly up it. Reeve couldn't quite get to the cache, which we saw, but landed a quarter mile from it, stopping quickly as the plane sank belly-deep in soft slush. Brad jumped out and sank almost to his waist.

Bob was in a hurry to take off, and while he and I filled the plane's nearly empty tanks with the cans of gas, Brad took Reeve's snowshoes and walked to the cache to get ropes, shovels, and more snowshoes. When he returned, reporting bad crevasses, Reeve tried to taxi the plane, but it dug into the slush up to a wingtip. An hour's digging was needed to get it out, and by then the weather was too bad to think of a takeoff. We spent an hour putting blocks under the skis to prevent their freezing to the snow and then snowshoed sadly to the cache.

On the way Brad and I each fell into a number of small crevasses. We pitched a tent and climbed inside as rain, unheard of at our altitude of nearly 9,000 feet, began to patter on the tent. Reeve was very unhappy. He had a small baby at home and no way to let his wife know he was all right. After some soup and cheese and crackers, we turned in. Nightfall brought a violent thunderstorm with torrents of rain that shook the tent. For a short time the temperature soared to nearly 60 degrees.

Bad weather continued all through the next day, with Bob wild to get home. The following day the snow surface was still soft, but Bob tried to take off along a runway we had stamped out with snowshoes the night before. The plane went nearly a half mile but kept breaking through the thin crust. When we joined him and turned the plane around, it plunged into a huge hollow with the left wing tip a foot under the snow. This time we dug down until the plane rested on ice and then shoveled a ramp, hoping Bob could use it to taxi out. Finally, after several tries with the engine at full throttle and Brad and me pulling for all we were worth, the plane roared up and out of the hole. Once more we reblocked it, and decided not to try again until there was a real freeze.

Two days later Bob made a major try to take off, but the crust was too thin. We spent much of the day digging the plane out of three holes. Once a ski tip was six feet down and the propeller nearly two feet below the surface of the snow. That time it took three hours of hard digging to level the plane and build a ramp. We completely unloaded the plane. Even then it took several tries, with the engine roaring and us pulling, to move it onto the surface, where we blocked it up. Bob, for the most part, was silent, and looked frequently at his wife's picture. The fifth day on the glacier the weather turned colder—29 degrees—and the clouds began to move. Bob turned the plane toward the sun to help remove the frost and began to lighten it. He practically stripped it, throwing out tools, emergency equipment, everything movable. He took a ball peen hammer and altered the pitch of the propeller—"to get more bite," as he said grimly. His jaw was set as he climbed into the plane.

Brad and I had brushed off the last frost, and we again reminded him that if he could not get the plane off, we could all walk out together. That did not appeal to him. He muttered, "You skin your skunks, and I'll skin mine." He warmed the engine well, gave a short wave, and took off down the stamped runway on his short skis. Little crevasses kept killing his speed. Again and again he broke through the crust and we saw that he could not get the tail off the snow. Beyond our runway on the right stood big blocks of serac ice, while on the left the slope dropped steeply to a partly frozen glacier pond a mile ahead. If he bumped off either side, we felt sure the plane would be wrecked. It bucked and bounced but Reeve kept on. To our horror, we saw him slide off to the left, then head straight downhill toward the pond, gathering speed. Just as we expected the splash, he lifted the plane off, skimmed the surface, gained 50 feet of altitude, and turned to avoid the mountain beyond. Reeve was on his way.

Slowly Brad and I began to breathe again. There was no chance for him to return with Russ and Norman; they would never get in. It was just the two of us now, with a long walk out to civilization. Bob was skinning his skunks. Now we had to skin ours.

We needed action ourselves after that. Putting some lunch in our pockets, and roped well apart to prevent crevasse accidents, we carefully threaded the cracks for four miles toward Mt. Steele, marking our route with quarter-inch painted dowels so we could use it even if clouds were down on the glacier. We kept the rope full-length and tight between us, for we remembered well the fate of Carpé and Koven in the crevasses of the Muldrow Glacier on Mt. McKinley five years earlier.

That evening, as we considered our problems, I was glad my partner was Brad. He was tough, a splendid companion, and very resourceful. We examined carefully Brad's small book of airplane pictures of the region. At once we ruled out a return via McCarthy. We had seen what that route would be like on the flight in, and wanted none of it. The fastest way out seemed to be by way of the Steele-Lucania Plateau, the route we had hoped to use to make the first ascent of Mt. Lucania. Now it would also be our route to civilization. To follow it would mean practically traversing the summit of 16,650-foot Mt. Steele, descending the 9,000-foot east ridge that Walter Wood had climbed, descending the Wolf Creek Glacier for 30 miles or more to the Donjek River, crossing it, then walking 30 miles farther across wilderness tundra and brush to Kluane Lake, after crossing the smaller Duke River en route. The alternative was to try a much longer route involving crossing two passes and descending 20 miles down an unknown glacier to the upper Donjek River Valley, then walking 40 or 50 miles to Kluane. There was no argument. Reasoning that any-

*Mt. Lucania. We landed on the Walsh Glacier at lower left, advanced through
the crevasses to the big cirque, and ascended to the plateau.*

thing Walter Wood could get up we could get down, we chose the Steele Plateau route.

We took off the next day to organize the food and equipment we would take with us to Mt. Steele, also setting aside an additional pile of food for 25 days to be left as a cache at the point where the much longer route would begin if we were not able to gain the Steele Plateau. Where we were now, food was no problem. We had four men's food, but food might become a problem on either route during our long walk out to Kluane Lake.

We decided to sled supplies to where the two routes separated. Toward this point we began to move 50 days' supply of food, a Logan tent, a Primus stove, two saucepans, 15 gallons of gas, two heavy Wood Co. sleeping bags, two air mattresses, part of a tent for use as a tarp, and a minimum of warm clothing: a total weight of more than 300 pounds. We also had Brad's 9-by-12 cm. Zeiss camera and film packs. Everything else was to be left behind: tents, clothing, camera, food, and his beloved Fairchild aerial camera—all carefully arranged and covered by a tarpaulin. I also took from the winter cache Russ Dow's uncle's heavy police revolver, for I knew it was important to Russ. There weren't many shells, but it was our only firearm and might prove useful.

Our gear was far heavier than clothing and equipment in use today. The Logan tent weighed 15 pounds dry and 22 or 23 pounds wet or with the bottom iced up. The Wood sleeping bags weighed at least 12 pounds each when dry. We had no down clothing. The stove and fuel containers were heavy, and our packboards weighed six pounds apiece.

That night it rained, and rain and light snow continued for the next three days. Working despite the weather, however, we were able to set up Camp II on June 26, nearly halfway to the base of Mt. Steele. We had put together a sled that had been flown in in pieces, but the wet snow made sledding difficult. As we neared 9,000 feet, brief clearings revealed the rib we hoped to climb from the upper end of the Walsh Glacier to the 14,000-foot Steele Plateau.

Light snow fell nearly continuously, but during a few hours every day we could pack loads and search out the route ahead. We put camps close together and by relaying loads kept our trails well broken. Working on snowshoes, by July 1 we had left our emergency cache and pitched our fifth camp at about 10,500 feet at the head of the upper basin of the Walsh Glacier. Here we assembled 450 pounds of food, fuel, and supplies. Above us our ridge led toward the plateau, 3,500 feet higher, but seemed to end in a mass of seracs silhouetted against the sky. Beyond lay the plateau, which we called our Shangri-La.

In the snow basin the sun produced an almost suffocating heat. Mountains surrounded the basin on three sides, and when the snow and ice walls reflected sunlight, avalanches poured down. One fell 6,000 feet off the vast east face of Lucania, but our camp was safe. We dried everything and even had snow baths, for the temperature reached 94 degrees Fahrenheit, but the moment the sun went under, we had freezing temperatures again. After the snow stiffened, we grabbed the chance we had been waiting for and began a reconnaissance of the ridge.

First we had to work out a route through a small, steep ice wall where unconsolidated snow hid many bad holes. This was delicate work. We inched our way through a nest of crevasses and finally over a bergschrund, then pushed on up steep snow to the bottom of the ridge. Above us rose a continuously steep ridge, where we had to kick or cut steps. With considerable effort, we reached about 12,000 feet and rested. By midnight, we were back at camp. The ridge, with its steep snow, was no place for heavy loads.

The next day was cloudless and our thermometer reached 114 degrees. We abandoned the tent we were using as a tarp, eight gallons of gasoline, an air mattress, and one big sleeping bag (light sleeping bags had not then been developed). If we could leave behind one sleeping bag and mattress, we could move more quickly. That night we both climbed into the same end of one of our rectangular sleeping bags. We managed to squeeze in, but were so crammed that we could barely breathe. That system didn't work. Then Brad seized our pliers and removed the heavy zipper at the bottom. One of us climbed in the top and the other in the bottom; and that way we could fit, with shoulders against feet. As we soon learned, however, one person's head always seemed to be downhill. We drew lots to see who would have which end, but eventually alternated. From then on, that was how we slept (or tried to sleep). Occasionally I would hear Brad mutter something, but sound didn't travel well. I would imagine he was commenting on the snow conditions, when finally it would dawn on me he was saying, "Quit kicking me in the ear!"

On July 3, before midnight, we had brought all the food and gear that remained halfway up the narrow ridge to a tent whose platform we had carved out of ice and snow. Across from us rose the stupendous 6,000-foot wall of East Lucania, with Mt. Hubbard and Mt. Vancouver appearing beyond. The weather didn't last and, as we feared, a major snowstorm struck soon after our tent was up. We were well dug in, but concerned about avalanching from the slopes above. By eight the next morning, two feet of snow had fallen and our tent was nearly buried by drifts.

Since storms might follow storms, we decided to keep working ahead with a succession of short, steep relays, even if our progress was very slow, marking the route as we went. Much of the snow was knee-deep, and occasionally even waist-deep, but we carefully worked up as far as a big serac we had seen from the camp below. Here we set up another camp, this time at more than 13,500 feet, among huge ice blocks on a shelf of deep powder snow. It snowed hard on July 4, but during clearings we were able to reconnoiter a route higher, working our way between huge ice blocks. This led us to a long, gradual slope that we felt would take us onto the plateau. Much relieved, we returned to camp to have bacon and Ovaltine before climbing into our single bag. The temperature was now 10 degrees.

The next day we moved everything to the edge of the plateau at near 14,000 feet. Here we had food for nearly 30 days, plenty, we hoped, for an attempt on Mt. Lucania, for that was why we had come.

A major problem ahead was our route to civilization from the plateau. We knew that the 9,000-foot ridge that Walter Wood's party had climbed was too steep for campsites, and once we started down from the plateau we would be committed—there would be no coming back for further loads. From the base of the ridge we hoped to push on as rapidly as we could for Burwash Landing on Kluane Lake, at least 60 miles away as the crow flies, and across the Donjek River. We would need to move fast, for we could not carry more than 10 days' worth of food along with our camping and climbing gear.

By the evening of July 7, snowshoeing in soft snow, we had crested the plateau and established our camp there in a wild snowstorm. The plateau, our Shangri-La, was windy and very cold, but we were there. Reaching it had been a major objective. Now we must climb Lucania.

In the morning an inventory showed that we had carried to the plateau food for 25 days. That seemed just as well, for snow fell all day until 4:00 p.m., when all clouds disappeared in a magnificent clear-off. The air was bitter cold. Eighteen inches of snow had fallen, but we packed our gear, a tent, and a week's food, and pushed a smaller camp to the base of Mt. Lucania, several miles away, setting up the tent at midnight. We had to drop down somewhat from the point where we first reached the plateau, but we were in good position now, with everything depending on snow conditions and weather.

Camp on the Steele-Lucania Plateau, with East Lucania in the background

We woke at dawn to a clear sky. How glad we were that we had pushed on the night before despite the −8 degree weather and the wind. After a big breakfast, we began the 3,500-foot climb, but not speedily because the snow seemed almost bottomless, and even with snowshoes we wallowed. When Brad took off his snowshoes, he half-disappeared and used a lot of energy getting back on top of the snow again. We shared the lead across a 40-degree slope, making great zigzags. If the weather had been warmer, the route would have been swept by avalanches, but it remained cold.

After we had gone four hours without resting, a steeper slope led us to the col between Lucania's second and third summits, but we needed great effort to get there. On the 40-degree side slope a wind crust had formed but not strong enough to hold us. Without snowshoes we went through the crust and deeply into the snow below. With them on, we had to stamp hard to break the surface enough to secure a footing and keep us from sliding off the mountain. We solved this problem by smashing the crust with our ice axes, and then stamping forward.

The crust beyond was dry and wind packed, and to our delight we could climb the steep slope beyond to the top of the second peak wearing crampons. The weather was still cloudless and cold. The wind had turned

Climbing Mt. Lucania: a 3,000-foot treadmill of climbing powder snow. (See articles in Life, *Sept. 27, 1937, and the* American Alpine Journal, *Vol. III, 1938.*

*R.H.B. and Washburn on the summit of Mt. Lucania. The camera was tied
to an ice axe with a shoelace.*

almost calm. A snack at the col had increased our stamina, and our enthusiasm was high, even though our watches showed 3:00 p.m. already. The summit lay ahead of us along the ridge, 800 feet above and nearly a mile away. Feeling that nothing could stop us, we continued steadily ahead until 4:30, when we climbed the last few feet to what we thought was the summit, only to find that the ridge went on to a slightly higher point farther on. We dropped down a bit and moved steadily on. Thirty feet ahead, at the end of an airy knife-edge ridge, was the true summit. Carefully we belayed each other along to the top, where we let out yells of victory.

Below us to the west the slope plunged down so steeply that there seemed to be nothing supporting us. On the opposite side, crevasse after crevasse emerged through what appeared to be a slope of deep, soft powder snow. Mt. Logan looked close enough to touch, and the giants of the area from Mt. Fairweather to Mt. Bona stood out clearly, including Mt. Hubbard, Mt. Alverstone, and Mt. Saint Elias, whose shapes we knew so well. Closer by, we could look over the top of Mt. Steele, which appeared to be nearly as high as we were. Our summit at first seemed big enough for only one of us at a time, but we carefully flattened the snow a bit. Brad tied his camera to an ice axe with a shoelace and managed to get a picture of the two of us on top. The temperature was near zero but amazingly there was still no wind.

It was now 5:00, and we had miles to go to return to our camp. We were tired too, but with an experience like this behind us we felt we could do anything. Soon we were back to our snowshoes, where we found our uphill track a great help on the descent, at least if we always pushed the heel of each snowshoe down hard to avoid tripping. When we reached camp more than 11 hours after leaving it, we barely had our boots off before falling asleep.

The next morning, with the temperature at -10 degrees and a biting wind, we snowshoed back to our camp near the pass. Here we discarded all the gasoline but one gallon, keeping our frying pan, one stove and burner, and most of our clothes. We cut most of the floor from our tent and kept only one pot. Since the ridge off Mt. Steele was too steep to pitch a tent on or to carry heavy loads down, we were determined to cut our loads of 60 pounds each. That evening, in preparation for the big move, we carried 50 pounds apiece to a point about 500 feet below the summit of Mt. Steele, and marked the trail.

In the morning the weather was still holding. If we could get down the ridge, weather would no longer be of such importance. We carried our last

*The top of Mt. Steele,
with trail markers left
by Walter Wood two
years earlier.*

loads to the cache we had left the night before, piled them in two 75-pound packs, and then crossed the northern shoulder of Steele. Before having a big lunch, we sat on our packs looking at the Steele summit. What a pleasure to be enjoying a rest with the knowledge that the top of Steele was soon to be ours too. The climb to it was a bit more than we expected, however, for we had to change to crampons and cut a few steps to reach the summit. Again the panorama was extraordinary, and this time we could look down 9,000 feet onto Wolf Creek Glacier (now known as Steele Glacier), our route out. It curved to the east, leading to the dark trench of the Donjek River. We couldn't see Kluane Lake, but saw the hills beyond it, and they looked a very long way off.

An amazing experience on top of Mt. Steele was finding the tips of trail markers emerging from the highest snowy hump. We quickly uncovered them. They had been left there by Walter Wood on August 15, 1935, and were frozen in too firmly for us to move except for some pieces for archival purposes. Climbers had long argued that the height of snow peaks might vary as much as 40 feet a year, but here was evidence that at least on

WASHBURN

The ridge used to descend Mt. Steele. Tracks can be seen on the summit cone.

one high, snowy peak in the Yukon, the top point had remained roughly the same for at least two years.

Our thoughts now quickly turned to our descent. Walter Wood's small party, carrying no loads, had climbed up and down the 9,000-foot East Ridge in one day. Knowing that was a major encouragement. Since the ridge dropped off very steeply, before we started our descent we eliminated still more weight. We abandoned our last air mattress, nearly four pounds of food, and one of our two rucksacks. We cut off the tent guys and the rest of the floor of the tent. We would sleep in our one bag on our six-pound packboards. We kept 19 pounds of food, an amount we estimated should get us to Kluane Lake if all went well, but we still carried 60 pounds apiece.

We snowshoed down the first 1,500 feet, though the slope was very steep for snowshoes. We then abandoned them at a small plateau and put on crampons. The steepness continued, with one area of about 50 degrees, and occasional patches of ice. Where there was a strong crust, we made good time, using crampons. When the crust became breakable, in places we would go in to our knees, even to our waists, and it was exhausting work. The slope was far too steep for snowshoeing now. The descent seemed to go on forever, and the last 1,000 feet were the worst. We had abandoned our crampons too soon, for the slope became steeper, a sort of frozen, windswept scree, with no belays possible. Finally, at 8:35 in the evening, we finished our 9,000-foot descent, our legs and feet soaked by two feet of slush in the final gully.

There seemed no level place to camp, but we weren't particular. I still carried our bamboo tent pole, and on a patch of rocky moraine we pitched the tent to keep off the glacier wind. Then we had a hot drink and crawled into the opposite ends of our sleeping bag. That night our legs had cramps, but we didn't care; we were over Steele, over the hump at last. Wolf Creek Glacier and the Donjek River were our targets now. Burwash Landing on Kluane Lake still seemed far away.

The next morning, stiff but very refreshed and confident, we ate a leisurely breakfast and then looked for a food cache that Walter Wood had left somewhere at the base of the ridge. We never found it, but we didn't look particularly hard, for we knew he had left a major cache on a bluff some 10 miles or so down the glacier, and we were anxious not to lose time on our way out. Nine hours and 13 miles later, after packing along a crevassed, irregular ice surface with frequent detours, we left the ice and continued along soft gravel moraines. With great anticipation we approached the bluff holding Walter Wood's cache. We felt sure that Walter's expeditions ate well, and we could hardly wait to see what was there. As we climbed the bluff, however, we discovered with dismay that bears had reached it first. They had devoured or smashed and destroyed everything in the cache. Bits and pieces were strewn over a large area, and the only intact item was a small jar of Peter Rabbit peanut butter, on which we pounced.

The empty cache changed matters. We had been counting on help from the two caches, but now we must do without either. That night we went on two more miles before making camp in a meadow above the glacier floor. It was our first night off snow and ice in nearly a month, and we had a grand sleep. The next day we kept on for 16 miles and 16 hours, sometimes on ice, more often along soft moraine, and sometimes on the edge of woods. Side streams swollen to torrents by warm weather that melted the mountain snows were our worst problem. Our feet and legs became numb crossing them, especially one that was waist-deep. We were now getting well below 4,000 feet, and here at last we abandoned our long underwear. We stopped to eat, then continued on, and at 10 p.m., near the Donjek River, found a cabin. Excitedly we entered it, but it was empty. Since we found no water handy, we went on to the Donjek, where we lay down on the sand.

In the morning we checked our food supply carefully. It was getting low, and once across the Donjek we would have 30 miles of woods and tundra to cross. I still had Russ Dow's old police revolver, which we had hoped would help us secure food on the way out. On our way down the Steele Ridge, whenever we stopped we commented that there must be game we could get somewhere in all that greenery, but so far we had seen nothing whatever, not even a squirrel.

All morning we searched up and down the riverbank, trying to find a ford. Since the water was deep, flowing furiously, and icy cold, it formed a much greater barrier than we had anticipated. When I tried to ford it, I was quickly washed off my feet, to be snubbed in by Brad's rope. He also tried with the same result. Even with rocks in my pack, the combined depth and pressure of the water were too great. There was no driftwood for a raft, and we had no axe. Cold and uncertain, we stopped for a small bite to eat. Our food had gone quicker than planned. Our tremendous energy output made us always hungry, and now we regretted leaving food at the top of the Steele Ridge.

We realized that if we could go downstream along the Donjek, we would eventually reach the Kluane River, and somewhere there find Indians, but fast-flowing Wolf Creek entered the Donjek below where we were, and if we could not cross the Donjek now, we could hardly cross it after larger streams came into it lower down. If we went downstream, we would be trapped. Upstream, however, the Donjek seemed to emerge from the Donjek Glacier, about 11 miles away. All we had to do, we reasoned, was to go upstream to the glacier, cross on the ice, come down the opposite bank, and find a trail to Kluane that was occasionally used by hunting parties.

Since our packs felt heavy and we were getting tired, we carefully cached in a tree our extra clothing, one packboard, and Brad's camera and film packs. In our one rucksack we put all our food and a pint of gasoline. On the packboard we tied the tent, the sleeping bag, and the kitchen (one pot, two cups, one knife, one fork, and two spoons). Then we started upstream along the spongy riverbank, trading loads every half hour.

In midafternoon Brad heard a squirrel chattering. I brought out the old police revolver, which I had fired twice at a target at base camp, when it had seemed to fire high and to the left. The squirrel kept up his chattering as I walked around the tree trying to get a good view of him. Carefully I aimed and fired. The squirrel hastily moved to another branch; Brad groaned. The third shot hit the branch the squirrel was sitting on and down he came.

While I was trying to get a shot at the squirrel, Brad noticed some patches of small mushrooms. He gathered a couple of handfuls and asked me what I knew about mushrooms. I said, "If there's a death ring around a mushroom, like the one on the deadly amanita, I know it's poisonous. What do you know about them?"

Brad replied, "I heard once that if you cook mushrooms with a piece of silver and the silver turns black, the mushroom is poisonous." We were both dubious about the accuracy of this idea and anyway neither of us had a quarter.

The mushrooms were small, light brown, and numerous. They didn't look poisonous, but we couldn't tell if animals had been eating them. Brad said, "Jim Huscroft once told me that if you don't eat the brightly colored ones or the white ones, mushrooms in the north are okay." That convinced us.

Within minutes, the stove was lighted and the squirrel was skinned and in our single pot, along with the mushrooms. We watched the pot as if our lives depended on it. The soup was tasty, but there wasn't much meat on the squirrel. Brad said it was like eating piano wire.

Each of us looked dubiously at the other as we began slowly eating the mushrooms. They had no flavor and seemed to be composed mostly of water. We didn't eat all we cooked, but stored some uncooked ones in our packs and again turned upstream toward the distant Donjek Glacier. As we walked, I kept turning to look at Brad to see if he was all right. I noticed him looking curiously at me, too. Maybe Jim Huscroft had been wrong.

Walking on spongy ground was bad enough but two side streams flowing into the Donjek nearly cut us off. One we managed to ford, but the other, formed by meltwater from the East Walsh Glacier, was a torrent. Painfully we turned up it and finally came to where it spread out into 11 streams, all flowing fast and ice cold, with the main channel nearly waist deep. We rested on the far side, ate our last cheese and a handful of raisins, then pushed on. As we slowly neared the ice of the Donjek Glacier, we made a dismaying discovery. The Donjek River did not emerge from the

The Donjek River and the Donjek Glacier. We walked along the ice to
where the river becomes braided (left center) and crossed there
(picture taken 40 years later when the glacier was smaller)

Donjek Glacier. It flowed alongside the glacier in a deep canyon carved
from solid rock. How far away the source of the river began we had no idea.

Getting onto the ice was easy and at first the walking was not bad.
Then we ran into a jumble of seracs, ice ridges, and crevasses, where we
made slow forward progress. We sorely missed our crampons. At 9:00 p.m.
we stopped for soup, then kept on until well after midnight, when we
draped our floorless tent over our two ice axes tied together, with the sleeping bag resting on a patch of fairly flat moraine. We estimated we had covered 14 or 15 miles since trying to ford the Donjek. The river was fast and
narrow here; on the other side we could even see small birds. Big seracs
ahead seemed to block the route, but we were too exhausted to worry about
the next day. We ate a few raisins, lay down, and tried to sleep. We had
taken off our long underwear too soon.

We didn't rest long, but took time to cook breakfast: half a cup of cornmeal and two strips of bacon. Then, despite wearing shoepacs, Brad did

some brilliant ice work. He carved a staircase along an ice knife-edge 60 feet long, then cut an ice bollard from which we roped down 20 feet to a platform. We had left all but one rope behind and had to extend it with a packboard clothesline.

Then, with astonishing suddenness, the ice ended. Ahead lay the river, but no longer in a deep channel about 100 yards across. Braided streams spread out into dozens of channels across huge gravel flats. Farther upstream the river narrowed again and we could trace its course to mountains 20 to 30 miles away. The mountains were far too distant for us to reach with our limited food, but our focus was elsewhere. The sight of those big braided streams was electrifying. Here was our chance.

We were hardly off the ice, however, when we surprised a grizzly bear, which surprised us. Where he came from we didn't know, but he was half a mile away before I thought of Russ Dow's police revolver in my pack. More of the same mushrooms were growing on the gravel and we put several handfuls in the pack. Then we reached the first of the braided streams, roped up, and plunged in. The water was icy and the footing uncertain, for in some places we sank knee-deep into accumulations of fine sand, almost a quicksand. Fortunately these were in pockets, not in large areas. We had several hundreds of yards to cross, and moved as fast as we could, for the cold water and the wind were numbing. We angled from stream to stream, trying to cross where the current was least or the footing best. At last, with more than a dozen big streams behind us, we reached the final two. All along we had feared these would be the worst, and they were.

The first we forded despite water over our waists. Just beyond the last one, a bank with bushes and trees beckoned, but the water looked too deep and swift to ford. It was the main channel. No matter what was ahead we were now too cold to go back. As the heavier, I went first. Brad belayed me to the end of the rope, 75 feet, where the current swept me downstream and him too. At this moment fortune helped, for the pack and duffel bag we carried were both water-repellent and buoyant. Swimming and bouncing off the bottom, we were aided by the flotation. When I reached a bush on the far side I was so cold I could hardly drag my body out of the current. Brad was in the same condition. The crossing had taken half an hour.

Our hands were so numb that at first we couldn't untie the duffel bag. Then we pulled out our sleeping bag, stripped off our clothes, and climbed into our separate ends. There we shivered uncontrollably for almost half an hour. All we could think of was how lucky we were to be across.

A cool wind that blew down the river valley soon partially dried our clothes. We didn't want to lose time and so we put them on, traveling along a game trail that more or less paralleled the riverbank. Downhill at last. Not many miles on, we again heard a squirrel, and this time I got him with the first shot.

Within minutes the squirrel was in our single pot along with lots more mushrooms. Again the soup was tasty, but again there wasn't much meat on the squirrel. We felt better anyway and kept on. Travel on the game trail was the best we had had in a long time, and when next we put the sleeping bag down, we had traveled 10 miles downstream.

At first light the next morning, stiff and weary, we ate a few dried baked beans and started out. Our loads were light now and we made great progress. The most exciting moment came when we saw ahead a big arctic hare. He looked enormous compared to the squirrel and very meaty. We whispered a plan of action. I was to get as close to him as I could, then shoot him; Brad was to go around behind him to try to head him off if I missed or at least to see where he went. I knew a little about rabbits. If I walked straight toward him, he would think I was after him and run quickly, but if I walked in his general direction, headed a little to one side, he would think I had not seen him and sit tight. I walked this way as close as I thought I could get, then turned to fire, but to my horror there was Brad directly beyond the rabbit, his hands spread as if to chase him back. I didn't dare speak or shoot. For a few seconds none of us moved, then Brad gradually eased to one side and I got him—the hare, not Brad—with the first shot.

Out came the pot, and soon he was in it, cooking merrily. With anticipation we waited and sniffed the steam. Finally I announced him cooked, and what a feast we had. Perhaps he wasn't the most tender hare in the world, but he gave us the best meal we had had in days. That night we reached a point about opposite the part of the river we had first tried to ford. We had had to walk 30 miles to cross 200 yards!

The next day we swung to our right, away from the river. We had just crossed an area of muskeg bogs at the head of Burwash Creek and were walking wearily along when we heard a strange noise, a sort of jingling. I looked at Brad and he looked at me. We each wondered if we were getting lightheaded, but we both had heard it. The jingling became louder, and in a moment I saw a man's hat rising and falling behind some bushes. A small pack train of 10 horses with supplies for a cabin near the Donjek was coming along a trail we had not yet reached. Two Indians and a young, weather-beaten Frenchman were with the horses, and to say they were amazed to see us is an understatement. They seemed stunned at our joyful greeting and could not understand where we had come from. When they asked where we were going, we quickly replied, "Anywhere you are going, and then to Burwash."

Our long detour was over. We went with them three or four miles to a cabin, where that night they roasted the leg of a mountain sheep. It was the most delicious meat we had ever tasted, but Brad, after warning me not to eat too much because our stomachs had probably shrunk, did just that and was sick all night. I felt better the next morning than he did, and so with an Indian to show me the ford, I recrossed the Donjek—this time on horse-back—rescued the packboard with the camera and film left in a tree, and returned to the cabin. What a difference it made to be on a horse and with someone who could locate the ford! The following day, after a most uncomfortable 10-hour, 25-mile ride on unpadded wooden pack saddles, we reached the cluster of cabins at Burwash Landing.

That night Gene Jacquot, the delightful owner of the Burwash Trading Post, treated us to a feast of fresh whitefish from the lake, fresh string beans and lettuce from his garden, more sheep steaks, and a remarkable lemon meringue pie he made specially for us. Fortunately by now our stomachs were nearly back to normal.

At Burwash Landing, Pan American Airways had built an emergency airfield for their Lockheed Electra planes flying between Whitehorse and Fairbanks. As yet it had never been used for passengers. Pan American had also established at Burwash Landing a weather station that was very useful for forecasting weather over the Saint Elias Mountains. This station was able to report our safe arrival and to send cables to our families.

Apparently the information caused a bit of a stir, and a day later, July 20, a Pan American passenger plane, piloted by our old friend Joe Crosson, arrived in perfect weather, took us aboard as passengers, and flew us to Fairbanks in time for dinner. It was suddenly over, as if we had just awakened from a dream, but no dream could have made us appreciate so much the luxury of a bed, a chair, and a full meal.

I had one other small adventure before returning home. Brad flew to Juneau from Fairbanks the next morning, but I wanted to go down the Richardson Highway, which I had not seen, and continue on by boat. A driver of a small truck, who was leaving for Anchorage anyway, had agreed to take me. The second day after our arrival, I entered the Fairbanks Drugstore at 6:30 a.m. to have breakfast before our departure at seven. The drugstore shelves were crammed with patent medicines, camera film, alarm clocks, women's stockings, and toothbrushes, the normal mixture of a modern drugstore. Just inside the door was a quick lunch counter with stools, where a man who entered just ahead of me sat down. Nobody else was in the store except a young female employee, who had coffee perking and a blender roaring as it digested a combination of canned milk and strawberry jam to produce the day's ice cream.

I asked for coffee. As she set a cup down, I noticed that the coffee was swirling around in the cup. At the same moment I saw the chandelier overhead swinging around too. The blender kept roaring noisily, and stupidly I wondered if it were shaking the store. Then things began to happen. The store began to vibrate violently; a ripple ran along the shelves, tipping over everything. Alarm clocks, bottles of Sloan's Liniment, and candied cherries went down together. As I jumped up to move away from the chandelier, the girl behind the counter screamed and ran to the front door. She had her hand on the doorknob when the other man put out an arm and stopped her. It was well he did, for a moment later one of the steel guy ropes supporting a big sign over the doorway snapped and came down hard on the front entrance, leaving the big sign hanging crazily. If the girl had gone out, the broken cable would have struck her. One small earthquake shock followed another. There seemed no danger in the drugstore if one wasn't standing under a shelf or a picture, but nearly everything on the shelves fell on the floor.

Since the shocks did not last long, soon the street was full of people. I went outside and heard a truck driver telling of big slides on the Richardson Highway. He was shouting, "There was water, water a squirtin' up outta the road." His story was quickly corroborated, and I found that the road was out and the railroad too. No trains would leave until several trestles had been carefully checked.

I was anxious not to miss my boat, and since road and train service were out I figured I had better see at once if there were a plane to Anchorage. There was, with room for just one more.

A week later, I was strolling about Montreal, still in ski trousers and shoepacs, waiting for the train to Boston, when I passed a newspaper office. The window was full of recent news items and to my amazement there was my picture and a front-page story of our Lucania climb. The National Geographic Society had certainly been busy. Shocked and embarrassed, partly because of my clothes I suppose, I quickly returned to the station. Thereafter I reached home with no further surprises.

About a month later I received a letter from Bob Reeve that read:

Dear friend Bob,

Been intending to drop you a line. . . . Say that sure was some route you covered coming out. *How did you ever* get down that ridge on the east side of Steel.

By the way, three weeks ago I was flying the Fairchild 51 (the ship we used) down the Columbia Glacier on skis with a load of timber when the motor quit cold . . . , and I had to make a forced landing in the ocean. I had to swim to shore. We got the ship out at low tide, repaired the motor, and flying regular again, none the worse for the dunking. Trouble was a broken timing gear. Don't say we hadn't luck on Lucania. I've only flown the ship four or five hours since we returned from that flight. . . . I don't mind forced landings but I sure would have hated to walk out from there. . . .

Bob

CHAPTER VII

K2

1938

THREE MONTHS AFTER returning from Mt. Lucania, I was busy with graduate work and a full teaching schedule at the University of Pennsylvania, when late one evening the telephone rang. Charlie Houston was calling from New York. Almost his first words were, "Can you go to the Himalaya this summer?"

Adrenaline shot through me. I was wide awake. "What do you mean?"

"Well, the club has received permission to send a small party to K2, and they've asked me if I can get a group together."

Giant K2, the second highest mountain in the world, was already a legend. Questions raced through my mind. Could I get a leave of absence from my teaching? Should I go? We would probably need to start the following April. The expedition would take close to six months, and if I went I would be putting off summer work on Aubrey again, but to go to K2 was a chance I couldn't miss. Alaska had been exciting, and Lucania's 17,150 feet had seemed high, but exotic India and 28,250-foot K2 were something else. This was a jump into the big leagues. Was I up to it? I didn't know, but everything within me said, "Do it, do it, do it!"

The next day I went to see Professor Shelley, the chairman of the English Department, prepared for stern questioning about whether I was serious about my teaching career, but to my surprise and delight he listened carefully and then stated at once that if I didn't go I would always regret it, and that experiences I would encounter would make me a more interesting teacher. Suddenly I *loved* Professor Shelley, whom before I had only liked and respected. I left his office walking on air. His only proviso was that I provide substitute instructors for my courses. I had already sounded out friends who were teaching the same courses and they were glad to help and to have some extra money.

The months that followed had many moments of pure pleasure, for I loved everything about the planning for the expedition. Our departure date, of course, was very important. It depended on when the Zoji La pass into northern Kashmir could be crossed in the spring. That date should be about the beginning of the second week in May. Travel to India by boat would require a month, and so departure from the U.S. would need to be in early April.

Now I could focus on K2 and the Karakoram, that marvelous 100-mile stretch of barren rock, snow, and glaciers northwest of the main Himalayan Range that contains a compact area of 30 peaks over 24,000 feet, and more peaks over 25,000 feet than any region in the world. K2, in 1938 usually written on maps as Mt. Godwin-Austen (for the famous British surveyor-general who first triangulated in the Karakoram), has become generally known by its original survey designation, K2 (or Karakoram 2, Karakoram 1 being Mt. Masherbrum). K2 has no native name, for it is so far from any village that it lacks the identity, myths, and legends of Mt. Everest. It lies on the border between northern Kashmir (now a part of Pakistan) and China's Xinjiang Province, an area known in 1938 as Chinese Turkestan. No attempt to climb this most remote of all the world's great mountains had been made since 1909, 29 years earlier.

In 1938 very few peaks in Asia had been climbed. Our situation was in some respects similar to that of Jacques Balmat and Dr. Paccard in France 150 years earlier, when Mont Blanc had not yet been ascended and little was known about the effects of altitude on climbers. In fact, most mountain expeditions in Asia before 1938 had been turned back. No wonder I approached the coming expedition with both exhilaration and a certain uneasiness I had never felt in Alaska.

The two previous K2 attempts especially interested us. In 1902, an international party had reached an altitude of more than 21,000 feet just below the crest of the northeast shoulder, where they were stopped by deep powder snow overlying hard, black ice. Seven years later the famous Duke of the Abruzzi had selected the southeast ridge for an attack. His guides had found no campsite on the south side higher than 18,245 feet, and so they had moved around to the west ridge, where, at 21,800 feet, they had gained a col they named Savoia Pass at the head of the Savoia Glacier. They were stopped there, but later the duke, with three guides, moved to Bride Peak (Chogolisa) and reached a height of 24,600 feet, the world altitude climbing record until the Everest expedition of 1922.

The most recent expedition to the Karakoram had been a French one to Hidden Peak (Gasherbrum 1), which left Askole on April 17, 1936, with an entourage of 650 porters. Bad weather had stopped it just below 23,000 feet. We were particularly interested in this expedition, not only because it was the most recent to visit the Karakoram, but because Charlie, through friends, had been able to secure the agreement of Captain Norman Streatfeild of the Bengal Mountain Battery to be our transport officer. He had been transport officer for the French party.

Telephone exchanges between Great Neck, New York, and Philadelphia became frequent, and Charlie and I began to get together for occasional weekends in New York to discuss personnel, expenses, clothing, food and equipment, Sherpas, porters and a host of other concerns. It was a great pleasure working with Charlie, who quickly became my best friend. We had been close on Crillon in 1933, and I had greatly regretted being unable to accept his invitation to join him in 1934, when he made the first ascent of Mt. Foraker. Since then he had also distinguished himself on Nanda Devi and would have gone to the summit if the night before the summit climb he had not eaten a can of meat that turned out to be contaminated. Charlie is a brilliant problem solver, and we had great fun working together. How he was able to do what he did for the expedition as well as his work at medical school at Columbia University, I don't know.

Charlie sounded out Terris Moore and Dick Burdsall about joining our party. These two had astonished the climbing world in 1932 by both surveying and climbing 24,500-foot Minya Konka (now Gongga Shan), a remote mountain in Szechwan thought by some before their expedition to be higher than Mt. Everest. Terry could not go with us, but Dick could, and this kind hearted, mild-mannered engineer was the perfect man to become our expedition treasurer. None of Charlie's companions on the British-American Himalayan Expedition could get away, nor could Spencer Chapman, an English climber we also admired greatly, who had climbed Mt. Chomolhari on the Bhutan border. On the other hand, we had an outstanding American climber, one of the two who had overcome Mt. Waddington after 16 expeditions had been defeated. This was Bill House, a legend at Yale, whom we had not yet met. Bill, a forester, had only limited expedition experience, but already had become one of the outstanding rock climbers in the U.S.

When Bill met us at The American Alpine Club in New York, we took out the club's big photographs of K2 by Vittorio Sella. These we placed around an inverted wastepaper basket and looked at possible routes. We saw none but it was a most successful meeting.

One final member came through Farnsworth Loomis, a member of the 1936 Nanda Devi group. He could not come with us but offered to pay the way of Paul K. Petzoldt, who had no expedition experience but had started a guiding concession in Grand Teton National Park. "Farnie" had climbed with this big Westerner and spoke highly of him as a companion and a climber.

Food had become my particular problem, and we decided we would need three kinds: food for the one-month, 350-mile trek to the mountains, food for the reconnaissance below 20,000 feet, and a smaller amount of high-altitude food for use at our highest camps. High-camp food, we finally decided, should be pemmican of a type that had proved very satisfactory on the Nanda Devi expedition. Our type, consisting of dried meat, cereal, and raisins, could quickly be turned into a nutritious stew. Meat was a major problem, since many Kashmiris are devout Muslims and Hindus, who would not allow canned beef or pork to enter the country. Our plan was to save our pemmican for the highest camps and use other meats, such as dried beef or tinned fish, lower down. In order to get this meat through customs, we agreed that I should relabel cans and keep a record of what the cans really contained. Accordingly, chipped beef became pumpkin and corned beef hash became spinach, but this required finding old cans of the right size, soaking off the labels, and reusing them.

The need for such deception seems crazy today, but at the time there were many strict fundamentalists in Kashmir. We were told that if we were driving in Kashmir and suddenly had to choose between striking a man or a cow, to choose the man. We could pay for him, but hitting the cow was a serious religious matter. If we killed a cow, a mob might kill us.

As on our Alaskan expeditions, dried vegetables came from Mrs. Kelly. We had hot cereal and dried fruit for breakfast. Lunch usually would consist of cheese or sardines, with biscuits and chocolate. We had no coffee, plenty of tea, and one-third of a pound of pure sugar per man, per day. We knew that our chocolate would have to be shipped through the Sind Desert from Karachi in midsummer and we feared it would all melt. Accordingly, I went to the Baker Company in Milton, Massachusetts, who made for us a special chocolate called Javatex, which could withstand a lot of heat. It did that, but later, on the expedition, we preferred malted milk tablets presented to us in quantity by the Horlicks Company. For special occasions on our long expedition we had two quarts of rum, one of them Demerara, 152 proof.

In Alaska Brad Washburn had taught us the advantage of packaging our food in man-per-day units. We put one day's ration for two men in one bag, and three such bags in a larger bag. The larger one became our standard unit. Five such bags would provide the equivalent of five days of food for six men. In this way we could quickly provide food as needed by large or small parties.

In 1938 in the U.S., few if any companies were making clothing or tents suitable for mountain expeditions, and none made climbing equipment. Most of our clothing and equipment, therefore, came from European sources, and by 1938 standards it was very good; but down clothing, modern high-altitude double boots, lightweight tents, and freeze-dried food items were unknown. We used two-piece Flint suits, made to measure, of double-thickness Grenfell cloth. These also had been used on Nanda Devi in 1936. We had marvelous light underwear, and sweaters, mittens, and a scarf, each made in the Shetland Islands. These we could use in layers.

After much discussion about snow goggles and ventilating them, we selected a model that had been used on Everest. Boots probably were the most important item of all. Ours were made to measure by Robert Lawrie of London: expertly made leather boots with toes high enough for an insole. Since we chose our own type of nailing, I selected edge nails all around and tricounis in the center. Socks to go with them were of different sizes and marked by colored tape. We were to wear puttees too, something new to me, to keep snow out of our boots. Hats for the mountain were Balaclava wool helmets, while for the march in, most of us wore sun helmets because of dire warnings from the British about sunstroke, but we drew the line at cummerbunds. For the six Sherpas we bought similar boots, suits, and sleeping bags. Tents were British too. A Meade two-man model, seven-by-four feet, weighing 12 pounds with pegs and poles when dry, seemed good for small campsites. We also had a Logan tent and another pyramidal one for base camp.

European expeditions had worked on weight problems, and our sleeping bags for K2 were far superior to the one Brad and I had used on Mt. Lucania. They were double down bags lined with red flannel, the inner with a hood, and both tapered. Total weight was seven and one-half pounds. They were our most expensive item. Air mattresses weighed four pounds each and were only half-length. We bought light packframes rather than packboards, and Eckenstein crampons with two-strap bindings. We had a few pitons and karabiners and standard Manila climbing ropes.

Packing 4,000 pounds of food and equipment for shipment halfway around the world was a problem. We weighed out dried vegetables, cereals, rice, and macaroni into small, paraffin-coated bags. Plywood knockdown boxes that could be reassembled quickly in Kashmir for use by horse or porter carriers were constructed as well. Many items were coming from England, where David Robertson helped with the selection. Our Condrupp stoves, Primus type, had special pressure chambers for operation at high altitudes, supplied by the maker. Pemmican came from Denmark. Finally, on April 1, all American items were packed and loaded on a freighter bound for England, to be reloaded there onto the P&O liner *Comorin*, together with our purchases from England. This ship four of us would board at Marseilles for the long voyage to Bombay; we would have our supplies with us.

Thanks to the American Alpine Club, loans, and the generosity of many friends, we met our estimated cost of $9,000 for six men for six months—at that time a considerable sum. To have six or seven weeks on K2, we needed to be away from home for almost half a year: a month to get to Kashmir, a month to go 370 miles to the mountain (350 on foot), and a similar amount of time to return.

On the evening of April 14, when Paul Petzoldt arrived from Wyoming, we five Americans were all together for the first time. We had a splendid dinner at Luchow's Restaurant, thanks to Oscar Houston, with 22 family members and friends to see us off. At midnight, Burdsall, House, Petzoldt, and I embarked on the *Europa* for Cherbourg.

The next day John Case and his wife invited us to have drinks with them in First Class. In his younger days John had been the outstanding American climber, making new routes in the Alps with the English alpinist George Finch. Together we looked at pictures of K2 we had brought with us, and after much discussion decided that the only way to climb it might be to add an extra ridge.

The following night a fine-looking man of about our age came up to us and said to Bill, "Aren't you Bill House? Haven't I seen your picture in the *London News*?" He was Jim Gaul, Harvard '32, en route to Turkey as an archaeologist. Since we were looking at a map, and there was furious discussion about routes across Iran, Afghanistan, and China, as well as our route home from Kashmir, Jim Gaul wanted us to look for places of archaeological interest on the way. At the end of a fascinating evening, he suddenly blurted, "I'd give a lung to go with you. Who knows what you may find? Just a pot shard will do it. Why, man, it's lifeblood to an archaeologist and worth its weight in print. Just a pot shard, just a pot shard."

Later Dick and I climbed the ladder from D deck to the crow's nest, to the great surprise of the watchman. We had tried to take the normal route to the crow'snest, but inadvertently went through the crew's quarters in

House and Burdsall

doing so. The crew were all elsewhere and never knew that in their quarters I saw posted an official German map of the future world. All of Europe, except the USSR and the British Isles, was to be German, as well as all French and British colonies in Africa. Britain and Russia were shown cross-hatched, meaning they were to become semiautonomous. We slipped out of the crew's quarters fast, but in later years I remembered the map and the prophecy of Germany's future.

In Paris the president of the French Alpine Club received us, along with Pierre Allain of Henri de Segogne's 1936 expedition to Hidden Peak. With members of the expedition as our guests, we had another lively dinner. When they asked Paul what he did, he said he worked on a ranch as a cowboy. "Cowboy?" they said, thinking of milking problems. "How many cows?"

"How many cows? About a thousand."

"Ooh la la. How many milkmaids?"

"No milk, no bulls," he announced.

They were quite overcome, puzzled over it, and finally shook their heads and gave up.

They insisted that it had been scientifically proved that no one could physically stand being over 20,000 feet for more than two weeks; to plan food for more than that, they said, was crazy. They laughed at our having practically no pitons, and the next day Bill and Paul in fact did buy a few more in Paris. I also bought an ice axe that I liked, but the shaft must have been dry, for I broke it on the Baltoro Glacier early in the expedition.

The fruit trees were blooming in the north and the vineyards were ripening in the warm sun in the south as we went by train to Marseilles, where after a bouillabaisse dinner on the waterfront we boarded the *Comorin*, which would take us to Bombay. Comorin and Bombay—the very names were exciting! We quickly checked to see if our boxes from the U.S. and England were aboard. All were there, and though apparently they had had rough handling, the only damage seemed to be to Charlie Houston's windproof suit, which was drenched in honey since a nail had pierced a large tin.

The ship, we found, was largely filled with English officers or civil servants going to posts in Asia, some to places we had never even heard of. We were the only Americans aboard and received a lot of attention. Most of the younger passengers were a carefree crowd, having their last holiday before returning to work or beginning it in the wide expanses of Asia. The older ones were experienced travelers, sometimes having combined hunting trips with exploration; and John Rymill, whom I came to know, had led a recent expedition to the Antarctic, described later in his book *Southern Lights*. His knowledge of cold-weather equipment was the best I had found anywhere.

The 100-mile trip through the Suez Canal at seven and one-half miles per hour was hot, though fortunately we had a south wind. On either side were deserts, sometimes with camels going 'round and 'round raising water, and once we saw canal guards with slung rifles racing their camels. In the evening the lights of Africa were on our right and Asia on our left, while above us in a clear sky with thousands of stars we made out the Southern Cross. The next day a good breeze rushed us into the Red Sea, but later the wind dropped and we realized what it meant to be traveling "posh," as we were *not* (port out, starboard home). By April 30, our ship was off Perim Island, the key point in British defense of the Red Sea.

On May 1 we stopped at Aden, one of the driest places on earth, situated in a circle of great hills separated by an isthmus from the mainland. Dick and I took a 30-mile ride around the area to see the native village and the great water tanks, supposed to have been built for the queen of Sheba. The Persians reconstructed them so well about 600 A.D. that they held water until 1928, when artesian wells began to be built. The Muslim women in the village wore chadors that completely covered them, but the colors were often bright red or orange or sky blue.

Four days later we had our last full day aboard the *Comorin*. Two Oxford professors, traveling independently, gave me letters to prominent friends in Oxford, asking them to help me when I returned to academic work on Aubrey. Rymill and Colonel Smith, of the Australian Antarctic Expedition, insisted that we have champagne cocktails together, and Paul distinguished himself by swallowing five.

We had a day in Bombay before boarding the frontier train to Rawalpindi, crossing the Sind Desert in India's hottest month. The day before departure we put to good use. Since Bill House and Paul Petzoldt had noted we were short of fixed rope, we went to the rope section of the bazaar to buy some. Naturally, no bazaar rope had any tensile strength markings, and it was hard for us to tell a rope's strength by merely looking at it. Accordingly, we would stop at a shop, select a rope of the size and weight we were looking for, and ask if we could test it. The shopkeeper always agreed, and so we would throw an end of rope over a beam and hang on it. It would usually hold Bill and me, but when Paul added his weight the rope would break and we would all fall on the floor—to the delight of a crowd of urchins and older onlookers who began accompanying the show. On our third or fourth attempt we found a rope that would hold us and bought several hundred feet.

We also had time to visit members of the German Nanga Parbat Expedition, who were traveling on a freighter that had arrived two days earlier. Most of the party had gone, but we had a pleasant visit with Bechtold and Schmaderer. Afterward we visited the Parsee Towers of Silence, the place where the dead are exposed to birds. The gardens surrounding the towers were beautiful, but the omnipresent vultures were sobering. We also went on to the handsome "hanging gardens of Bombay." On our return, newsboys with billboards were shouting, "American Karakoram Expedition in Bombay!"

We had drinks with the manager and his friends at the hotel, then were off to the station to rent bedding, pay a thumping bill for excess baggage, and secure a maund of ice (80 pounds), which would sit in a big tray in our compartment to cool it during our torrid train trip north through the desert. (I wondered if the ice had been cut in some New England pond near Exeter and shipped to India in a covering of sawdust as ballast.) At 8:30 sharp the great Frontier Mail pulled out of the station and we began to investigate dinner possibilities in the dining car.

That trip through the bleak desert baking in the brilliant sunshine was not enjoyable, but all seemed part of our entry into the storybook world ahead that Kipling referred to as being beyond the frontier. At Rawalpindi,

HOUSE

Captain Norman Streatfeild

Capt. Norman Streatfeild, our blue-eyed, black-haired, vivacious transport officer, greeted us, along with the six Sherpas who had been selected in Darjeeling by Bill Tilman, and had come by train to Rawalpindi. Captain Streatfeild was a brisk, spirited, authoritative British artillery officer whose expertise in his work for us was immediately obvious. He introduced the Sherpas, who looked very competent and friendly, gave orders about our baggage while we had tea, then bundled us into a taxi to go to a hotel. His keenness about the expedition was clear. He wanted to be one of the party and not just a transport officer.

Streatfeild was amazed at the small amount of our baggage and told us how different we were from the French, whom he had escorted to Hidden Peak two years earlier. We realized in no time that we had found a gem. Norman's eyes would flash as he spoke of some of the pleasant places on the route in, and the big Stilton cheese he had brought as a gift; then he would look serious as he spoke about the problem of when the Zoji La (pass) would be safe to cross.

Twelve hours after our arrival, we met Charlie Houston's train from Lahore. Examinations at medical school had delayed his departure from

New York until five days after the rest of us left. He had taken the *Queen Mary* to England, followed by a very expensive flight to Lahore. From there a 12-hour train ride had brought him to Rawalpindi on May 9 as planned. At last we were all together.

In two trucks and two cars, we set off for Srinagar, 180 miles away. First we crossed the pass at Muree and continued along the canyon of the Jhelum River, a road often closed by mud slides, a common hazard in the Karakoram. After passing customs at Kohala, we were in Kashmir, which then was a separate state. Finally the gorge opened into the beautiful green fields of the Vale of Kashmir, 90 miles by 25, an oasis in a dry region of brownish rock. We had a glimpse of distant Nanga Parbat beyond the circle of the Pir Panjal Range, before reaching a poplar-lined road that we followed mile after mile to Srinagar, the old summer capital of the Mogul emperors. Every other tree was lying where it had recently been cut down, the result of a small accident the maharajah had suffered when he ran into a tree.

We were to stay at Nedou's Hotel, very central, and not on one of the many houseboats we saw moored along the Jhelum River. Nedou's was then a distinguished hostelry with attractive grounds, and adjoining rooms spread out from the central building almost like motel rooms.

I was awakened in the morning by a polite, crisply turbaned servant bearing a tray with a teapot, cup and saucer, and an apple. Since it was already light, I was bursting to get out to see the city. I drank a cup of tea, ate the apple, and wanted hot water for shaving, but nobody came. My room was some distance from the main part of the hotel and I could see nobody about; the servant had disappeared. Anxious to get out, I poured out a second cup of tea, used it to soak my beard, and was almost shaved when the servant suddenly appeared. The horror on his face at that moment I will never forget. "Ne, sahib!" he shouted, "Ne, sahib!" and seizing the tray he disappeared through the doorway, leaving me completely embarrassed to be caught in such an undignified undertaking, and also only two-thirds shaved. He did return shortly with a pitcher of hot water, but the look on his face indicated that it was below his dignity to serve barbarians.

To the great pleasure of the Sherpas, after breakfast there was much unpacking of gear sent from New York. It didn't take long to decide that our knockdown plywood boxes were too large for 50-pound loads, and so our first task was to reduce the sizes of the boxes as we put them together.

Paul quickly took charge of our repacking at Nedou's, showing the Sherpas how to use our automatic screwdrivers. They were so fascinated that at first they would screw and unscrew boxes several times just for fun.

We liked them at once. They were good humored, eager to work, and regarded everything about the expedition as a circus to be enjoyed. I was busy with the food, trying to be sure I knew where high-altitude food, "ordinary climbing" food, and bulk food for the march in were packed. Meanwhile, Dick and the captain were arranging a transfer of funds to Skardu so we could avoid carrying loads of Indian coins there for daily payments farther on. Beyond the Balti capital, paper money was generally not known or accepted, and so by arranging in advance to pick up coins in Skardu, we saved weight and worry about getting it there.

Finally the Zoji La was reported open. We had a marvelous final moonlight paddle into Dal Lake, with its fields of blooming pink and white lotus, the moonlight ducking in and out, horns sounding in the distance, and the cooking smells of curries, spices, and ghi sometimes engulfing us. Little bazaars lighted by burning torches were full of life, Hindu temple bells kept ringing, and we seemed in a dream world. When we returned at 1:30 in the morning, wedding drums were still throbbing in the distance.

The next morning, we were up early to load the lorries for the 18-mile drive to Woyil Bridge, where we were to meet our ponies. Ahdoo, the cook, strutted around in my old Swiss boots, polished as never before, giving orders about his cooking gear. The Sherpas, meanwhile, perspiring cheerfully and wearing their high-altitude jackets to impress the Kashmiris, climbed in among the duffel bags, disappearing almost completely except for their new felt hats, worn derby-style, and their delighted grins. We climbed aboard, waved, and in the highest of spirits watched as Dal Lake, with its lightly curling morning mists, slipped behind us. We were on our way, starting our one-month journey to base camp.

At Woyil Bridge 25 ponies of the one hundred that were offered us were selected amid great confusion, and loading began again. Finally we were off, this time on our own feet, for the hot 17-mile march along the Sind River. The first day out is always tough. Dick developed blisters and Paul claimed that the sweat dripping off his nose at one time averaged three drops a step. On our arrival at a camping place, we each chose a Sherpa as orderly, a system favored by the Sherpas and useful to all of us, though definitely not part of our American climbing tradition. My man Phinsoo, a Nepalese, was an old Everest porter and the humorist of the party. He had a pug nose and a constant grin, wore a huge black hat of which he was very proud, and carried an enormous kukri (curved knife) in his belt.

In the morning Phinsoo awakened me with a cup of tea. We ate our breakfast standing in the rain, with water pouring off our pith helmets.

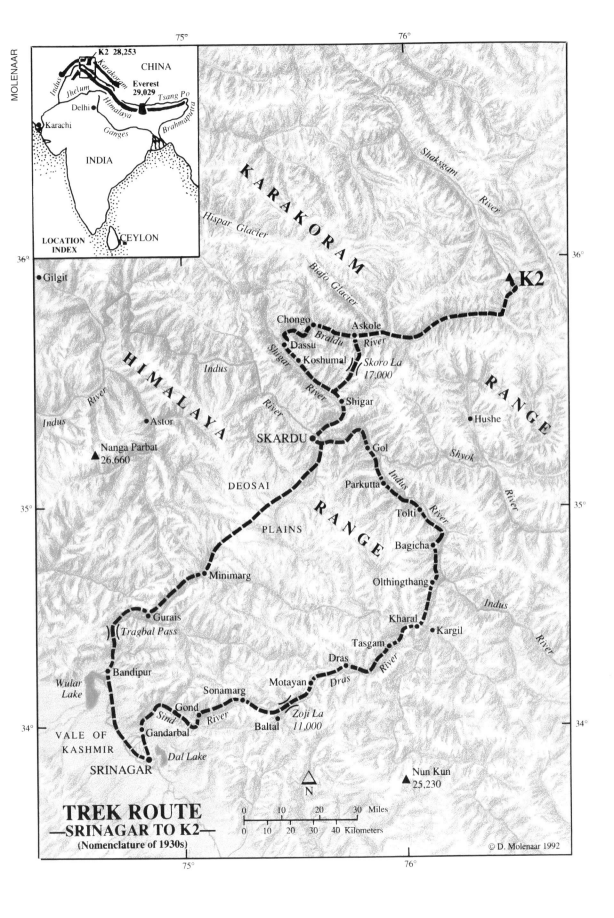

MOLENAAR

LOCATION INDEX

K2 28,253

CHINA

Everest 29,029

Tsang Po

Karakoram

Indus

Jhelum

Himalaya

Delhi

Karachi

Ganges

Brahmaputra

INDIA

CEYLON

Gilgit

Shaksgam River

KARAKORAM

Hispar Glacier

Biafo Glacier

K2

Chongo

Askole

Dassu

Braldu River

Koshumal

Skoro La 17,000

Shigar River

Shigar

Indus

River

Hushe

SKARDU

Gol

Nanga Parbat 26,660

Astor

HIMALAYA

RANGE

Shyok

Parkutta

Indus

DEOSAI

Tolti

River

PLAINS

RANGE

Bagicha

Olthingthang

Minimarg

Indus

Kharal

River

Gurais

Tragbal Pass

Kargil

Tasgam

Dras

River

Bandipur

Dras

Wular Lake

Sonamarg

Motayan

Dras

Gond

Zoji La 11,000

VALE OF

Sind

River

Baltal

KASHMIR

Gandarbal

SRINAGAR

Dal Lake

Nun Kun 25,230

N

TREK ROUTE
—SRINAGAR TO K2—
(Nomenclature of 1930s)

0   10   20   30 Miles

0 10 20 30 40 Kilometers

© D. Molenaar 1992

That day we did only 14 miles, partly through a canyon, to Sonamarg, with 17,000-foot peaks around us. There were traces of avalanches here, but nothing compared to what we saw before we reached Baltal at the foot of the Zoji La. Part of the dak bungalow at Baltal, where we expected to spend the night hours until midnight, had been smashed recently by a winter avalanche, while across the slope from us another slide had scattered tree trunks like a box of spilled matches.

To avoid avalanches in the pass, we planned to leave a few minutes after midnight and climb by moonlight, but another wild scene began before our departure. It was pitch dark when we stepped outside, except for flaring resin torches. The ponies were expressing their displeasure in every way they knew. As we stumbled along a path, our boots crunching the frozen snow, a slightly luminous patch of sky showed us that somewhere there was a moon. Up a snow chute we went, black walls hemming us in and the slope becoming steep enough to make us kick in our toes to keep our footing. The step kicking seemed to go on forever. The light was eerie and nobody spoke. Only the sound of boots on crusted snow prevented the feeling that this must be all a mysterious dream. Then suddenly we were out of the chute in broad moonlight with a large, friendly full moon lighting everything. Ice gleamed on the slopes above and the valley widened ahead. We crossed old avalanche tracks, stumbling around huge ice blocks brought down by slides months earlier. There a cold wind told us we must be near the top of the pass. Snowy walls still rose above us but moonlight revealed ahead the bleak country of Baltistan, with mile after mile of snowy peaks extending to the Indus River, to Ladakh, seemingly to the end of the world.

Dick took a barometer reading and found we were at 11,000 feet, but it was too cold to linger and so in semidarkness we followed tracks down to where a crude bridge, slick with ice, crossed a stream that became the source of the Dras River. By six we reached Machoi, a small resthouse, where we had a belated breakfast. Caravans were everywhere. The drivers had black beards and wore big boots. Most had charms sewn on their coats; they were tough men, much more impressive than the Kashmiris. When they said, "Salaam," they looked you in the eye.

Caravans from the east were loaded with numdahs (rugs), Tibetan tea, and bales whose treasures we could only imagine. Many of these caravans used dzos, great shaggy animals with huge heads and rings in their noses. Dzos, a cross between yaks and cows, are much valued, for they combine endurance with a degree of docility. These shaggy brutes, with hair over their eyes, reminded us of their wild-looking drivers. Both clearly could absorb great physical punishment. Luckily our ponies had pushed right on, for soon the trail was choked for a mile or more with floundering horses and grunting dzos. One caravan in trouble would stall the rest, and sometimes loads and even animals slipped down the snow slopes into the river. In the space of an hour, we passed the carcasses of several dead ponies.

Some five miles from Matayan, we had another meal before going on to the resthouse there. En route I found a bear track made by a Himalayan red bear. Snow leopards were supposed to be numerous, but we saw no tracks. Matayan was full of mud and manure, but nothing could have bothered us that night; we were all across the pass and finally in Baltistan.

The next day, en route to Dras, I had a thrill when I saw scratched on a shiny chunk of marble cliff the letters HHG-A, 1861-2-3. We were following the footsteps of Henry Haversham Godwin-Austen. That night we paid our pony men and hired others. As we skirted the swollen Dras River the next day, in places the water had washed away the path. In one of these gaps, according to a driver, one of our ponies had slipped into the swift water. "Horse go in water," he shouted. "Much work. We get him out. Saddle gone, load gone, cook very angry."

Good old Ahdoo, we thought, always so anxious about his master's belongings. If anyone could get the load, he could, but a few more words from the pony wallah changed our ideas and made us yell with relief. No wonder Ahdoo was anxious, for the lost load contained only his own bedding. Then temporary panic set in at the thought that the load might have been the one with *all* the stoves for the mountain. That night we separated the stoves into separate boxes and made other separations.

The air was becoming hotter on our side of the Dras-Shingo River. The rocks were hot and the reflected light was dazzling, but across the river we could see terraced hills of green barley and groves of mulberry and apricot trees. We were thankful to reach Kharal, where our river met the Kargil River, and to cross on a modern suspension bridge. The Baltis, we were quick to recognize, have been fine engineers for generations. They not only had constructed paths across precipitous walls by ingenious systems of braces and switchbacks, all without using mortar, but their irrigation ditches ran mile after mile across barren cliffs, some of them dating no doubt from the time of Alexander.

Dick and I would have liked to take a couple of days to see the old Buddhist city of Leh, but pressure to reach the mountain was too great, and we agreed to save our visit for the return march.

On our ninth day of trekking, we reached the Indus River, one of the greatest in the world, for which India is named. Following the river the next day, we entered the domain of the rajah of Tolti, where we were immediately visited by a delegation from the rajah, all wearing flowers in their hair or behind their ears, with an invitation to play polo. We respectfully declined, but accepted an invitation to watch the Tolti players.

Eight players, including the rajah, who was in spotless white with rosebuds on his turban, rode wildly up and down a field surrounded by stone walls, where most of the residents of Tolti sat as spectators. A small irrigation ditch crossed the middle of the field and a large mud puddle helped to protect the goal at one end. Just before game time, the water in the ditch was turned off, and the game started when a rider galloped down the field with a ball and, not slackening speed, threw it in the air and whacked it ahead. There was mad pursuit, with haymaker swings at the chipped wooden ball that frequently just missed knocking off someone's head. At times skirmishing was furious, but at others the rajah would receive the ball and ride ahead for an easy goal. If the ball entered the mud puddle, however, he would not go after it but call one of the players to get it out for him. Then there would be explosions of muddy water, which the crowd loved.

Between chukkers, there was some ceremonial hookah smoking, probably bhang, a kind of hashish with tobacco. The rajah had a carved silver hookah with a stem at least three feet long. The great man had a few puffs, then handed it to his prime minister, who, in turn, passed it somewhat condescendingly to the other players. Later we had tea with the rajah and presented him with cigarettes and chocolate.

On May 25, after an arduous 20-mile march through an area where only cactus grew, we advanced through a violent sandstorm to reach the Skardu Valley. The canyon walls had opened, and ahead we saw a medieval-looking mud and wood fort prominent on a huge outcrop above the town, with green fields surrounding it and 17,000-foot peaks above. After the confinement of the canyons, the capital of Baltistan gave a fine feeling of open space.

We no sooner had our tents up beside the polo field when we had a visit from the rajah of Skardu, a fat, self-important person dressed in purple, whom we didn't care for, and later a visit from the rajah of Shigar, a 12-year-old boy, accompanied by his munshi (teacher). The wazir (governor) of Baltistan also came and the tehsildar (mayor) of Skardu. All of these were intelligent officials who spoke excellent English and were delighted to tell us of new developments in Skardu and neighboring Shigar. They also told of visits to Leh in Ladakh, also the wazir's territory, and how Tungan refugees from Chinese Turkestan recently had ridden into Leh with maunds of gold. The wazir had confiscated four maunds (320 pounds) from one group and told of a single Tungan who had reached Srinagar with eight maunds of gold, all he could take away of his store of 100 maunds when fighting in Chinese Turkestan began. Who was fighting whom, the wazir didn't know.

Since we were now halfway from Srinagar to K2, we took a rest day in Skardu to pay off our porters, make an arrangement for future mail and telegrams, and secure 75 pounds of coins to pay our coolies. We also bought tsampa (barley flour) and rice for the Sherpas and other odds and ends for the kitchen, including extra sugar, for on the route in we had been drinking two quarts of tea apiece a day with sugar. There was time also for me to do an article for the *Times* of London.

That evening we had our first baths in two weeks. Then, wearing everything from shorts to high-altitude trousers, we walked through a blooming flower garden to the residence of the wazir, who was giving a formal dinner for us. There were embarrassing moments. At the door, where we were instructed to take off our shoes before entering a large room with silk rugs, sizable holes were exposed in the socks of two of us. Later, as we sat on the floor and ate with our fingers from mounds of rice and various small bowls of spiced meats and sauces, we felt like barbarians who had arrived in a sophisticated community. Sauces dripped down our jackets and tears fell from our cheeks as the hot curries took delayed effect, and when we drank from the silver goblets before us, we suddenly found that one of us had two goblets, and the wazir had none. Most of us stopped eating with the feeling that the sauces were still cooking away merrily in our stomachs, but red-bearded Paul Petzoldt loved hot food. He ate all in front of him and three extra helpings besides. Finally, on cramped legs, we tottered into the hallway, where water was poured on our hands and we washed our faces, then stumped to a reception room for soothing almond custard.

We learned much from the wazir about Balti ways. He told us that Baltis are rarely violent people, with most disputes being about water rights. There is no such thing as infidelity in Baltistan, where people can marry for a year, a day, or any length of time. We took this to mean that Baltistan is a man's world where the man makes decisions, but apparently the women have certain rights, too.

The tehsildar, an enthusiastic tennis player, said that he regretted our departure in the morning, for we would be unable to play tennis with him. We saw the court, with its unusually large spaces at the back and sides sur-

Crossing the Indus River near Skardu in Alexander's barge

rounded by purple turban cloth. The top of the net was red and hung with gorgeous red tassels.

The evening was too soon over. We were escorted to the resthouse by the wazir and the other gentlemen, preceded by torch bearers. We had met gracious hospitality and, in addition, wisdom, sophistication, and humor. We were sad to be leaving.

At Skardu in the springtime the Indus River is wide and swift, and in 1938 there was no bridge. Instead an ancient ferry was in use, whose massive planks were locally reputed to have been put together by Alexander's men. Before we shoved off with our load of three horses, five sheep, seven goats, and 17 people, the steersman, a huge Balti, who manned an enormous sweep oar in the stern, paused to spread wide his arms and pray loudly to Allah that we should not be drowned.

Everybody worked. Narrow paddles and sticks lay on the planks of the ferry, and young and old alike, without semblance of rhythm, hacked furiously at the water as if the devil were chasing them. The riverbank shot by alarmingly fast as we swept downstream in a diagonal course that brought us to shore nearly half a mile below our starting point.

From here 12 miles of hot walking through soft sand brought us to Shigar, a prosperous town, where we camped on the polo field. The rajah

Balti porter

and his munshi were in Skardu, and again we were feasted in a most hospitable way, this time with five kinds of cakes, cinnamon tea, and Tibetan butter tea. Some huge, platter-sized delicacies, made of fried ghi and sugar, were of eggshell thickness, while others were thick and very heavy. The room where we ate had fine wood carvings and rich carpets from Turkestan.

At Yuno, 18 miles away, we had trouble. Porters for the next stage demanded triple the wages the wazir had told us to pay. The Yuno men, pushed by two troublemakers, believed they had found easy money. The captain increased our offer but refused to pay their exorbitant demands. They had been smoking bhang and were becoming excitable. One of the ringleaders began jabbering at the captain offensively and the captain pushed him away. The man stepped backward, tripped, and fell down. At this the crowd of 70 men surged forward threateningly. They were angry and so were we.

The hindmost men shoved the foremost toward us and one man struck Ahdoo on the head with his rope. That was too much for the Sherpas. Ice axes in hand, they started forward to carve the enemy to pieces. "Let us at them, sahib, we do not like these men," Pasang pleaded. "Let us at them." The sight of the Sherpas with their ice axes and Phinsoo with his big kukri was too much for the Yuno men. They ran, yelling threats as they went.

One of them threw a stone that knocked down Bill's tent, where he had his camera. Bill yelled and picked up a stone, too. Paul heard Bill yell, thought he had been struck, and, picking up a large rock, dashed after the enemy like an angry bull buffalo. As he went, his foot struck a guy rope of another tent and it went down too. He didn't notice. His size, his anger, his red beard, and the great rock he brandished had immediate effect. We could hear the Yuno men running for minutes afterward.

Fortunately, the munshi's son had accompanied us and he went to see the porters while we huddled in a council of war. It was getting dark, and while we were talking, the Sherpas set up a guard. They placed each man's ice axe by his sleeping bag, with the spare axes stacked military style like cutlasses in the center of our ring of tents. The Sherpas, on their own initiative again, took turns guarding the area of the camp with ice axes and the kukri.

In three-quarters of an hour the munshi's son returned. He said the Yuno men were again smoking bhang and being urged by two men to swear on the Koran not to go on unless they were paid their highest price. He told us we would need to go back to see the tehsildar. A zhak, a goatskin raft, was available, and it was decided that in the morning the captain and I should return in it to Skardu.

That night nothing happened. In the morning the captain and I climbed down to the Shigar River, which we had been following the previous day, to our zhak. It consisted of 28 goat bladders tied to a framework of slender poplar poles, on which we were to sit an inch or two above water level. The whole contraption weighed less than 100 pounds and could easily be taken apart and carried upstream. The moment we stepped gingerly aboard and sat down on a waterproof jacket someone let go of the raft. Then, with loud prayers to Allah, we and our ragged boatmen went bobbing and spinning downstream.

For the rest of the morning we were completely in the hands of our boatmen, who had long sticks but no paddles. The raft grounded on sandbars and spun round and round in minor whirlpools; when we approached rapids, the boatmen put down their poles and prayed loudly as we tossed and spun and held on. Most of the time one or two of them would be blowing up leaky bladders—even ones we were sitting on—or splashing water on the exposed skins to keep the sun from cracking them.

Our shoes and clothes amazed the boatmen, who were not worldly types. One of them had six toes and another had a half-inch part shaved down the center of his head with long hair hanging down over his ears. When the zhak finally reached the Indus, we went booming downstream, but despite their best efforts, we failed to cross to the far shore until we were some two and a half miles below Skardu.

We paid the happy boatmen and trudged to the tehsildar's house, where dozens of shoes beside the door indicated that court was in session. Inside we found the wazir and the tehsildar sitting in thronelike chairs. Court was immediately adjourned and we were escorted to the wazir's garden, where over tea and an onion omelet we told the reason for our return. The tehsildar at once offered to return with us but finally agreed that a well-known chuprassi (a sort of police captain) should accompany us. With that settled, we learned what we had interrupted. A new tax collector was needed, and the wazir was trying to find the right man for the job. His system was to tell a riddle or a story that required a solution and to select the man with the best answers. There was no nepotism here. Instead, as in some modern business schools, a case system of problem solving was used to find the best man.

Stories of Balti customs followed. To our amazement we learned that in valleys where glaciers had disappeared, sometimes new, artificial glaciers are constructed by villagers. Glaciers are treasured in this dry country, for meltwater is the source of practically all irrigation. The last glacier to be started, we were told, had been made 35 years earlier by the grandfather of the present rajah. It had been built to an ancient formula, with ice blocks coming from male and female glaciers (their difference was not made clear). These blocks were deposited in a high valley and covered with charcoal and thorn bushes, on top of which 50 goatskins of water were placed. The water was to help keep the ice cool and to augment the ice supply when the water froze in winter. After 20 years of gradually adding ice and snow, the glacier became strong enough to support itself and send a constant supply of water in the nonwinter months to the dry fields below.

At first light we were awakened by a stocky chuprassi, originally from Hunza, with three saddled horses. He had been ordered, he said, to bring the two strike ringleaders to Shigar for trial. In no time at all we were in "Alexander's barge," again floating swiftly down the Indus but in a craft with more control than our zhak. Five hours later we were in Shigar, where again we drank our fill of cinnamon tea and ate sticky cakes, then rode on to Yuno. Now and then we could strip off handfuls of half-ripe mulberries as we rode painfully along, damning Balti wooden saddles, until at last we reached camp. There the others had been busy too, improving the tents and teaching the Sherpas the proper use of the rope—both endeavors that paid off weeks later. The chuprassi had a magic touch. The next morning the porters who had blackmailed us were all smiles. "Win some, lose some," they seemed to say.

The trail continually crossed bare slabs, requiring great care, sometimes descending close to the river where the air was cold, then again up as much as 1,000 feet higher along the cliffs. Fourteen of the men, all from Satpura village, had been with us since Tolti. They had not supported the strike, were always cheerful, and now put backbone in our porter train. It was good they did, for the climbing was steep; the river roared below, with a constant churning of stones and heavy thumps as boulders were swept along by the current. The following day was worse, for the track rose and fell some 3,500 feet on the way to the first village where we could camp. The route crossed or wound around slabs falling sheer to the river, a better route for barefoot porters than for climbers in nailed boots.

Tiny villages existed in every green oasis of our vertical desert. Often people asked for medical help, but there was usually little we could do. Some brought gifts of apricot kernels. Charlie was the only doctor some of the patients had seen since the Duke of the Abruzzi's expedition 29 years earlier, and some we were told had not seen a doctor for 40 years.

Charlie had successes, some of them unusual. Once a man came to him with a rope bound very tightly around his head, announcing that a headache was splitting his head in two. Charlie cut the rope and made a quick cure that vastly impressed onlookers. Another time, after a man described his wife's illness, Charlie had the impression that calcium would help her, but he had no calcium. His eye fell on a huge bottle of calcium tooth powder that Paul's friends had given him as a joke. Charlie poured out half of it for the man and said that his wife should take some of it daily with milk. Weeks later, when we saw the man again, we found him deeply grateful. His wife, he said, was cured.

Charlie had a far more difficult problem at Hoto, the last village before Askole. Paul, who had never been ill in his life, came down with a worrying 103-degree fever, with symptoms Charlie was unable to diagnose. The next morning Paul felt a little better and insisted on going on six miles to Askole, although this meant crossing a 200-foot gorge over the river on a Balti rope bridge.

These bridges are made of three ropes of twisted, braided willow twigs: one rope for the feet and two higher ropes on either side as handrails. As one walks, the ropes creak like an abused wicker chair and sway alarmingly, both sideways and up and down. One tries to watch his feet and not the waters rushing violently below. If he falls, there is no help for him. Tatters of broken willow side pieces flutter in the cold wind rising from the river as he starts down the bobbing, swaying rope to the low point of its sag, stepping over sticks that hold the handrails apart, and then begins the steep climb to the other side. The captain had told us that on his previous expedition a bridge had overturned when two expedition members leaned on the same handrail at the same time, leaving them hanging from one cable high above the river until rescued.

The porters hated these bridges. One porter at least was blindfolded and carried over on another man's back. The bridge we now crossed was an old one and we treated it with respect, aware of the Balti maxim: "No bridge should be repaired until it is broken." The bridge held, and we all crossed successfully, including Paul, but at Askole the next morning his temperature was 104.4 degrees.

We were still a week away from the mountain and arriving later than we had hoped. Paul's mysterious illness could become a disaster to the expedition if we all had to wait at Askole for his improvement. Charlie Houston was both the expedition leader and the doctor, and he at once made clear the fact that he would not leave Paul, who in his present condition could no longer walk. He stated that the rest of us must go on to the mountain. He and Paul would come after us as soon as possible. We hated splitting the party. On our long trek we had developed strong team feelings. Unfortunately, however, our days on the mountain were limited. If we were to accomplish what we had set out to do, the rest of us must go on.

In Askole scores of eyes watched our every move, some Baltis getting so close that we could feel their breath as they watched us using knives and forks. This "togetherness" infuriated the captain, who would wave his arms and cry "Nikel jao, nikel jao" (go quickly), and sometimes throw water at the boldest.

Balti is a Tibetan-type language, but its inhabitants are a melting pot of races, with some showing definite Greek or Russian features. In Askole everyone wanted work. When it came time to hire men for the carry to the mountain, some 300 yelling coolies burst into the compound where we were trying to question individuals in an orderly fashion. Some came over the thorn-topped walls, others knocked over piles of stones, and for a few moments a maelstrom of human beings seethed through the camp. Finally the Sherpas, with the help of the Satpura men, established order, and the first 50 loads were given out. The rest we gave out the next morning as camp was broken.

We all felt strong emotion when, after a brief breakfast together, the party separated, for we knew we might never meet again during the expedition. Paul thought he was dying, and Charlie, who was doing everything he could think of to improve Paul's condition, was obviously depressed. Charlie had lived K2 for six months, and now he might never even see the mountain, but he didn't mention that. He insisted we go on.

Our advance party, which left Askole with 70 porters and 12 men carrying food for the others, crossed the end of the Biafo Glacier, made famous by William and Fanny Bullock Workman in the early 1900s, and camped near the Dumordo River that flows from the Punmah Glacier. Early in the morning, when the water was lowest, we got a rope across, and everyone forded the swift water, thus saving a six-mile round trip to a rope

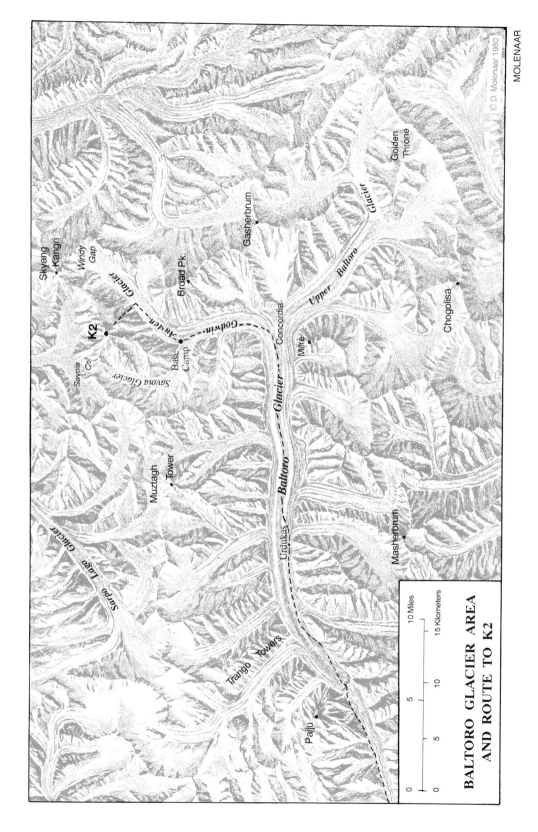

MOLENAAR

© D. Molenaar 1980

Skyang
Kangri

Windy
Gap

K2

Savoia
Col

Savoia Glacier

Base
Camp

Broad Pk

Gasherbrum

Golden
Throne

Glacier

Upper Baltoro

Concordia

Mitre

Chogolisa

Muztagh
Tower

Urdukas

Baltoro Glacier

Masherbrum

Surdu Lago Glacier

Trango Towers

Paiju

0   5   10 Miles

0   5   10   15 Kilometers

BALTORO GLACIER AREA
AND ROUTE TO K2

bridge upstream. What we had gained, however, was lost by a dispute the next day about porter wages. Our treasury was practically empty, but we finally compromised and went on. The third day from Askole we reached Paiju, where there were a few trees and the porters could cook chupattis for their meals on the glacier.

The spires and pinnacles around us were amazing. Some looked like old-time pictures of the Alps, only there was no chamois standing on a sharp summit. We passed frequent bear tracks and a place where snow leopards had been eating two ibex, apparently swept down by an avalanche. At one place the distant top of K2 was visible; it looked very steep.

Before us now lay the black, ugly lower section of the 40-mile-long Baltoro Glacier, with its slippery ice and loose rolling stones. The porters gathered together and prayed before climbing onto it. Our first night there was unpleasant, the silence constantly interrupted by sliding stones falling into some glacier pool, but our second night, at Urdukas (13,340 feet), was pleasant, for among huge boulders at the side of the glacier we camped on grass and flowers for the last time. A spring was flowing, and across from us we could see the Trango Towers, the Muztagh Tower, and peaks at the edge of Concordia. It was here that Pasang Kikuli shouted, "Sahibs, look see, look see." We looked, expecting to see ibex or some other game. Instead, in the distance, we made out Charlie and Paul picking their way through the rocks on the glacier.

When they reached us, they poured out their story. The fever had mysteriously gone just as it had come, and they had caught us by forced marches. Paul hadn't even lost his appetite. After three pint mugs of tea and huge quantities of cheese and crackers, he hoped there would be a "really large pilau" for supper.

The next day we had our first view of Masherbrum, a big peak. We wondered how members of James Waller's party were doing in their attempt to climb it from the opposite side. Ahead of us extended a vague line of ice towers, rising 50 to 200 feet above the glacier, that the Abruzzi expedition had referred to as the "Baltoro ice ships." That day we passed the Muztagh Tower, swathed in cloud, and camped on bare ice. Up-glacier, the Mitre jutted skyward, a savage wedge of upthrust black slate, with giant Gasherbrum beyond.

Our fifth night on the glacier we were at the edge of Concordia at about 14,000 feet, perhaps the most extraordinary mountain view in the world, but clouds were down and we could not see the summits of the spectacular Gasherbrum peaks, Chogolisa, or the Golden Throne to our right, or Broad Peak ahead. Our quarry was close, however, and the next day we began climbing up the Godwin-Austen Glacier straight toward an incredibly high, ghostly summit that appeared momentarily, nearly 20 miles away, through a rift in the clouds. K2 at last!

As we ascended, we began to feel the altitude, but the 80 porters were moving fast now, for the end of their long carry was in sight, and Charlie and I had scarce time to select a hollow in the moraine as a site for base camp before they were upon us. They put down their loads and demanded pay at once, for they wanted to get a good start on their return to Askole before nightfall. A frenzied counting-out of annas and rupees began, with presents to the Satpura men who had stood by us so well.

When the porters left, we gave a coolie leader 45 stones and told him to throw away one each day and then return to base camp with fewer men to pack us out the day all the stones were gone. If all went well, and children didn't play with the stones, that meant they would arrive on July 26.

That night after the tents were up and supper was cooking, we took stock of our situation. Thanks especially to Captain Streatfeild and Charlie, we were all now 370 miles from Srinagar, camped below the great southern face of K2 at 16,500 feet near the confluence of the Godwin-Austen and Savoia Glaciers. The giant southeast wall of the K2 pyramid rose above us, while directly across stood the huge bulk of Broad Peak with its three summits, the highest of them 27,132 feet above sea level. To the right of Broad Peak, we could look down to Concordia and beyond, with the Gasherbrum group and beautiful Chogolisa standing prominently. The occasional rumble of avalanches that broke the silence made our location all the more impressive.

We quickly agreed that K2 is every bit as precipitous as the Sella pictures showed. We could hardly take our eyes off the face that rose above us with its steep slopes, complicated ridge systems, rock gendarmes, and avalanche couloirs. It was possible that routes could be forced there, but we hoped easier ones would appear elsewhere. Our instructions from the council of the American Alpine Club were to make a thorough reconnaissance of the mountain. Once that was accomplished, we were free to push as high as we were able.

Though we had done well so far in getting our expedition to the base of K2, the history of high-altitude climbing was sobering. We were a small party to reconnoiter and attempt to climb the second highest mountain in the world, 28,250-foot K2. The greatest climbers in the world had so far been unable to climb any 8,000-meter peak. Mt. Everest had turned back seven expeditions led by famous English climbers with the loss of several men, including Mallory and Irvine. Six climbers had died on Kanchenjunga, which had withstood five assaults, while 26,620-foot Nanga Parbat, K2's neighbor to the east, had turned back four expeditions with a loss of 28 lives, including some of the most distinguished German climbers.

We were cheered by the knowledge that Charlie Houston, our leader, had gone high on 25,645-foot Nanda Devi. Dick Burdsall, now 42, had reached the summit of 24,890-foot Minya Konka in Szechwan in 1932. Bill House, Paul Petzoldt, and I, however, had never climbed higher than 17,000 feet, and therefore how we would acclimatize to high altitudes was unknown.

The history of attempts on K2 suggested that even if we all remained healthy, the odds against our small party's going high were great. K2 had turned back an international expedition in 1902, and a very large and well-equipped expedition led by the Duke of the Abruzzi in 1909, for the best Italian guides were unable to find a route up the mountain. Would we be able to succeed where they had failed?

One fact was certain: We were all eager to go high.

The morning after our arrival we were still acclimatizing when we split the party to begin the reconnaissance. Streatfeild and I with three Sherpas went up the Godwin-Austen Glacier to have a look at the Northeast Ridge, while the four others headed around the southwest corner of K2 to the Savoia Glacier, planning to ascend it to what the Italians named "Savoia Col" at 21,800 feet. The Duke of the Abruzzi had not found a route beyond the col, but since his guides had had no great difficulty reaching that point and since Sella's pictures of the route beyond looked encouraging, we thought this could be the place for a high advanced base, with not much over 6,000 feet left to climb on the mountain.

House and Houston, despite stormy weather, reached the cirque below the col on June 16 at more than 19,000 feet, and the next day began the ascent to the col. Unfortunately, however, they found hard ice where the duke's guides had had hard snow. It was not a route for Sherpas, who had no crampons, and it would become a dangerous avalanche slope after each storm. Though they had gone above 20,000 feet, they turned back.

Meanwhile, Streatfeild and I had picked a route through some wicked crevasses and established a cache four miles up the glacier. The day House and Houston were turned back on the west side, Streatfeild and I left base

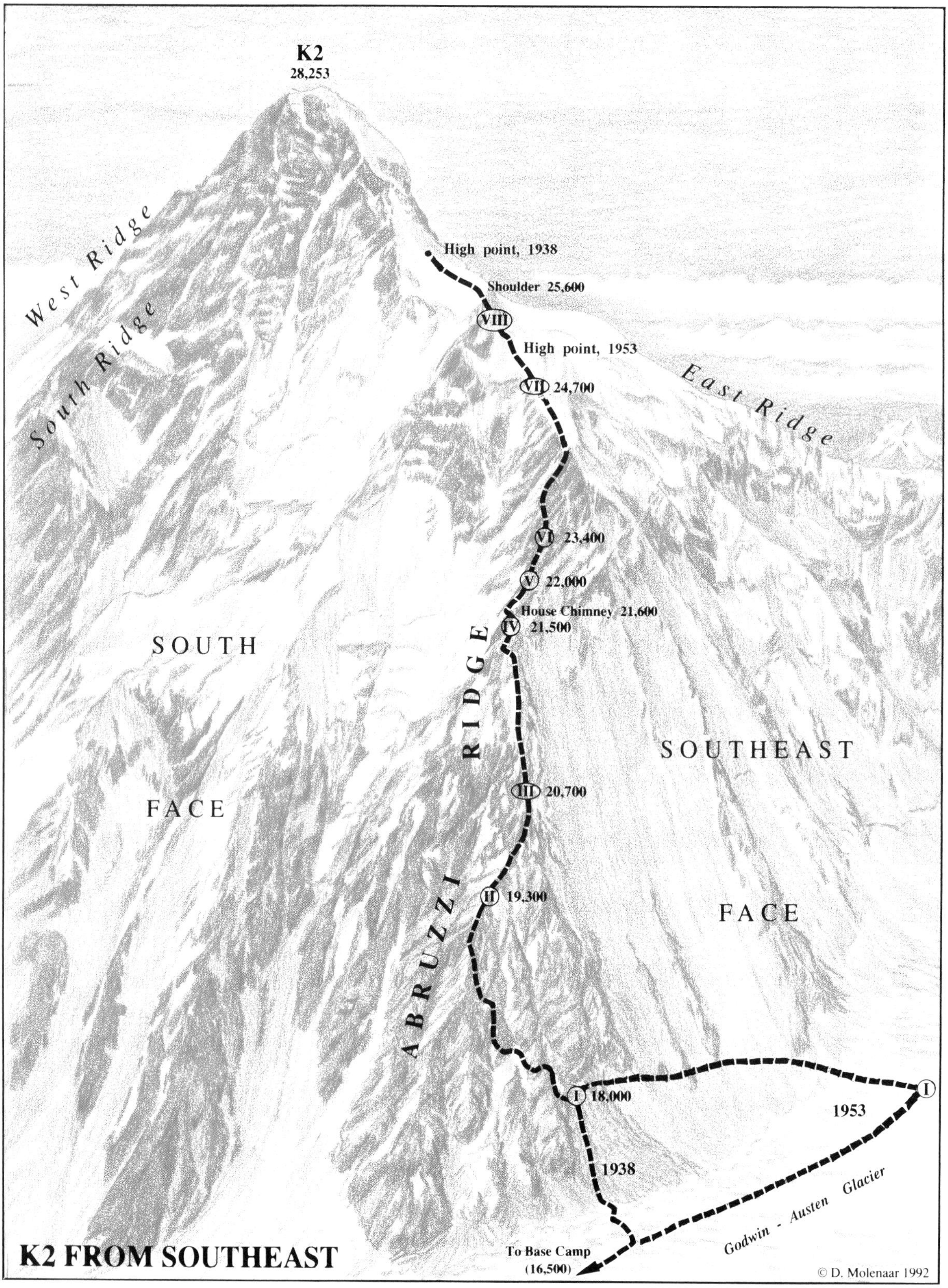

MOLENAAR

K2
28,253

West Ridge

South Ridge

High point, 1938

Shoulder 25,600

VIII

High point, 1953

VII 24,700

East Ridge

VI 23,400

V 22,000

House Chimney 21,600

IV 21,500

SOUTH

R I D G E

SOUTHEAST

FACE

III 20,700

II 19,300

A B R U Z Z I

FACE

I 18,000

I

1953

1938

Godwin - Austen Glacier

K2 FROM SOUTHEAST

To Base Camp
(16,500)

© D. Molenaar 1992

for the long Northeast Ridge, which the Guillarmod-Eckenstein Expedition had tried to climb in 1902. It was a very long ridge, more than 20,000 feet high for at least one mile, with a very steep climb to the summit at the end. Snow held up a careful reconnaissance, but by June 22, when we were joined by Houston and Burdsall, we had examined several approaches to the Northeast Ridge, including the back side; on all of them we found hard ice where our predecessors had had snow. Such routes would not be possible for the Sherpas, and so seemed eliminated for us.

House and Houston the next day climbed to nearly 19,000 feet on the Southeast Ridge but, like the Duke's guides, found no campsite. They did, however, make a different discovery. In a small saddle about 1,000 feet above the glacier they found some small pieces of wood. That marked the site of the Duke's only camp on the ridge we now named for him. In a way that find was encouraging, for it showed we were not alone in being thwarted by K2's defenses. If anything, it made us feel more challenged, more determined to establish some kind of a camp higher on the mountain. So far, however, the great mountain had stopped us and we were becoming discouraged. We had looked over every route that seemed feasible by 1938 standards. To make matters worse, Petzoldt had another attack of fever and needed rest.

PETZOLDT

Three Sherpas watching avalanche on west face of K2

Bill House and I now returned to the Savoia Glacier and climbed a snow couloir and a rock rib east of Savoia Col. This was some of the hardest climbing of the summer, but we acknowledged it to be a failure too, since the route proved too difficult for packing loads. It stormed hard that night, driving snow through the smallest tent openings. After the snow stopped, we again looked at other possible routes, but soon the sun came out and began causing great booming avalanches that convinced us there was no future in climbing these snow couloirs. We returned to base.

On the Godwin-Austen Glacier

Camp II at 19,300 feet

Meanwhile Houston and the captain had climbed to 20,000 feet on the Northeast Ridge, but returned to agree that the route would require cutting too many steps for the Sherpas to use. For the next four days it snowed, then on the last of June we all packed loads to the Abruzzi Ridge. We were not sure that a route existed here but considered it our last hope, for the north side of K2 is in China, and we had promised the India foreign office we would not try to go there.

The Abruzzi Ridge is not a true ridge; it consists of a series of little ridges, with couloirs between, which rise to a black rock pyramid about 7,500 feet above the glacier. Above that, a sloping plateau of snow leads to a rock cone partly draped in ice, pieces of which occasionally fell while we were on the mountain, starting tremendous avalanches down the east side. After a heavy snowfall these slides would shoot clear across the Godwin-Austen Glacier and our route from base camp, and even start up the peaks on the other side. Fortunately, they would normally go down the huge snow slopes at the eastern edge of the Abruzzi Ridge, well away from our tents.

Petzoldt was now feeling himself again, and we established him and House in a camp near the base of the ridge to find some form of campsite. The next day the rest of us packed our final loads to this advanced base, and to our joy that evening learned that the reconnaissance party had found a little snow pocket where tents might be pitched above a steep ice gully.

The next day House and Petzoldt continued their reconnaissance while the rest of us moved up to the glacier camp, now established as Camp I; and the following day they were established at Camp II in the little snow pocket. They found no good place for Camp III, but determined that a couple of small tents might be pitched on top of a small, sloping rock buttress if rock platforms could be constructed. One bad couloir had to be crossed on the way and there were many loose rocks, but the route up from Camp II, along the rocky edge of the 7,000-foot snow slope that borders the right side of the Abruzzi Ridge, continued to "go." Two ice traverses and a steep ice gully required special care, and so House and Petzoldt put in 900 feet of fixed rope.

By July 10, we had a strong base on the ridge at Camp II. Houston and two Sherpas had brought back the last loads from the Northeast Ridge, and Houston and Petzoldt had been established at Camp III to continue the route. Camp III was very exposed, being set on a rock platform built up three feet or more on the outer side, just large enough to hold two tents. There was no protection from the more or less continuous wind or from rockfalls.

Camp II and track along the ridge

Above Camp III, a rotten rock ridge rose 1,000 feet to a short cliff, which Paul climbed by a difficult overhanging crack. 20 feet higher and to the left, they found a gentle slope for Camp IV. That same day House and I with three Sherpas carried loads to Camp III, and were in camp when Houston, Petzoldt, and two Sherpas were carrying loads to Camp IV. To our dismay, the ridge above us was so rotten that rocks dislodged by the climbers began bounding down 500 to 1,000 feet directly into our little camp. We were in the line of fire and had to keep dodging the whizzing rocks as best we could. Both tents were punctured at least once. When the fusillade first began, two Sherpas were in one of the double-ended Meade tents making some tea, but a fist-sized rock screamed through the middle of the tent, in one side and out the other. We heard a muffled cry of alarm and a Sherpa exploded out each end of the tent. Fortunately neither was hit, and Bill and I were unharmed too, but the tents needed considerable patching and were never quite the same. After that we agreed that nobody should be in Camp III when climbers were on the route to Camp IV.

The next day, as all seven of us climbed on that miserable loose-rock ridge to Camp IV, we understood the problem, and we also appreciated the fixed rope in the overhanging crack. House and I, the next reconnaissance team, were left at Camp IV with 10 days food, mainly pemmican, which so far we were able to digest. The next day's reconnaissance we knew would be a crucial one, and so it turned out. When we had examined the ridge from the glacier, we had always commented on a bump of reddish-yellow rock that interrupted the ridge angle. This we all considered the major difficulty with the route. Now, from our tent, we could stare directly at this obstacle, a vertical, nearly 100-foot-high band of rock that crossed the ridge and barred access to what lay above.

After breakfast that chilly morning, we armed ourselves for the attack with 400 feet of extra rope and a few pitons. I had a vague hope we could pass the rock base by climbing a steep snow slope to the west, but when we reached it we found ice so steep and hard that after a few steps we gave it up. Cutting steps at more than 21,000 feet is very exhausting. We now tackled the short ice slope leading to the rock cliff, but even cutting up those 75 feet took us nearly an hour. Beyond we headed toward a shallow chimney that dents the cliff face, because two other routes we had previously considered now looked at least as hard and each had an overhanging cornice at the top.

Ten or 15 feet to the right of the chimney, a tooth of rock jutted from the base of the cliff. Here I cut two big steps in the ice, tied on to the flake, and prepared to belay Bill, the more experienced rock climber. I must admit

I was happy to leave this lead to him. From my belay point, I could not see into the chimney, but I had a good idea of what he was up against. Even getting to the base of the chimney was tricky and time-consuming. There Bill managed to get in a piton. As I found later, he then climbed about 20 feet, straddling the chimney, before being forced to inch his way higher with his back on one side and feet on the other. He had put his crampons in his rucksack before starting up the rock and they now kept catching, threatening to topple him when he made a move. Snow or rocks he knocked off fell straight down the snow chute directly below him, and then on some 5,000 feet to the glacier.

At 40 feet, a toehold gave him a rest, but he could not get in a piton. Since I couldn't see Bill, I had to judge what was happening by his heavy breathing or an occasional "Damn!" For several minutes the rope lay still. I was afraid Bill would become so tired he couldn't move and yelled that maybe he should come down. Bill didn't like the idea though he was getting tired; he considered it safer to move up than to try to descend on the sloping holds. Cautiously he continued up 15 feet, and here he found the first real foothold. Above, the chimney narrowed. One more rest and he reached the top, 80 feet above me. What a relief for both of us. From the time he had left me, it had taken two hours.

The day was a cold one, my stance was awkward, and I had become stiff and half frozen. In my cramped position, could I have held him if he had fallen, or would we both have gone down the chute together? I will never know.

After warming hands and feet for a few minutes, I followed Bill's impressive lead. The reconnaissance and climb together had taken about four hours.

To our delight, above the chimney easy snow slopes led upward for several hundred feet, and after a bite to eat we climbed these to a place just below a rock buttress, where we decided Camp V should be. We put some fixed rope in the chimney before returning, and the next day carried 25-pound loads up the chimney and on to Camp V. The strain on the arms was exhausting, however, since there were no good footholds most of the way. We were climbing before the days of Prusik knots and Jumars! Thereafter we rigged an aerial tramway and used it to hoist loads to the top of the chimney.

While we were above the chimney, Houston and Petzoldt arrived at Camp IV with big loads, including mail. We never imagined receiving letters at 21,500 feet. What a surprise! We treasured those letters, some of them mailed only five weeks earlier.

Camp V—22,000 feet

Tents at Camp VI before damage done by the big storm

The next day we put more rope in the chimney and carried up additional loads. Then, when the others arrived with the Sherpas, we helped to establish Houston and Petzoldt in Camp V. At that point they took over the lead, and the following day while House and I worked our jury-rigged aerial tramway to move loads to the top of the chimney, they climbed over a series of rock buttresses and across three ice couloirs to a point at the foot of the huge black buttress that formed the top of the ridge. They reported a possible site for tents at about 23,400 feet.

We were glad to have ample supplies at Camp V to last out a storm, for at this point the weather changed. All night, wind and snow battered the tents. When the wind dropped a bit about nine the next morning, Houston and Petzoldt started out with loads, hoping to establish Camp VI. As House and I were about to follow 20 minutes later, the others returned, their beards iced, their hands and toes on the verge of frostbite. They had gained scarcely 100 feet. As the violence of the storm continued, we began to worry whether this was the big storm we had been anticipating. Three Sherpas were with us, including Pasang Kikuli, one of the few survivors of the Bechtold party caught high on Nanga Parbat in 1931 in a big storm. Pasang was probably the most experienced high-altitude climber in the world. At least he had been on more high mountains than anyone. As the storm increased, he said to us seriously, "Just like Nanga Parbat, sahibs."

But it wasn't, for the following morning the wind dropped, although light snow continued to fall, and we decided to pack higher. Houston and Petzoldt went ahead with light loads, hoping to push the reconnaissance upward, while Bill and I followed, with heavier loads, belaying the Sherpas carefully. It was cold and there was loose rock, but all went well until the base of the black buttress, where the others had left their loads. It was not a place where anyone normally would think of camping. There were two small, sloping ledges not far from the 5,000- or 6,000-foot drop to the glacier. Everything else was steep. The Sherpas were marvelous at building walls, and with their help we constructed small ones, up to three or more feet high, and filled in behind with rocks to make small tent platforms. On one we pitched a tent, left our loads, and departed.

Meanwhile Houston and Petzoldt, after considerable trouble finding a route, pushed upward some 500 feet and put in a couple of fixed ropes. Here the wind whipped away one of Petzoldt's mittens, one of those little happenings that under severe conditions can make the difference between life and death. Fortunately, there was a spare pair at camp.

The weather seemed to be deteriorating, but the next day while House and I with the three Sherpas moved up to Camp VI with 35-pound loads, Houston and Petzoldt pushed the route on to the top of the Abruzzi Ridge at about 24,700 feet. There they cut steps horizontally across a 45-degree ice slope toward a maze of ice blocks that had fallen off the summit icefall. Beyond, the slope rose at a 30-degree angle.

That night we held a council of war. We realized that two more camps would be required for an attack on the summit. We also knew that our safety margin was getting very slim. Long storms in the Karakoram are well known. We had had no storm longer than a day for two weeks, but the weather gave every indication that the long-overdue big storm was about to strike. The climbing in several places had been very difficult under good conditions, and we realized that a big storm could trap us on the mountain. The last expedition to the Karakoram, the French Hidden Peak group, had been pinned down for two weeks by a furious storm, and on Nanga Parbat, as mentioned, another bad storm had forced a famous German party, through lack of supplies, to try to retreat to base camp while the storm was raging. The porters to pack us out were due in seven days, and they would

The ice traverse at 24,750 feet

need to leave the next day whether we were ready or not, because they would have no extra food.

If perfect weather could have been guaranteed, there might have been time to establish two more camps and to reconnoiter a route to the summit, but this would have left only two or three days for the descent, an impossibility in storm. Great ominous columns of threatening clouds already loomed to the south. With this fact facing us, we made a decision: to pack a camp for two men to the highest point Paul and Charlie had reached, from where the next day, weather permitting, they would have a chance to move as high as they could, with the hope that they would get far enough at least to see a route up the summit cone. The plan meant giving up our hope to reach the summit, but at least we would extend our route up the mountain.

Deciding to abandon our plan to gain the summit was the hardest decision of the whole expedition, because climbing the mountain was the aim of all of us. After discussion, however, we all sadly agreed that going down was the right action. If we had known then how many climbers on K2 in a similar position to ours would die in later years because they failed to descend before a major storm, our decision would have been easier to make.

The next decision, of course, was who should go higher, for all four of us were in good condition. We did not dare trust the Sherpas to carry loads while doing the delicate rock climbing above Camp V. Load carrying now was up to us. At our high altitude, without prior acclimatization, the maximum the four of us could do would be to establish for two men a camp consisting of a tent, sleeping bags, mattresses, and a stove. Charlie and Paul had had higher acclimatization than Bill and me and were going strong. Charlie also was the leader, but as always he left the decision to our vote. Paul physically was possibly the strongest of the four. We voted that Charlie and Paul should have the honor. Bill and I would establish them at Camp VII and return to VI.

The weather was no worse the next morning when we started out. As we were about to leave, Pasang Kikuli looked so unhappy at not accompanying us that we relented and gave him some of the load. It was slow climbing with our packs, crossing rotten rocks and slabs with great exposure, and belaying much of the way. The night before I had accidentally eaten a chunk of undiluted, uncooked soup, and my stomach was objecting. After a hard four hours of packing, our feet were cold, and at lunchtime on a shelf below the top of the ridge, we rubbed them vigorously.

From our eyrie, we seemed to look straight down on the crevasses and rock bands of the Godwin-Austen Glacier and could trace its flow from Windy Gap below Skyang Kangri, to its meeting with the Savoia Glacier (which comes from the west side of K2), and on to Concordia. Here the ice disappeared, but we could see the line of the Baltoro peaks, where the ice flowed west another 30 miles to the beginning of the Braldu River. Beyond Concordia, we could see the gleaming white slopes of Chogolisa, where the Duke had climbed so high (and Herman Buhl later would be lost), while farther west Masherbrum's distinctive summit rose above surrounding peaks. We were higher than Americans had ever climbed before.

We did not reach the ice slope where the others had cut steps until 3:00 p.m. The pitons protecting the traverse had melted out and had to be replaced, but Charlie and Paul could do this. Bill and I would need to leave at once if we were to reach camp before dark. There were quick "Good lucks," and we started down with Pasang, each wishing he could be one of the two to stay behind. Our descent was slow, but we reached the worried Sherpas at Camp VI before dark.

On July 21, five days before the porters were to arrive, Paul and Charlie made their final dash—if dash it can be called at more than 25,000 feet. It was cold and they were each wearing four light Shetland sweaters, wool underwear, flannel shirts, and windproof suits, plus two pairs of wool mittens and gauntlets. There was little wind, but they had barely enough clothing. To avoid the seracs that intermittently fell from the summit cone, they kept to the western side of the summit plateau, climbing sometimes on ice, sometimes in knee-deep snow or breakable crust over powder snow, a terribly tiring combination. By noon they reached the shoulder Dick Burdsall had surveyed as being 25,600 feet high, where there was a good campsite. After eating, they kept on through a mass of fallen ice blocks and eventually reached the rocks of the summit cone, where Paul climbed a bit higher. At the base of the cone, he found a flat space suitable for a camp. He thought the route above would be less difficult than some of the climbing we had already done, but there was not time to find out.

Late in the afternoon, when they returned to camp from 26,000 feet, the weather appeared to be breaking. Despite their great fatigue, they began considering a descent to Camp VI, but the clouds cleared suddenly, and gratefully they decided to stay. Their matches had not been lighting well. Soon they were down to their last one, but it lit, and gave them a warm supper.

The next morning as clouds began forming above the lower Baltoro peaks, Bill and I were delighted to welcome Charlie and Paul at Camp VI. There were high cirrus clouds and a ring around the sun. After they rested, we all began the descent to base camp, thankful not to be descending in a storm. Sunny weather had caused considerable melting, and we found lots of loose rocks and also smooth slabs where we had climbed up on snow. We reached the chimney, descended it, and spent the night at Camp IV.

We were strung out across a steep ice gully below Camp III the next day when a shout from Pasang alerted us to a huge boulder bounding down the gully toward us. We all jumped aside and ducked as the boulder crashed into a rock projection and exploded, sending jagged splinters flying. Grazed but unhurt, we thanked Pasang, who said the "snow man" had told him to look up at that exact moment. It was the mountain's farewell shot.

We slept at Camp II, and in the morning Burdsall appeared with two grinning Sherpas to help us down. The air seemed thick, almost as if we were breathing soup, although even at base camp we were nearly at 17,000 feet, much higher than any summit in the Alps. Suddenly we all felt desperately tired, not an uncommon feeling for those descending from high altitudes.

What a reunion and dinner we had! We learned that during our absence Dick Burdsall and the captain had been down the Godwin-Austen Glacier and had mapped peaks east of Masherbrum. They had also ascended the glacier to Windy Gap, where they could look directly into the Shaksgam and the country north of K2—all a part of China.

On the next day, July 25, the porters arrived, one day early and with no extra food. It was lucky we were there when they came.

We had done our best and completed the reconnaissance of the remote and magnificent mountain. We deeply regretted not gaining the prize of the summit, though we had gone much higher than had seemed possible two weeks earlier. Obviously there were thoughts of, "If only we had had another week," but they couldn't take away what we had accomplished. Charlie had been a great leader who fully deserved reaching the summit. We had pushed hard, descended just before the storm (which did come), and returned to climb again.

On the way to Askole we realized that we had lost a lot of weight and expended more energy than we imagined. Askole seemed almost a metropolis, although it had seemed very small when we saw it for the first time. Many people were there waiting for Charlie to appear, for the word that a distinguished doctor was about to arrive in Askole had brought people from as far away as 40 miles. He did his best but for most there was little he could do. At Askole we crossed the Braldu River on a 100-yard rope bridge, the same one we had been over before, and then climbed over the Skoro La (16,644 feet), a shorter route to Shigar and Skardu.

The Skoro La is a pass normally blocked by snow early in the season. When we reached the summit, snow was actually falling, but we had no difficulty. During the long 5,000-foot descent, we stopped for lunch. Tse Tendrup, the captain's Sherpa, had just removed lunch from his pack when a great boulder, dislodged by porters above, bounded down, took a crazy hop, and landed on his pack. It was time to get out.

When we reached the Shigar River, apricot trees everywhere were loaded with fruit. We could hardly tear ourselves away. The munshi was at home and again provided us with a magnificent tea. He engaged two zhaks to take us to Skardu the next day. We raced them, and our zhak was ahead until we were almost across the Indus, when, as we were shouting derisive remarks about our opponents, we ignominiously grounded on a sandbar. We were still struggling as the others, with great grins and suggestions that we swim, went slowly by us and on to the shore.

Again the tehsildar gave a sumptuous tea, with enormous mulberries and pakorhas, pieces of vegetable dipped in whole wheat flour and fried. After we had stuffed ourselves, the tehsildar brought out two tennis rackets and asked me to play with him. It was not the moment I would have chosen. Fortunately, however, there were 30 or 40 solemn, turbaned "ball boys," most of them elderly, who competed in chasing the balls and bringing them to us. We had a stirring match, though the quality of the tennis will not be discussed.

On August 4 we left Skardu for the six-day pony ride across the high Deosai Plateau to Srinagar. This meant that Dick and I would miss our side trip to Leh, but the Deosai route was too good to miss. On the way we passed a large and ancient Buddhist carving, and long before we topped the Chota Burzil Pass there were splendid views of Nanga Parbat. When we reached the Gilgit Road, traveling was easy, though still we had to cross the 11,586-foot Tragbal Pass. A lorry had been ordered to bring us the last 20 miles to Srinagar, and while we waited for it a barber, armed with hundreds of chits from satisfied sahibs, offered to improve our appearance. He was so good, and our beards and long hair were so quickly altered, that the Sherpas hardly recognized us. That night we were ensconced in a luxurious houseboat, costing a dollar apiece a day, with three big meals and tea thrown in. Lotuses were blooming, the breeze was sweet, and suddenly we felt we had found the mythical land of the lotus eaters and would stay forever.

*Houston and R.H.B. at railroad station in Khanaqin, Iraq. Here House contin-
ued to Bagdad, while the others headed north to go to Istanbul.*

CHAPTER VIII

Overland from
Peshawar to Istanbul
1938

ON OUR RETURN FROM THE MOUNTAIN, we had various discussions about the route we should take on our way home, but all agreed we should go overland. In April, while in Paris, Dick Burdsall and I had gone to a Russian Intourist office and bought inexpensive tickets that would take us from Pahlevi on the Caspian Sea to Baku in Azerbaijan by boat, then across the mountains to Batum, thence by boat again to Novorossisk in the Crimea, on to Kiev, to Berlin, and to Bremen to take our boat home. Charlie was especially interested in trying to get permission in Kabul to cross the Oxus, enter the Soviet Union, and proceed west from there via Moscow. Bill House wanted to return fairly rapidly, but was ready for what might turn up.

I wanted to see something of India before heading west across Afghanistan and therefore left Srinagar before the others, whom I would meet in five days in Peshawar. The choukidar took me to a bus for Rawalpindi and put my lunch on the front seat. Soon, however, a holy man with three disciples came along, a man so holy that he was given the front seat and I was respectfully demoted to the bench behind, where I sat with the three chelas. Second class on a native bus! What a comedown from the company of wazirs and tehsildars!

That began a fine visit to Delhi and Agra that ended when I took the Frontier Mail to Peshawar, where I went to the Cantonment, currently circled with triple barbed wire and closed at night. Streatfeild had reported that the Faquir of Ipi was attacking British outposts and causing a lot of trouble among the local tribes. Sentries in outlying areas had their rifles chained to their wrists so that they would be less likely to be killed for their weapons.

We learned also that to keep the area peaceful, the British stationed the best polo players in the army at Peshawar, and had a polo match once a week to which local chiefs were invited. After the games, these chiefs would be invited to have a chota peg of whiskey, which was rarely refused. With these inducements, the British kept a fragile peace. Streatfeild told us what these local chieftains often said as they departed, "Thank you, Colonel Sahib, for the polo game and for the chota peg. Very good. The war will not start for two weeks!" The following week there would be a repetition of the polo game.

At the Peshawar dak bungalow where I stayed, I quickly found that travel to Kabul could be arranged by an Afghan official who was not available at the time. That night one other visitor was at the bungalow, an English electrician who had recently returned from Nepal, where he had been electrifying the royal palace. He hadn't seen anything of Nepal, for he ate in his room and was escorted to and from work by Gurkha soldiers, but he was well paid, and each morning he received as baksheesh a new bottle of whiskey and a new box of cigars, items supposedly essential to Englishmen. The electrician was to take an early bus south to Bannu, where there was fighting. He was greatly worried about the Faquir of Ipi's men. The next morning at five, when he left to catch a bus, I sleepily wished him a good trip. Two hours later he was back, saying that his journey south had been delayed.

"Why?" I asked.

"I couldn't take the bus—the blighters blew it up!"

What arrangements he made later I never knew.

That afternoon the others arrived without Paul, who had decided to stay on and work for two Americans, a Dr. Johnson and his wife, controlling members of a religious cult in the area. Paul was enjoying India and the pay was very generous.

The next day we went to the Afghan government office in Peshawar, a place probably used only occasionally. The official who met us was a dignified, well-educated Afghan who normally may have been a doctor in a Peshawar hospital. He first made sure we were vaccinated against cholera, then made a speech about the needs of Afghanistan for medical help. Next he led us to an adjoining room where a large wooden box with a slit in the

This auto took us from Peshawar to Kabul.

top stood on a table. It might have been a large ballot box. We had no idea what was in it. He said he would leave us to our consciences and then see what he could do about visas. We looked at the box and at each other; it was huge. We were very short of funds, but we had some silver rupees, each almost as large as an American silver dollar. Somebody said, "Let's drop in a chip and see what happens."

Charlie dropped in a rupee and the box bonged loudly. The box was empty. We dropped in a couple more, and waited. In a moment the suave gentleman returned and began writing out simple visas for us, meanwhile advising us strongly not to use alcohol and to be wary of cholera. Afghanistan was now open to us and we quickly arranged for a car to take us to Kabul the next day.

Two roads led through the Khyber Pass: one for camels and horses and one for motor vehicles. The latter road, a great engineering achievement, wound through low hills, a 36-mile stretch protected by a line of forts. We could easily see that whoever controls the hills controls the pass.

Before entering Afghanistan, our passports were examined three times in 15 minutes. Beyond the last checkpoint the valley broadened, with just as many forts and steel-plated sentry boxes as before. As our lonely car went slowly along, we had the feeling that we might be sniped at any time. In a few places the driver advised us not to look out the windows because of snipers, and once or twice even made us duck out of sight. Each time we stopped for water for the car, we saw scowling faces and men with rifles. Many of the men wore tremendous cartridge belts, with cartridges crossing the chest in three places. They fingered their rifles as if they loved them. Big, hardy, full-bearded men—we could tell at a glance that they would love a fight. Once we stopped near a fort to get water for the car. Nobody was in sight when we stopped, but 10 seconds later five men were standing, rifle in hand, at various vantage points of the fort.

Dates and oranges were growing luxuriantly at Jalalabad when we stopped for tea, but we drove on to Nimla for the night. The next day, despite brake trouble, we reached Kabul. Outside the city a soldier took our passports. We refused to leave them with him, and so he climbed aboard. Twice more we were stopped, and each time a man climbed aboard. The car groaned on to customs, where one man left after an hour, then we went on to the police station and the hotel. Shortly after lunch, an American named Payne came to see us. He was teaching at Ismailia College and said he was THE American in Afghanistan, there being no others. He would not talk much in the hotel, saying in a lowered voice, "Too many spies everywhere." Outdoors he was critical of a lot of things. He made me doubly glad I had turned down a job offered me during my senior year at college to go to Afghanistan to tutor the king's son in English.

The next morning we started working on entrance visas to Iran and Iraq and exit visas from Afghanistan. Soldiers and police were everywhere and we were constantly watched. No pictures were allowed, and we felt distinct hostility toward strangers. At the British legation we met Major McAnn, who told us of the difficulties and dangers of crossing Afghanistan. He would help us if he could, he told us, then mentioned that in Kabul there was another American who was trying to cross Afghanistan to Iran.

"Would you object to taking this other American with you?" he asked. Naturally we exclaimed, "Of course not." "So be it then," he said. "Come back later." On our return he told us that the Royal Afghan Mail truck drove from Kabul to Herat once a month. He had obtained places for us on it and said we should be ready to depart from the hotel at 6:00 the following morning.

We were up at 5:00 a.m. to have breakfast and pay our hotel bill. The manager had made it out for 20 Afghanis too much, and then left for an all-day funeral where he could not be reached, knowing that the police would not let us depart unless the bill was paid.

Outside the hotel in the morning sat an old Dodge truck, open in the back. In the cab was a woman of indeterminate age, a Miss Taylor, who

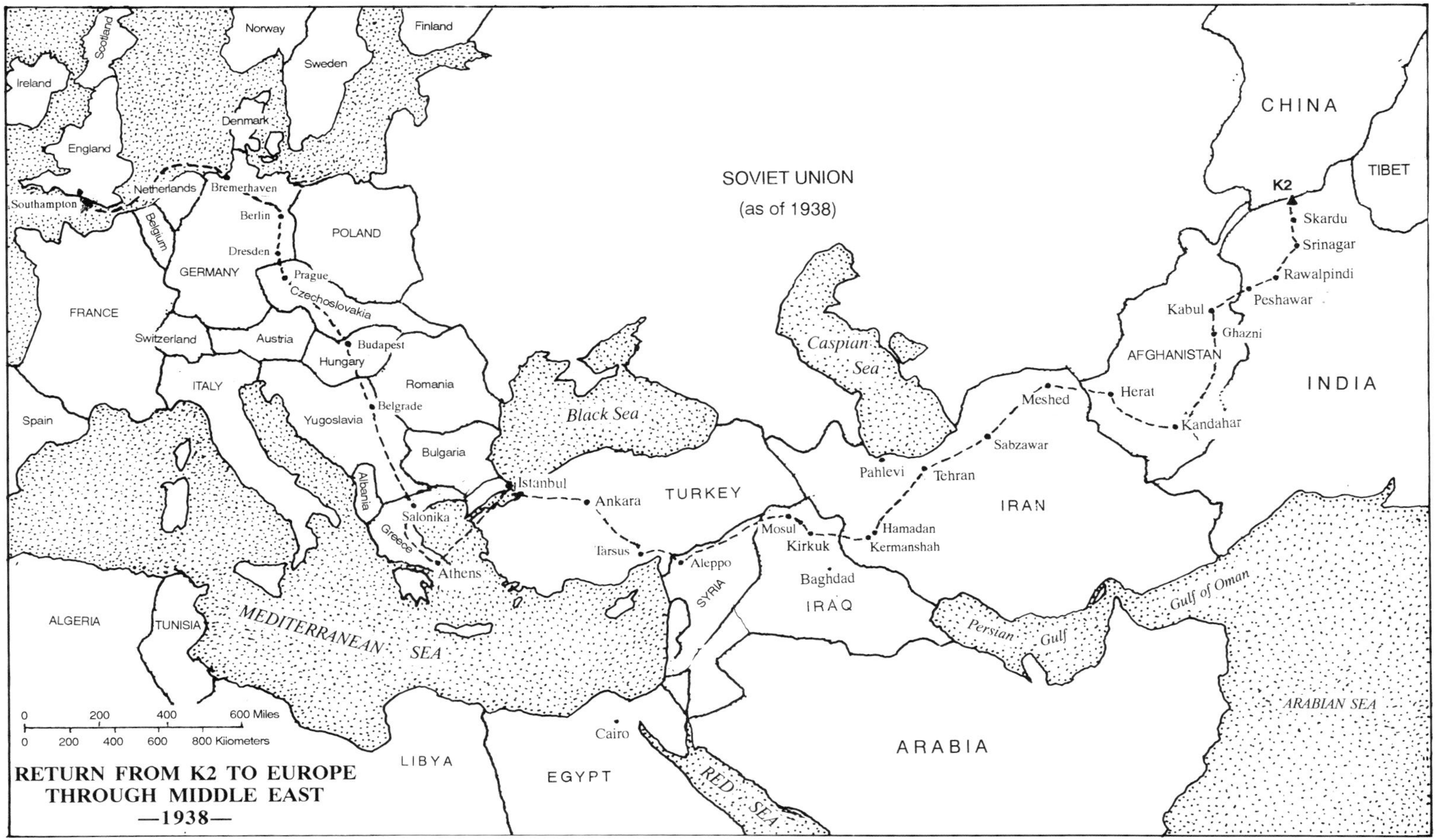

RETURN FROM K2 TO EUROPE THROUGH MIDDLE EAST —1938—

MOLENAAR

spoke American English. She told us that for several years she had been working as a missionary in the Deccan in southern India. In addition, she said that in a dream God had told her to return home to Kansas by way of the Khyber Pass and Riga, Latvia, because she had good work to do on the way. Obviously she looked on us as potential to be worked on and she talked continuously. What were we to do? The driver, obviously, did not care for her, and when there was a delay of several hours and she disappeared, we hoped he might start without her. We were becoming optimistic when suddenly she appeared and climbed back into the cab. "You wanted to leave me, didn't you?" she said sternly. "But God wouldn't let you."

The seats of the lorry were hard where we sat, crowded in with 15 or more turbaned Afghans including two women completely veiled and clothed in black. The mail was stuffed under the front seat, tied in loose bundles with string. As we bounced along, letters would occasionally slide into the middle of the truck to be kicked back under the seat. Several men wore big cartridge belts but the passengers were friendly; and we were all soon of the same dusty color as the loose surface of the dirt road that whirled up behind the truck and descended on us in a cloud.

The driver was obviously not a man to cross. Frequently he jarred the truck to a stop when camels or sheep stampeded across the road. Herds of fat-tailed sheep were everywhere, some with tails a foot across, and a few wearing two-wheeled contraptions that kept their tails from banging their private parts when they ran. The camels were often driven by wild-looking nomad women wearing red gowns, many silver bracelets, necklaces, and strings of coins. Fierce guard dogs were always with them, many wearing spiked collars to protect them from wolves.

Unfortunately trouble developed in the left front wheel and we stopped in Ghazni to fix it when only 90 miles from Kabul. We spent the night at a resthouse where we had a fine pilau, but were anxious to move on. Miss Taylor ate with us, ordered for us, gave us advice, tried to convert us, and almost drove us crazy. Dick Burdsall, a Quaker, the mildest of men, was more understanding than the rest of us and we asked him to ride with her in the cab while the rest of us rode in the back.

We left Ghazni after a few changes in the back of the truck. It now held a huge drum of gasoline, more bales of carpets, and three women shrouded in black. A few men had left us. The country we were crossing was wild, but forts or graves were never more than a mile apart. At a place called Mokur a barrier across the road stopped us for cholera inoculation. Our passports stated that we had been inoculated, but the driver and the other passengers had not. It looked as if we would be stopped for three days. While we were wondering how to move on, a dark-complected Afghan politely offered us a hookah, then invited us into his mud house. We did not understand a word he was saying. Inside we squatted on soft Afghan rugs and were served a huge platter of excellent white grapes. The next course was green tea served in delicate little cups. Our only regret was that between each filling one of the men took a corner of his turban off the floor where it was used as a tablecloth, and wiped out the cups.

Meanwhile we were exchanging English words and Pushtu words with our host. Camel was ISHTAR; sweet tea—CHAI SCHAREEN; passport—KITAPCHA; rifle—TOFA'NG, a wonderful onomatopoeic word with emphasis on the last syllable. One could almost hear a bullet whining off into the distance. Our host had tried desperately but unsuccessfully to communicate with us in Pushtu, Farsi, and Urdu, and finally, in an inspiration, indicated that he had sent for somebody who could talk with us. The man sent for came, but unfortunately his only foreign language was Russian. We felt very ignorant. When we left the house, we offered our host cigarettes and other things but he would accept nothing. He would not let us take his picture.

We learned that another truck had come in and was leaving for Kalat. Intensive bargaining followed and we were allowed aboard, including Miss Taylor, who also had been inoculated previously, but as we were starting a man jumped in and threw out Charlie's bag. For a few moments things were tense, then our host came to our rescue, gave us an armed escort, and raised the barrier. A mile down the road the escort left us.

The new truck had wide cracks between the floorboards, causing dust to stream over us inches deep until everything was unrecognizable. The driver, who wore a black patch over one eye and looked like a pirate, stopped for evening prayers, with a mullah in front leading the praying, and behind him a line of ferocious, devout men. One wild-looking Afghan, who wore a gilt-trimmed red velvet vest, held down his prayer rug with his 1892 English rifle.

What worried us more than the condition of the truck was Miss Taylor. While they were praying, Miss Taylor would call down to the men in English, "That won't do you any good at all, it's really the worst thing you can be doing." The Afghans did not understand a word she was saying, but her scolding tone was unmistakable. We were afraid that if they became angry at her, they would take out their anger on us, too.

The next morning we made good time through an unpopulated area with only a few black nomad yurts showing habitation, and in midafternoon reached Kandahar, the Pushtu capital and Afghanistan's second largest city. We wandered through the huge bazaar, admiring the brass, copperwork, and carpets. After a pilau for dinner, we had another stroll in the bazaar, where I bought some soapstone carvings. I had become separated from the others in a dimly lighted section of the bazaar when a huge Afghan came out of a shop, stopped in front of me, and spat on the ground. We knew that many fundamentalists who hated foreign "unbelievers" lived in Kandahar, and people had spat on the ground when they saw us many times before, but this man was twice as big as me, looked like a fanatic, and was making very hostile gestures. Whether he had a knife, I couldn't tell. All I could do was step around him and start walking, though I was plenty scared. He kept my pace, walking one step behind me. Shopkeepers were watching and I hoped they would prevent his attacking me from behind. Some of them grinned, others spat and looked sourly at me, and a few looked apprehensive. After 10 or 12 steps he dropped back and I kept on.

We did not leave Kandahar until dark. That was a rough night. The lorry lurched from bump to bump, jarring every bone in her and in her passengers. Hour after hour we slowly went on. Dawn found us on the banks of the Helmand River, where without even a look around I fell asleep on a heap of Persian carpets. When I awoke, hours later, the truck in front of us was being unloaded before being driven across a pontoon bridge. Coolies were staggering across with loads weighing up to 200 pounds.

Once across we had a long wait, which we spent eating melons and watching a donkey. He refused to cross the bridge and was being walked over it by a man who rested the donkey's front legs over his shoulders. A mile farther, we stopped for the day at Girishk. Here we bought a dekshi and boiled some tea. We were living largely on yogurt, nan (Afghan flat bread), melons, and tea. Yogurt, Charlie told us, was always safe if we spooned off the top layer of dust.

At six in the evening we set out again. The evening air, delicious after the hot day, brought wild outbursts of song from our companions as we headed across the desert. Charlie and I began to sing, too, and we alternated with them. They sang Afghan, Turkic, Pushtu, and Persian songs, and I don't know what else. Some were long, wailing ballads, with a chorus where we all clapped and shouted together.

At 1:30 a.m., when the truck stopped for a couple of hours, we lay down beside it and slept. At dawn we were off again. More delays followed, but two nights later our truck pulled into the Herat serai (guarded courtyard).

Bus crossing the Helmand River

In the morning we moved to the resthouse, which seemed luxurious. Piles of Persian carpets were everywhere, and a first-rate choukidar quickly brought us hot tea, good eggs, and marvelous grapes. Herat, the biggest city in western Afghanistan, was dominated then by its huge castle and seven tall minarets. After checking in with the police and visiting the Iranian consul to arrange a private truck to take us to Meshed in Iran, we went to the bazaar, the great mosque, and the tall minarets. For a small sum I was allowed to climb a precarious bamboo scaffolding inside one of them to get a view of Herat.

That night the lorry drove at a furious pace to the border. The steering wheel had so much play in it that I would not have wanted to drive it, but we had no accidents. With us were four soldiers who demanded transport to the border. We did not dare refuse. At the border six hours of arguing in Charlie's best French and money payments were needed to enter Iran. Miss Taylor had no money. We looked at each other questioningly, but of course we could not leave her and we paid. All cameras were sealed and we were charged four tolman each for permission to take cameras across the country.

Our main problem came at a cholera inoculation station, where the officer in charge insisted that we stay for five days. Again there was arguing to get permission to go on, received only after every single article we possessed was handled and examined. Fifty yards farther there was a customs inspection. Since the head man was having a siesta, we went to a teahouse where we had bread, tea, and eggplant with sour cream. Afterward we needed more arguing to go through customs.

Bus travel in Afghanistan

Beyond the border and the many checkpoints, many farmers were asking for rides. Since practically all had melons, we began giving rides for a melon apiece, only to find quickly that if we kept on we soon would become a melon wagon. We continued to bang and bounce over the washboard roads with our sulky driver at the wheel until 8:30 p.m., when he announced motor trouble. Fortunately there was a small restaurant nearby where we had a good stew, then fell asleep on the flagstones of a serai veranda.

Up at dawn and away, with no mention of the motor problem, we were soon halted to pick up a very surly general whose car had broken down. The country was flat and we could see the great mosque of Meshed long before we entered the city.

At the office of the British consul we found charming people who were living as if in a walled camp. No Persian was allowed inside. A note to a barber might cause the bearer's arrest and a jail sentence.

Fortunately, at the hotel we met a young Englishman named Bellingham, who had been traveling around the country as guide for an American lady. We gave him information on Afghanistan and he took us to Haroun al-Raschid's magnificent shrine. There were four great courts, each a mosque in itself, with great silver doors, beautiful mosaics, tiles, and inlaid glass. Muslims were visiting from many countries. This great mosque had been open to "infidels" for only two years. When it was first opened, fundamentalists massacred 2,000 people in Meshed. Police were still on guard everywhere, and we were told that only a few Westerners had been allowed to enter the mosque.

Since we needed some Persian money, I went to a bank to exchange 30 Indian rupees legally. The exchange took exactly three hours, and I signed my name exactly 10 times. That evening we left Meshed, passed through Nishapur, where Omar Khayyam is buried, after dark, and eventually spent part of the night sleeping on the veranda of a serai in Sabzawar.

The next morning we had not gone far when the driver developed a high fever from a return bout of malaria. We stopped where there were date palms, a few mud houses, and quantities of pistachio nuts, which at first seemed to be the only food there. The driver's temperature was 103.5 degrees, but after six hours he felt well enough to go on. Charlie and the driver alternated driving until we stopped at a small village for the night. The following morning we reached Tehran, where we quickly left Miss Taylor with missionary friends, who welcomed her. She thanked us and we departed, relieved that the last part of our relationship had been less strained.

We were not impressed with Tehran despite its size, the broad streets, and the three-horse droshkies driving fast. Few cars were in use. Traditional clothing had been recently forbidden in Iran, so that nearly everyone looked as if his ill-fitting Western clothes had come from a secondhand store. Many soldiers marched in the streets. We had decided not to go to the most expensive hotel in Tehran, the Ferdozi, and when the driver took us there, we told him to keep driving around and we would tell him when we saw something closer to our price. After a while we saw a large building with a shabby entrance and went in. It was a hotel too, and we rented the entire ballroom for a song. Some hours later, we found we had not been as smart as we thought. We were staying in the Ferdozi after all, having entered it by the back entrance.

At the American embassy the next day, we met a recent Cornell graduate about our age who was the bottom man at the embassy. He was delighted to meet us, hated Tehran, and told us what to see in town, including the tremendous roofed bazaar with its great variety of silver ornaments and rugs.

I had already realized that because of our many delays, I could not possibly get to my classes on time at the university if I went with Dick across the Soviet Union. Accordingly, I decided to take a direct route west, retaining my Russian vouchers.

Early in the morning of September 8, traveling with a cheerful Iraqi driver who agreed to take us to Bagdad, Dick, Bill, Charlie, and I began our last drive together. Dick wasn't with us long, however, for we left him at a railroad junction to await a train to Pahlevi on the Caspian Sea. I was sorry not to go with him, but felt I had no choice.

Soon afterward we were stopped for two hours by police and released only after the driver paid a 20-tolman ($14) bribe. Then in order came a blowout, engine trouble, and a flat tire. Our driver remained cheerful, however, even after being forced to pay another bribe. In Hamadan we had a long stop for repairs to the car, then went on to Kermanshah, where we stopped about 11:00 p.m. at a resthouse. A play was going on and we went to sleep to the sound of flutes.

In the morning our cheerful driver drove leisurely in order to reach the Iraq border in the afternoon, when a friend of his went on customs duty. Our arrival time was good for all of us. Our bags were not carefully inspected, though every photograph in Bill's and Charlie's possession was examined to make sure it had not been taken in Iran. They had to pay more money for taking their cameras out of Iran than for taking them in, though the cameras were still sealed and they had never been used. No wonder Iran was not our favorite country. Through judicious bribes, the driver took a 140-tolman rug out with him. Some yards ahead we reached the border of Iraq, where we were courteously received and went through customs and formalities in two minutes, but our driver sweltered for two hours before he got his things through.

At the Khanaqin railroad station Charlie and I said good-bye to the driver and Bill House, who were continuing to Bagdad. Bill then would go to Beirut, while we were headed toward Istanbul. As we waited for our train to Kirkuk, trying to keep cool with lime juice and soda, the stationmaster told us we were lucky to have missed the warm weather when it was 130 degrees Fahrenheit. "Now," he said, "it's only 115." At 9:00 p.m., when we climbed into a third-class compartment, the thermometer was still well over 100 degrees.

As the train rattled across the arid desert with a full moon shining, we bounced around on small board seats. At 7:00 a.m. at Kirkuk the heat was already debilitating, but we weren't there long. After a hasty breakfast we boarded a huge modern bus for the ride across the desert. Only two other passengers were with us: an English lady and the daughter of the kind British consul at Meshed. This delightful 10-year-old told us about her dogs, ducks, and other responsibilities, and also fed us lemon drops.

We were still crossing flat desert when we came to Erbil, a Kurdish city on a rocky mesa, possibly the oldest continually inhabited city in the world. An hour or two later we passed Jonah's tomb before crossing the Tigris River, passing through the remains of the walls of Nineveh, and entering Mosul. The bus stopped at a fine resthouse where there were many English newspapers. While idly leafing through a copy of the London *Times*, I was taken aback to find I was reading something I had written. The *Times* had also printed a summary, sent from Srinagar, under the heading, "Fine Achievement of American Climbers on K2."

Mosul had much of interest, but we had to move on. We hired a small Chevrolet to drive to Tel Kochek (Tall Kushik) in Syria, where we could take a train. The road was bad, the temperature well over 100 degrees, and we were grateful to reach the Syrian border. Here, after a splendid Arab dinner with local beer, we boarded a Turkish railway car bound for Aleppo (Haleb), very satisfied with our progress. The compartment was cramped and for the second night in a row we didn't get much sleep, but about 6:00 a.m. we bought some grapes, and soon afterward an Armenian boy gave us each a cake made of bread and meat. We had never seen anything like it before. It made a fine breakfast. A gift of grapes pleased the boy very much but his present had no ulterior motive.

At Aleppo we changed trains, much regretting not having more time there. The minarets were very different from those we had seen. We purchased bread and wine before the train left, and soon crossed the border into Turkey, winding slowly up through mountains. Our carriage was empty and the country wild, with old forts or castles on hilltops. The people, probably largely Kurds, wore bright clothing and looked very rugged. We were following a deep gorge with cliffs high above when we lay down on wooden benches to sleep.

At dawn a crowd of Turks poured into our compartment and stayed with us to Ankara, where another crowd entered. After another night, we reached the Sea of Marmara and continued along the beautiful coast to the Bosphorus in Istanbul. From the ferry we had good views of the city. Someone had suggested that the YMCA would be a good place to stay, and so we took a taxi there, where after a long conversation in broken French we were allowed to stay.

The next morning we met the secretary of the YMCA, an American named Baker, who was most helpful. We lunched with him on some fine kabobs before he took us to a magnificent underground cistern with a high roof and striking pillars. We rode around it in a rowboat. While waiting for the departure of the Taurus Express, we visited grand old empty Hagia Sophia, with its magnificent veined marble columns; the glorious Blue Mosque; and Topkapi, the former palace.

I waved to Charlie as the express for Paris pulled out the evening of September 14, but the following morning I was away too, on the Russian boat *Svanetia* bound for Athens. This new boat was almost totally empty in the first and second classes, but jammed in the third, with Greek refugees sleeping all over the decks. I shared my second-class cabin with a Palestinian Jew and an old Greek. On board were two American girls Mr. Baker knew and I talked with them a good bit. The only apparent difference between the first and second classes that we could discover was that at dinner one had black caviar and the other red. In the evening we passed the trenches of Gallipoli, now very peaceful, and woke to find the island of Euboea off our starboard bow with glimpses of Mt. Hymettus ahead.

At Piraeus, where we landed, a friendly Greek who had lived in the U.S. steered me to Athens, where I checked my bag at the Salonika station before phoning old friends, the Crosbys, at the American School of Classical Studies. I would have loved to stay in Athens but there was no time.

After a splendid lunch with the Crosbys I left for the Acropolis. Rain was streaming across it in gusts, but I had a splendid time there. I felt deep, deep pleasure standing in the Parthenon and looking out through the great entrance to where the storm clouds were sweeping across the bay. There was the same breathtaking feeling I had experienced at the Taj Mahal, a feeling of something too noble and beautiful to be man-made.

Too soon I was on board a night train again, this time sharing my compartment with a young Greek engineer from Salonika. In the morning he promptly showed me around the city and the waterfront, where red-hulled sailboats were rocking in the blue water. Then again I was on my way, enduring a rough roadbed as we moved north through Macedonia and Kosovo, where the peasant women still wore bright clothing. Early in the morning we were in Belgrade, though I saw little of it.

Budapest I loved, but I caused quite a sensation when I walked out of the station wearing shorts and my tropical topi. I saw the old fort and walked along the Danube, which did look blue in the afternoon sun. The cosmopolitan nature of the people eating in restaurants along the river signified my return to Europe. I had a good dinner, read a newspaper about the dangerous situation in Czechoslovakia, and returned to the station to take my train to Prague.

The train did not stay in Prague long and I was soon traveling through the Sudeten area. Many passengers in my car were Germans fleeing Czechoslovakia and the threat of war. Soon I was in Germany, following the handsome Oder River to Dresden. Again I wished I could stop. At three in the afternoon we reached Berlin, where I went straight to the Nord Deutscher Lloyd office, and found there that I must take a boat train to Bremerhafen at 1:00 a.m. My travel plans made in Istanbul were working out.

I bought a bun and was sitting on a bench eating it when several drunken Germans came up who were sure I was a refugee from the Sudetenland. They were all very friendly, questioned me about Czechoslovakia, and offered me beer, but I was glad when they disappeared. I still had a good deal of time after dinner before I could board the boat train, and so went to a movie. It was dripping with propaganda.

On the train I shared a compartment with an intelligent, pleasant young German. His uncle, who lived in Chicago, had sent him a boat ticket to the U.S. He was allowed to take with him out of Germany only 15 marks but this was not what worried him, and he was very worried. He said he wanted to leave Germany because there was going to be a war. He was 19, of draft age, and afraid despite a deferment that he would not be allowed to sail. I found him an unusually fine person and have often wondered what happened to him, for he was not allowed on the boat. I was glad when the *Bremen* left the dock, for I had come to dislike thoroughly the spirit of fascist Germany.

We sailed at midmorning to Southampton, where Charlie came aboard. Together again, there was much to tell, but the best news was that the expedition film had turned out well. On the boat trip to New York, we both had writing to do, and I began reviewing for my imminent Ph.D. preliminary exams. When we landed on September 26, we were met by all the Houstons. That night I was home again in Philadelphia.

*R.H.B. at Jenny Lake before climbing a new route on Mt. Moran
in the Tetons*

CHAPTER IX

Five Miles High, the Alps, and Exeter

1938-1940

I REACHED PHILADELPHIA A DAY BEFORE my work began at the university. On the boat from Bremerhafen to New York, I had found it easy to slip back into a more normal routine, and so the shock of beginning another academic year was lessened. Charlie and I had agreed to write a book about the expedition, and on the boat coming over I had suggested the title *Five Miles High,* which we eventually used.

The expedition was in debt and since the movies taken by Charlie and Paul were good, we all began to lecture when we had the opportunity, to reduce our indebtedness. I gave a number of talks with the movies in the Philadelphia area and one the following February at my old school, Phillips Exeter Academy in Exeter, New Hampshire, where my brother was teaching. The talk was unusually well received. Many faculty members and students asked questions about the mountain attempt and our subsequent travels.

A couple of days after my return from Exeter, a big surprise was a telephone call asking if I would take a teaching position in the English Department at the academy. The man calling me was Dr. Lloyd, head of the English Department, who said he had the enthusiastic support of principal Lewis Perry. This offer was a bombshell. I was progressing well with my graduate work toward the Ph.D., and had found plenty of thesis material on John Aubrey in the Bodleian Library at Oxford. If I continued in my career at the university, however, I saw a future in which as I climbed the academic ladder, most of my spare time and my summers would be spent publishing scholarly papers, perhaps largely on minor matters of academic interest. I had lived and breathed a broader world and the thought of concentrating on academic criticism did not thrill me. I talked to my brother, who was eager that I should come. He stressed the top quality of the students, who came from all over the U.S. and some foreign countries, and the pleasure of teaching books of your own choosing, with the students seated around the table with you in seminar fashion. I was getting tired of the constant noise of trolley cars and trucks drowning out what students were saying in my university classroom. Also, I was aware of the pleasures of the outdoors surrounding Exeter and its proximity to the White Mountains, the ocean, and skiing. Most important, the teaching would be more stimulating, and I could do what I wanted with my summer vacations.

I went to Exeter to see Dr. Perry, whom I had regarded as a minor deity when I was a student at the academy. He greeted me graciously and affectionately. He told me that my salary would be almost doubled. Exeter, he continued, probably could always keep a salary scale as good as the ones at Amherst and Williams Colleges. More important to me, he stated that if I were asked to go on a major mountain expedition again, he would arrange a leave of absence for me and would make this permission part of our agreement. That did it. I notified the University of Pennsylvania of my decision and prepared to settle in Exeter in the fall.

This meant losing a pleasant social life and my departure from many good friends in the Philadelphia area, including Bill Child, my oldest friend, and Howard Lee, my former Exeter roommate, both of whom were colleagues in the Penn English Department.

During the fall, I focused on a more challenging form of teaching as I sat at a table with 12 students. Meanwhile, two matters besides the writing of *Five Miles High* brought together the four of us who had recently crossed Afghanistan together. One was a letter from Miss Taylor in Kansas to Dick Burdsall. It told nothing about how she had gone from Tehran to the middle of the North American continent, and failed to mention whether she had indeed gone through Riga, Latvia. Instead, there was a check for something like $12.56—the equivalent of what we had paid for her at the Afghan/Iran border.

A more immediate problem was that Paul, basically through no fault of his own, was in jail in India charged with manslaughter. He was asking our help. Through the American consulate in Calcutta, we sent funds for legal help, and after considerable difficulty he was released.

All through the winter and spring of 1939, I kept working during spare time on *Five Miles High*. Bill House and Dick Burdsall were writing sections, but Charlie and I were doing most of it. Photographs had to be selected too, and drawings were being done by an artist. In June the book was complete, and in July I read the proof for Dodd, Mead & Co., the publisher. It was to come out in September or October, in time for the Christmas sales.

With a light heart, I boarded the *Normandie* in late July and headed for Switzerland to meet Adams Carter and other friends. Some of my Christmas vacation during each of the previous five or six years I had spent at the Carters' delightful family home in Jefferson, New Hampshire. Interesting people were always there, frequently unusual foreigners, as well as Ad's father and mother, whose company I enjoyed. The big house had a fine view of Mt. Washington and was ideally situated for skiing or winter climbing in the White Mountains. It had helped Ad to become a great skier, a member of the United States Ski Team in Europe in 1934.

Ad had asked me to join him for three or four weeks of summer climbing in the area near Kandersteg in the Swiss Oberland. With him was another American friend, Peter Hunsaker, and also two slightly younger Englishmen, Peter Palmer-Thompkinson (known as Tony) and Tom Bird, both good skiers but not experienced climbers. Ad had begun his own climbing in the Kandersteg area many years earlier and knew the best guide, Kilian Oggi, at whose home we could stay. I joined one climb that the others were taking with Kilian and from then on Ad and I did the leading, making one or two new variations of routes on our own.

At mountain huts it was not easy to get world news but we did learn from hutkeepers that war was appearing more likely between Germany and Poland. The Germans were getting very aggressive and almost all the Swiss we met were apprehensive. We saw Swiss mountain troops maneuvering and we talked about how the U.S. Army could make good use of mountain troops too.

Other people were concerned about a coming war. We had just come down from the Altels when Tony, who had a reserve commission as a second lieutenant in the Royal Flying Corps, found a telegram ordering him to report to his unit. We gave him a big farewell dinner and saw him off on the night train. We never saw him again, for he was shot down in the Battle of Britain. The next day we climbed the Balmhorn, and when we returned found a similar telegram for Tom Bird, who had a reserve commission in the Rifle Brigade. When we next saw Tom, he had been wounded four times and was a major serving as aide to Jumbo Wilson, the British Army's senior officer in Washington.

Ad remembered he had promised his mother that before returning to the U.S. he would see an old family friend living in Germany. He bade Peter and me a hasty good-bye and took off for Germany. Peter and I were planning to do one more climb, but when the German news announced that the Poles had raped and murdered a number of German nurses and thrown their bodies in the river, we decided to move too. A night train took us to Paris, where we arrived about five in the morning, having heard no news on the train. As we carried our bags into the station, newsboys began hawking the day's first papers. I bought one and was soon surrounded, for the newsboys had only a few. A large headline read, "Les Huîtres Sont Ici" (Oysters Are Here) in one-inch black type. Over it, very hastily printed in smaller type, was a simple statement in French, "The Germans have invaded Poland."

Peter left at once to see if he could get an earlier passage home, while I went to get a ticket to England by train and ferry. I wanted to see Norman Streatfeild before leaving Europe. Everything in Paris was confusion. Men were being called up, shops were closing, and there was worry on every face. My return ticket to the U.S. was on the *Bremen*, a ship that the papers announced had disappeared. On the boat train and during the channel crossing I heard much sober conversation, with a few older men talking about World War I. When we reached London, I learned that England and France were at war with Germany. Almost immediately sirens sounded an air-raid alert, caused, it turned out later, by some Dutch planes.

At Nord Deutscher Lloyd, I was politely told that my ticket on the *Bremen* would be refunded in the U.S., but they could not do it there. The official mentioned that the *Washington*, sailing to New York from Southampton, might still have passage. I rushed to its office and joined a line of hopefuls. All tickets seemed to have been issued when the loudly dressed woman in front of me reached the clerk. She insisted that she have a first-class cabin and would not take no for an answer. The annoyed clerk finally said, "This is the last ticket, move on please," and he gave it to me.

Since the *Washington* was sailing in two days, I had time to phone Norman Streatfeild, now a major at Aldershot, and go down to see him. He also would be sailing in two days, "going to France," he told me in great confidence. We had a fine dinner and evening together and I departed after breakfast. He was taking with him to France the film he had exposed on our expedition. Later we learned that he showed it several times to troops.

R.H.B. skiing at Exeter

It was probably with him on the destroyer that took off some of the last men to leave Dunkerque—a destroyer torpedoed and blown up as it left the beach. (In his will, Norman left this film to Charlie and me.)

The voyage on the *Washington* was an experience. The boat was crowded, everybody with a story of what he had done when war was declared and rumors about submarine sinkings. At night the ship was fully lighted, the spotlights shining on a huge American flag painted on each side. Daily news bulletins were eagerly devoured. I wondered if the Germans were planning to change the map of the world as I had seen it changed on the map in the crew quarters where Dick Burdsall and I had blundered the year before. It did not seem possible that the Germans would try to do it.

As I found out later, Peter Hunsaker managed to get a ticket on the *Ile de France*, sailing from Cherbourg. On it were my brother Bill and also Gail Oberlin, whom I had not yet met. Meanwhile Ad Carter could not get out of Germany. For a time he took a job with friends, then managed to get to Italy, and home from there.

Back in the U.S. I returned to Exeter. I liked my students and advisees, and thoroughly enjoyed my teaching, including taking students of the Outing Club on ski trips and nearby climbs. When the spring of 1940 brought a national registration for the draft, I drew a very high number and my brother a fairly high one. Like everybody else, we did not know what the future would bring, but I decided to do some summer climbing while I could. When June came, Bill and I headed for the Canadian Rockies, where we did several climbs. I had not been there before and quickly got a feeling for the Canadian Rockies and the Canadian huts that has never left me. I did one climb with Rex Gibson, a Canadian from Edmonton, which two years later led to his participation in the Alaskan Test Expedition.

A good friend who was in Banff at the same time was Dr. James Monroe Thorington, who had brought me into the American Alpine Club in 1935. He took us to the home of Belmore Browne in Seebe, where for the first time I met that delightful artist, hunter, and mountain climber whose biography I was to write in later years. Belmore graciously put aside a canvas he was painting to show us the home he had built after World War I. It combined comfort and frontier character, the latter coming from the beams, the huge moose and mountain sheep horns, and over the central fireplace the large American flag that, wrapped around his waist, he had carried almost to the summit of Mt. McKinley on his third try, thwarted at the last moment by a furious blizzard. His attempts to climb Mt. McKinley were legendary. I never forgot that first meeting with him.

From the Canadian Rockies we drove to the Tetons, where Bill House met us for more climbing. We camped with Paul Petzoldt and made a new route up Mt. Owen, but Bill, as a forester, was called away to fight a forest fire. My brother Bill and I climbed the Owen route on the Grand Teton, taking along a couple from Philadelphia who were inexperienced climbers. Then, on Bill House's return, he and I climbed the east ridge of the Grand Teton, a long climb that required good route finding and brought us down to the upper saddle just as it was getting dark. On the way, a severe afternoon thunderstorm, with strong lightning strikes, set our ice axes humming. We could feel the electricity in our hair too, and were glad to get away from our exposed ridge and off the mountain.

Through Paul Petzoldt we met Betsy Cowles and her brother-in-law, Macauley Smith, both of whom he had been guiding. With them, Glen Exum, and Paul Petzoldt, we climbed the steep north ridge of the Grand Teton, all of us leading in turn. It was a fun climb. I believe it was the third ascent of the ridge. Next we made a new route on Mt. Moran; and Bill, Betsy, and I made a couple of other climbs, including the east ridge of Nez Perce, before the season ended. The only injury (very minor) on any of our climbs that summer came when the woman from Philadelphia sat down heavily on her upturned pair of crampons and arose with them embedded in her rear.

Phillips Exeter Academy, a fine old school, where R.H.B. taught from 1939 until 1976

Shortly after returning to Exeter, I had conversations with James Bryant Conant, president of Harvard, about his son Jim, an Exeter student and president of the Lantern Club, which I advised. Jim had done some climbs with me, and his father had made some climbs in Switzerland. Mr. Conant wanted to do a rock climb in the White Mountains and asked if we could all do one together. With my brother's help, I agreed to take father and son up the "Pinnacle" on Mt. Washington.

The crux of the climb requires ascending a 20-foot wall with small holds. President Conant was a good sport, but using the small holds exceeded his skill. Accordingly I belayed him from above as Bill helped him to climb onto his shoulders. With encouragement he climbed up a foot or two, but slithered back just as Bill looked up. Bill swears that Mr. Conant then called up to me, "I'm afraid I'm standing on your brother's face!" He finally made it.

The day was successful in more ways than one, because we talked much of the time about how mountain troops could be useful to the American army. Conant was to meet with General George Marshall in a few days and promised to discuss with him the importance of beginning to train such troops.

U.S. Army rations on Mt. Wood

CHAPTER X

The Wood Yukon Expedition

1941

IN THE FALL OF 1940, Bill House, Charlie Houston, and I asked the American Alpine Club to discuss the part it might play in national defense. Ad Carter and Walter Wood were also active. Walter had asked me to join his expedition to the Yukon the following summer and I had agreed. He now asked me to help him set up an exhibition of up-to-date mountain equipment to show Major General Woodruff, a senior army officer. The display and the discussion that followed obviously made an impression on him. General Woodruff's reaction may have triggered a letter afterward, on December 20, 1940, to the American Alpine Club from Colonel Harry L. Twaddle, acting assistant chief of staff of the U.S. Army. This letter asked for information on essential items of mountaineering equipment that could be of use to the army. There was no mention of mountain troops.

The idea of having mountain troops, however, was very much in the air, fueled particularly by the spectacular winter successes of Finnish ski troops in attacking Russian motorized vehicles.

A detailed reply to Colonel Twaddle's letter listed 21 items of equipment and where they might be needed, based on regional and temperature differences. At the same time, the club council asked Kenneth Henderson to prepare a mountaineering manual that could be used for the instruction of troops or the average mountain hiker. In March 1941, Walter Wood phoned me to say that he had had an urgent request from Brigadier

General Twaddle to come to Norfolk, Virginia, to discuss important mountaineering matters. I was asked to come with him.

At army headquarters at Old Point Comfort, we met General Twaddle, Colonel Walker, and Lieutenant Colonel Hurdis. They knew of our planned summer expedition to the Saint Elias Range and asked a hypothetical question. "Suppose we wanted to take a dozen men 100 miles through mountainous country with no people in the area. How would we go about it?"

"Would we have a map or photographs?"

"The map would not be detailed but you could have photographs."

In that case, we said, you could work out a route on the photographs, but you would need to backpack a lot of supplies if no people are living there, or else drop food to the men.

This latter idea was seized on. "Where would you drop the loads?"

"If the mountains are in the northern area where there are few people, there will likely be glaciers running through them or high alpine valleys. In either case, one can drop supplies to places determined by photograph even if there is nobody there to receive them."

The army apparently had had no experience receiving air-dropped supplies, and they doubted that army or air force planes had ever made such airdrops. The enthusiasm of our hosts rose.

The discussion turned to our expedition, where we were going, and what we were planning to do. Before we departed we were offered and accepted the services of two B-18 bombers to carry out experiments during our expedition. We suggested that there could be problems with dropped loads being covered by snow before being found or loads being dragged into crevasses by wind. We were asked to work on these problems.

Soon after this meeting, I joined Walter at Whippany, New Jersey. He had a friend in the area with a small plane and the desire to help us. How to prevent parachuted loads from disappearing under snow before they could be found was our first problem. Walter had a good idea, suggested to him by Anderson Bakewell, a member of our expedition who had long been interested in airdrops by firefighters in Montana. We found a wooden box, then went to a hardware store and bought a half-dozen rattraps with strong springs. We attached a trap to every side of the box. We then bought three-foot pieces of wood and some red cloth, which we tore into separate flags. We nailed a flag to one end of each stake and attached the other end to a rattrap on the box. The stick was placed so that it would lie flat if the trap were cocked and jump upright if the trap were sprung.

The next move was to experiment with springing the trap. We found that one string carefully placed would restrain all the traps from opening. When a box was parachuted, this string would break and the traps would release, erecting every stake with its flag. The purpose, of course, was to add to the box's visibility at a time of heavy snow. No matter how the box landed, at least one flag would be more than two feet above the box and so would help with its location.

Walter's friend took him and the box in his plane, with a parachute and static line attached. When Walter pushed out the box and parachute over the Whippany airport, the chute filled, the rattraps opened, and the box with multiple flags flying made a successful landing.

The second problem we wished to solve was how to separate the chute from the box, for we feared a strong ground wind could cause the chute to drag the box, possibly pulling it into a crevasse or other undesirable place. Our solution was to light a fuse before throwing out the box. The fuse would burn to a point where it would destroy the connection between the chute and the box, leaving both free. Separation of the chute was a problem, for the man lighting the fuse must know the length of time it would take to burn away the connection, as well as the length of time the parachute would need to be in the air before landing. In mountainous country, the height above the surface of a drop might vary considerably. Also, the fuse might go out, not cause a complete separation, or burn through before the box landed. At any rate we did not then find a better solution. Later Walter bought some timing devices that had much the same problems.

We also made brief experiments in free dropping without a parachute, for we believed many items could be dropped on snow without damage, especially if placed in multiple sacks. There was no snow in Whippany at the time, but we threw out sugar and flour in multiple sacks with no damage except to the inside containers—the food was unharmed.

Soon after our return from General Twaddle's headquarters, Captain Jackman, who was to be the army observer on our expedition, wrote to us and I arranged to take him climbing in the White Mountains. I liked him at once, found he had done some backpacking, and hustled him off to Ad Carter's house in Jefferson, New Hampshire. The weather was not good, but after we managed to do a little rock climbing, both Ad and I concluded he would be a useful member of the expedition.

Jackman, who was involved in operations and training, found the Quartermaster General's Office especially interested in the expedition, although it was in no way involved in the test we were making for General

Twaddle. When Jackman arrived in the Yukon, he had both army and navy survival rations, which I had agreed to test with him.

I left Boston on June 16, headed for Whitehorse, where I would meet the rest of the Wood Yukon Expedition. Reaching Prince Rupert at 1:30 a.m. on June 22, I promptly went to the Central Hotel, where the clerk announced that every room was taken "except the best room in the house, but that, of course, is too expensive."

"How much?" I asked.

"Oh," he said, with awe in his voice, "it's a very fine room, but it costs $1.50 a day." I took it, and well after sunrise was awakened by a radio blaring out the amazing news, "Germany has invaded Russia."

What changes the invasion would make in the European war was the main topic of conversation on the *Princess Charlotte*, the boat taking me on to Alaska. We reached Skagway the morning of June 25, where I boarded the Yukon White Pass Railroad for the all-day, 100-mile trip to Whitehorse. Walter and Foresta Wood and Albert Jackman met me at the station. A couple of hours later we were eating moose steak for dinner when the roar of big planes overhead told us that our two B-18 bombers had arrived. Minutes later the town seemed to have been invaded by the American air force. There were four pilots, three sergeants, an executive officer, and a special parachute officer, sent from Fort Benning, Georgia, to help us. The flight commander, Earl Jacobson, we soon discovered to be witty and well organized. He agreed to leave at 3:00 a.m. the next morning if the weather was good for a flight to base camp, about 160 miles from Whitehorse.

Two days later, on the Fourth of July, we had our first airdrop, throwing out several parachute loads and bulk food in multiple sacks without parachutes. From the air, we could tell that the chutes landed well near base camp, but a long streak of flour across the tundra showed where at least one free-fall had come to grief. A radio report later from Anderson Bakewell, who had gone in earlier with a light pack train and François Bée, told us, however, that we had lost only 45 pounds of sugar, 50 pounds of flour, and 10 pounds of rice—not at all bad considering the amounts dropped.

A couple of days later, we circled Mt. Logan, Canada's highest mountain, and made the first flight over the summit, proving that it is not over 20,000 feet high, as some had claimed. (The 19,625-foot height seemed accurate.) On the way we parachuted loads along a glacier we would visit later in the summer. There we would test the plan proposed to General Twaddle some months earlier.

BAKEWELL

R.H.B. with a Dall sheep

It was four years since Brad Washburn and I had climbed Mt. Lucania, forded the Donjek, and finally reached Burwash Landing on Kluane Lake. What a difference now! We had horses, packers, and an easy crossing of the Donjek ford. Beyond the river every bend in the glacier valley brought back memories of how, short on food, we had worked out a route across the mountains to get from the far side of Mt. Lucania to Kluane Lake.

Soon camp was set up along the Wolf Creek Glacier and we began reconnoitering the route up Mt. Wood, our major climbing objective, now the highest unclimbed mountain in North America. Jackman fitted in well, as did Andy Bakewell, from the American Geographical Society, and Bob Sharp, a top-notch glaciologist. One of the test items Jackman had brought with him was an experimental tent made by Bestor Robinson of the Sierra Club, which Bob quickly took with him on a geology side trip. On his return a few days later, he was very critical of it. Jack and I were to test it more fully later.

After several days of backpacking, we were ready to begin our climb of Mt. Wood (15,885 feet). Before we left, Walter wanted to get some meat for base camp, and I won a shooting contest to see who would secure it.

The next morning with Andy, an experienced hunter, I started out, carrying his 30.06 Remington rifle. After a good climb and some long stalks to avoid 17 ewes and lambs who would have given the alarm, I crawled across an exposed slope to where I could see eight rams about 125 yards

F. WOOD

Wood and Bakewell retrieving box parachuted onto Mt. Wood

away. One of them stood up and I fired. I could not tell where my bullet struck; the ram just stood there while the others raced away. I fired again and again and he dropped. He was stone-dead when Andy joined me and we went over to him. Each shot was in the same area, but I had held a bit low. The ram was a beautiful animal with a large set of horns, and I hated killing him. We cleaned him, with Andy doing most of the work, and together carried out a huge load of meat and the head.

The following day, the Woods, Bakewell, Jackman, and I began our climb of Mt. Wood by packing 60-pound loads to 8,000 feet at a place where box 1 had been dropped. We found the box and parachute with all flags flying. The fuse and dynamite cap used to separate the chute from the box after its landing had worked. If the wind had been blowing after the landing, the chute would have blown away, leaving the box.

We moved higher in the morning, packing through a heavily crevassed area to about 10,000 feet, where we decided to put Camp II. About 600 yards beyond, we located box 2, where it had landed on a bridge over a huge crevasse. It was hard to reach, but by belaying carefully, we unloaded it, secured the loads on two packboards, and pulled the rest in the parachute to a safe place.

Variable weather slowed us, but on July 22 we all packed heavy loads through crevasses and up a steep ridge to about 11,500 feet, where we set

WASHBURN

Mt. Wood (15,885 feet)

up a tent. In the afternoon we reconnoitered to at least 14,000 feet and saw a route ahead to the top. On our return to the tent, we found we had a stove but no utensils. That was easily solved by putting the coffee in my hat, cooking in the coffee tin, and using army ration tins as cups. In the morning we returned to Camp II and moved the others up to join us. Shortly after we set up a second tent, furious gusts of wind, followed by snow, battered both tents.

Two days later, when the storm had cleared, we set off to reach the summit, but it was still very windy and cold, even wearing our high-toed Bass boots. We had climbed above 14,000 feet when Foresta said she had no feeling in her toes. We took off her shoes and socks and tried to warm her feet; I even put one foot against my stomach, but after 20 minutes her toes were still white. We told her she had to go down.

I felt that Mt. Wood should be Walter's mountain. This was his second year attempting to climb it; accordingly, I took Foresta back to camp. She kept stating that her feet were all right, but we knew better. At camp, her feet were painful—frosted, not frozen, but if she had kept on, she certainly would have been a hospital case and probably would have lost some toes.

It was nearly 7:00 p.m. when the others returned with icicles on their beards and moustaches. They had had a very cold day, reaching the nearly 16,000-foot summit four hours after we left them.

In our spare time Jackman and I had been testing various items for the army, including Bestor Robinson's tent, which, as directed, we pitched as a one-man, two-man, three-man, and four-man tent. We did not like any of them, especially if needed in areas of high wind and snow. Among other items still to be tested were army and navy survival rations. The army pemmican sent to us looked like a cake of compressed oatmeal cookies, but seemed to be made mostly of ground peanuts, whole oats, and fat. The navy pemmican looked more like the Danish pemmican I knew so well, but was very sweet, with a sickly smell of vanilla.

We were about to combine a three-day survival test, living on the army survival rations, and searching for the first army test box of several we had parachuted onto the slopes of Mt. Walsh. Up at five to prepare a breakfast of hot army pemmican and hot army chocolate, Jack and I were soon away. The rations could be eaten cold as well as hot. Each meal was to consist of a bar of pemmican weighing one-third of a pound, plus two squares of fortified chocolate.

Wolf Creek was running high and Jack and I had an exciting crossing before starting along an unnamed glacier, which we called Sheep Glacier because of the many tracks on it. That night we camped with clouds all around us, but in the morning we were off with 50-pound loads, including items for the Walsh climb, on what turned out to be a very hot day.

We reached the Valiant Glacier, whose surface was wet with melting snow, and finally came to a stream six to 10 feet across, with side walls four to five feet high. Water two or three feet deep was running very swiftly. We followed its windings for 15 minutes until we saw a place where I felt we could cross. Cutting a step, I lowered myself onto it, and making a long stretch, reached my foot to a piece of ice on the opposite side. Using my axe, I pulled myself over and waited for Jack. Jack did not like it. "I'm going to throw my pack over first," he said. I thought he was going to untie his load and throw parts over separately, but instead he tried to heave the whole pack. He slipped, and he and his pack splashed into the stream.

In a moment Jack was racing downstream as if in a bobsled run. The walls were smooth, he had left his ice axe behind and had no way of getting to his feet. Glacial streams have a disconcerting way of suddenly dropping down a hole to the bottom of the glacier and continuing there, but Jack had no concept of this danger as the flow rushed him around corners with smooth ice walls. I chased after him and thrust my ice axe at him. "Grab it," I yelled. He thought I meant his pack, which was plunging downstream just in front of him. As he grabbed it, he swept past me, going fast. I cut across two curves of the channel and pushed my axe in front of him again. This time he grabbed it and I hauled him out. "My pack," he gasped. I rushed along the bank, caught up with it 100 yards farther on, and gaffed it with my axe. The current was so strong that all I could do was hold it against the pull of the stream. With Jack's help, we hauled it out. Then I showed him what happened a couple of curves ahead, for there with a roar the stream poured into a great hole, dropping to the bottom of the glacier.

Jack's hands were bleeding from small cuts and he was very cold, but otherwise unhurt. The sun was behind a ridge and it was now early evening. I gave him dextrose and my parka. When he opened his pack, there was his long underwear, still dry. Going back upstream, I recrossed and retrieved Jack's axe. Then we continued, with wet clothes hanging from our packs. Jack was still somewhat wet, but he didn't lament his luck at all—he had seen the stream disappear.

I had an aerial photograph, taken I thought in 1939, but actually in 1936, showing a glacier mound near which we had parachuted a load. Jack and I were cold, the light was waning, and we could not find the mound. (What I didn't realize was that the glacier had carried the mound half a mile below where it had been when the picture was taken.) We began to have trouble distinguishing heights and distances, but we finished our pemmican, took some dextrose tablets, and kept searching. The box we were looking for held a tent, and we had none with us. Finally the need to bivouac became obvious. Leaving Jack, I went on a bit to see if there was a more sheltered place ahead. In so doing I found the mound, but we still could not locate the parachute in the semidarkness. It was now 2:30 a.m. We blew up our air mattresses, put down our sleeping bags, and I was asleep before Jack made the discovery that his bag was wet from his fall in the stream.

At four it began to rain. I dressed quickly, put my sleeping bag in the duffel and scrambled up the mound. There was more light now and immediately I spied the parachute and box. Letting out a yell, I rushed to it, ripped the top off with an ice axe, and in three minutes we had the tent pitched and were in it, just as the rain started to pour down. "Timing," I have often said, "is everything."

While we were asleep a wolf had circled our tent. In a couple of places, his tracks had sunk so far that he must have spent quite a bit of time there. Jack's watch read 5:00. We had our last pemmican and then set out for a cache several miles away, where we were to pick up supplies to take to base camp. On the way we felt strangely tired, whether from our diet or the hard work we could not tell. Clouds were thick at the cache as we pitched the tent. When I looked to see what was there, right away I noticed a bottle of ketchup. We looked at each other, quickly seized the bottle, poured out cupfuls, added some wet snow, and drank it all. I have never cared much for ketchup, nor has Jackman, but the army survival diet must have lacked something. Our pemmican test with dextrose tablets had given us sufficient energy for very hard work, but we were ready for real food again.

The cache held an eight-man portion of corn soup. We cooked it all, along with some bacon, ate it, and with full stomachs quickly drowsed off again.

Waking at 12:30 p.m. by Jack's watch, we washed the soup pot, struck the tent, packed up 40-pound loads, and headed for base camp. Hot weather had changed the route and there were great areas of glacial mud and a big surface stream to detour around. Here we noticed that Jack's watch had stopped. We thought it was early afternoon, but it began to grow dark. We felt outraged. How could it do this? Could it be an eclipse of the sun? The sun could not go down in the middle of the afternoon and leave us in the middle of a very unpleasant place. We had been in the clouds for the better part of three days. During this time Jack's watch, having been drenched in the stream, had slowed and finally stopped.

The approaching darkness hurried us on. By mistake we got on the wrong side of the big glacier stream, whose roaring grew louder and louder as more tributaries poured into it. Warm-weather melting had swelled all the streams, and one we had great trouble crossing. Jack, carrying a heavy pack, teetered forward and backward on a rock in the middle. I was sure he was going headlong into the frothing water, but he made a valiant recovery and we went on.

Finally we reached a flat place where the water spread out in many channels. In semidarkness we took off our trousers and underwear and plunged in. The first two channels were good, but in the third one I got in over my waist and barely kept from being swept downstream. Probing with the axe, I found a more shallow place and crossed. Jack followed. That night crossing was too risky. We never should have done it, but a warm bed on a rainy night is a great enticement.

By now it was dark. Steady rain had set in, but we knew more or less where we were. For an hour we stumbled across tundra until we saw what looked like the chalk cliffs of Dover. "Have you ever seen this before?" I asked Jack. "Gosh, no," he replied. We struggled toward it. At once the cliff turned into a 12-foot bank and we knew where we were. In five minutes we were in camp eating a can of grapefruit apiece. That marked the end of our test of army pemmican and the beginning of our last expedition objective, the climb of Mt. Walsh.

Near base camp a bear had eaten, without apparent discrimination, coffee, onions, arsenic (for curing skins), powdered milk, vegetables, jam, and crackers. We had concern for our food parachuted on Mt. Walsh, but considered it out of the normal range of bears. On August 12, we had a long search for the second box dropped on the route to Mt. Walsh. It lay in an area of big crevasses, seracs, and 50-foot-wide glacier lakes. We were not far from the base of Mt. Steele, and while Jackman continued to look downstream for the box, Walter and I went to his old cache at the base of Steele, the one Washburn and I had never found in 1937. The glacier was 50 feet higher than when the cache was made, but we found it and almost everything in it was still good. Brad and I had searched within 100 yards of it. On our return to where we had left Jackman, we found a note saying that he had found the box. It was unbroken, though it had been dragged by the parachute to a hollow between big crevasses. The fuse had burned through but the parachute had not separated from the load.

The next day Jackman and I set out to force a route up the Whirlwind Glacier icefall to reach boxes parachuted higher. Nobody had set foot on this glacier before and that added to our zest. We found the icefall treacherously crevassed, with old snow covering many cracks, and hanging seracs on the sidewall above the most logical route. I led cautiously on a double rope, with an additional loop at the end for further protection. At about 8,300 feet we had lunch in a tangle of crevasses. We were on steep slopes cut by layer after layer of parallel cracks, like a flight of steps.

We pushed forward up the middle, curving to the right to avoid some large blue caverns with overhanging icicles. I had just stepped across one dubious place when I heard a cry behind me. We always kept the rope fairly taut and I stopped Jack quickly. He was in a crevasse up to his shoulders, his feet dangling free. Out he came, his nerve not lessened at all. Dubious snow bridges were beyond and we negotiated them with great care. Above were huge crevasses, which Jack referred to as drydocks, and beyond what looked like a corridor on our left leading to clear snow. For 200 yards all went well and then at the last moment a lateral crevasse too large to cross cut us off.

WASHBURN

The Saint Elias Mountains: (at left) Kennedy, Alverstone,
and Hubbard; (center) Walsh, with Queen Mary showing over
right shoulder; (right) Vancouver, Wood, and Lucania

We seemed to be completely stopped. Up to now, we had been wearing snowshoes because they spread our weight, but as I reconnoitered to the far right I saw a steep slope that might provide a route if we took off our snow-shoes. That worked. Traversing across this slope above a giant blue cavern, we reached a smaller crevasse. Here, after returning to our snowshoes and doing considerable probing, we crossed another large crevasse on a small bridge. Ahead all looked well for 100 yards, and when we arrived good for another 100 yards, and so on. As we wound up and up, the slope gradually became less crevassed and steep. Before we knew it, we were in the upper valley. We were through! It was the longest, most difficult crevasse work I had ever experienced.

Upward we went, and at about 10,000 feet saw a flag about 150 yards ahead. A parachuted box was buried but the flag was showing. A smaller load of skis was not far away. These, with some effort, we unpacked, though our boots did not fit the bindings. We took one pair of skis with us to a point above the upper crevasses where we could use them as a sled. It was now 6:00 p.m. and the snow had frozen, making our nearly 3,000-foot descent to camp safer. By nine we were back in camp, to be met with hot soup but gloomy faces. The others had had a bad day. A falling stone had given Walter a nasty crack on the head. He had a mean headache and a possible concussion.

Fortunately, in the morning Walter felt better and we decided to move up as far as our lunching place of the previous day. Walter went slowly but steadily all day.

Up before 3:00 the next morning, I cooked breakfast and we were soon following the route we had marked by black-tipped dowels. At the steep slope, Jack slipped but caught himself with his axe. From there to the skis we had left, all went well, and we were soon screwing on to them the Robes carrier, a packboard-sled combination we were to test. We piled 250 pounds onto it, pulled it to the box we had found the day before, and camped. On hard snow, it worked.

In the morning we sledded four miles with 350 pounds, then climbed nearly 1,000 feet to a col where two boxes had been dropped. The first box was buried with one whole flag showing, while the only indication of the other box was the tip of its topmost flag. Six inches more snow and we never would have found it. "Hurray for rattraps," we cried.

The camp we set up there had spectacular views of Mt. Vancouver, 60 miles away, now the highest unclimbed peak on the continent, and all the way down the Hubbard Glacier to Mt. King George (which we had named in 1935).

We had never known such a stretch of clear weather in the Yukon before and did not dare pass up a summit attempt on Mt. Walsh. The weather looked bad at 4:00 a.m. but better at five, when I started cooking breakfast. An hour later Walter was leading through some nasty crevasses right toward the rising sun. "Watch that crack," he called to me.

"Everything ought to be frozen now," I yelled back.

"It's not. I just went into that one you are standing on."

In the next 15 minutes, he put a leg into two different crevasses. Then I took over the lead, which we continued to alternate for the rest of the day, kicking and occasionally cutting steps. Of course, sometimes I put a leg in too.

The route went around crevasses, then up a steep slope to a more or less horizontal knife-edge ridge. Four snow- and ice-encrusted towers had to be passed, and then steep rock and snow to the top. Walter was leading the last part, but he stepped aside and all three insisted that I go first to the

Wood and R.H.B. at the summit of Mt. Walsh

summit. Mountaineering is a team sport and what we had done was a group accomplishment, but I felt the courtesy of the others and knew what they had been thinking when they reached the summit of Mt. Wood.

Films of cloud brushed across the summit, but we could see Hubbard and Alverstone, Alaska boundary peaks, and far to the south Fairweather and Crillon. Clouds blotted out Vancouver and Logan, but we had glimpses of our old companions, Steele and Lucania. How the toil of the ascent dropped away from us in that breathtaking half hour. We felt uplifted in spirit as well as in body, for the climb had been a battle all the way. At 5:00 p.m. we started down on a four-man rope. By 9:30 we were back in camp.

The next day Jack was sure he heard an airplane. We were in the tent and could not hear it, but burst out with hopes of an airdrop with mail or news. Outside none of us could hear the plane or see it anywhere, though Jack yelled that it was very near. Then we found it. A bee, 20 miles from the nearest greenery, was resting on Jack's hat and humming loudly.

On the morrow we had good skiing, trying out Swiss two-piece skis and folding skis, all meant to fit in a rucksack. Then we loaded the sled and started down, the sled pulling us but controlled by ropes from behind. The weather was deteriorating as we descended the icefall, snow was falling steadily, and avalanches were pouring off the cliffs above the Whirlwind Glacier and down into the Steele Cirque. That night was our last on the glacier, for in the morning we were off to base camp with 90-pound loads. Skiing with such packs is very tiring and we all had some spills. Jack had one bad one. When I reached him, he had blood all over his moustache and was wiggling his nose with his hand to see if it was broken. His knee and right shoulder also hurt and he had a pain in his chest, possibly from a cracked rib, but he insisted on going on. Great fellow! All four of us had become close friends on the expedition. In fact, our whole group went well together, including Foresta Wood, and Bob Sharp, the glaciologist; and Frank Bée, the always helpful French Canadian from Burwash, who after a big meal one day ate several pieces of survival experimental chocolate because he thought it was dessert.

During the expedition, two and one-half tons had been dropped with less than a six percent loss. We had also proved that fast travel in unknown mountain areas could be accomplished by experienced climbers using air supply. The expedition had accomplished all its objectives. I returned to Exeter by way of Seattle and the Great Northern Railroad, but floods in the Middle West stopped our train at a siding and I arrived at school a day late.

William N. Bates with his two sons, W.N.B., Jr., and R.H.B.

CHAPTER XI

World War II: The OQMG and Mt. McKinley

1941-1944

I WAS HARDLY BACK IN MY OLD DORMITORY when I received a letter from Lt. Col. L. O. Grice of the Office of the Quartermaster General (OQMG) in Washington, asking if I could meet him in Boston a few days later to discuss problems of mountain and winter warfare. I met him at the Essex Hotel near South Station. Grice was a square-built, balding, tough-looking man with a no-nonsense approach. Arriving when I did was a large, slightly lumbering, genial man of about my age, who introduced himself as Paul Siple. I knew that name at once. He was the Boy Scout who had gone to the Antarctic with the Byrd expeditions and been highly praised for his work there. Paul exuded friendliness and we liked each other at once.

Grice asked us questions about our experience in cold-weather areas and the clothing and equipment we used. He was frank in his statements that the army needed help in getting better equipment. Alaska was already a concern of his, for reports had come in requesting better clothing. Grice also referred to the European war and the need for preparations if the U.S. became involved.

Over dinner Siple told us of work he had been doing for his Ph.D. In the Antarctic he had found that his face would freeze much more quickly on a cold windy day than on a quiet day of equal cold. Trying to quantify the problem, he took a container holding a cubic centimeter of water and timed how long it would take the water surface to freeze over in various degrees of freezing temperatures and wind velocities. From his data he was trying to work out a chart of what he named *wind chill* temperature equivalents. Paul obviously knew Antarctic conditions well and his scientific attitude made his use to the army obvious.

A few days later a letter from the quartermaster general of the army to Principal Lewis Perry of the academy arrived requesting that I be granted a leave of absence to come to the War Department as a civilian to work on mountain and winter warfare problems and equipment. No faculty member had left the academy to help national defense up to that time, but others would surely be needed in the future. I was eager to go. During the summer I had become very interested in the army's problems and realized that in matters of cold weather and mountain clothing and equipment, our army was way behind the times.

It took a few days to get a replacement teacher for my classes. In fact, I was still marking a set of papers in early October when Dick Niebling, a bright graduate student at Yale, arrived to take my place. In the years that followed, he became a pillar of the Exeter faculty.

On reporting to the standardization branch, supply division, of the OQMG in the Railroad Retirement Building the next day, I entered a world very new to me. Gruff Colonel Grice was almost affable. I was assigned a desk and a part-time secretary, and one of the employees, Franz Fraze, was assigned to introduce me to the mysteries of the War Department.

The office consisted of about 20 people, including secretaries, with experts on boots, gloves, clothing, wool, plastics, and so forth. Somehow I had the feeling that the branch had not always been bustling with activity, but there was action now. Colonel Grice was constantly on the phone or dictating, and he obviously needed more help. Apparently I was the first specialist on winter or mountain items to arrive, but Paul Siple and Bestor Robinson, whose tent I had tested in the Yukon, were supposed to arrive soon. Meanwhile, I read reports and learned how new items are officially adopted for army use.

The standardization branch came into being because all items of clothing and most items of quartermaster corps equipment were used by all services of supply (such as the ordnance corps, and signal corps), and by the arms (infantry, artillery, and cavalry). There was as yet no action toward standardizing army, navy, and marine items, but no item of quartermaster issue could be adopted without the approval of our standardization branch. Its decisions, therefore, were very important, especially to the army ground forces.

One of my first jobs was to fly to Chicago to display items of army clothing to a meeting of manufacturers. They were to be given a chance to see items they might want to manufacture. I was to help Colonel Grice to answer questions on the purpose and use of the items.

Almost immediately on my return, I was given a file with a seventeenth endorsement. This file had been making the rounds of the army for nearly two years. It had started with a packboard somebody had wanted standardized to carry mortar shells. This request had been endorsed to other branches of the army that wanted a packboard to carry other items. Several different shapes and sizes of carriers were requested as the original document went back and forth between the services, army ground force headquarters, and the OQMG. The final packboard endorsement was a very bad compromise, and since far better packboards for general use were available commercially, I indicated such and ended the file's travels.

When I learned that Colonel Grice had been given an opening for another person to work on mountain and winter warfare equipment, I recommended Bill House, who quickly came to Washington to be interviewed and accepted. It was fine having Bill's judgment and companionship.

One of the problems facing our office at the time of Bill's arrival had to do with field overcoats for use in Alaska and other cold-weather areas. The Alaskans asked for sheepskin-lined coats, but shearling, the trade name for sheepskin used for clothing, was in tight supply. Both the army and navy air force wanted shearling for jackets and boots, and the demands for our growing army would far exceed current availability. Many manufacturers were recommending coats with various cotton, wool, and pile linings, some woven, some knitted. Could any of these be used instead? Bill and I were not scientists, but we decided on a test. We asked our clothing experts to make immediately 14 standard army coats identical except for linings. Two would use shearling (one first-grade shearling and one second-grade). Two or three coats would have different thicknesses of pile fabric, while the rest would have various linings.

At Beltsville, Maryland, there was a cold chamber belonging to the Department of Agriculture. Bill was able to borrow it and some soldiers from Fort Myer to serve as guinea pigs. We also borrowed a specialist from the Bureau of Standards to place thermocouples on all the men in order to read their skin temperatures. We tried to get soldiers who were about the

same size so that the coats would fit everyone equally. We procured a fan
and tried to give a similar amount of wind to all the men as they stood for
half an hour each in each coat. The test was not perfect, but we learned
that the thickest coats were the warmest no matter what material was
used—*as long as the exterior was windproof.* The thickest pile seemed just as
good as the shearling for warmth. Pile was also much lighter and would dry
far more quickly when wet.

Colonel Grice felt that we had settled the problem and that the army at
least would specify a good pile fabric liner instead of shearling. A few days
later there was a big War Production Board meeting on shearling to which
I was sent to represent the OQMG.

Soon after the meeting started and the small quantity of available first-
grade shearling was announced, a furious argument began between officers
of the army and navy air forces, each claiming a prior need for all the first-
rate shearling. Apparently, when getting first-rate shearling, a large amount
of second-rate shearling is produced. Some of this second-rate shearling, it
was stated, could be made available to the army, which had a lower priority
than the air forces. When the army was asked how much shearling it wanted, I announced that it didn't want any. There was sudden shocked silence.
You could have heard a pin drop. "You mean the army doesn't want any
shearling?" I answered that it did not and stated that our tests had shown
that for army purposes, pile fabric was superior. That practically broke up
the meeting.

Later experience showed we were right. Warmth is equivalent to thickness of insulation in still air, whether in a house or in clothing.

Bestor Robinson had now come on duty as a major. He was a lawyer
from San Francisco who had had brief experience in the army in World
War I and was active in the Sierra Club. Bestor became head of our unit.
Paul Siple came in about the same time and began working on maps of climate in different parts of the world. These could help long-term planners
to define what items would be needed where and at what time of year.

It had been obvious to Bill and me that the army had no historical
information on how armies had fought in the mountains in the past and
what had been learned about clothing and equipment from these wars.
Through Jackman, we had Adams Carter hired to translate German documents on the bitter fighting in Austria in World War I. Currently Finnish
ski troops were fighting the Russians brilliantly, and so it was also important to know what the Finnish and Russian armies were wearing, including
their use of skis and snowshoes.

Reasons for the secret successes of the German Gebirgejäger in Norway also needed to be examined. The only real resistance to these Germans had come from French Chasseurs Alpins, aided by mountain-trained British and Polish troops near Narvik. Few remember that the Allies in World War I had lost more men in battles near the Isonzo than at Verdun, or that the Italians had lost more than 200,000 men in the mountains of the Tyrol. Ad Carter's quick translations of European military documents helped me to bring him into the OQMG in charge of QM intelligence.

Reasons for the British defeat at Narvik were carefully examined, for it had been thought that British units that had had mountain training would be too much for the Germans. Then certain facts came out. The British in Norway had various units variously equipped. The skis did not fit men wearing mountain boots or the clump-soled service shoes worn by regular infantry. The ski boots had stiff soles, and those wearing ski boots could not walk well wearing them. Other items of equipment were also not well adapted to use in Norway, but the mismatch of boots and shoes was the worst.

Jack was now working at G3, Army Ground Forces Headquarters, in Washington, and we frequently got together. He showed me the U.S. Army report on the boot problem at Narvik and we decided to do something about it: to draw up a basic specification for a boot to be designed by the QM for use in climbing, walking, and skiing. It was to be suitable at temperatures of -30 degrees Fahrenheit, to have a high toe permitting use of big insoles, and to have a large opening for easy drying and insertion of the feet in cold weather. I recommended that a single thickness of dry tan leather be used, for easy drying, and also that an effort be made to produce a Bramani-type moulded rubber sole, with cleats. Jack had a request for such a boot sent from Army Ground Forces Headquarters to the OQMG, where loud were the exclamations when it arrived. Nobody knew I had anything to do with initiating the request, but the boot people of the QM, after moments of horror, responded manfully.

One of the problems was finding a Bramani sole as a model. During the summer of 1939, Ad Carter and I had seen, in Switzerland, boots with cleated soles made of hard rubber. The advantages of such a sole over leather with attached boot nails were tremendous. The boot was less cold and there were no nails to wear down and make the soles slippery or to tear off, thus weakening the boot, but where could we get such a sole to show to the bootmakers? The sole we had seen was made in Italy, and at first we could not find anyone who had brought such a sole to the U.S. Finally a pair was found to be used as a prototype, and though the boots that emerged from our specifications weighed nearly three pounds apiece, they met the qualifications called for. The mountain boots, as they were called, were used successfully by our mountain troops, and later by many American climbers in the years right after the war. They were warm and practically indestructible. Jackman and I felt good about our action.

About this time I was sent as an observer to winter maneuvers in northern Vermont, where I met General Robinson, commander of the Second Division, who placed me next to him at dinner, asked lots of questions about cold-weather clothing and equipment, and took me with him when he reviewed the troops on a cold morning. I noted that the soldiers had good-quality light wool shirts and trousers but wore heavy overcoats and ordinary service shoes or service shoes with galoshes over them, all poor items for mobile troops in winter. It was clear that better boots, light windproof clothing of the type we had been using on expeditions, and warmer layers of clothing would add greatly to the comfort and mobility of the troops. I made a full report on my return.

Jackman and I left Washington early on December 7, 1941, to spend a day rock climbing at Bull Run, Virginia. We did a number of short climbs, had good views of the battlefields, and with no idea of what had been happening elsewhere that day began to drive back to Washington. Traffic soon became extraordinarily heavy for no reason we could imagine. We finally got back to the city and passed a large crowd surrounding the Japanese embassy on Massachusetts Avenue.

We turned into Jack's driveway and opened his front door. There was a hail from his wife, who was upstairs, welcoming us. "You've got to put your uniform on now, Jack," she called.

Jack looked disgusted. Army officers in Washington had not been wearing uniforms, probably in order to conceal how their number had grown.

"Doggone it," he said, "now why did they have to do that?"

She came to the head of the stairs. "Haven't you heard? The Japanese have bombed Pearl Harbor." It was the first we knew of it.

Pearl Harbor changed everything. There was a great sense of urgency and expansion everywhere. In no time at all our office was moved to Temporary Building A, a row of connected, flimsy, two-story buildings next to the old, beautiful, and sedate Army War College, and across the river from Bolling Field. About this time I learned that my brother was to be commissioned in the navy at the end of the academic year.

The QMC, and in fact the whole army, needed creative ideas at the time of Pearl Harbor. It was full of affable, well-intentioned people who, partly from lack of funds and voter lack of interest, had not kept the army up to date. Equipment for the standard infantryman in 1940 was not much better than it had been in World War I. There was a saying that the army was ready to fight in Maine in the summer and Florida in the winter, but not the other way around.

Ad Carter had been learning more about Swiss mountain-troop equipment, and we secured another pair of Swiss army skis capable of being separated into two pieces and carried in a rucksack. When needed for skiing, the front piece slipped into a socket at the front of the back piece, and they were locked together. Jackman and I had made brief tests of similar skis in the Yukon, but they needed further testing. In February Ad and I went to Mt. Washington to use these skis, along with a sled and various items of winter clothing. We camped in Tuckerman Ravine, skied over the headwall, and tested everything. The skis turned out to be very stiff. The sled was even less successful, especially in soft snow. Problems existed with the clothing as well.

By now we had many prototypes of mountain, cold-weather, and emergency equipment that had been adapted from civilian models for army use. Developments had been made rapidly, and there was great need for testing before procurement began, as our brief work on Mt. Washington showed. Many other prototypes under development would not be available for cold-weather testing until early spring, when even Mt. Washington would not be a useful area. The need for a major test we discussed with Colonel Grice, and he agreed to attend the April meeting of the American Alpine Club, where Walter Wood was now chairman of the Defense Committee, to ask for help in testing equipment. What Colonel Grice did not know was that Brad Washburn, now a consultant for the army air force, was planning an air force test of winter clothing just as we were, and he would be at the American Alpine Club, too.

The result of the meeting was complete agreement that there should be a joint testing expedition with help from experts in the American Alpine Club. Brad and I were instructed to see the quartermaster general, who became keenly interested in having a joint expedition with a well-coordinated plan. It soon developed that the air force wanted the OQMG to organize and conduct the test work, and so Lt. Col. Frank Marchman, a senior quartermaster corps officer, was placed in command, with me as his executive officer. (I had just been commissioned a captain in the quarter-

The SE approach to Mt. McKinley (Denali), showing why early explorers had such trouble approaching the mountain from the coast

The Great Gorge is at the lower left center. The ice in it is 3,800 feet deep, moving down at three-and-a-half feet a day.

WASHBURN

The U.S. Army Alaskan Test Expedition (May 1942). Left to right, front row: R.H.B., Wing Commander Webb, LTC Marchman, Nilsson, Washburn; 2nd row: Moore, CPT Lund, CPT Bollerud, Hendricks, CPT Jackman; 3rd row: SGT Gabriel, SGT Musser.

master corps (QMC).) The supply division of the OQMG was eager to begin procuring cold-weather clothing and equipment items for the winter of 1942-43, but buying our untested items and spending millions of dollars would result in serious errors we were sure, and the quartermaster general backed us up. Procurement must await test results.

The first question was where the tests should be held. Walter Wood and I had discussed testing in the Yukon area we knew well, but Brad Washburn urged Mt. McKinley, and we soon saw that he was right. Mt. McKinley was a peak in American territory, higher and colder than anything in the rest of North America, with McKinley Park headquarters nearby and American air force planes not too far away in Anchorage, where the air force had a base. Mt. McKinley, rising from 2,000 to 20,000 feet, offered a tremendous variety of cold-weather testing.

After considerable effort, the following list of personnel for the Alaskan Test Expedition was approved.

American Alpine Club: Sterling B. Hendricks, Terris Moore, Einar Nilsson, Walter A. Wood, Jr.

Army Air Forces: Pvt. William Goddard (musher), Second Lt. Paul Hansen, Capt. Harold Lund, Sgt. Wilbur Musser (cook), Bradford Washburn

Army Ground Forces: Capt. A.H. Jackman, Sgt. Peter Gabriel

Medical Corps: Capt. Jack Bollerud

Royal Canadian Air Force: Flight Lt. Peter Webb

Royal Canadian Army: Capt. E.R. Gibson

Signal Corps: Lt. Waldo Elmer

Quartermaster Corps: Lt. Col. Frank G. Marchman, CO, Capt. Robert H. Bates

Thirteen of the party had former Alaskan experience. In addition, Sgt. Gabriel was a former Swiss guide and ski instructor, Capt. Gibson was probably the most experienced Canadian mountain climber, and Flight Lt. Webb was a technical expert of great competence in the design and manufacture of all sorts of fabrics.

Two months to the day after Colonel Grice's meeting with the American Alpine Club, all personnel were in Alaska, though there had been delays owing to the Japanese attack on Dutch Harbor. By the time I arrived, Wood and Washburn had begun parachuting loads onto the Muldrow Glacier, and also on areas of the Harper Glacier at about 18,000 feet. We had some 30 items to test, mostly clothing and equipment but also a mountain ration, cold-water soap, and such experimental medical issues as Chapsticks and paper underwear. We were to test cold-weather clothing items from underwear to parkas, as well as packs, packboards, crampons, sleeping bags, snow goggles, sleds, tents, skis, and snowshoes. That was a lot to deal with.

By June 20, the main part of the expedition had crossed the McKinley Fork of the Kantishna River and the 30 miles of mosquito-infested muskeg leading to Cache Creek and McGonagall Pass at the edge of the Muldrow Glacier. Heavy rains had made the glacier surface soft and mushy. Private Goddard had driven the loaded dog team to the base of McGonagall Pass, but conditions on the Muldrow were so unfavorable that he and the dogs were sent back. At this point decisions were made about which items were to be tested on the upper and lower areas of the mountain, and responsibilities were assigned. Because air support would be necessary throughout the expedition, it was essential that one member of the party stay in Anchorage to provide radio contact and supervise the loading and dropping of test items. Walter Wood, who would have enjoyed being on the mountain as much as anyone, was the best man for this responsibility.

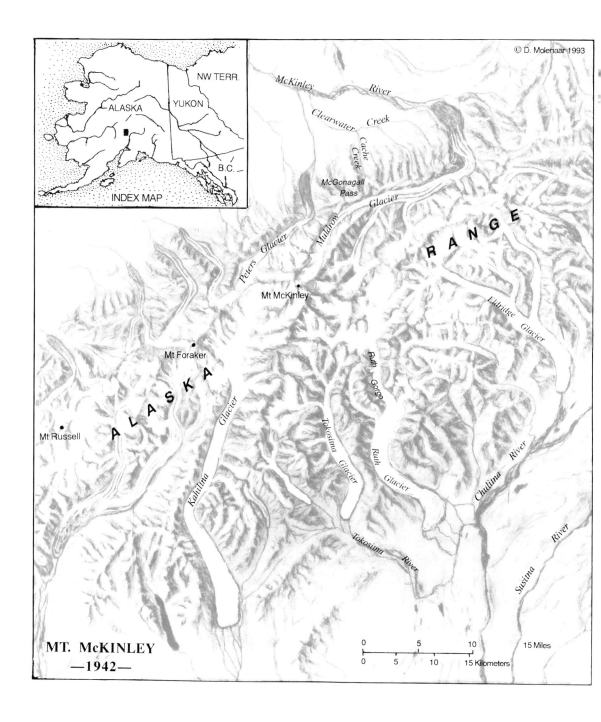

© D. Molenaar 1993

MT. McKINLEY
—1942—

WASHBURN

Camp at 10,800 feet near head of the Muldrow Glacier; Browne Tower at left

Tests were carried out on the southwest fork of the Muldrow Glacier, as well as on the main glacier, where Moore, Hendricks, Nilsson, and Gibson found a good route through the crevasses and seracs. By this route, access from base camp to the middle testing area at 10,000 feet was fairly easy, especially if traveled at night when snow bridges were firmer and progress safer. (Crevasses, however, were always on our minds. Washburn and I, traveling a full rope apart, once simultaneously put a foot each in a large covered crevasse that lay at an angle to the normal crevasse structure. Such hidden crevasses could be more than 200 feet deep, and some were large enough to hold the *Queen Mary*.) At the only point where there was danger from overhanging seracs, the distance was short.

At base camp the temperature rarely went below freezing, while at 10,000 feet, eight miles up the Muldrow, the night temperature would go to zero, cooling quickly when the camp was curtained from the sun. Sudden storms were encountered at both areas, including one at base camp that blew down several tents and rolled away a 75-pound boulder that was guying one of them. There was plenty of rain, hail, and snow to test rain gear and water-repellent clothing.

Most of the parachuted items had landed safely, but a generator dropped near base camp was not located for two weeks and then found to be completely smashed, since its parachute did not open. On another occa-

Terris Moore

*Einar Nilsson with
snowshoes he made*

sion a sled dropped from a DC-3 caught on the right stabilizer and hung
on until the pilot could shake it off. Moving loads up the Muldrow taught
us a lot about our sleds, snowshoes, ropes, ice axes, stoves, and other gear,
but did not show how our tents, mummy sleeping bags, warmest clothing,
and especially footwear would work in extreme cold and wind. Accordingly,
Colonel Marchman assigned four of us the work of establishing camps on
the Harper Glacier in what we called the high-test area. There we would
find arctic winter in early July.

On the Fourth of July, Moore, Washburn, Nilsson, and I climbed up
the glacier and established an intermediary camp at 12,000 feet on the
lower part of Karstens Ridge. We were about 2,000 feet above a large
crevasse where Hendricks, during an earlier reconnaissance, had roped
down 70 feet to recover a box dragged in by a parachute. (Nearby, Moore
had also made a crevasse recovery.) Now, two weeks later, Moore suddenly
needed help himself because of an inadvertent Fourth of July explosion.
Moore and Washburn were cooking supper in one tent, and Nilsson and I,
in a similar two-man tent opposite, were looking forward to their efforts
with keen anticipation when we heard a loud explosion followed by a
scream and a cry of, "Look out for the other stove." Somebody lurched
through the door of the other tent, followed a moment later by a second
body that crashed into our tent, bringing it down on our heads.

Capt. Rex Gibson

Nilsson and I crawled out. Washburn, still wearing his Canadian Mounted Police hat, had been cooking rice over a lightweight, experimental pressure cooker, when the wire catch holding the lid parted, blowing off the lid. Washburn was leaning over the stove when the lid struck him in the head with great force, momentarily stunning him and showering Moore's exposed neck with boiling rice. It could have been worse, because the thick hat Washburn was wearing cushioned the blow, and Moore could have been facing the stove instead of being turned away from it. Moore plunged out the door, followed by a somewhat disoriented Washburn. Moore received a second-degree burn on his neck and at once left for base camp to get medical attention. I went with him. Captain Bollerud, the doctor, was at a lower camp, and we all returned together to base.

Hendricks and Jackman took over for Moore and me, and with Washburn and Nilsson moved up Karstens Ridge, past Browne Tower to the Harper Glacier. At base camp we learned that no more testing was needed in the lower areas, and so three of us, with the recovered Moore, moved up to the Harper too. Gibson, Webb, Moore, and I all carried good loads up Karstens Ridge to a camp at Parker Pass at 14,600 feet. Our tents were hardly up when two army B-24 planes flew over the Harper Glacier, dropping a string of parachutes. (DC-3s could not fly high enough to reach this area, and it took great persuasion on Walter Wood's part to get B-24s to make the drop.) All seemed to arrive safely, but one missed the glacier entirely and floated off somewhere beyond the north peak. (What was in it, we learned later, was gasoline for the stoves.)

On the way up the ridge, Rex Gibson had talked disparagingly of the experimental mountain ration we were eating and the lack of what he called real food. The mountain ration had been developed with the idea of reducing the weight of food mountain troops would need to carry. As far as possible, water had been eliminated from the ration, even to the point of including dehydrated ice cream. The ration was a balanced one but only if all parts of it were eaten. For instance, there was plenty of candy, which could be used on the trail, but little pure sugar.

I sympathized with Rex Gibson, tried to make him feel better about our test, and was careful to make him my tent-mate when we set up our two-man mountain tents. While we cooked supper shortly after our arrival near big granite blocks above the Muldrow Icefall, Rex continued to grumble about the food, but he admitted he was tired—wasn't getting enough energy—and we soon turned in.

The weather was deteriorating as Washburn and Nilsson joined us and camped with us that night. Hendricks and Jackman arrived in the morning too. All had been short of food. Now that the B-24s had come, we would be in good shape.

When the storm kept us in our tents the next day, Rex repeated his criticisms of the ration and refused his share of the candy. That night as usual I slept soundly, but was occasionally awakened by Rex, who was very restless. A couple of times he said something, but when I sleepily replied there was silence, and each time I dropped off to sleep. It was beginning to be light when this happened once more. Rex murmured something and I answered. He was breathing very hard. When I sat up to look at him, I saw that he seemed to be having some kind of fit. His eyes were so rolled back that mostly white showed, his face was a gray-white color, his forehead was furrowed, and he had lost consciousness. I was afraid he was dying, but gradually his breathing slowed, he moved his eyes, and came to, sweating as if he had been working hard. He muttered something I did not understand and became unconscious again.

At this I rushed over to the other tents and announced that Rex was having convulsions. I wanted to get in touch with Dr. Bollerud at once, but the radio had not been working well and had been taken apart. It was obvious that the convulsions were putting a great strain on Rex, and I wanted to keep up his strength. Water was already heating and I quickly made some tea and put a great deal of sugar in it to give Rex energy. He was still unconscious when I returned to our tent, but soon his eyes flickered and he regained consciousness. At that moment, I thrust the cup in his hand and made him drink the tea. He gulped some and said it was too sweet, but he did drink it all. I went back for more tea and Rex drank that too. He had no further convulsions.

We did not know how long we would be without radio communication, so at this point Moore and Jackman, both rapid movers, left for base camp as fast as possible to alert Captain Bollerud and start him up the mountain to see Rex. Half an hour later, when Washburn had the radio

Washburn radios base camp from upper Harper Glacier.

Climbing Karstens Ridge. Camp where the pressure cooker exploded appears in right background.

working again, we talked to Captain Bollerud direct. His quick diagnosis was that the problem had something to do with lack of blood sugar and to continue what we were doing.

During the next four days, Rex became gradually able to sit up and then to stand, although all movements of his back hurt him. On July 20, he was able to walk well enough for Hendricks and me to start down to the 12,000-foot camp with him. During this descent, he was constantly in great pain as we worked down through deep snow at first and then along the narrow part of the ridge. At one place, where 25 steps had been cut in steep ice and any slip would be extremely difficult to hold, with 4,000 feet dropping off below him, he moved with the instinct of a born climber. What agony that descent cost him we could only guess. Only a very courageous man and a great mountaineer could have put up with the suffering, for as we learned later he had fractured four vertebrae during the spasms and shortened his back by nearly two inches!

On his return to Ottawa weeks later, he was given a medical discharge from the Canadian army. (He had been accustomed to a high-sugar diet. The mountain-ration sugar was mainly in candy, which Rex would not eat. Heavy exercise without sugar was the cause of his spasms.)

Above Karstens Ridge looking toward the summit

WASHBURN

Einar Nilsson at 18,200-foot Denali Pass. To the left is the Muldrow
Glacier route and to the right the West Buttress route.

Meanwhile, Washburn and Nilsson had been working for three days at
17,000 feet or higher, retrieving loads parachuted on the upper Harper
Glacier. One load had caught in the rocks at the top of Denali Pass, where
its parachute hung over the slope that descends in a great precipice facing
Mt. Foraker. It is probably still the highest mail delivery ever made in
North America.

On the night of July 22, seven of us were camped at 17,800 feet,
including Moore and Jackman, who had carried 50 pounds apiece from
12,000 feet that same day. The weather was dubious the next morning, but

View from the summit of Mt. McKinley, north peak in background.
R.H.B. and Moore right center (small figures), at almost exactly the place
where Belmore Browne was stopped by a storm in 1912! They are
640 horizontal feet from the summit.

we did not want to miss a chance to reach the summit. Accordingly, four of us, each wearing different footgear and warm clothing, began a reconnaissance of the route to the top. At that altitude, daytime air temperatures were usually zero or below, dropping at night to about -23 degrees Fahrenheit, while the snow an inch below the surface kept to a constant -17 degrees. I was wearing mukluks, while others wore shoepacs, felt boots, and leather boots. We all wore crampons. Moore and I were on one rope, Washburn and Nilsson on the other. How far we should get we did not know, but we realized how much better off we were than Belmore Browne, Professor Parker, and Merle LaVoy in 1912, or Archdeacon Stuck and Harry Karstens in 1913. Unlike them, we were within easy distance of a camp stocked with food and equipment dropped from the sky.

We began by breaking trail through a foot of loose powder, changing the lead every 50 steps. When we stopped for lunch, we were close to the height of the north peak, with the weather improving. Climbing as rhythmically as possible, we reached the high shoulder that offers the first view to the west. The surface changed to rock-hard, bluish ice, which our crampons barely scratched. We were near the point where LaVoy and Parker had

On the summit: Nilsson, R.H.B., Moore (Washburn missing).
All were testing different kinds of boots and clothing.

sheltered while Browne, facing a furious storm, had tried to go forward on his hands and knees to the summit, 150 feet higher. Today was calm as we moved slowly along an easy ridge to what looked like the summit. The true summit, 10 feet higher, was 50 feet farther on.

On the summit my thoughts were of Belmore Browne and his companions, who had come so close and had such misfortune with the weather, and to our quartermaster friends and General Gregory, who had backed the expedition. I knew also that my father would be pleased. We were at the highest point in our country, a country at war. I felt our responsibility to do everything we could to help it. Brad wanted a picture of the three of us holding an American flag and we held it—backward I might add, because it looked right to us that way. Then we were off. In 55 minutes Moore and I were back in camp after descending directly toward the tents.

The next day, again doing more testing, Hendricks, Jackman, and Webb repeated the climb, rebreaking the trail most of the way. Webb, the first Canadian to climb Mt. McKinley, was not normally a climber. We regretted that Gabriel, Bollerud, and others who had done so much for our testing could not have shared more personally our success. It had been 10 years since the Lindley-Liek Expedition had reached the summit, and 29 since Walter Harper of the Stuck party became the first human being to reach the crest.

*R.H.B. testing paper underwear
at the highest camp ("stepping
hopefully into the New Year")*

On the night of July 24, a major storm from the west pounded the area until we feared for the seams of our tent. For the next two and one-half days someone had to go out into the storm every half hour to keep the tents from being buried by snow blown along the surface by the wind. It blew so fiercely that we could not cook, though we were able to make tea occasionally. The intense cold, the pressure of the wind, and the constant need to dig out the drifted snow made this the hardest test of the expedition.

After the storm we made our final tests, and Jackman and I spent half a day looking unsuccessfully for Belmore Browne's thermometer, left at the highest rocks of the Browne Tower Ridge in 1912. Later Hendricks left two minimum thermometers where Hudson Stuck had left his near the granite boulders at Parker Pass. The Lindley-Liek party, the only others to reach the summit of Mt. McKinley (in 1932), had retrieved Stuck's thermometer, which then registered approximately 95 degrees below zero, probably not a true reading. It was here that we found a cache of food left by the same expedition 10 years earlier. Pemmican biscuit, Knorr's dynamite soup, tinned sausages, and chicken, expertly packed in a large tin wrapped in a tarpaulin, were all in perfect condition. We repacked what we had not eaten and added army rations to the package.

We had given our clothing and equipment the most thorough arctic and mountain testing it could find in North America, and when we all gathered at base camp some days later, every man wrote his own evaluation of every item of equipment he had used. We had tested and photographed every item sent to us, including the paper underwear, an experimental medical item. Medical corps personnel and the OQMG had conceded that long underwear would be worn generally in very cold regions and often it would not be possible to wash it regularly. The medical corps idea was to wear soft paper shorts inside the long underwear and to keep changing the shorts. At the high camp we suddenly realized that we did not have a picture of paper underwear. Nobody wanted to pose for the picture, but finally, wearing my long underwear, I pulled on a pair of the paper shorts while Brad took a picture. Later that picture became famous, for Terry Moore, who loves jokes, had Christmas cards printed with the picture and the caption, "Wishing you a very Merry Christmas as I step hopefully into the New Year." He sent cards to a lot of my friends without my knowledge, and their delight was announced in a flood of letters.

Everyone now went to base camp, for our tests were finished. Sergeant Musser, the cook, made 118 doughnuts to celebrate the occasion, and the last ones were gone the next day. Near McGonagall Pass on our way down to Cache Creek, someone saw an unusual pair of leather ski boots resting in a rock recess at the side of the trail. They obviously had been there a long time. I took them, not imagining where they had come from, thinking that the Mt. McKinley Museum might like them. I put them down when we reached Cache Creek, and before I could say anything Terry Moore came over and in great surprise said, "Where did those come from? Why, those are my boots!" He opened one of the boots and on the tongue showed the mark "T.M."

"But, Terry," I said, "you've never been on McKinley before, have you?"

"No. I threw away those boots in 1931 after the Fairweather Expedition. They didn't fit quite right. I wonder if Allen Carpé could have picked them up?"

Gradually we solved the mystery of the boots. After Moore threw away the ski boots on the Fairweather Peninsula, Allen Carpé, a member of the party, must have retrieved them, thinking them useful for some future expedition. The next spring he was on the Muldrow Glacier of Mt. McKinley with Theodore Koven, part of the ill-fated Mt. McKinley Cosmic Ray Expedition, whose members were on the mountain at the same time as the Lindley-Liek party.

The Lindley-Liek team, on returning from the top of Mt. McKinley, found two tents pitched by members of the Cosmic Ray Expedition on the upper Muldrow Glacier, but nobody in them. Fresh snow partly covered the only tracks, and the last diary entry had been made the day before. Continuing on down the glacier, they found Koven's body face down in the trail, where he had been trying to get back uphill to his camp. He had a bruise on his face. They followed his tracks back to a crevasse, into which he and Carpé had apparently fallen, and from which, hurt, he had emerged. Some of the crevasses in the area were more than 200 feet deep, and Carpé's body was never found. Their only rope was found at the tents.

The Lindley-Liek party started to sled the body down the glacier but they had only one rope. A short time previously, their party nearly had a fatality of their own when Ranger Grant Pearson fell into a big crevasse unroped, and dropped 40 feet before his big pack stuck, enabling the others to extricate him. The Lindley party wrapped Koven's body in a tent, marked it with an upended eight-foot sled, left it, and continued on down the glacier.

Two months later, the body was recovered and brought back to Koven's family by Andy Taylor and Merle LaVoy, sent there for the purpose. Only the very tip of the eight-foot sled was visible above the snow when they reached it, but they dug it out and on it slid the body to a point below McGonagall Pass, where a horse could be brought. Here the boots were found.

On our return, all requested changes in items were incorporated as recommended and the ensuing specifications were approved. I had a special interest in one of the items. My neck sometimes gets cold and a sweater normally does not have a collar or open at the throat. Harold Lent, a knitting expert on our QM staff, one day was talking to me about sweaters, when I mentioned that I would prefer a sweater that could protect the neck. In no time at all, Lent, with my help, worked out the design for a medium-weight sweater with a neck that could be opened for ventilation or buttoned closed. This item, known as sweater high neck, was a hit with our expedition and later became a favorite overseas. (Commercial variants of it are still extensively used.)

Not long after our return, Bill House received a coil of nylon rope from a manufacturer. The loss of the Philippines to Japan had severely reduced supplies of Manila hemp rope, and Bill had been working with two or three companies to produce a synthetic substitute for our mountain troops, who had recently been activated. The company that sent the rope claimed for it

WASHBURN

Testing "my" sweater

a high tensile strength, much more than that of our standard 3/8-inch or 1/2-inch Manila rope.

When the rope arrived, someone said, "Let's try it." An end was wound around one of our desks on the second floor, where we had our offices, and I quickly put the rope around a thigh and opposite shoulder to go out the window to test the rope with a "classical rappel." What none of us realized was the amount of stretch in the rope. As I went out over the windowsill, my weight came on the rope and it stretched, dropping me well over a foot as the rope lengthened. My legs dangled outside the window of the office below. Immediately there was a loud scream that almost made me let go the rope. The secretary at the window below thought she was witnessing a suicide. All the surrounding windows filled with faces as I rappelled to the ground.

Shortly after I returned to my desk, where we began discussing the desired amount of stretch in the rope, Colonel Doriot and the quartermaster general (General Gregory) arrived, both looking as expectant as boys on the first day of the fishing season. "Bub, Bub," Colonel Doriot commanded, "show the general your little trick." So again we threw the end of the rope around the desk and I roped off. Both men chuckled. There was something about the new rope and the use of a desk and a window for a quick test that touched their fancy. Both were imaginative, pragmatic men, who gave all of us a free hand in trying out new ideas.

By now, our Special Forces section was practically complete. It consisted of a remarkable group of dedicated men, inspired and driven by the initiative, personality, and example of George Doriot (formerly a distinguished professor at the Harvard Business School), perhaps the most intelligent man I have ever known well. Colonel Doriot (later General Doriot)
worked at least six days a week, often seven, at the office, and probably
most evenings at home. As chief of the military planning division, he set a
splendid example for the men and women working there. Several of his old
students he had brought in for special positions, including quiet Bill
McLean, later acting president of Stevens Institute.

Well integrated into this group were others with special experience in
areas of severe or wet cold, or in desert, tropic, jungle, and mountainous
regions. This group included Terris Moore, businessman, bush pilot, and
later president of the University of Alaska, who in 1932 had made the first
ascent of Minya Konka in China, a peak then thought to be possibly higher
than Mt. Everest; Bill House, a distinguished mountain climber (with first
ascents of Mt. Waddington and Devil's Tower, and a fine climbing record
on K2); and Adams Carter, who had climbed in many parts of the world
and was a former member of the American Ski Team.

By far the most famous man in the section, indeed in the OQMG, was
Sir Hubert Wilkins, pioneer Arctic and Antarctic explorer, who had also
lived with the aborigines on their terms in Australia and pioneered submarine travel under the Arctic ice cap. He was as modest as he was bold and
imaginative, and he had worked with people from many countries, including Japan and the Soviet Union. There was also Jim Ford of the American
Museum of Natural History, who had lived with Eskimos on St. Lawrence
Island and helped them build an oomiak; and Bob Woodbury, basically an
artist, who as a private in Panama had discovered that the canal was completely unprotected from approach through the jungle, and with the con-
nivance of the commanding general had personally placed a dummy bomb
on the main lock of the canal, causing consternation.

Three imaginative California mountain climbers were now also members of Special Forces: Bestor Robinson and Dick Leonard, both lawyers,
and Einar Nilsson, an engineer. There were visitors too, like Vilhjalmur
Stefansson. Bradford Washburn, head of the Boston Museum of Science,
also worked at the office for many weeks, as did Fred Wulsin, who had
explored in Mongolia, and briefly L. L. Bean, of shoepac fame.

It was now clear that the OQMG needed a place where on short
notice tests could be made on clothing and equipment under severe cold

conditions. The success of our Mt. McKinley test proved that. Our first step was to rent a room at an ice cream plant in Washington, DC. The temperature was constantly at 20 degrees, and we could ask the owners to cool it to zero if we wished. Sir Hubert Wilkins and I made several trips there to test wool underwear, mittens, and Eskimo-style survival suits. These were two-piece pile suits with two-piece windproof poplin parkas and trousers to go over them—more or less copies of Eskimo skin clothing in different materials. Sir Hubert and Jim Ford had developed them to provide emergency survival gear for pilots of air transport command planes flying across the Arctic.

Our testing area in the cold chamber of the Eskimo Pie Company, with its rows of Popsicles, chocolate-covered ice cream, and exotic frozen delights, was too limited. It took too long for us to get cold, and to speed up our cooling we would usually eat some confections off the shelves, permitted of course by the company. I vividly remember Sir Hubert, with his distinguished Vandyke beard, standing in long underwear, chewing a Popsicle to increase his cooling and looking disdainfully at the rows of frozen desserts.

That cold chamber had still air, and we began to look for an area for more realistic testing. Shortly after Christmas of 1941, we decided that some region developed for the Crimson Project might be of use. The Crimson Project was a plan to build a chain of airfields across Canada to Baffin Island so that fighter planes, with their need for frequent refueling, could be flown from factories in California across the U.S. and Canada, to Greenland, Iceland, and on to England. Airfields were already being built, or were in existence, north of Winnipeg at The Pas, Churchill, and Southampton Island. Shortly after Christmas, I made an exploratory trip to see whether we could use one of these as a base for testing. I arrived at Winnipeg in the dead of winter, where a mysterious banner in the center of town read, "May all your rocks go in the house." It was a welcome to curling teams from all over Canada, who were about to begin a tournament.

At The Pas, north of Winnipeg, there was no hotel, but I rented a room for the night from a fine old Scot, who poked the fire with a long narwhal tusk. The next day, at Churchill, I found a small air force detachment guarding a huge airfield. Churchill was very cold, -30 degrees to -40 degrees Fahrenheit every night (with marvelous auroras), and about 10 degrees above to 10 degrees below zero in the daytime, often with wind. Indians and Eskimos with dog teams were numerous, and not much effective outside work was being done by the troops. It was a place where we could test for extreme cold, but not many troops would be subjected to such low temperatures, and Churchill was too remote for easy access.

In Washington we decided to look for a test area closer to home, with somewhat less severe conditions. After consulting the weather map, I went to Devil's Lake, Wyoming, one of the coldest areas in the continental U.S. A small army installation there could be made into a testing station, though again access was not easy.

By this time Bruce Dill of the Harvard Fatigue Laboratories had come to our office to take charge of our testing programs. He was very interested in an opportunity for cold-weather testing in a woolen mill in Lawrence, Massachusetts. The mill had a large area not being used that could be cooled to zero or lower; it had been used to separate lanolin from wool. Dr. Forbes, also of the Harvard Fatigue Laboratories, who was well versed in techniques applied to industry, was available for direct work there. Our office rented the building and installed Dr. Forbes with a few QM troops. A large fan was provided for controlled testing of wind-proof materials, and a "copper man" was made available for scientific testing of fabrics.

During the winter of 1942-43, the Second Division was sent to Wisconsin for winter training. Skis were issued to all troops. In midwinter a maneuver was held near Land o'Lakes, and I was sent as an observer. Night temperatures reached -40 degrees, and the weather during the whole maneuver was cold. The troops had previously been at Fort Sam Houston, Texas. Most of the soldiers were very poor skiers and they hated the snow and cold. When a break came, they would write in the snow with their ski poles, "Good old Fort Sam" or "Take me back." During the maneuver, troops received some frostbite, and I reported the need for better training on care of the feet under cold conditions.

Colonel Doriot was interested in long-range planning. What would happen if the Germans forced the Russians back to the Urals? How could we support them? He suggested that we try to find out. This forced me to read up on ports and weather conditions in the Kamchatka Peninsula, ice conditions in the Chukchi Sea, and normal months when the Lena and Kolyma Rivers were frozen. A few days later at the Pentagon I was scolded by a colonel who considered any such investigations none of the quarter-master's business. Colonel Doriot, however, considered the whole world our business. Who knew when we might be fighting in Yugoslavia, Japan, Korea, or China? We were responsible for knowing immediately what army items would be needed anywhere in the world and at any time. That meant

BRADLEY

Three observers on maneuvers at Land o' Lakes, WI. Left to right: unknown, LTC Lyons (British), and R.H.B.

a lot of study of temperatures and precipitation for Paul Siple's group, and work with Knight Ames on a program to chart basic clothing requirements for each month, for each major region, listing also additional items possibly needed for special local conditions.

Summer in Washington can be very hot. A week's leave at Ogunquit, Maine, where my father and his sisters were staying, was a pleasant interlude. When I returned I found an answer needed for the general commanding the Air Transport Command. His planes were flying over a lot of cold water, and he wondered about the floatability of the cold-weather survival outfits we had made for his pilots, including recently delivered insulated boots. The fastest answer, of course, would come from a nonscientific test we gave ourselves. Accordingly, Sir Hubert and I drove to the Bolling Field swimming pool in survival suits, wearing insulated boots. We both got into the pool and timed how long it took before our suits became waterlogged. At first we rode high and dry, with air in the boots and between layers of clothing, but after five minutes the water began to soak everything and became a drag. Swimming then became very hard work.

Our test completed, we got out of the pool, dripping water, looking like a couple of bedraggled snowmen, and began walking to our car. To get there we had to pass the front of the main Bolling Field building. During our test we had failed to note the arrival of a four-motor plane, and we reached the front of the building at the exact time a small group of beribboned officers was being met by a welcoming committee of generals. We were leaving a wet trail and tried to sneak out of sight, but one of the incoming visitors saw us and shouted, "Sir Hubert, what are you doing here?" He was Hap Arnold, the commanding general of the U.S. Army Air Force, who had just arrived after making the first U.S. flight from Australia. He knew Sir Hubert well and had recognized his face and beard despite our disguise. As the generals and the new arrivals stood around, we dripped and answered questions while they interjected stories about Australia and the flight. At that time I was asked to come on a future occasion to test the size of all plane seats, especially tail gunner seats, for use when wearing survival clothing. Later I did. I enjoyed entering the planes and trying out the seats while wearing bulky clothing. As might be expected, many of the seats felt too small.

By now, the mountain troops (known to the Press as ski troops) had become the 10th Mountain Division, the first such "elite" division in the American army. They were training at Camp Hale, Colorado. The British Lovat Scouts were about to begin training in the Canadian Rockies too, and the British hoped that American items of clothing and equipment could be used by the Scouts, while perhaps items of Scouts' equipment might be used by the 10th Division.

To consider these matters, the British Barclay Mission, a group of three experts under Brigadier Barclay, came to the QM to discuss the pros and cons of British and American clothing and equipment for mountain warfare. One of the experts was Frank Smythe, an outstanding English climber and the author of many books on mountaineering. When we at Special Forces examined the British equipment, we clearly preferred our own. The British likewise preferred their own, but found various American items they wished to use while the Scouts were in training in Canada. After a conference at the OQMG, the mission was to visit Camp Hale, and I was sent along as guide. I had just been made a major, and was now equal in rank to Smythe and the other British experts.

Camp Hale impressed them but, like me, they thought emphasis should be placed on mountain and rough country work rather than on skiing, and there should be more training of small units working independently. At the end of their visit, we went on to Camp Carson briefly to see another "light division." It was here that I found my friend Belmore Browne, of Mt. McKinley fame, giving survival training. That morning he had been showing how shelters could be made from a parachute. As usual, he was fun to be with, and we lunched together on an elk he had shot during a training exercise.

For many months the Japanese presence in the Aleutians had been a sore point with Americans and plans were being made to force them out. Special Forces became involved in the clothing to be used. For footwear in this continuously wet area we recommended shoepacs. We also recommended ponchos and our latest field jackets, sweaters, and trousers. When the time came for the American landings, I was disappointed, for I had hoped to go along as an observer. Bob Orr was selected instead. Doriot had other plans for me, though I didn't know it at the time. The general commanding the force refused to use the new equipment we sent him—in fact, he had it thrown overboard—and insisted that his troops use Blucher boots, leather boots with a double sole. These boots are useful in areas of occasional rain, but in areas of continual wetness they eventually become soaked and then are extremely difficult to dry. The result was a lot of trench foot and many unnecessary cold-weather casualties in the campaign. The Attu campaign proved to the chief of staff that we knew what we were talking about.

By the fall of 1943 all our major QM items for the war in Europe had been approved but none was in use overseas. Army rules stated that stores of old items always must be used first, and no new items could be issued without the specific request of the theater commander. Since the theater commander and his officers had seen none of our gear and clothing, none was being ordered or produced in any quantity. Doriot, now a general, solved this problem in his own way. When key army officers were about to go overseas, he offered to show them the latest clothing and equipment and to outfit them with it. Each officer who came to our showroom was given clothing in his size and a new type of duffel bag to carry away his loot. In this way, knowledge of what could be made available reached the battle zones.

There was no question about the new equipment being better than the old, and European theater interest soon appeared. Before this time we had done a lot of testing of our own items. For instance, I had been ordered to give the hardest use possible to the new field jacket, field trousers, and mountain boots. I took with me Bob Woodbury, who carried an assault rifle while testing the clothing. We drove from Boston to Whitehorse Ledge, near North Conway, New Hampshire, where we squirmed through brush and slid down granite slopes so vigorously that we gave a year's normal wear to our jackets and trousers. From there we went to Mt. Washington for further testing.

On our return, the fabric people were amazed at the amount of wear we had given the clothing. These tests proved the value of the big pockets we had fought to have built into the field jackets, and also showed that the plastic buttons being used broke easily. (Later we found that the buttons even broke when jackets were strapped too tightly when baled for shipment.) Snaps replaced the buttons.

We all agreed that a suit that could be inflated or deflated (based on temperature and the wearer's exercise) would logically provide the best clothing, but we never found any good basic plastic clothing until the end of the war, when a one-piece suit developed for use in the Aleutians became popular among civilians as the wet suit, an item still much in use today.

An unusual question was whether we could supply a dog harness in case of fighting in the Arctic, where dog teams might be needed to supplement mechanized travel. Jim Ford borrowed from the Smithsonian, complete with harness, a famous stuffed dog, Balto, lead dog of the team that carried serum to Nome, Alaska, when the town was stricken with influenza. Balto we used as a model for a dog harness and also in lieu of a Christmas tree in December 1943. We hung a bottle from his neck and surrounded him with holly and presents.

Shortly after that Christmas I left for Alaska, where Caspar's Cutthroats and other Alaskan units were to hold maneuvers in the Talkeetna-Chulitna-Susitna Triangle, heavily wooded country between Mt. McKinley and the coast. It was a cold midwinter maneuver. The temperature was -30 degrees to -40 degrees Fahrenheit every night, with very little daylight. At dawn, a rosy glow would gradually appear, hang in the sky, and eventually merge into sunset. Plenty of trappers, Indians, and Eskimos were in the Alaskan force, and when frozen vehicles delayed the food supply, word went out to get a moose or two. That took no time at all.

Late one afternoon, when I was about 60 miles from maneuver headquarters, a signal corpsman brought me a field telephone and said I had a call. An officer told me to be at headquarters at 10:00 a.m. the next morning to be picked up by a plane and flown to Anchorage. How I was to get to the plane he left up to me.

For the next several hours I used my orders to bum rides on weasels and trucks, finally reaching headquarters with time to nod off for an hour or two. When the plane arrived, I found that the pilot did not know why he was sent to pick me up. I was the only passenger. On the flight to Anchorage, we passed large bunches of caribou, but my thoughts were elsewhere. What was up? At Anchorage, I was told to call a Washington number, which I did. On the other end of the phone was Clinton Morrison of our office. All he said was, "Boy, do we have something for you! No, I can't tell you over the phone. Get back here as soon as you can."

That was the beginning of one of the most interesting periods of my life. In Washington, General Doriot was eager to see me. He said that some of the officers to whom he had given new equipment had sent a request through the office of the theater commander for a test by a whole battalion in combat. I was to escort 1,000 sets of items to Italy and see that they had a fair test.

CHAPTER XII

Italy

1944

FOR THE NEXT COUPLE OF WEEKS I was busy conferring with General Doriot and getting my orders. I was to tell nobody when and where I was to go. General Doriot stressed the importance of the mission. All the work we had done for the past two years would be practically useless, he said, if we could not get our items to the troops in combat. The results of the test would be of great importance to the whole QM, to American manufacturers, and to the combat efficiency of our army. Two men to accompany the items had been requested, and the shipment was to be given top priority to get it to the Fifth Army in Italy fast. I was to be in charge and could select the other officer to go with me. For this purpose General Doriot strongly recommended a former OSS (Office of Strategic Services) officer, now in the QM, named Michael Slauta.

Mike was a Lithuanian-American who hated the Nazis (and Russians) and looked and talked like a GI. He was very tough, intelligent, and practical, a fine companion for our mission, but I saw him only briefly before we boarded a Liberty freighter in South Philadelphia. When I went to get my orders, the man who cut them said there was only one way to get the shipment out immediately and that was by making me a task force commander, which he did. I became the commander of what was probably the smallest task force in World War II: two people!

The night before my departure I spent at home in Philadelphia, but did not even tell my father where I was going, though he realized that I must be going overseas.

The next day Mike and I reported to the Philadelphia quartermaster's office, and in the evening boarded a Liberty freighter without knowing where we would land. The ship's skipper, an elderly man who had spent his life on ships in the Great Lakes, greeted us seriously and assigned us to the small cabin called "the hospital." He indicated that he did not care much for his cargo. We had lots of steel rails that he hoped would not shift in a high sea, and a deck load of chlorine gas. The most amusing character on the ship was the chief engineer. He had a fund of funny stories, interrupted frequently by comments about how he wouldn't be on that bridge for anything when "those damn German planes start attacking." The shaft alley was where he would be—"the best bomb shelter in the world."

Mike and I settled in for a long voyage. First we learned that we were going to Hampton Roads, Virginia, to become part of a convoy. We sailed early in the morning, keeping a look out for U-boats, since sinkings occasionally still occurred along the East Coast. We anchored in Hampton Roads near a dozen other ships. For nearly two days we were anchored there while more and more ships arrived, until there were more than a hundred. No one was allowed on shore, and there wasn't much to do but look over the whole ship, talk to the officers, and get to know the navy first lieutenant in charge of the Bofors ack-ack guns. In case of attack, my station was to be on the bridge, and Mike was to be with the ack-ack.

We had a long voyage on our Liberty, for the convoy moved at the speed of the slowest vessel. We passed the Azores and went on through the Pillars of Hercules to Gibraltar, where parts of the convoy separated. An attack by German planes there was anticipated, but nothing happened. From Gibraltar we skirted the dry North African coast. The days stretched on but still we didn't know our destination. One morning, just at daybreak, we anchored. We could see palm trees and lemons growing, but we could not go ashore or at first even find where we were. Finally we learned that we were in the harbor at Augusta, Sicily. We spent a day and a half there, then pulled anchor and headed for Naples.

Thirty-one days after leaving Philadelphia, we dropped anchor in Naples harbor, where we could hardly have arrived at a more dramatic time. Vesuvius was erupting and a tremendous cloud of black smoke billowed thousands of feet into the air. Bits of grit even fell on our ship's deck, while after dark the flows of burning lava descending from the crater glowed. At frequent intervals we could see masses of fiery rock tossed into the air, usually to fall back into the crater, but sometimes showering down outside the lip, and so increasing the lava flows. Fires occasionally were started and blazed furiously, perhaps consuming trees, buildings, homes—we could not tell. A full moon rose, lighting the many ships anchored in the harbor and adding to the unreality of the scene. The officers on board were sure that the eruption would guide hordes of German bombers to raid the ships in the harbor, but none came.

The next morning early, Mike and I went ashore to the port office and presented our orders. The officer in charge glanced at them, then nearly jumped out of his shoes. "A task force," he shouted. "My God, nobody told me a task force was coming! What is this?"

After I calmed him down, he ordered a jeep to take us to Fifth Army Headquarters at Caserta. Here, in the huge palace of the former king of Naples, we met General Sullivan, the Fifth Army quartermaster and a friend of General Doriot. He asked about the items we had brought and announced that arrangements had been made to send them to Anzio at once for testing in combat. Mike and I would go with them. Sullivan took us to lunch at the colonels-and-generals mess, where we ate from the beautiful china of the Queen of Naples.

Our test items were to be loaded onto an LCT (Landing Craft Tank) for the route around German-held territory to our troops in the small Allied beachhead at the towns of Anzio and Nettuno. The Germans were launching heavy attacks on the beachhead, and so ammunition had top priority as LCT cargo. We were told that despite our high priority our gear could not be moved to Anzio for at least a week.

Mike and I were eager to get on with the test and felt somewhat frustrated, but since we had a free week we decided to find something useful to do. That evening Mike met a couple of OSS men and learned that some of their operatives who had been outfitted with the new items at the OQMG were now in Yugoslavia at Tito's headquarters on the island of Vis. An OSS pilot who was flying to Vis daily offered to fly us there. Since we had no assigned duties for a week, we jumped at the opportunity to interview men who had already been in combat with our items.

Early in the morning a small plane flew us to Bari with our pilot friend. Bari had been shattered by an explosion in the harbor and the whole area looked desolate. The OSS officer in charge looked at me somewhat suspiciously, but thanks to Mike's OSS connections, orders were cut for us to fly to Vis. We crawled into a B-26 filled with cartons and boxes of Spam, butter, and canned fruit, and flew out across the Mediterranean. We flew so far east that we thought the pilot was going to land on the mainland, but he dropped down toward a small island with a tiny landing strip and we were soon unloading at Vis. Soldiers wearing British uniforms and American caps marked with a red star immediately surrounded us and began to unload the plane. A few British troops and a couple of OSS men looked surprised to see Mike and me.

The OSS men were wearing some of our new items, but they had not been in combat. Other OSS people were operating on the mainland and occasionally after dark would bring in Allied airmen who had been shot down and taken in by partisans. At the moment none of these men were on Vis.

Tito's headquarters were on the island but unfortunately we never saw him. Troops were drilling on the cobblestone street leading to the harbor. The clatter of marching men told me before I saw them that they were wearing clump-soled British boots. British troops were in charge of the training and, as I had already noted, the food boxes we had flown in quickly acquired British markings, although their original stencils named origins in California, Oregon, and our Midwest. Yugoslavia was considered by the Allies to be in the British orbit, but Tito clearly wanted to keep his options open. The little harbor, center of life on the island, was dominated by a low white building with two wings, each equal in length to the main part that faced the water. Large inscriptions on each section had been carefully lettered. They read: Jivio Drug Stalin, Jivio Drug Churchill, Jivio Drug Roosevelt. (Long live Comrade Stalin. Long Live Comrade Churchill, Long Live Comrade Roosevelt.)

Since the sun was blazing hot, our pilot suggested a swim in the harbor before lunch. It didn't seem possible that we could be so carefree when men were fighting for their lives on land we could easily see. At lunch we heard many stories of pilots being rescued, and of meetings with partisans, but little of use to our mission. Our return flight in the afternoon was uneventful. We believed that General Doriot would have approved our initiative, but did not think it necessary to discuss our venture with General Sullivan.

Grim stories were going around about the battle for the Anzio beachhead. Enemy attacks had been repulsed so far, partly with help from navy guns, but the situation was still critical. The port was being bombed by night and shelled daily. A few days before our arrival, a big shell had landed on the jetty, killing seven young lieutenants who arrived at the wrong moment.

Late one afternoon, we drove to Pozzuoli and boarded our LCT. In it, well-loaded trucks with our gear were already in line. Unloading at Anzio was to begin as soon as we touched the jetty. German submarines had been trying to intercept supplies on their way to Anzio, but recent navy successes against them had made the trip safer. The LCT seemed completely dead until after dark, when there were quick movements and we slid out of the harbor. The LCT was far quicker than the Liberty we had been on, but the throbbing motor was noisy and could be heard by submarines at a considerable distance. We were strongly cautioned about showing lights.

That night we did not undress and did not sleep much. We saw occasional lights in German-held territory along the shore, and at dawn were about 3,000 yards outside the harbor of Anzio and Nettuno. We nosed right in. The jetty had a gaping hole and buildings along the shore showed considerable damage. Few people were in sight. Truck motors already had been started, so that the moment the gangplank banged down, the first truck drove off, followed in disciplined order by the others at short intervals. An officer at the dock told me to report to Colonel Holcombe, the corps quartermaster, and a jeep took us to his office in a house in Nettuno just off the shore road.

On the way we saw plenty of evidence of heavy shelling: partly destroyed buildings and cars, and over everything a film of plaster dust and dirt. All Italians had been evacuated and we seemed to be driving through a dead city.

Colonel Holcombe, a pudgy, cheerful, and very efficient officer, greeted us warmly. He told us that we had just missed a tremendous German attack, when the elements of 13 German divisions had tried to carry out Hitler's orders to destroy all Allied forces on the beachhead, an area now about 10 by 15 miles, all under surveillance from the hills farther inland and subject to daily attack by planes and artillery.

We were to be attached to the quartermaster of the Third Division, a unit originally comprising Californians, now true veterans who had become one of the most experienced American forces in Italy, having fought their way from North Africa and Sicily to Salerno, Naples, and Anzio. Their heaviest fighting had come in their recent defense of the beachhead, which GIs were now calling "the world's largest German concentration camp," for German troops surrounded the U.S. Third, 34th, 45th, and First Armored Divisions, three British divisions, and two special elite regiments. The American generals who had planned the amphibious landing had no idea the Germans could react so fast and gather such strong forces.

Before we drove to the Third Division Quartermaster Headquarters, Colonel Holcombe took us to the "castle," Fifth Army and QM Headquarters. The castle was a massive stone building, with a deep cellar that had been separated into several rooms, each lighted by electricity supplied by generators. There I met the corps commander and some of the most important generals on the beachhead, including General Truscott, the tough Third Division commander who, while training his division to move fast, had become known for the "Truscott trot." "Iron Mike" O'Daniel, who distinguished himself later in Vietnam, I particularly liked, and I met many others. All were pleased that new clothing and equipment items had reached Anzio, and it was quickly decided that all officers at different times should see them and have a chance to ask questions about them. I was impressed by the quality of these men.

At the castle we also met Major Goodwin, the number two man in the division QM and the senior officer living at Acciarella, where he drove us. Goodwin was a stocky man of obvious competence, who spoke seldom but made his words and his presence felt. We learned that the roads at Acciarella drew a good bit of shell fire and that two-thirds of the 15 or 20 farm buildings there had had some artillery damage. He was concerned about where we would display our items and said it would need to be done carefully, for any unusual gathering of men drew enemy fire.

From the group of farm buildings where we were to stay, we could look across the mostly level and drained Pontine marshes to hills 10 miles away held by the Germans. The oldest of the buildings was the command post, where Mike and I dumped our duffel in a small, doorless brick stable in the side of the building, facing the hills.

From our stable that night we looked out on constant flashes of German artillery firing from the hills and heard the thump of incoming shells and the distant chatter of burp guns and heavy machine guns. That night and every night we were blacked out, for German bombers made nightly raids. These planes we learned to identify by the sound of their engines, just as we quickly learned the different sounds of incoming and outgoing shells. Spitfires and Hurricanes rose to meet the bombers as our ack-ack began firing, sending streams of brilliant tracer bullets arching into the sky. We could hear our fighters go up but could not tell what success they had. A couple of searchlights were trying to find the German bombers. From over on the opposite side of the beachhead came the crump of bombs. Someone murmured, "The First Airborne's getting it now." Then the air show was over, but the gun flashes in the hills and the dull growl of artillery in the distance continued.

The next morning we were driven again to Colonel Holcombe's little office. It was a bright, sunny day, and a GI with his shirt off was sunning himself on a nearby rooftop. We were at the door of the building when suddenly a shell we never heard crashed into a yard a couple of houses

R.H.B. at Anzio demonstrating
the latest army clothing, helmet,
and boots

away. Shrapnel hissed around and the man who had been sunning quickly disappeared, fortunately unharmed. Colonel Holcombe went with us to a small building, where we were to explain the use of our new items to a few officers at a time from all the beachhead divisions. Items were to be issued immediately to a battalion of the 30th Infantry Regiment (about 900 men), whose officers we were to talk to first.

From then on we held one or two sessions a day, explaining to officers in what ways the new items were better than the old. At Caserta I had been asked to check the equipment of the hospital nurses, who were working under dangerous and muddy conditions. A large hospital area, plainly marked, had been shelled several times, probably unintentionally, for the crowded conditions on the beachhead seemed to make such shelling inevitable. The nurses basically needed army boots because of the mud everywhere, and also field jackets. Many of them already had them but I recommended that a regular issue be authorized for all nurses.

One night Mike and I were driven slowly to an area of the front line where the Third Division combat patrol was setting off on their regular night mission of probing enemy positions and preventing enemy platoons from infiltrating. Men in the patrol were all wearing our new clothing and using the large pockets in the field jackets. Their faces were blackened and they were a tough-looking crowd. One of the youngest was a kid named Audie Murphy, who already had a reputation as a daring marksman with incredibly quick reactions. It was pitch dark outside the patrol tent, and if we had not known the night's password we could have been in serious trouble. When the patrol returned, we talked with the men. It had been a quiet night: a short firefight with an enemy patrol that had then retired. No known casualties. They liked the new clothing. No suggestions. I asked permission to spend a night in a foxhole as a useful experience but the officer in charge would have none of it. We drove back slowly with dim lights, careful to avoid mined areas.

General Sullivan, to whom I had reported at Caserta, had approved all our items except shoepacs (Barker boots), made famous by L.L. Bean. He considered these boots with their rubber bottoms and leather tops "new-fangled," and said they should not be issued. The MPs on the beachhead, however, stood in the mud all day directing traffic, and they came to me to see what could be done about their constantly wet feet. Under the circumstances, I let them try the shoepacs, which had come to the beachhead with the rest of the items. They liked them at once. This, as it turned out later, was a very useful test.

Several buildings at Acciarella were hit while Mike and I were there, and one night there was a big bang. A house that partly blocked our view of the hills was struck on the corner toward us. If the shell had landed a yard to the right, it would have burst in our open stable. On another occasion, about noon, when a self-propelled gun began firing one burst after another, we took shelter behind the house. The gun, probably an .88, was sweeping the area, with shells landing about 200 yards apart. We quickly figured that the bursts would strike on either side of us, and they did. Often at night we would hear the chug-chug sound ending in a big explosion of "Anzio Annie," the German .280-mm railroad gun that our artillery and planes were never able to knock out. It fired mainly at the harbor and its position frequently moved.

Since our QM troops were tired of training and waiting for the big move, when some Texan suggested holding a rodeo, Major Goodwin thought it a good idea. A couple of hundred yards from our farm complex a low ridge protected a field from enemy view. It was here that the rodeo could be held. At an informal QM meeting of GIs and officers, it was decided that the rodeo should have "wild cow milking into helmets," "bareback horse races," a betting booth, and a concession stand.

The day of the rodeo was beautiful. Three cows were located for the milking and several horses were rounded up. The riders were to race in pairs bareback, with the horse with the fastest time the winner. A betting booth was set up, and a GI wearing long earrings and dressed in an Italian skirt and a woman's blouse enclosing two apples kidded everyone into betting on the race. Mike could not resist being a rider, though he had done little riding before.

The race course was a straight stretch of field, a little over 100 yards long. I cheered as Mike mounted Anzio Annie's back. He had a colorful scarf at his neck and exuded confidence. The horses started together, urged by smacks from behind by their handlers, and thundered down the stretch. Two-thirds of the way Mike was slightly in the lead, but at this point, something happened and he flew off, landing on soft ground, shaken but unhurt. The two most spirited horses, Kraut Killer and Beachhead Beauty, were yet to race and they ran neck and neck, with Kraut Killer the winner by a nose. Afterward, a libation of Cyprus brandy was doled out, and everyone declared the rodeo a great success.

Time was passing. Soon all American officers on the beachhead had seen our new clothing and equipment and a battalion of the 30th Infantry, whose men were testing our items, was ready to write its report. This task was assigned to a young captain who hated writing. He also had his regular duties to attend to, and asked for my help. By now I knew the unanimous opinion of officers and enlisted men on every item far better than anyone, and so I wrote the report for him. He looked it over and signed it. Mike made covers for it with the Third Division's blue and white shoulder patch, and I took it to General O'Daniel and General Truscott for signature.

I knew how anxious General Doriot was to get the report. If it were approved by the theater commander, factories could begin production at once. If it were not approved, most of our work of the past years would have been nearly useless, and our new items might never reach men in combat.

General Truscott and General O'Daniel glanced at the report, looked pleased, asked a question or two, and signed. The next morning early I was at the airport, ready to board the daily Cessna mail plane to Naples. Its route was out to sea and not over the German-held, intervening land. That day's pilot, normally a fighter pilot, had flown neither the plane nor the route before; his only map was a small road map. I sat in the copilot seat with him while a signal corps officer, also going to Naples, sat in the rear. We were hardly in the air and away from the beachhead when the pilot showed me islands in the far distance and asked me if I would hold the plane steady toward them while he took 20 winks. He said he was exhausted, and looked it. Keeping the plane on course was easy and I held it steady. After a bit, the pilot opened his eyes.

"Why didn't you waken me?" he asked. "We've overshot it. There's the Bay of Naples now."

As he headed the plane toward the coast, and I was looking for the city, there was a great bang and the plane was thrown around violently. A hole appeared in the wing a couple of yards from my window, and black bursts erupted all around, mainly over us. I jammed on my helmet for lack of anything better to do as the pilot put the plane in a steep dive. I was so sure we were going to try a crash landing that my immediate thought was what to do with the secret report if we landed safely. Then we pulled out of the dive so suddenly that my helmet fell off. The black bursts now were way above us. The pilot, who was swearing, turned the plane northwest, on the land side of the mountains along the shoreline. He had mistaken the Gulf of Gaeta, in German hands, for the Gulf of Naples. The ack-ack that had penetrated the wing next to me had not exploded, but had knocked out the aileron. The pilot murmured, "We haven't any lift; I can't get over those mountains."

We were flying at less than 1,000 feet above the ground. The pilot turned the plane 180 degrees and headed east toward Cassino, looking all the time for enemy aircraft. A ridge running from the sea to Cassino, held by the Germans, was the front line. The low point was near Cassino, and the pilot headed straight there, passing over the town of Formia, where we could look down on German soldiers walking in the streets. Some were looking up at us. I grabbed a fallen helmet and put it on, mentally urging the plane to go faster. The plane did not have much lift, but we skimmed a low point in the ridge, and a few minutes later touched down at Naples. As we got out, the signal corps captain and I looked at each other. During the flight we had exchanged helmets.

From the airport I went to General Sullivan's office and from there to see General Mark Clark. Clark was pleased that the report was so favorable, mentioned the cold-weather casualties of the preceding winter, signed the report, and sent me to General Gruenther's office. I did not see Gruenther, the army commander, but the next morning returned for the signed report and received orders to fly to theater headquarters in Algiers.

This flight was smooth. Soon after landing I was on my way to the office of General Eisenhower's quartermaster, where I met two Texans, Lt. Col. Jack Finks and Maj. Richard Lewis, both of whom became good friends. They told me it would take a day to get the report signed, but said they would get it done. Meanwhile I had time for a bath at the plush Algiers Hotel, where I was billeted. I also had a look around the Casbah, after seeing some of the handsome buildings in the city. Thanks to Jack Finks, the report was soon approved, but I was told that General Middleswart, the theater quartermaster, wanted to see it and me before it was sent to the U.S. for action. The next morning there was a flight to Oran, where the general's office was located.

As I waited at the Algiers airport to be summoned to the plane, an officer came up with a briefcase. He asked if I were cleared for secret material; I said I was. He then asked if I would deliver the briefcase to an officer who would meet the plane at the airport at Oran. Of course I agreed. Immediately afterward I was told that my plane was ready. Two pilots boarded it, but apparently I was the only passenger. It was a DC-3 with bucket seats.

I sat down in the middle of the plane and watched as we took off and gained a few thousand feet. Then I pulled out of my pocket the day's copy of the *Stars and Stripes*, the army newspaper. We were flying smoothly over desert as I opened the paper, leaned back, and began to read. Suddenly there was a small click. My shoulders went back as the emergency exit directly behind my back opened and my newspaper whisked out the opening. Tightly holding a fragment of newspaper in each hand, I looked straight down 5,000 feet to the desert. Fortunately my arms were spread as I read the paper, and my elbows projected enough on either side of the window so that our speed did not provide enough suction to pull me out of the plane. I moved quickly to another seat. If I had fallen out, what a mystery there would have been!

Oran probably has many interesting things to see, but I never saw them, for after leaving the briefcase with the officer who had come for it, I went straight to General Middleswart's office. We hit it off immediately. He was interested in our test items and also in what I knew about the 10th Mountain Division. He had before him the list of QM items to be shipped to Italy for the 10th and asked my advice. I suggested several changes, such as eliminating the old-style ski boots, which were useful only for skiing, and even then did not fit the ski bindings well. He made the changes.

My basic mission was now complete. The report and official request for the new items were on their way to Washington. How I wished I could be with Doriot and my companions in Special Forces when they heard the test results, but even more I wanted to return to Anzio and be with Mike, for I learned that the breakthrough from the beachhead had started. In Algiers I said good-bye to Jack Finks and flew back to Naples, where I found a cable instructing me to stay with the Fifth Army and do what seemed best. Wonderful orders!

The next day I found Mike, who had been waiting for me in the Anzio area. He had not been idle. During the breakthrough, the Third Division had cut off and bypassed certain enemy units holed up in strong positions on a hill near Roccamassima. One of them kept firing at supply units as they went forward, but Mike solved the problem. He yelled for a mortar, got one, and dropped a shell neatly right on the hilltop. Out came 33 Germans with their hands up.

All movement was now toward Rome. In a hurry to get there, we accepted a ride in the back of a truck of the 88th Division with Mike's friend Lt. Pete Credidio. Along the whole route we saw evidence of tremendous Allied firepower. Cisterna, the town where the Germans had had their headquarters, had been turned to rubble. Mined areas already had been marked, and along the roads lines of smashed German half-tracks, command cars, trucks, and motorcycles showed the deadly effect of our control of the air. Burned-out tanks, both German and American, revealed the intensity of the fighting. The basic German force had now retreated beyond Rome, but they had left behind forces to harass or block the advance in every way possible.

Near Palestrina we came across a graves registration unit collecting point. Since Mike and I had been asked by the OQMG to find if the new plastic body bags were improvements, we stopped to find out. The Seventh Infantry had run into heavy tank fire at this point and several men had been killed, including Lt. Col. Toffey, the regiment executive officer, one of the most popular officers in the division. Little did I suspect at that moment, as I looked at him, that years later his fine son would be a student I knew at Exeter. The men at the collection point had no new body bags but they had heard of them. Later, at the Nettuno cemetery, we found that the new bags were far superior to the old ones.

We passed through the Pope's woods, where every tree along the road had explosives tied to it, unexploded because of the speed of the advance. As we began reaching the outskirts of Rome itself, Colonel Wolfer, the Third Division quartermaster, came by in a jeep and yelled at Mike and me to join him.

We drove into the city with crowds lining the streets. Most were women and old men. A few threw flowers or offered drinks of wine. All looked tremendously excited and happy that Rome apparently had been spared. Finally, we joined the swarm of people before the Victor Emmanuel monument. We did not speak Italian and few Italians spoke any English, but emotions were beyond the bounds of language. One well-dressed Italian woman tried to speak Latin with me, but after a few words we were stopped.

An American sergeant came out on the balcony where Mussolini had addressed crowds. Everyone roared approval. The sergeant made a short speech but it was hard to hear him. Since we were all weary, Col. Wolfer dropped us off at Mussolini's Fascist Museum, a treasure house where we were to be billeted with men from the 30th Infantry Regiment.

The place was full of Ethiopian spears and swords, huge Albanian flags, and fascist symbols and shoulder patches, together with small models of Romulus and Remus. I found a couple of Russian flags, undoubtedly captured in Spain, and trophies from the Isonzo campaign in World War I, as well as stacks of forged Greek thousand- and million-drachma notes. The 30th Infantry commander gave orders to throw everything out, but Mike and I managed to rescue a few Ethiopian spearheads and some flags to send back to the OQMG.

We were with men of the battalion who had tested our new items and we asked lots of questions. Two of the officers we knew were very enthusiastic about the way they had worked during the breakthrough, especially about the field jackets with the big cargo pockets. We made these two company commanders turn out what was in their pockets to show what they had carried in them during the advance. They were amazed to find that each had carried more than a dozen useful items in his pockets. The GIs had used their pockets mainly for K-rations and ammunition, but they were enthusiastic, too.

We had been told in greatest confidence the date of the invasion of Europe, and when that day went by and no action was reported we became worried. We had heard nothing about the weather in the English Channel. A day later, news of the delayed invasion came crowding in.

The Third Division was to garrison Rome, while the other American divisions continued pursuit of the retreating Germans to the north. Mike and I now had a breathing spell to check out what we had learned from the GIs wearing the new equipment during the drive from the beachhead. We had heard of heels on our new combat boots coming off and went to a salvage operation to see what we could learn. The rumor was true. We found a number of practically new boots with one missing heel. Immediately we cabled this information to the OQMG, counted the number of boots we found in this condition, and sent back samples to our office, along with some captured Albanian flags and Ethiopian spearheads salvaged from the trophies thrown out of Fascist headquarters. The boot problem, we found out later, was caused by trying to save metal. The men writing the boot specifications had made the heel nails too short for severe army use.

Since we were beginning to get requests from the OQMG about specific items, we needed transportation to do our work. With Fifth Army help, we were assigned a jeep and driver. Quickly learning that salvage operations were the best place to find out about army clothing deficiencies, we had the main depot set aside for our examination all new items that came in, as well as any unusual German or Italian items.

We also visited a British-American camp where instruction in mountain warfare was being given by six or eight junior officers from the 10th

Mountain Division under Capt. Edward Link. They had been sent to Italy a few weeks ahead of us to learn the best way to train small units in how to move in the Italian mountains, and to give that training.

The Fifth Army kept moving ahead and we kept with them, interviewing GIs and one division quartermaster after another. The front line was soon north of the Arno. The Germans evacuated Lucca and Leghorn, and for two or three days Leghorn became a no-man's-land. Mike and I entered it under eerie conditions, hoping to find new German clothing and equipment before it was grabbed by Italian peasants. Our office was eager for ideas based on German or Italian items. Our own combat boots, for instance, had used the German idea that boots need to be higher than service shoes in order to keep trousers inside them and out of the mud. Leghorn was heavily booby-trapped and we secured little useful material.

In July the quartermaster of the Fourth Army, which was being formed to land in southern France, asked me if I would like to go with him. I said I would and went to General Sullivan for permission to apply, but he refused. Some time later, word came from General Doriot that Mike Slauta was to go and I was to keep on with the Fifth Army.

Before Mike left, we were assigned to train the whole Fifth Army in how to use their new clothing, especially footwear, in the winter, showing methods to prevent trench foot or frostbite. We carried out this assignment at the spa of Montecatini, where one division after another came for rest and relaxation. At Montecatini there were big bathtubs, where after-hours Mike and I usually managed a good soak. We had Ed Link and Jack Clement summoned from their mountain training and set up regular shows for both officers and enlisted men, with special emphasis on the layering system and how to adjust clothing to amount of exercise as well as temperature. We emphasized the advantages of shoepacs, showed ingenious ways of drying socks, and told how the "buddy system" can help prevent frostbite. Clement, a born comedian, put on a striptease of layers that made the GIs howl.

The previous winter in Italy, frostbite and trench foot had caused heavy infantry casualties, though most men eventually returned to duty. I did not know at the time that in the winter months following our work, there would be a tremendous decrease in casualties from cold and trench foot in Italy. (I later received the Legion of Merit, with specific mention of this work.)

I said good-bye to Mike with great regret, not only for the loss of his companionship but because the real action was beginning in France.

About this time General Sullivan asked me if I would do a favor for General Clark and take over to the commanding general of the British Eighth Army a pair of shoepacs. Apparently the word had gone around that shoepacs were the best footwear for mud and cold. Picking up a duffel bag with several sizes of shoepacs, I drove through the British lines to Rimini, where I was well-received by the Eighth Army commander, with whom I had a pleasant chat. He had never seen such boots before and was obviously very pleased.

Seeking information, frequently I drove along the Florence-Pistoia-Lucca highway, turning north toward the Gothic line, where German troops, well dug in, were preventing further Allied advances. During this period, I had a fine reunion with my old friend Albert Jackman, now a major with the 10th Mountain Division. My influence at the salvage depot helped him to secure for his outfit a complete cook set, a prized item, which was of great use to his troops later. I also saw in Jackman's unit my former Exeter student Bill Wright, whom I had recommended for the mountain troops. Another Exeter student of mine, whom I looked for but failed to find, was Hugh Evans, who had also been 18 when I officially recommended him to the Advocate General's Office. He later was decorated for knocking out a German machine gun on Mt. Belvedere.

CHAPTER XIII

Body Armor and the End of the War

1944-1946

I N LATE NOVEMBER, TO MY SURPRISE, I received orders to go to Paris, en route to Washington, for discussions. In Paris, I reported to my old friend from Special Forces, Bestor Robinson, with whom I quickly shared information about the use of the new QM items in France and Italy. Bestor was especially interested in the training program that Mike and I had given to the whole Fifth Army at Montecatini the previous summer. He hoped that something similar could be carried out in France.

From Paris I flew to Prestwick in northern Britain, and from there boarded a C-45 with bucket seats for a flight to the U.S. After flights in DC-3s, this plane felt huge. The wings seemed to go out, out, out. During our long flight of nearly 14 hours we had good views of southern Greenland and thousands of blue and greenish icebergs beyond, and then the weather below us socked in. The pilot seemed undecided about something and he finally told us, "I don't know whether we're going to land at Gander [Newfoundland], Baltimore, or Bermuda." To passengers eager to get home, there seemed excessive latitude in that statement, but gradually Gander and Baltimore were scrubbed and we did land in Bermuda. The next day we reached Baltimore and I went on to Washington. There I had a grand reunion at the OQMG with General Doriot, Bill House, and our Special Forces people.

After a weekend in Philadelphia with my father, I returned to the OQMG for a briefing concerning my final important mission overseas.

This was to learn the best way to use Doron, a secret bulletproof material, made of laminated nylon and phenolic resins combined by pressure and heat to be used as body armor. It was heavy, and so tough that a diamond saw was needed to cut it. I was given pieces of various sizes and also a few thick nylon pads that had some power to stop low-caliber bullets or grenade fragments. My orders were to take this material to Italy and find the best way it could be used in combat. All pieces not brought back were to be destroyed.

Directly after Christmas I left for Paris again, this time with Clinton Morrison and Alec Daigneault, two keen young members of Doriot's staff. We were to attend a major conference on cold-weather operations, after which I was to go to Italy with my pieces of Doron.

In Florence, after bringing General Sullivan up-to-date, I went to the Fifth Army Medical Corps Headquarters for information on the most important body areas to protect outside of the head. I checked records of men wounded and killed in action and quickly learned that in Italy mortar and artillery fire were the greatest sources of casualties. Protection for the chest and neck were most needed. Returning to the main salvage depot in an abandoned tobacco factory, I persuaded the tailor to make two sleeveless vests with slots where I could place slabs of Doron. He also put together pads of soft nylon to give neck protection.

The next step was to visit a division commander to get his evaluation of the sleeveless vests and learn in what other ways Doron should be tried. The campaign to rout the Germans from the Apennines and push them beyond the Po River would soon begin, and it was possible we could get some kind of a test in combat that would be helpful in the future campaign against Japan.

I went first to the 34th Division Headquarters, where I was warmly greeted by the commanding general. He invited me to have breakfast with him and his regimental commanders the next morning, when I could show them what I had and ask their advice. This I did. We had just sat down, however, when an officer reported that two 34th Division soldiers had been taken prisoner the night before. There was brief speculation about whether they could reveal anything important about plans for the coming campaign, and then, as I was being asked to speak, another officer came with an urgent message that he said was secret. The general said, "Let's have it," and the officer said, "President Roosevelt is dead." Complete silence followed, then a whole series of questions about whether his death would affect the course of the war and the world afterward.

Finally, I had a chance to show my Doron and ask for suggestions about its use. All the officers were keenly interested and asked what penetration Doron would stop. Most suggested that the best way to use it would be in a jacket or vest. One of the regimental commanders asked me to come with him after breakfast for further discussion, and I gladly accompanied him to his command post.

He asked whether he could personally test the Doron with his .45 service pistol. I said he could, and we stepped outside and placed a small square of Doron against an earth bank. This piece of Doron had been fired at before, and it showed a soft place in the center where a bullet had struck but not pierced. The colonel aimed at the soft place 15 feet away and fired. While we had been getting ready for the test, the clerk in the office had become more and more interested, and just as the colonel fired, the clerk poked his head out the door to watch. The bullet struck the Doron and ricocheted, striking the clerk in the head. There was little velocity in the ricochet, but the clerk promptly collapsed on the ground, thinking he was dead. The clerk was not a man used to combat. The colonel, after seeing that the clerk was unhurt, enjoyed the moment enormously. He also was impressed by the strength of the treated nylon, and said that he would be glad to help my project in any way. In the ensuing advance to the Po River, one of his infantrymen was selected to wear one of the vests with the Doron inside.

When this fact became known to the soldier's buddies, one of them quickly offered me $100 for another vest, which showed that infantrymen going into combat probably would not mind carrying the extra weight to get the extra protection.

During the advance, the 10th Mountain Division distinguished itself in breaking through the Gothic lines of the Apennines and continuing on to the Po. The German retreat became rapid, but there were strong areas of resistance; for instance, at Lake Garda, German .88s took a heavy toll until the lake roads were cleared. The much-feared German mountain troops and the Fourth Parachute Division were dug in in the mountains beyond the lake, contesting every advance. One morning I was about to leave for Lake Garda to see the 10th Mountain Division quartermaster and some infantry units when General Sullivan saw me and called, "Come on, Bates, we're going to see the chief."

When we arrived, the chief of staff was on the phone. "Both of them?" he was asking, "And upside down? You think the partisans have the gold, too?" In a moment he put down the phone and explained to us and others that Mussolini and his mistress had been captured by partisans as they tried to escape to Switzerland and both had been immediately hanged.

He had hardly finished when the phone rang again and I heard him say, "White tablecloths, you say? Well, I don't know. Tell them to hold off until I get back to you." He turned to us, "That was Pat at the air force. He says German troops are waving white tablecloths. It looks like they're folding up." He went back to the phone. General Sullivan left quickly and I went to my jeep to continue to Lake Garda.

The people I wanted to talk with were at the far end of the lake, and Ducks (amphibious armored vehicles) were being used to get there, since tunnels on the roads on both sides of the lake had been blown by the retreating Germans. One man in the Duck with me was Bob Livermore, a well-known American skier, now with the 10th Mountain Division. He was vigorously asserting that all of the peace talk was hogwash, for the Germans could hole up in the mountains for months, and slow or stop any American advance. He did not know it, but Hitler had given the order to the German mountain troops beyond the lake to stay and die to the last man rather than retreat any more. Bob also did not know what I had just heard. German generals were surrendering, and the war beyond Lake Garda was ending, too.

When the end of the war in Italy was announced, the reaction of the troops was amazement. They could not believe it could end so suddenly. Some were silent and serious, while others shouted, "I made it!" but most merely spoke of getting out of the army and going home. The war in France, and even more the war against Japan, were worries, but at the moment that part of the war seemed far, far away.

Suddenly partisans with red armbands and neckerchiefs seemed everywhere. Most of them were waving a rifle with one hand and raising a clenched fist in the other. For a few days, they drove captured vehicles wildly until they could get no more gas. How strong the communist element was among the partisans, it was hard to tell, but there were a great many red armbands.

A couple of days later General Sullivan said that a large German quartermaster depot had been reported being held by partisans, and he asked me to go there and find out what could be used by German prisoners, who were quickly becoming a troublesome supply problem.

I took a driver who could speak Italian and we located the warehouse. Armed partisans, who were controlling it, lolled outside, and I sensed a definite coldness on our arrival. It was clear that many partisans took the attitude that the depot was now their property and not anyone else's. One man spoke good English and he courteously showed me all over the warehouse, with its stacks of German clothing and rations, and a few minor items. I made a mental survey, jotted down estimates in a small notebook, said good-bye to the apparently well-educated English speaker, and left. I saw sullen looks on many faces as I departed.

General Sullivan was interested in my report and quick to realize that the stores would disappear unless we placed a guard over them at once. The next day I returned with another officer to record the exact amounts of food available for prisoners. When I arrived, sullen faces again greeted me. One man pointed to a house next door and said in heavily accented English, "Your friend have accident." I went to where he pointed and stepped in. On a table lay a corpse, with burning candles in large candlesticks surrounding the body. It was the man who the day before had spoken English and shown me around the warehouse. The room was full of men with guns who looked distinctly unfriendly. I was not wearing sidearms and would not have pulled a gun under the circumstances anyway. My fellow officer had already gone outside and was getting in the jeep. I merely regretted the death, glanced at the warehouse, and returned to our car. I knew that if the U.S. Army was to use those supplies, they must capture them from the partisans first and do it fast. That afternoon, troops were sent to the warehouse, but most of the stores had already been removed.

It was not long before the war ended in Germany also, and again I received orders to report to Paris. This time I had no difficulty with the flight and found that I was to join Mike Slauta and Adams Carter in interviewing German prisoners at Bad Tolz, the former German mountain-troop headquarters in Bavaria. The three of us had a grand reunion there before beginning our interviews with German quartermaster officers and a few line officers.

These interviews brought out interesting facts. The German quartermasters, far from being the superefficient warriors we had imagined, had made just as many mistakes as we had, probably more. The last clothing item that the German QM people were working on was a reversible overcoat parka. Two of them could be snapped together to make a tent. It was a very complicated item to make, expensive, and in my way of thinking a bad piece of clothing. For instance, if you made your overcoat into a tent and wanted to get out into a storm, you had to take your tent apart and put on the wet coat. A tent of this kind in the OQMG had been Bestor Robinson's "baby." Fortunately, only a few of our items had been made, but

the Germans had secured one and were starting to make a similar item of
their own.

We learned little of value from the German prisoners except that their
items of cold-weather clothing, boots especially, were not warm enough to
stand up against the severe Russian winter. Practically every prisoner told us
that we would soon be fighting the Russians, and that they (the Germans)
had been fighting against communism. Many stated that they were professional soldiers and eagerly volunteered to join the American army.

We finished our interviews with the belief that our quartermaster items
were better than those of the Germans, but the Germans probably had
given more thought and training to getting hot meals to troops in combat
under cold-weather conditions.

I was to return to Paris, then to Italy, and await orders to return home.
The return to Florence was uneventful. My only unfinished business was to
destroy the pieces of Doron not returning with me. I took a boat down
Lake Garda, which had now emerged from army control, and consigned
my pieces to the bottom of this very deep lake.

Soon afterward, from a DC-3, I had my last look at the great Duomo
in Florence, and the following day, again in a C-45, flew across the
Atlantic. This time I arrived in New York, and received a welcoming glass
of milk from the Red Cross. In Washington I found a phone call waiting
from the number-two man of the FBI, a Mr. Tolson. He was very anxious
to talk to me about how I had used the Doron, and asked me to come to
see him the next day.

I did, and got the grand treatment. Not only did we talk about how to
use body armor, and the FBI's concern that gangsters would get hold of
some of it, too, but at one moment Mr. Tolson pushed a button on the wall
beside his desk and a whole shooting gallery opened up. Here we took
some of the Doron I had brought and fired German and Italian revolvers at
it, as well as the more penetrating U.S. police special revolver. The Doron
stood up well against all side arms, but a rifle bullet punctured it easily.
Afterward I was shown all around the FBI headquarters, including laboratories where a flake of paint could reveal what make of car it came from, or
a spot of blood could lead to the conviction of a murder suspect. It was
clear that Mr. Tolson was offering me a job when I left the army, but I told
him that I did not want the FBI to be my lifework.

At the QM I received a desk job with the title Assistant for Product
Analysis. It was a promotion, but far less exciting than what I had been
doing. In Special Forces we began concentrating on the war in Japan, hold-

ing conferences by teletype with quartermaster officers in Hawaii. We would ask questions that would be sent by scrambler code, and almost immediately answers would be decoded, unscrambled, typed, and shown on a screen in front of us. Our planning was based on the prediction that the Japanese in Japan would fight as furiously as they had on Iwo Jima. The dropping of the atom bombs and the sudden ending of the war in the Pacific surprised us all.

There was still much to do in summing up the experiences of the quartermaster corps in World War II. I also had to make decisions about my future. Exeter, I learned, had already engaged its teachers for the coming year. Various other job opportunities were proposed, but I had already decided to return to Exeter in the fall of 1946.

Meanwhile, Walter Wood, then military attaché at the American Embassy in Ottawa, asked for help in carrying out a plan called Operation Muskox. This was to be an expedition using Canadian and American over-snow vehicles to cross the Canadian Arctic in midwinter. The party was to determine whether the Canadian Penguin or the United States Weasel could be used best in opening up or defending northern Canada. The leader of the party was to be a Canadian and the plan was proposed by Canada. Walter Wood, who knew the Canadians well, came to me and Bill House for help. General Doriot fully approved the idea and it was decided that I would be involved in planning the American part of the venture and Bill House would go as the U.S. quartermaster observer. Our basic idea, of course, was to field-test American and Canadian clothing and equipment in a period of extreme cold.

The Studebaker Company, which had developed the Weasel, admitted that their engines did not last long under hard use. This flaw might have meant the end of Weasel participation, but Walter Wood had an idea for solving the problem. He knew that the U.S. Air Force had many gliders in stock, with no likely future use by civilians or the military. These gliders were expendable and Muskox people could have any number they wanted. Since the expedition would at all times have radio contact with their base at Churchill if a Weasel motor burned out or some other supply item were urgently needed, a glider with a pilot could be flown to the expedition and the glider landed exactly where wanted. The glider then would be written off and the pilot would become a temporary member of the expedition.

Since the Canadian authorities were skeptical, Wood arranged a demonstration of glider use at Ottawa. He invited me to see how well gliders could solve the problem, and since I was slated to sign for the Weasels, I accepted Wood's urgent request to come. The day of the test found me standing in a U.S. glider behind the seat of the pilot. To the left of the nose of the plane rose what looked like the supports for a pole-vault bar, but instead of a bar a nylon rope ran across the space between the supports, and from the middle of the rope hung a ring. The ring was tied to the nose of our glider.

In the plane with me were two very suspicious Canadian pilots, who were loudly expressing their opinion that whatever happened, the blasted thing would not work. Fortunately for me, I had a good hold of the back of the pilot's seat, for suddenly a DC-3 rushed past us nearly at ground level and, as a hook on the DC-3 caught the ring between the stanchions, we shot like a sprung arrow into the sky. The nose of the glider tilted upward, and I had to hold on hard to keep from being flung backward. The two pilots had not been holding on to anything and so both of them went tumbling backward to land in a tangle in the tail. Crestfallen, they crawled slowly forward, but by this time our long nylon rope had leveled off and we were being towed smoothly at the same height as the DC-3.

The snatch had been very smooth, but it was still necessary to see how accurately the glider could be landed. At 5,000 feet we released the tow rope and glided. We were in a silent world where the pilot could turn and twist with great ease. It was like being in a maneuverable balloon. We could distinctly hear sounds on the ground as we circled down, our glider pilot showing us that it was impossible to put the glider into a spin. Gradually we came lower and made a soft landing on the exact spot selected in advance for that purpose. The test was successful; the plan to rescue Weasels was adopted.

Soon afterward we said good-bye to Bill House in Washington and told him we would meet him at Churchill, Manitoba, when the expedition started. This we did not long afterward. I left Washington on an unusually warm day when the temperature rose to 60 degrees Fahrenheit and arrived in Churchill, where the temperature was nearly -40 degrees. Good work had been done to organize the force.

The next morning, which was cold and very windy, most of the inhabitants of Churchill gathered in small groups as the engines of the vehicles began to start. There was a variety of clothing, especially among the Indians and local whites, but all faces were either sunk deep in parka hoods or shielded by scarves and wool hats, with only the eyes showing. When each member of the expedition was in his place, Pat Baird, the leader, gave the signal to fire an old brass cannon to announce their departure.

Passing through the Suez Canal.

*Eric Shipton, whom I met
at Zermatt.
The Matterhorn is behind.*

Tsering Yangdon, her mother and son, with us in the garden of her house in Kathmandu, where she and her American husband were working. (Taken several years after we first met.)

The Peace Corps group in Tansen. (Left to right) Martin, Stevens, Marchand, Clayton, R.H.B., Nishihara.(Sitting)

*Old friends: (Bottom row) Dorcas Houston, Ann Carter, Barbara Washburn.
(Middle row) Charlie Houston, Adams Carter, Bradford Washburn.
(Back row) R.H.B. and Gail.*

*Passing the colors at base camp: Clinch (left),R. H. B., Wang Zenghua, and
Chang.*

At Tenzing Norkey's home in Darjeeling. (Left to right) George Russell, Tenzing, R.H.B.,

Camped with view of Dhaulagiri. Gail (center) and John Case (far right)

Thereupon the vehicles, half-obscured by smoke from their exhausts, slowly set out. What a test they would be giving their clothing, their vehicles, and themselves! I didn't envy Bill the cold ride, but I did envy him the experience.

Some weeks later Walter and I flew to Churchill and boarded a Canadian Air Force plane for the flight to Victoria Island. A vast, snowy landscape, known as the Barren Lands, spread before us as we flew north from Churchill. Our friends of the Muskox Expedition had been crossing lonely country, especially after leaving Baker Lake. Once or twice we saw their old tracks before we reached the windswept ice of Coronation Gulf. Near Victoria Island the ice was smooth, and we landed close to the Muskox vehicles on the south shore, well north of the Arctic Circle. The ice where we landed was 12 feet thick, strong enough to support the heaviest bomber. Far below the surface we could see seaweed frozen into the ice.

A dog team reached the plane first, and Bill House, obviously a strong member of the team, was an early arrival. Bill took me to a cluster of Eskimo igloos, where I met an Eskimo acquaintance of his who spoke good English. A frozen seal was in the outer passage, but the interior of the igloo was warm and a bit stuffy. Bill spoke highly of his companions but told of difficulties with the machines. The short days had also severely limited their hours of travel. He also praised highly the intelligence and adaptability of Eskimos who were accompanying them.

Apparently the Canadians were somewhat reluctant to resupply engines by glider, though one engine had been brought in successfully. The team still had a long way to go: along Coronation Gulf to the Coppermine River, then south to Great Slave Lake and on to Edmonton.

Walter and I climbed back in our plane and were soon over the Barren Lands on the way to Churchill, where we found much activity. Logistic support for Muskox was about to change its location to Yellow Knife on Great Slave Lake, and since a glider might be needed there for emergency use, it was to go too. The DC-3 helping with the move to Yellow Knife was already loaded, but the pilots agreed to pull a glider too, though it had some spare parts in it.

Walter and I were to go in the DC-3 with two pilots, while another pilot climbed into the glider. Using the customary nylon rope, the plane pulled the glider slowly to the end of the huge Churchill runway, where the pilots revved the motors a few times. Walter and I were sitting on piles of gear in the back of the plane, for all seats except the pilot's and copilot's had been taken out. As we started down the runway, which tops a bluff, one of

the pilots yelled to us that we had a heavy load and to get as far forward on
the piles of gear as we could. We did, staring out the windows as we slowly
gathered speed. Two-thirds of the way down the runway we were airborne,
but the weight of the glider was so great that it didn't rise and pulled our
DC-3 back on the runway!

Walter and I stared at each other in alarm. We heard an exclamation
from the pilots, but the plane kept on. Outside we could see the runway
going by faster and faster, but still the plane did not rise again. Then we shot
off the end of the runway, looking down on jagged tree stumps 80 feet below,
where I expected to crash at any moment. But we didn't. Somehow the plane
kept on flying at the same level, pulling the now airborne glider behind it.

A worried voice told us to keep as far forward as we could and not to
move around. One pilot was swearing at whoever had loaded the glider.
Fortunately the heavily wooded area west of Churchill that we were flying
over was flat, and for what seemed like hours we kept flying over forests at
almost the same low level until we had used enough gas for the pilots to
relax. Once, hundreds of miles from any habitation, we flew over a small
lake where a man was driving a dog team. He stepped on the brake,
stopped the team, and swung around to look at us. We were so low we
could see his face clearly, and he looked absolutely bewildered. "What is
this?" he seemed to be thinking. "One airplane pulling another—now I've
seen everything."

When the glider cut loose above the airfield at Yellow Knife and we
circled and landed beside it, we had a great feeling of relief. All of us in the
plane and glider climbed out knowing we had been through something. As
we found out later, the sergeants who had loaded the glider knew nothing
about the weight it should carry, and had put in lots of heavy nuts, bolts,
and spare parts that far exceeded the authorized load.

Several weeks later, Bill House was back in Washington. He had had a
rugged trip getting to Great Bear Lake and Great Slave Lake, but the rest
of the trip he had found slow. Bill was ready to leave the QM now and so
was I, though I had been asked to make it a career. The peacetime army
held no charms for me nor did the State Department, though a job there
was suggested. Schools also were looking for headmasters, and Harvard
offered a job as Assistant Dean of Freshmen, but I had other ideas. I
enjoyed Exeter, the students, and my teaching. I did not want to become an
administrator or a headmaster. I did want to complete my work for the
Ph.D., however, an enterprise which at this point meant only writing a thesis. I had done the course work and had completed all examinations.

Before the war I had planned to do some new work on John Aubrey, but during the war a detailed and scholarly book had been published that used much of the material that I was counting on using. It was too late to work on Aubrey, even though I still found him fascinating. Then I did the logical thing. I went to Philadelphia to see Professor Harbage, a Shakespearean scholar, chairman of the English Department at the University of Pennsylvania. He was glad to see me, understood the problem at once, and was eager to help. "What do you like? What would you enjoy doing?" he asked. I admitted that I especially liked mountains. "Fine," said he, "You've lost too much time already. The main thing is to get your degree as rapidly as you decently can. We recently have had a thesis on the literature of the sea, so why not one on the literature of the mountains?" "Wonderful," I said, "I'll do it."

Before Bill House and I left Washington, however, we did something we had long talked about: We took a first step toward getting back to K2 by visiting the Indian ambassador. He was an experienced diplomat, who could not have been more cordial or more emphatic that the time was not right for an application. "Later," he kept saying. "Things are difficult right now. Maybe next year or the year after."

That put K2 on the rear burner for both of us, and I turned to reading or rereading books that I knew had portions dealing with mountains. The American Alpine Club library, with its outstanding collection of books, was obviously where I should be working. Fortunately, Charlie Houston's family invited me to live with them in Great Neck while I was working in New York, and I gratefully stayed there for much of the time between leaving Washington and beginning teaching again in September 1946 at Phillips Exeter. Something different I looked forward to was having Charlie Houston in Exeter, for he was opening a clinic there with two other doctors.

CHAPTER XIV

After the War

1946-1951

RETURNING TO EXETER after the intense years of the war was something of a shock, but there were advantages too. I loved being able to go into the New Hampshire countryside practically every day, with good classes providing the necessary challenge and contrast. Almost the day when school began in the fall of 1946, three students arrived at my door to ask if they could form a mountaineering club with me as the adviser. Naturally I was delighted, and thereafter we explored local cliffs together with mutual enjoyment, both fall and spring, with occasional weekend trips as well.

My brother, Bill, had started recreational skiing at Exeter, and now there were many ski meets in which our boys could compete. In the natural course of events, our program became very popular. Students wanted a ski team, which we did our best to coach, though neither of us was in any way a professional. At first the team competed only in slalom or giant slalom, but the schools to the north of Exeter had begun competing in four events, and soon we were building a 30-meter jump on the hillside of a local farm pasture and competing in jumping and cross-country skiing, too. The ski team became an enjoyable part of my winter life in Exeter, with lots of early morning risings and long drives to meets, or visits to northern areas when snowless periods at Exeter denied the team snow on which to practice.

I also became adviser to the Lantern Club, the school's literary society, based on the Elizabethan Society at Yale, with funds to entertain writers or scholars visiting the school. In addition, I ran the program to bring a succession of outstanding lecturers to the academy on Sunday evenings. No wonder time went fast.

One of the boys I met on his arrival was George Russell, whose parents were worried about him because he had a heart murmur. Charlie Houston was starting the Exeter Clinic with Henry Saltonstall and Dr. Gilbert, an older, well-known Exeter doctor. I had great confidence in Charlie and persuaded the senior Russells to let him examine George's heart. He did, and determined that the heart murmur was slight, something George would outgrow. Meanwhile the best thing he could do was to get lots of exercise.

He had been held back from sports and other activities because of the murmur, but now the door was opened and he leaped out. George became an ardent member of the Exeter Mountaineering Club, and during his four years at the academy we became lifelong friends. He developed into a fine all-around athlete, competing in cross-country, wrestling, and lacrosse, and during his final years at the academy was president of the Mountaineering Club and an outstanding climber. Later he became a wrestler of Olympic caliber.

In the summer of 1947 I completed work on my Ph.D. thesis and received my degree. That left me free for climbing the following summer.

My college roommate, Waldo Holcombe, who had become an expert pilot, suggested that we fly his small plane west in the summer of 1948 to do some climbs. Accordingly, one afternoon Wac, as he was known, picked me up at Sanford, Maine (near Ogunquit), and we flew as far as Erie, Pennsylvania. The next day twelve hours of flying brought us to Bismarck, North Dakota, from where we flew to Calgary and Banff. Our arrival over Banff and the subsequent landing were memorable. Strong crosswinds were pushing us about. As we approached Banff, Wac asked in his quiet way, "Do you see a small town on your side?" "Yes," I replied, "I see it every once in a while." "That's odd," said Wac, "I often see one on my side, too." When we landed, the wind was blowing at more than 40 miles per hour and we had to tie down the plane immediately. After some climbs out of Banff, we flew to Jackson, Wyoming, did some more climbs in the Tetons, then flew on to Rawlins, Wyoming, to pick up Ruth Holcombe, Wac's wife, who was to return East with us.

This return flight was also eventful. When we stopped at Ann Arbor for gas, a young fellow filled the tank but put the cap on backward. We did not notice, took off, and were 500 feet up when the motor quit and Wac had to make a very quick turn in time to get back across a fence to the field. At first we did not know why no gas was reaching the carburetor. The next day the temperature was in the high 90s when we stopped at Auburn, New York, to gas up again. The engine was warm and we quickly took off.

We had gained a little more height than the day before when the engine again quit. Once more, Wac got back to the field, but in the opposite direction from which we had just taken off. This time it turned out that we had carburetor icing, something we did not know could happen on such a torrid day, and something that is now automatically prevented. Despite the forced landings, I had confidence in Waldo and his plane, and made more flights with him.

That fall, my father, almost 80, had moved from Philadelphia to Boston to be nearer his sisters, and Bill and me. While there he had a fall, and it was determined he should stay at a nursing home in Cambridge. Bill and I frequently went to see him before he died.

I never knew a finer man. He was intelligent, very kind, and scrupulously honest. An internationally known scholar who wrote many books on ancient Greek dramatists and their works, he was also a distinguished classical archaeologist. He combined learning with common sense and judgment, and was the center of a close-knit family. The trips he and I made together to visit Civil War battlefields during spring vacations are some of my finest memories.

CHAPTER XV

The Saint Elias Mountains Again

1951

WALTER AND FORESTA WOOD had invited me several times since the end of the war to join them in their glacial studies and climbs in the Saint Elias Mountains, but for one reason or another I had not been able to go. In 1951, everything seemed clear and I agreed to fly to their camp on the Seward Glacier, with the hope that we would be able to climb 15,015-foot Mt. Hubbard, or another of the big unclimbed peaks. Hubbard had tempted us in the winter of 1935, when we were mapping the heart of the Saint Elias Mountains, but our cartographic work did not give us time for the enterprise. Plans for the climb were also proposed several times prior to 1951, but none developed. Now the time seemed right.

The major purpose of this Arctic Institute of North America party was glaciological research, but the expedition had also agreed to test experimental clothing and equipment for the army, and this I agreed to do. A key member of the team was our old friend Professor Robert Sharp of the California Institute of Technology, now one of the world's leading glaciologists, and the kind of man to be with when the chips are down. This year he planned to sink aluminum pipe to a depth of more than 1,000 feet on the Malaspina Glacier to secure information on the internal flow of glacial ice. The whole expedition was to be supplied from Yakutat, using a ski-

Mt. Alverstone (14,565 feet) (left) and Mt. Hubbard (15,015 feet)

wheeled Norseman airplane flown by veteran pilot Maurice King. He would take off on wheels and land on skis near a base camp perched on a nunatak on the Seward Glacier, 70 miles inland.

Surrounding this camp was a circle of magnificent peaks, including Saint Elias, Logan and King Peak, Lucania, Vancouver, Cook, and Augusta. The only greater mountain belvedere I know is Concordia, at the upper end of the Baltoro Glacier in the Karakoram. I had asked George Russell, who had just been graduated from Exeter, to join the expedition. I knew he would be a great asset, but his parents had other ideas and he was unable to go.

In late June I arrived at Yakutat, where I found Walter and Foresta Wood, their daughter Valerie, and John Case. Dr. Sharp's group was already at work on the Malaspina Glacier, and Peter Wood, Nicholas Clifford, Geoffrey Hattersley-Smith of the Canadian Defense Research Board, and Paul Townsend of the U.S. Quartermaster Corps were already at base camp.

Our first indication of a serious problem came on our flight from Yakutat to base camp. Maury King was flying us in the Norseman over the seracs of the upper icefall of the huge Malaspina Glacier when the engine began to lose power. There was absolutely no place to land in the icefall below, but we did not have far to fly. We held our breaths as Maury coaxed the straining plane up over the lip of the icefall to where he could glide across the Seward Glacier to our camp on the nunatak. Since the plane recently had been completely checked over by a mechanic, Maury King was deeply concerned about the cause of the trouble.

The next day King went over the motor as carefully as he could, tried it out, and flew the plane to Anchorage to install a new engine. Meanwhile the glaciologists began digging an ice pit and I began testing army equipment. A key test was to wear experimental insulated rubber boots while using army skis with balata ski bindings. The latter would fit any boot, but without the tightness necessary for good control. I put on boots and skis, and on my first run, poling hard, skied down a rough slope. Just as my pole was coming down, I struck a chunk of ice that pushed my left ski sharply to the left. My descending pole drove clear through my left rubber boot and through my foot.

John Case, who was nearby, helped me to pull out the pole and take off my boot, which was wet with blood. "How did you get the hole in the bottom of your foot?" he asked, not realizing that I had driven the pole clear through my foot. He helped me to limp back up the hill to my tent, where Foresta cleaned the wound and gave me antibiotics. Fortunately I had not struck a bone; four days later I was starting to ski again.

While we waited for the return of the Norseman to fly us to the base of Mt. Hubbard, the weather was fine and we were able to make short trips locally; then bad weather intervened, but by July 14 King returned, and Walter and I flew with him to make a reconnaissance of our projected route on the mountain. It looked as if a landing could be made at about 6,000 feet, with a potential route through three icefalls leading to the Hubbard-Alverstone Plateau at 13,000 feet. We decided that Case and I should be landed to establish a camp and investigate the first icefall, while Walter returned to base to make arrangements for parachuting.

Case and I waited for the regular night freeze and then began to mark a tricky route through the first icefall. The key was a somewhat fragile snow bridge that we hoped would last. It was here, miles from any grass, that we saw a cony. When he saw us, the poor thing panicked and dove into the nearest crevasse.

The next day, Walter parachuted loads onto a smooth area at 8,000 feet and on the col at 13,000 feet. Climbs of Hubbard and Alverstone, both unclimbed boundary peaks, could now be attempted without days of heavy backpacking. A week of bad weather now held us up, and so when the plane finally came in with Walter and Peter Wood on July 24, John Case had to go out in it to Yakutat to return to work. We were now a party of four: Walter and Peter Wood, Nicholas Clifford (later provost at Middlebury College), and me.

The route Case and I had marked out led us quickly through the first icefall, for the thin bridge was still holding, and we found two parachuted loads near the second icefall, where we camped. Rising at 3:00 the next morning, we worked out another tricky route through the second icefall and continued on through the third to the 13,000-foot plateau between Hubbard and Alverstone where loads also had been dropped. With Hubbard and Alverstone rising close above us, we had grand views looking out across the Ice Field Ranges. How easy it seemed to have food and shelter awaiting us on the plateau, so different from the heavy packing and sled hauling we had done on the opposite side of Mt. Hubbard during the winter Yukon Expedition 16 years earlier.

Since we were eager not to lose good weather, we were off again early the next morning. We led around old avalanche debris, up a slope deep in powder snow, and between two big crevasses. Kicking steps, we zigzagged upward to the edge of a small cirque. East Hubbard, later named Mt. Kennedy, had dropped below us now and Alverstone was looking lower too. Slowly we moved onto windpacked snow on the summit ridge and finally onto the summit itself.

Such moments are exhilarating. Vast snowfields surrounded us, snowfields locking up more than half the surface water in North America. Nearby rose Mt. Logan, Mt. Saint Elias, and farther away to the southeast, Mt. Fairweather. Closer stood Mt. Vancouver, but our base camp, under a cloud cover at 8,000 feet, we could not see. There Maurice King was about to take off with Foresta and Valerie Wood on the first leg of their return to New York and Valerie's coming-out party. We were standing on the summit, enjoying the panorama, when we heard what seemed to be the roar of a plane taking off. It was obviously our plane, for no other was in the whole region. Walter turned to Peter and remarked, "There they are now. They'll be over us in five minutes to get some pictures." Walter and Peter continued talking as I looked in the direction of base camp, hoping to see a plane come through the cloud layer. It was at that moment that I heard what sounded like a distant backfire. The others, who were talking, did not hear it, and I thought it best not to discuss what I had heard.

The plane did not appear in five minutes and, since a biting wind was making us very cold, we dropped down below the summit to a more sheltered place. There too the wind began to freeze us, so we descended to our high camp. The weather again was looking dubious.

The next morning, though the weather was cloudy, it seemed likely to hold long enough for us to try Mt. Alverstone, about 500 feet lower than Mt. Hubbard, but a more difficult climb. A shattered granite rib on the east side appeared to provide a good starting point.

On either side of the fractured granite rib, hard ice, covered with a thin veneer of snow, looked very uninviting, but when we reached the end of the rib we were forced onto it. Better snow seemed to lie to the north, and we cut steps gingerly across 55-degree ice to the top of an ice mass whose bottom hung out over the great northeast face. Above this we crossed a small schrund that provided a short traverse to hard-packed snow. Each step was delicate. Gradually we angled around to the north to gain better snow. Below, as clouds moved in, we caught glimpses of the site of our high camp on the 1935 Yukon expedition. Beyond us now was the summit, topped by a great 40-foot cornice that hung out over the northwest wall. Since our reconnaissance flight had shown us this danger, we carefully belayed one another toward the edge. Then we turned our attention to weather in the southwest, for the storm was approaching fast.

Half an hour later, as we began the delicate traverse across to the top of our rock rib, a furious blast struck us. A screaming wind whipped horizontally across the snow, stung our faces, and seemed bent on knocking us from our steps. We were thankful to reach the upper part of the rib, but the surfaces had quickly glazed over and now were slick with verglas. Axe handles, parkas, mittens, and beards also iced over, so that our descent required constant care. One gust threw me clear off the rocks, but my ice axe held and I was back in a moment.

When we reached our snowshoes at the bottom of the rib, snow and sky blended in a "whiteout." In the morning we had not believed bad weather could move in so fast and had failed to place trail markers from our camp to the rib. Now our morning tracks were completely obscured by wind and snow. Unfortunately the fast-changing wind prevented using it to help our navigation. If we did not go in the correct direction we could easily fall into hidden crevasses. When we put on our snowshoes and stared into the snow and driving wind, we felt that we might not find our tent that night. Trying to play safe, we found the best shelter we could and waited. After about an hour, a slight lifting of the clouds showed us more of the slope and from then on finding our tent was easy.

That night and for the next two days it snowed. On July 31 the weather cleared, but nearly two feet of snow had fallen. Normally after a storm in a crevassed area one waits for the snow to settle to provide indications of lurking crevasses, but we were concerned about Foresta and Valerie's flight with Maury King and were anxious to get to base camp in the vague hope that a message could have been dropped there at our tents while we were high on the mountain. We started down.

I led, with Nick Clifford behind me and Walter and Peter Wood farther back, on a separate rope, taking pictures. Nick and I kept well separated because of crevasse danger, but partway down the glacier we reached what I was sure was a crevasse. I brought Nick up to give me a closer belay. Standing in snowshoes on unconsolidated snow was not the best place to be a belayer, and Nick was not a very experienced one. Too hastily I said, "It may be a big one, but I think I can jump it. Give me a good belay." Probing was impossible, for the surface powder was more than ice-axe deep. Most big crevasses in the area had been well bridged, however, and feeling well belayed, I started across.

Halfway, the snow dropped out under me, and instinctively I lunged for the far side. My axe touched nothing solid and I dropped as if someone had sprung a trap. Five feet below the surface the rope checked, and I grabbed it with both hands; then it began running free. The side walls shot by as if I were in a car speeding down a tunnel. Again a jerk—violent this time—and I could feel the rope stretch. My pack was hurled over my head to hang mainly from my right shoulder, leaving me suspended by my waist loop and hanging head down.

I was hanging free, unable to touch either wall of the crevasse, and at least 40 feet below the surface, my head pulled down by the weight of my 60-pound pack. Holding the rope in one hand but unable to get any other purchase, I struggled to get my pack back into position as I swung around. It was impossible. Reluctantly I dropped it. The pack broke through a thin screen of snow about 60 feet below me but I never heard it land. Since the crevasse was still wide where it broke through, it likely went on another 50 feet or possibly 100. The impetus given by my releasing the pack made the rope turn, and I began to go around and around like an apple on a string. I was also bobbing up and down slowly, too, as if on a yo-yo, as the rope stretched and contracted. Each year's snow had left a distinct layer in the crevasse, and I felt I must be rising and falling somewhere between the level of 1895 and 1915. One layer showed a lot of volcanic ash, perhaps from the great eruption of Katmai, which I passed several times going up and down.

Fortunately, when I had first put on the rope, I had tied in a few feet from the end, where I left a small loop to be used in case of crevasse problems. I now unwrapped this loop from my waist and placed a toe in it, losing one snowshoe in the process. That was much better, for now the toe could take much of my weight, previously shared by my waist and arms. My arms had kept some of the force of the fall from my simple waist loop and I knew I had not broken any ribs.

Almost at once I heard Walter call down, "Are you all right?" He had seen me fall and rushed forward. Clifford, carrying a big pack, had been pulled over on his face by the sudden jerk and the rope had run out, breaking two of his fingers. Walter helped him to anchor the rope, and now payed out to me another rope with a loop in the end. It curled like a vine around my belay rope, but when it eventually reached me, I put my other foot in that loop. We had not yet learned about Prusik knots, and so used the old Bilgiri method to get me out. This meant stepping from one rope onto a second rope, where the loop was held higher; then, after the first rope was raised and secured, stepping back onto it again, and so moving higher a step at a time. The first nylon laid ropes had a lot of stretch, and at my first transfer I lost a couple of feet. Since my belay rope went straight to my waist, the strain on my arms was still considerable, but I knew I would soon be out and began to look at my surroundings more closely.

It was a big crevasse. I could see several hundred yards in one direction and maybe half a mile in the other. With the exception of a few old holes in the snow bridge I had fallen through, all covered by the last storm, the crevasse seemed completely bridged. Unfortunately, I had struck one of these old holes. The light filtering from above colored everything a light blue, a

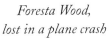

Foresta Wood,
lost in a plane crash

Walter A. Wood

lovely, ethereal color. There was no sound. I felt I should speak in hushed tones as if in a cathedral. Directly above me I could see blue sky. Slowly I was moved up to the icicles growing on the bottom of the six-foot-thick bridge. I climbed hand over hand past them and emerged into sunlight.

Since I had lost one snowshoe in the crevasse, progress to our camp below became slower, but by the middle of the afternoon old route markers led us to camp. That night Walter shared his sleeping bag and air mattress with me, and the next day we pushed on to base camp through softening snow. We found no message there.

When August 2 came, we were disturbed that we had seen no sign of the Norseman since leaving base camp, while various planes, apparently flying search patterns, were appearing. One even buzzed our camp. On August 3 we again saw search planes; and on August 4, when two more army planes appeared, we took skis, snowshoes, rope, and ration boxes, and marked out in the snow the word NORSEMAN? The lower of the two planes, a ski-wheel-equipped air rescue C-47, now swung over and dropped a note asking us to mark the temperature, wind direction, altitude, and direction of nearest crevasses. A postscript was added: *Norseman still missing.*

The next minutes until the C-47 landed down-glacier were terribly long. Immediately we loaded our gear, and after an interminable wait the plane took off, with the help of JATO (jet-assisted takeoff), for Yakutat. The pilot could tell us only that the Norseman had been missing since July

27, and that it was believed Foresta and Valerie Wood were aboard. Bob Sharp was helping to direct the search.

When our plane landed at Yakutat, we stepped almost immediately into a waiting B-17, piloted by Major Bradburn, a fine officer, who flew us back and forth over King's normal flight route from the Seward Glacier to Yakutat. We saw no trace of the missing plane. Some of our searching was done as low as 50 feet, but since four-engine bombers are not the best for such close-in search, a wire was sent to Terris Moore, asking for his help.

My old friend Terry, now president of the University of Alaska and still one of the finest bush pilots in the country, then owned the only small plane in Alaska capable of landing on skis or wheels. When Walter's telegram reached him, his plane was on floats and he was about to take off on a flight to Maine. He canceled the trip at once and the army air force agreed to speed his action by flying his ski-wheels equipment to Yakutat, where they would be attached to his Piper Super Cub on his arrival.

Despite poor weather, Terry took off, avoiding the mountains by flying down the Alsek River, but lowering clouds forced him to land on an unmapped part of the river near a small island. When the clouds lifted, he flew on to Yakutat and landed in a small irrigation pond. We were greatly relieved to see him.

Bad weather on August 5, 6, and 7 now delayed our search, but on August 8 all planes were out. Moore and I flew to the Seward base camp, from where the Norseman had taken off, and for a week we combed the areas nearby that the big air force planes could not cover so thoroughly.

Terry had some exciting flying as he searched valleys where Maury King, flying off-course in a whiteout, might have wandered. Terry had problems with his own small plane, and made two emergency landings while flying alone. The first time he thought the cause was bad gasoline. Accordingly, he drained the tank and strained all the gas through his hat. The second forced landing showed that carburetor icing was the trouble, something easily corrected. Finding the cause made him feel better, for he had been flying over areas where no forced landings were possible.

To get from base camp to Yakutat, Maury King would have had to cross Yakutat Bay after leaving the mountains, flying over water for about seven minutes. Since we found no trace of his plane in the mountains, we began to search the beaches around Yakutat Bay to discover if any debris had washed up, for we now had come to the conclusion that our friends would not be found waiting for rescue and minor repairs. Something drastic must have happened.

Terry flew the beaches as slowly as he could, sometimes only 50 feet off the ground, but we found no trace of the lost plane. Bears were common on the beaches, and as we searched at low level one even stood up and stretched a paw toward us, perhaps thinking we were a big bird and edible. On another occasion a big wolf started to chase us down a beach, also probably thinking we were a bird. I yelled, "Terry, there's a wolf chasing us!" When Terry swung the plane around to see the wolf, the roar of the turning plane terrified the animal. The last I saw of him he was headed for the deep spruces at top speed, his tail between his legs.

Two geologists had been left behind at base camp when the Norseman took off. They told us that they had heard the plane for double the normal time after it left—20 minutes by the clock—and one of the two thought he had then heard a crash. What happened we may never know. The occupants of the plane were a brave and skillful pilot and two generous, courageous women.

Terry and I finally and sadly ended our search from base camp and took off for Yakutat to avoid a coming storm. We were flying Terry's ski-wheel plane, and were using skis as we took off from base camp. On our takeoff we struck a chunk of snow-covered ice. Terry was sure something had broken. Looking down, I could see the jagged edge of something, but what had broken I couldn't tell. It seemed to be a support for the right ski. Though the sky was clouding over fast, the Yakutat Airport reported a hole in the cloud cover over Yakutat.

It would take us about 10 minutes to fly across Yakutat Bay and we were both mindful of Terry's two recent forced landings. He told me that if we were forced down into the water, the plane would probably stay afloat for only a couple of minutes. He had an air mattress in the plane, and as we started across the bay he suggested that I blow it up. "If anything happens," he remarked, "it might give us some extra minutes." I blew it up, despite the small space in the cockpit. Clouds blanketed the ocean but there was still an opening over Yakutat. We reached it and Terry dove through. I deflated the mattress as we circled low over the field. Terry was asking the airport people if they could see anything broken. Since they couldn't, Terry put down the skis as well as the wheels. As we clattered to a landing in a shower of sparks, the local fire wagon rushed down the runway with us, ready to spray foam. Our wheel supports held and there was no crash. We found that the main forward support of the right ski had snapped on takeoff, and if we had landed on snow we would have crashed.

To this day King's missing plane has not been found.

K2, showing Abruzzi Ridge

CHAPTER XVI

K2 Once More

1952-1953

CHARLIE HOUSTON AT LAST had received permission from the government of Pakistan for an expedition to K2 in 1953, and he and I eagerly began talking about who might go on it. There had been no permission to go to K2 since 1939. We decided to meet all our applicants personally, since on major expeditions the ability to get along well with other members of a climbing party is as important as the technical skills of the individual. At the American Alpine Club meeting in December 1952, Charlie presented plans for the expedition and welcomed communications from prospective team members.

After many interviews in Exeter and considerable discussion, we selected a strong team of seven men, plus our British transport officer and Pakistan liaison officer. All the Americans were experienced mountaineers, though none we selected had climbed in Asia before. Bob Craig, Pete Schoening, and Dee Molenaar came from the Seattle area. All had made big climbs in Alaska, while George Bell, a former member of the Harvard Mountaineering Club, had made major climbs in South America. Art Gilkey, a brilliant geologist studying at Columbia, had guided in the Tetons and also climbed in Alaska. All were strong, husky, and much younger than Charlie and me, then 40 and 42. The two youngest were Art Gilkey and Pete Schoening, each 27. Dee Molenaar, at 35, was the oldest of the new men. We were a mixed group of American amateurs: a doctor, a teacher, an artist, an atomic physicist, a manufacturer, a geologist, and a businessman.

As part of my original agreement with Dr. Perry when I came to Exeter, the school granted me a leave of absence from the spring term to take part in the expedition. This made me available to leave the U.S. before

Capt. Streather

Schoening

Houston

Col. Ata-Ullah

Bell

Molenaar

R.H.B.

Craig

the rest of the team to tie up expedition loose ends in Europe and arrive in Pakistan in time to get supplies through customs and on to Rawalpindi before the others arrived.

On May 5, after a delicious dinner and send-off, I took the State of Maine sleeping car to New York, and in the evening boarded a flight to London. There I had a day and a half to make arrangements with Rob Lawrie about boots and to visit the Alpine Club. The next day it was on to Paris, where my hotel room at the France et Choiseul cost 1,000 francs, about $3. At Pierre Allain's store I bought crampons and an ice axe, and the following day flew on to Geneva, where the Swiss climber René Dittert and his fiancée gave me a great send-off for my Swissair flight to Cairo. Airline schedule changes kept me in Cairo for a couple of extra days, giving me time to see the Pyramids and the Sphinx and to visit the National Museum, where I had the Tutankhamen collection all to myself. Then, on the first day of Ramadan, Qantas flew me to Karachi. This time there was no sweltering trip through the Red Sea.

In Karachi I went to the Metropole Hotel, where stupidly I drank from a fresh carafe of water in the hotel room, and later had stomach problems. Karachi, like Cairo, was very hot, well over 100 degrees Fahrenheit, but more humid. Ambassador Hildreth was away and John Emerson, the chargé d'affaires, was not much help, but Bill Crockett, the administrative officer, was just the opposite. With his aid we found good rope and bought three rolls of 720 feet each for two annas a foot.

I also made arrangements for a customs man to help clear our gear when the *City of Carlisle* arrived via England. There was a shortage of grain in Pakistan and the movement of flour was restricted. We needed permits to take flour to Kashmir, ship film from Pakistan, and use our walkie-talkies and radio. These were eventually arranged. Finally, when the *City of Carlisle* arrived with our supplies from New York, a problem developed at customs, because the bill of lading showed 63 boxes, and the list Charlie had typed for me showed only 60. It took considerable diplomacy to get the chief appraiser, an honest old Scot, to pass all the boxes.

Major Goodwin of the Himalayan Club took me to a polo game, where I met Mr. Mueneddin, the director of health, and Vice-Marshal Cannon, chief of the Pakistan Air Force. When I talked to the latter about an airdrop on K2, he was very interested. He said fighter planes could do it using wing tanks to carry loads. Mueneddin, who had been head of the Gilgit Agency and was a friend of Ata-Ullah, our transport officer, phoned the secretary of defense and the foreign minister on my behalf. Meanwhile,

I found that our bags of flour, sent from the U.S., had reached the Karachi railroad station, but the bags had been badly torn by the hooks used by dock workers. All torn bags had to be resewed. This was done and I saw them loaded.

The next morning I was summoned to meet the foreign secretary, Akhtar Hussain, who was only about 30 but very impressive. We talked frankly, and at one point he pulled down a big map and asked me where I thought the boundaries were between Pakistan and China. Three lines were drawn across the map from east to west. I picked the northernmost line, the one showing K2 as being on the boundary between the two countries. "That's just what we think," said the foreign secretary, "but we don't know what's going on in those parts. Chinese may be there in the area north of Skardu. If you meet Chinese, you must promise me you will return right away. We are having lots of trouble with India now and we don't want trouble with China too." He said there were too many border problems to think of having airdrops. That I knew would disappoint Vice-Marshal Cannon, as it did me, but we left with a good understanding.

Karachi was full of excitement at the arrival of Secretary of State Dulles, former Governor Stassen, and a staff of experts, and to my surprise I received a large, gilt-edged invitation to attend a garden party for them at the American embassy. It was to be the biggest social event in years, and all ambassadors and government dignitaries would be there. Bill Crockett insisted I come, even though I had no formal clothes, and no dark shoes. He produced an old dinner jacket of his own that was several sizes too large for me and declared it would fit perfectly.

"Keep your trousers high and your elbows bent," he said, "You'll have a drink in one hand anyway, and you'll be shaking hands with the other. It will be getting dark soon after you arrive and nobody will notice."

With various misgivings, I accepted. The party was scheduled to last from 6:45 to 8:15. I arrived shortly after 7:00 and was warmly welcomed by the Hildreths, who headed the receiving line for Secretary Dulles and Governor Stassen. I asked the secretary about young Allen Dulles, whom I had known at Exeter, and who recently had been in a severe auto accident. Stassen knew Bill Saltonstall (the Exeter principal) well, and I had a friendly conversation with him too. I then began to mingle with the throng in the garden, where Bill Crockett soon found me and introduced me to the Japanese ambassador, and to Mr. Byroade and Douglas MacArthur, two members of the Dulles party. Just then the top security officer tapped me on the arm and announced, "The secretary of state would like to see you."

He took me to a brightly lighted, air-conditioned room, where Dulles, Stassen, and Hildreth were sitting with their jackets off drinking whiskey highballs and relaxing for half an hour before their plane departed. The bright light, of course, exposed my borrowed clothes, and my opening remark was, "Mr. Ambassador, I wish your administrative officer didn't have such long arms." Then I extended my sleeves. They all roared with laughter, and I felt at once completely at ease. Secretary Dulles remarked how nice it was to be among friends again for he had just come from India, where I gathered things had not gone well. He then inquired why we were going to K2 and not Everest, and asked lots of questions about our expedition.

Perhaps it was the whiskey, but I felt I was talking well and was certainly having a good time. They kept me there answering questions and chatting until their plane was called. Mr. Dulles was especially friendly and said I should be working for his brother. He said also that we shouldn't try to bring in an American plane, because it could spark an incident that would cause a lot of trouble, especially for him. When we separated as friends, the ambassador asked me to lunch the following noon.

On May 27, to my great delight, the plane with all members of the expedition came in. Then, after a round of movies and reporters' questions, we were spirited off to the embassy and air-conditioned rooms. The latter meant a lot to me, for the wet heat was very debilitating. In the afternoon the Crocketts gave a garden party for us with Japanese lanterns. It was all very festive. The foreign secretary and all the important Americans were there, as well as several Pakistani generals. Though it was an exhilarating party, all of us were exhausted by the time we got to bed at midnight.

We were up before four for our flight to Rawalpindi. What a pleasure to fly over the torrid Sind Desert, where local people claim the Hinges of Hell were forged. At Rawalpindi, Captain Tony Streather, our British transport officer, and Colonel Ata-Ullah, our Pakistan liaison officer, met us. Tony was young, keen, and energetic, while the goateed colonel was short, middle-aged, a bit portly, but very intelligent and quick to give commands. We learned that Ata, as we called him, was chief of Pakistan's medical services and a very devout Muslim.

Our welcome in Rawalpindi equaled the one in Karachi. We ate at Ata's house and stayed there or at the house of a general across the street. In the next days we met the chief-of-staff, General Sha Hamid, the adjutant general, and the major general in charge of ordnance. We had teas, lunches, and a grand dinner at Colonel Ata-Ullah's, where we met the political head of Azad (Free) Kashmir and other generals and dignitaries of Rawalpindi.

SWIEZYNSKI

R.H.B. and Charles Houston packing loads in Exeter, New Hampshire,
for shipment to Karachi, Pakistan

The next day the last of the boxes I had seen sent by rail from Karachi
arrived. The Sind Desert had melted everything possible, and the boxes
looked as if they had been dropped a dozen times from heights of 15 feet or
more. We repacked everything into the splendid aluminum yakdans that
Bob Dodson had had made for us by the Indian Aluminum Company. It
was all very tiring work, but Ramzan tea with the delightful Sha Hamids
revived us. Ramzan tea began at sunset when the daily fast was over. It consisted of lovely meat and pilau dishes, and ended with custards and coffee.

The next morning, leaving Charlie, Pete, and Ata to come later, we
took off for Skardu at the same time another plane was taking off for
Gilgit. The two pilots were Poles who had been fighter pilots in World
War II. They were real daredevils, who began to fly their DC-3s wing-to-
wing as if they were fighter planes, until bumpy air almost threw the two
planes together. At that they separated and the Gilgit plane began skim-
ming the cliffs and passes. Clouds blotted out Nanga Parbat, but we flew
under them, so low in fact that we seemed to ruffle the hair on the backs of
cows in a mountain pasture. When we swooped into Skardu, Tony and four

jeeps were awaiting us. We had flown in an hour and a half a distance that had required two weeks of hard walking in 1938.

A great crowd was waiting. The political agent and Major Khan drove us to town 11 miles away. En route, green banners with white lettering proclaimed Welcome; Zindabad America (Long live America); Settle the Kashmir Problem or Let Us Fight. As we stepped out of the jeep in Skardu, the rajah of Skardu and the rajah of Shigar put garlands of roses around our necks. Then we drove to the maharajah's summer resthouse, where we were to stay. Here we met 12 husky Hunza wallahs, our high-altitude porters, who already had walked for two weeks to reach Skardu. All looked tough and ready for action. (For political reasons, the more experienced Sherpas in Darjeeling were not available.) That evening, after a good pilau, officers told us how two men had captured the Skardu fort from the Indians by climbing above it and dominating it by rifle fire. The recent Kashmir war and the future of Kashmir were subjects that entered every conversation.

Skardu had grown from about 2,000 people to more than 7,000 during our absence. Jeeps and electricity had brought about major changes. When the first jeep and driver came to Skardu, we were told, welcoming Baltis brought eggs for the driver and hay for the jeep. The driver was a rascal, who nodded at the jeep and said, "It doesn't eat hay; bring more eggs," and they did!

On June 5, hundreds of people escorted us to the banks of the Indus, where "Alexander's barge" was waiting. On it we crossed, and then began our 125-mile march to base camp, a climb of more than 9,000 feet. It was far shorter than our trek from Srinagar in 1938, but long enough. In Shigar as in Skardu, people assumed that we could help them retrieve Kashmir from India's control. Our 16-mile trek beyond Shigar ended at Kochumal, a filthy village where strong wind blew so much dirt into everything that Charlie issued Aureomycin to all hands.

In 1938 we had stayed on the Kochumal side of the Braldu River practically to Askole, but our porters told us that route was now considered too dangerous and we should cross the river by zhak. A big raft, with 30 goat bladders supporting thin poplar boughs, finally appeared. The crossing looked dangerous and we shuddered at the thought of losing precious items. There wasn't much we could do about that, but we did distribute the contents of the money box to prevent a total loss of funds if a zhak overturned. Some of our porters would not go beyond Kochumal, and so I boarded the zhak with the police to make the first crossing and try to line up porters on the other side.

Houston crossing rope bridge

That first crossing was exciting. Many prayers were chanted as we pushed off. Waves made by big haystacks in the river swept the zhak through one set of rapids that the boatmen had not expected, but we got across.

The crossings took a very long time, even though Charlie cut the distance to be rafted by escorting all porters through waist-deep water to a big sandbar in the river. After each crossing, the raft had to be carried half a mile upriver. The boatmen worked hard, but 80 loads were still on the Kochumal side when at 6:00 the boatmen quit for the day. Unfortunately our bandobast (arrangement) had grown. We had Dr. Aslam, a physician, with 20 porters loaded with medical supplies for Askole; our worthless contractor with four helpers; and a group of four policemen and three soldiers, with four or five porters helping them.

The contractor, we found, had been paying the coolies only half what we had promised them, keeping the rest for himself. In the morning, when we sacked him, the porters cheered. After traversing small trails and crossing gravel slides that dropped off to the roaring Braldu, we reached our first rope bridge, about 300 feet long, which spanned a gorge. The cables dropped steeply at each end and hung low in the middle. Some porters would not carry loads over this swinging bridge with its danger of turning over, and the dismissed contractor, who was going on to Askole on his own, paid to be carried across, praying loudly, eyes closed, his face twisted with fear.

A mile farther, there was a second bridge, more dilapidated than the first. A Balti with a flower stuck in one nostril led the way. After we had crossed and were on our way to Chongo, we learned that the bridge had rolled over with a porter on it. He hung on, the cable was pulled back to its original position, and he was rescued.

The next day was one we had been looking forward to, for we reached a hot spring. There we had a glorious wash, both of ourselves and our clothes. The pool was about 15 feet in diameter and three feet deep, with a soft, springy bottom that a scientific member of the party examined. He declared that it consisted of six inches of compacted pubic hair.

Later we reached the fields and baked mud houses of Askole, the last village we would see. There we met porters Charlie and I remembered, and spent a fine afternoon taping and filming singing and dancing as different groups performed. Afterward we played the tapes for them, to their utter astonishment. The Askole people were living much as they must have lived for a thousand years. About three-quarters of them had goiter, which the use of iodized salt could have prevented.

We had sent ahead to Askole 2,700 pounds of atta (wheat flour). This we began to weigh into porter loads for their use during the trek to base camp and return. At first we couldn't get enough goatskins for the flour, and we weren't finished by dark when we stopped to eat by candlelight.

Refreshed by a half day of rest in Askole, we pushed on the next day to the great boulder at Korophon. Here a furious dust storm blanketed our camp, swooping up two air mattresses and dumping them a hundred yards away in an offshoot of the Braldu, where fortunately the Hunzas rushed down and rescued them. We dropped our tents during the blow and lay on them until the vicious wind was over. Our team had become an army of about 170 men, with nearly a quarter of them carrying food for the rest. When we reached the Punmah River with its rope bridge (our last), a quarter of the men would not carry a load across, forcing the more courageous ones to make multiple crossings. Once across, the porters announced that they would go no farther that day, but thanks to Tony, they were persuaded to push on to Bardumal, where we camped just before a soaking rain set in. Three of us got very wet trying to cover up atta and biscuits.

Capt. Streather looks for routes on Masherbrum (K1).

A bright sun cheered everyone the following morning, the last day of Ramadan. That afternoon we camped in a nullah (gully) near Paiju and issued candy and cigarettes all around. We had avoided a nasty climb across a cliff by using a route at the water's edge, and this brought us to camp early. The porters needed time here to find wood and bake enough bread for the next seven days (five to base camp and two back). En route we had seen a herd of ibex, lots of bear tracks, and even snow leopard tracks. Since the black, ugly snout of the Baltoro Glacier was now ahead of us, we issued cold-weather clothing to the Hunzas. We learned then that they were scared to wear red, because apparently it is a color that the guardian spirits like.

When we eliminated 22 porters next morning, we still had 147. Before these men started up over the slippery black ice and sliding rocks of the Baltoro, they paused to chant a melodious and impressive prayer. That night we camped in the moat of the glacier on a sandy beach called Liligo. Charlie and I had been looking forward to reaching Urdukas, a green hill-side at about 13,400 feet, and the next day we were there. Here, among giant boulders and clumps of purple saxifrage, we found tent platforms built for the expeditions of the Duke of the Abruzzi and the Duke of

The Abruzzi Ridge

Spoleto. Caves provided good shelter for the porters. From this belvedere above the glacier we could study the spectacular peaks lining the north side of the Baltoro, including Paiju, one of the most beautiful snow and rock peaks in the world.

At Urdukas we checked all loads carefully and discovered that Tony's boots and four pairs of high-altitude boots had been stolen. Sacks had been opened and then sewn up. This big loss had probably occurred when the night loads were left under guard on the Kochumal side of the Braldu.

Before our departure all the porters again prayed. No prayers in a cathedral could have been more moving. Magnificent peaks surrounded us, bracing mountain air bore the scent of flowers, and the porters' faces as they prayed showed deep emotion. That night and the next we spent on the glacier, with Masherbrum's great north face on one side of us and Broad Peak and the giant Gasherbrum peaks ahead.

Finally, on June 19, Charlie and I made an early start from our camp two miles below Concordia and continued up the Godwin-Austen Glacier to find a good place for base camp. Both of us were puffing hard by the time we reached the area of our 1938 camp at about 16,400 feet. The glaci-

Camp I on the glacier

er had changed but we soon located a satisfactory site nearby. Since we were short of money to pay porters, it was important that they reach base camp that same day, and with lots of encouragement they succeeded. The 2,500-foot climb from the last camp was a severe test of their stamina, and they looked happy when we put up our two largest tents for them.

At first light each man turned in the metal tag given him on his "enlistment" and was paid largely in paper money, a currency previously unknown to most of them. When three days later our last supplies from Askole arrived, we all turned out our pockets and managed to pay the porters who brought them, but with only four annas left over—less than two cents. More money had been requested from Skardu but had not yet arrived.

On the morning after our arrival, I was once more standing at the base of K2 looking up nearly 12,000 feet to a hanging glacier just below the summit. The broad faces of the mountain are either ice slopes or a maze of ice and rock gullies, cliffs, and gendarmes, much of it swept by avalanches, with ribs of rock rising toward the snow plateau that begins at about 25,000 feet. In 1938 we had reached it by climbing a prominent rock rib, which we named the Abruzzi Ridge. Our reconnaissance had convinced us that this

George Bell and others climbing above Camp II

rib gives the best access to the upper part of the mountain. The same route had been selected also by Fritz Wiessner, who a year later led the tragic American expedition that so nearly achieved the first ascent of K2. We were to find evidence of their efforts higher up, but now we must begin the tedious work of developing a supply line that eventually, we hoped, would take us to the summit. Our 1953 team was larger and more experienced than our expedition 15 years earlier. It was with confidence that we began our attack.

While the others developed the base camp and sorted supplies, Art Gilkey and I made an eight-hour reconnaissance up the Godwin-Austen Glacier to establish a route to Camp I. We hoped to find a shorter route than the one we had used in 1938, but crevasses and seracs frustrated us. Charlie and I were even more frustrated a few days later when after an early start we set out to find the route to Camp II, but became lost in an area of loose and exposed rock, cliffs, and gullies. The next day Charlie found it, together with a well-wrapped Logan tent and cans of jam, Ovaltine, and pemmican.

Camp II sat on a pocket of snow at 19,300 feet, with steep slopes on either side. Above it a ridge led to exposed rock regions, where in 1938 we

Lower part of the Abruzzi Ridge and Camp III

had received much stonefall. By July 8 we had packed 1500 to 1600 pounds of food and gear to Camp II, and found a slightly safer place for Camp III, about 200 feet below our former tent platforms. The Hunzas, who loved working with rocks, were a great help in building the new tent platforms on this steep slope. One was nearly 10 feet high on the downhill side and five feet wide, large enough easily to hold a two-man tent. The other was smaller and more exposed.

I had an abscessed tooth that was bothering me so much that Charlie gave me codeine and radioed to base camp to bring up a dental forceps to Camp II. While I stayed in Camp III, Charlie, George Bell and Dee Molenaar moved up to our old Camp IV, with George leading up the big gendarme we once called Petzoldt's Overhang. At Camp IV there was more evidence of the Wiessner party, a small treasure trove of cooking pots, Thermos flasks, and tins of jam, pemmican, and Ovaltine, all in good condition. The tents there were in shreds, but inside were three sleeping bags, all frozen and filled with ice. These bags we dried, and made good use of them later.

Above rose the House Chimney, the crux of the Abruzzi Ridge climb. Charlie led it neatly, and all three then moved up over 300 feet of exposed

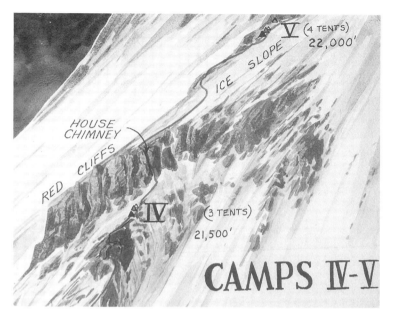

The House Chimney and Camps IV and V   *Camp VI and the black buttress*

slabs to our old Camp V (22,000 feet). Here they found trash and three more tent platforms.

Meanwhile, missing the fun, I had gone down to Camp II with Bob Craig. There, on July 10, Charlie pulled his first and only tooth, watched closely by Mohammed Ali, a Hunza porter whose companions regarded him as a wizard tooth puller. Charlie gave me Novocain and then did the job neatly and skillfully. It is probably still the highest extraction ever performed.

That evening a foot of heavy snow fell. Then two good days helped us, but on the night of July 13, a blizzard started that thumped the tents throughout the next two days. It was a nasty, 60-hour storm, with snow that threatened to push Charlie and Tony from their narrow tent platform at Camp III. Fortunately we had sent the Hunzas back to base camp before the storm began, for we felt that above Camp III they would be more trouble than help. They were not experienced climbers and would need food and more tent platforms if they stayed with us. Since stormy weather was coming at the time we had expected the best weather of the summer, we knew we must not lose a day of good weather.

After the storm Bob and I packed loads through deep snow from Camp II to III, and on our return saw ahead of us a huge chough (a sort of crow with a wingspan of three to four feet) attacking Bob's air mattress, which he had left outside the tent to dry. Each time the bird pecked the mattress, the rubber bounced back, enraging the bird, which screeched angrily at it, pecking it again and again. Before we were close enough to scare him away, the bird had won the battle, leaving the deflated mattress with seven big holes in it. Bob applied patches, but they didn't stay on well and the mattress was never the same again.

On July 17 we were again moving ahead, using a six-foot aluminum A-frame with pulley, designed by Pete Schoening, to pull loads to the top of the House Chimney, but the good weather did not last. Three days later, Pete, Dee, and I climbed to Camp 6 (23,300 feet), where we found two small platforms and the remains of two tents. In them, neatly arranged, were three packs, a stove, petrol, and three sleeping bags, with a handkerchief of tea in an empty stove box. This was the camp that three gallant Sherpas (Pasang Kikuli, Phinsoo, and Kitar) had left in 1939 in their desperate attempt to rescue the ailing Dudley Wolfe from a tent about 1,500 feet higher. They were never seen again. What happened to these gallant men, our dear companions in 1938, or to Dudley Wolfe, we will never know.*

We now began packing to Camp VI, with its platforms perched on an exposed section of the rock ridge only slightly less steep than the slopes above and below. Though the weather had definitely changed for the worse, on July 21 and 22 we brought up supplies. Above us the route led to the top of the Black Pyramid, the highest part of the Abruzzi Ridge. Storms during the next two days tried to push us off the mountain, and on July 25 it was so cold and windy that noses and toes were nipped. The next day, Bell, Craig, and Houston moved to Camp VI. Though some packing was accomplished thereafter, that was our last good day!

On July 27 the same three reconnoitered higher, to a point near our old Camp VII, while the rest of us packed to Camp VI. Once Bell was leading when a big rock rolled under his foot and he fell. A quick self-arrest saved him. It was a very cold day and Charlie nipped his toes. Despite our Mickey Mouse boots (insulated) and warm mittens, we were all on the edge of frostbite.

Storms on July 28 and 29 kept us in our tents, but the next day we all packed Gilkey and Schoening to what we called Camp VII cache, a small trough cut into the ice, a bad place for avalanches, but we found nothing

*In August 1993 some remains, probably of Dudley Wolfe and a porter, were found on the Godwin-Austen Glacier.

better. It was Pete's birthday. We had hoped to find a good tent site for these two, but since we found nothing better they stayed there. Five of us were descending a gully when a big rock roared down from above and exploded between Tony and me, sending fragments around us all. A much smaller rock did hit Tony hard.

The next day the weather was still bad, but in a great effort Gilkey and Schoening cut steps 500 feet higher, up a steep ice slope to the edge of the snow plateau. Here they found a reasonably flat surface, the best campsite since Camp II. That day nobody climbed up from Camp VI. Wind threatened to sweep off the mountain anyone on the slabs above. The weather had been so continuously bad that we were all getting worried about the number of days left before we must return to base camp.

August 1 dawned much like the day before. The clouds were higher, but there were also what seemed to me unmistakable signs that a big storm was coming. I told Charlie I thought the weather was too threatening to move. He agreed that it looked bad, but said he wanted to establish a team at Camp VIII. Accordingly, he, Craig, Bell, and Molenaar packed their sleeping bags, a tent, and some other necessities and left Camp VI. Streather and I remained in reserve. Light snow fell all day but there was no blizzard. That evening the others reported by walkie-talkie that they had all arrived after a hard day.

At daylight the next day the weather was just as threatening. Tony and I realized, however, that if we didn't move to Camp VIII now, we probably would lose any chance to reach the summit. We radioed the others, who said that bad weather and poor visibility were holding them in camp. When we told them we were coming up, they said they would come down to the Camp VII cache, where some loads had been left, and hope to meet us there.

Tony and I put on our warmest clothes, tied the tents securely, and began to climb. Snow flew in our faces as we moved up over steep, polished slabs with patches of ice and only small holds for hands and feet. Gusts threatened to push us off the ridge. It was a long, slow, 2,000-foot climb, with no ledges where one could take off his pack and have a bite to eat. We were two-thirds of the way to Camp VII when over the howl of the wind we heard shouts from above. The only word we could distinguish was "back." Whether it meant that the others were leaving the cache to go back to Camp VIII or telling us to go back we couldn't tell, but we had no desire to turn back.

We climbed on steadily, never stopping to eat because of the frigid wind. When we reached the cache, Tony pulled his bivouac sack from his parka and we wrapped it around us as we chewed date bars, chocolate, and

Camp VIII, with the tent smashed by the storm in the right foreground

biscuits. In some ways we had had good climbing, too cold to be fun but very exhilarating. We were now at 25,000 feet or thereabouts, it was mid-afternoon, and we did not know how much farther it was to Camp VIII.

A line of steps cut in hard green ice led steeply upward, partly covered by blowing snow. If we lost the route now, we would be in serious trouble, and so at the cache we lightened our loads before heading upward. We had not gone far, and I was wondering how much longer I could find the steps, when trail markers began to appear. Charlie had put them in. These were a godsend, for the snow now was sometimes knee-deep. We had to reach camp before dark, and thanks to the markers we did, after 10 and one-half hours on the ascent. What a great welcome the others gave us! They quickly pitched a two-man tent and brought us tea. The team was together again.

Camp VIII consisted of four tents, pitched near the edge of the great precipice that drops off thousands of feet toward the east. Above us rose the moderate snow slope that rises to the summit rock pyramid with its dangerous hanging glacier. We were all in good condition and probably within two days of the summit. We had 12 days of food, but *we must have good weather to reach the top.*

That evening the wind began to blow much harder, so hard that our tent started to lift off, and Tony and I both moved to the windward end of the tent, to try to hold it down. During a short lull, Tony used both of our ice axes to pin the tent to the slope. All night the storm blew, and it continued the next morning, straining the tent so badly that we feared the seams would rip. Snow sifted through ventilators and eyelets despite our efforts to close everything. The only communication with the other tents consisted of barely distinguishable shouts. No stove could be kept lighted because of wind currents within the straining tent.

We were thirsty, but trying to melt snow in our mouths made us so cold that we gave it up. I tried to melt snow in an empty tin by friction, beating it with a spoon, but it wouldn't melt. If we crawled outside the tent, we could breathe only by holding a mitten in front of the face to deflect the icy spicules hurled by the wind.

In the afternoon, during a short lull, we held a secret ballot to decide who should be the first two to make a summit try. Bell and Craig were the first choice, Gilkey and Schoening the second. Our plan was to establish the first two at our final camp on the next clear day—one day from the top! But the lull did not last.

That night again the furious wind pounded the tents. Seams in the tent Charlie and George Bell were in began to rip apart. All night they watched

Avalanche off Broad Peak. Such big slides sometimes crossed the Godwin–Austen Glacier to reach the base of K2.

as the tent began to disintegrate, hoping it would give some shelter until daybreak. At first light a very cold Charlie crawled in with Tony and me in our French tent we had thought too small for two. Big George went with Gilkey and Schoening. Our tent had an inside lining, and we three fitted so tightly that one man pushed against the fabric on each side, while the third lay uncomfortably sandwiched in the middle. Tony remarked that it was as if three men were living under a small cot. If one moved, all must move.

Day after day the storm continued. No stove would stay lighted, and without water our throats became parched. Gnawing at frozen meat bars chilled us and increased our concerns for our fingers and toes. As we lay in our sleeping bags, we continually flexed them to keep them from freezing. Hour after hour the wind continued to buffet the tents with no letup.

On August 6 Charlie was able to make a round of the tents and came back to tell us that George had two frostbitten toes and Bob had similar spots on his heels. The cruel wind continued, but the next day it dropped a little and we all crawled out. Art Gilkey emerged too, but when he tried to stand

Art Gilkey

he fell unconscious. When he came to, he told us that for a couple of days he had had a charley horse, a pulled muscle. Houston's examination, however, showed thrombophlebitis, a blood clot that was cutting circulation in his left leg. Art had been the most optimistic about getting all eight of us to the top, but this discovery changed everything. After brief, whispered discussions, we all decided to try to take Art down. There seemed almost no chance his condition could improve at Camp VIII.

We wrapped Art in his sleeping bag in the smashed tent, with ropes to pull him or slide him down the slope we had come up. Dropping the other tents, we took a little food with us and our sleeping bags, and began wading down through knee-deep snow, pulling Art. We had gone 200 feet when we realized that the whole slope was ready to avalanche. Tons of powder snow lay over the icy slopes with no bond. With great difficulty and a superb effort on Art's part, we worked our way back to Camp VIII. We couldn't pull Art through the snow, but he stood up on one leg, rested his weight on the shoulders of two men, and hopped back up the slope. The effort was exhausting for everyone.

We had avoided one death trap, but was there any other way down? To survive we had to find one. At this point Bob Craig and Pete Schoening remembered something and began to reconnoiter a rock ridge they had noted to the side of our route to Camp VIII. A couple of hours later they were back. They had descended to a rock rim and followed it down about 400 feet to an abrupt cliff, where a possible route could lead across to our Camp VII Cache, avoiding the avalanche slope. Their news electrified us despite the fact that the storm was again beginning to return with increased violence.

In the morning the weather was better and Art seemed better too, though it was very cold. We melted snow for tea and decided to wait a day, hoping Art's condition would improve. Clouds surrounded us and we couldn't see far, but since the wind had dropped, some of us climbed above camp. The slope was not steep. Schoening and Craig went up three or four hundred feet.

Radio contact with Colonel Ata-Ullah at base camp that evening gave no forecast of a break in the storm. "You are fighting now for all your lives," Ata said. "We here in base camp have been praying for you for many days."

The next morning it would have been suicide to try to descend. During the long day Charlie moved in with Art, and Pete Schoening joined Tony and me. Art was beginning to cough. Blood clots were entering his lungs. In the morning of August 10 Charlie came to our tent and shouted over the noise of the storm, "We've got to take him down . . . He'll soon be dead if we don't get him down."

The crisis we had dreaded had arrived. With Art in his sleeping bag, we wrapped him in the remains of the wrecked tent, tied a cradle of ropes around him, and using tow ropes began to pull him through drifts toward the slope above the rock rib. In all our minds was the memory of the fatal descent in storm of the Nanga Parbat climbers in 1934, but we concentrated entirely on the work at hand. When we asked Art how he felt, he would smile and say, "Just fine. Just fine."

Quickly the slope steepened and we all had to hold hard as gravity began to pull Art down. At first Craig and Bell were on the front ropes, with Houston, Streather, Bell, and me on the back ones. Schoening and Molenaar were scouting ahead. The new descent route was not a way we would have gone if we had had a better choice, but it was our only hope. This time there was no turning back.

Quickly our goggles froze over and our beards and moustaches began to grow icicles. We managed to tie two 120-foot ropes together and lowered Art down the steepest part of what was becoming a gully. Blowing snow kept those of us holding the upper ropes from seeing what was happening below.

Suddenly Streather shouted, "They're being carried down by an avalanche." We felt a giant downward pull on our ropes that threatened to pull us off. Then the pressure stopped and from what seemed a long way below, Streather shouted, "They're still there." The rope had started a powder-snow avalanche that roared over Craig and Art. Craig was not belayed and held on for his life as the rope stretched. The avalanche swept on, dropping thousands of feet more, leaving us all alive but shaken.

It seemed forever before we heard again from Streather that Art was belayed "on the edge of a cliff." At that we took turns in climbing down stiffly over crumbling rocks and ice until we reached the top of a small cliff, below which Art had been lowered by Schoening. Charlie and I were tied together on one rope; Bell and Streather on another. We were nearly frozen now, with numb fingers and toes, all on the edge of exhaustion. Schoening stood on a ledge belaying Art, his ice axe driven into snow behind a large, rounded boulder. Off to Art's left as we looked down was the narrow ledge that we called Camp VII cache. Below Art the ice gully descended steeply for two or three hundred feet, and then apparently dropped off into empty space.

Bob Craig, badly shaken by his close call with the avalanche, unroped and climbed over to the cache. The ice was hard, and Charlie and I were looking for a place to get our axes in for a safe belay so we could begin to slide Art horizontally toward the cache. Molenaar, who was below us, had tied in to a rope to Art, and Bell and Streather were still descending when what we feared happened.

Bell, whose toes were frozen before we started, slipped, pulling off Streather. At that moment something made me look up. A blurred figure above me, still on his feet, was desperately trying to stop, but he was sliding fast right into the rope between Charlie and me. I turned and slammed the pick of my axe as hard as I could into the slope above, but in a moment it was ripped from my hands as I was flung headfirst backward down the gully.

I knew that nothing could stop me now from the big fall, thousands of feet to the glacier below, but after two bounces suddenly I stopped. My feet were uphill, my hood jammed over my eyes, and a rope was wound round my hands. I seemed to be lying against an unstable rock that moved. I heard a groan from nearly on top of me and called, "Get me loose!"

The rope was pulled off my hands; I grabbed a rock and lifted my hood. I was half on top of Molenaar, both of us roped to something up the slope that kept the rope taut. Someone above us was yelling, "Get your weight off the rope." Above me I could vaguely see through the blowing snow someone struggling to get out of a tangle of rope. Just then I heard someone below me call out, "My hands are freezing." It was George Bell, who a moment before had been above me, but now was below and coming up over the edge of nothingness. He had lost his hat and pack, and was staggering up with his freezing hands held in front of him. His mittens had been swept off in the fall.

I stood up, releasing pressure on the rope, took off my pack, and thrust it in Molenaar's arms, saying, "Hold this." The walkie-talkie radio was gone from the top of my pack and my sleeping bag was half out, held by a single twist of line. I unroped and began to climb down to George. Fortunately I had a spare pair of wool mittens in my parka, and helped

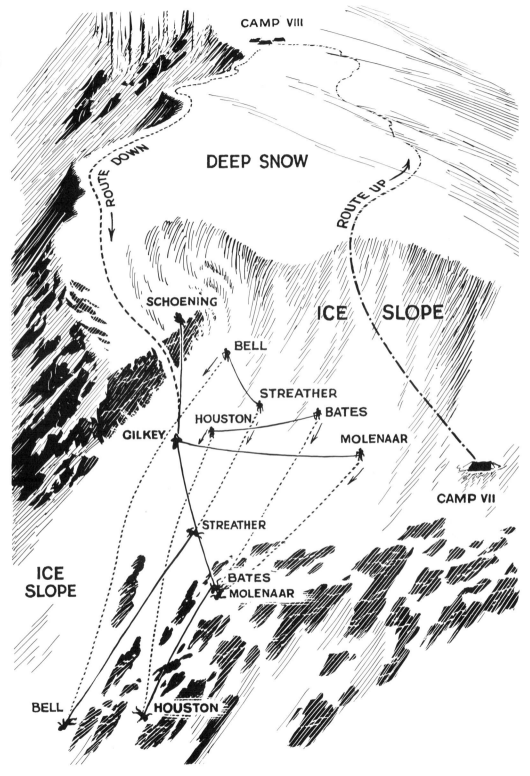

The big fall

George to put them on. George's fall had stopped just over the edge of the precipice.

On a narrow ledge below and to the side lay a crumpled figure. I climbed down and found it was Charlie. He also was held by a tangle of rope from above. I touched his shoulder. To my unspeakable relief he stood up. His eyes did not seem to focus as he repeated, "Where are we? What are we doing here?"

We would be too cold to move soon if we didn't get shelter from the wind. I shouted, "Charlie, if you ever want to see Dorcas and Penny again (his family), you climb up there right now!" That scared him. He turned and, well belayed, climbed quickly up to his belayers.

Without trying to sort out what happened, we set to work with our axes to hack out a space where we could pitch a tent. Fortunately the tent we carried had not been in one of the lost packs. It was our smallest two-man tent, but even so when Craig anchored it to an ice piton, the lower third hung off into space, where it was lashed by the wind. Craig had already driven in an ice axe up to the head to anchor Art. Until then Schoening was unable to relax his belay, which had saved five of us. Streather drove in another axe, and then with one tent up and the injured inside it, we began to chop out another platform to set up Pete's tiny bivouac tent. We were so exhausted that it seemed impossible to carve a platform wide enough for even that tent, which luckily had been cached on the ledge as a safeguard for Tony and me when we made the long climb to Camp VIII on August 2. When it was finally anchored with rocks and pitons, it still overhung in an alarming manner.

During our work on the tents, we were about 100 yards from Art, but because of a narrow ridge of rock that formed the side of the shallow gully where he hung suspended, we could not see him. We called to him two or three times while we were working but could not tell whether he could hear us over the roar of the storm. Craig, Streather, and I now roped up, crossed carefully over the low rock ridge, and looked across the gully where we had had the fall. We wanted to tell Art that we were all right, with tents up, and that we would be working out the best way to move him to the tents. What a shock! Staring into the wind, I thought my eyes were deceiving me. The whole slope was bare, with no sign that anyone had ever been there. Art and the embedded ice axes that held him were gone.

Craig and Streather joined me and moved out onto the slope. It was completely bare. My first thought was, "He did it to save us." Then I realized that Art could not have done it. There was no possible way he could reach the axes, let alone pull them out. No, a strong avalanche had swept him off the mountain. A few minutes before, while hacking out a place for the tent, I had thought I heard a hail from Art, and yelled that we would come for him as soon as we could. That may have been when the avalanche struck, though I never heard it over the noise of the storm.

We were numbed by what happened. Art was gone. It didn't seem possible that he had been swept away without a trace from the "escape route," where we had all been for the past several hours. We shouted, but the only answer came from the wind.

As we turned back to the tents, we were silent. We loved Art. He was one of us, and we had become a well-knit team—all for one and one for all. Now he was gone, and it was obvious that we had the fight of our lives ahead to get ourselves down, including the injured, the extent of whose hurts was not yet clear.

I crawled into the bivouac tent, but Schoening asked me to go to the slightly larger Gerry tent, where Houston was in a state of shock. I wrapped the inner part of my sleeping bag around him and put the outer under the feet of the four of us, who were crammed into the little tent with our backs to the ice ledge and our feet resting against the part of the tent that was hanging over space. We kept telling one another not to put weight on our feet. Fortunately the wind was dropping. We began to assess injuries and try to figure out how the miracle happened that had saved us all.

George Bell, whose hands and feet were in bad shape, was jammed into one end of the tent. He had lost his glasses in the fall and also the spare pair that was in his pack. Dee Molenaar had a cut in his left thigh that was stiffening, and also a painful rib. He lay in the tent doorway and insisted on using his down jacket to warm Charlie, who sat between Bell and me, with my arm around him. At first Charlie was in shock, but after his shivering stopped, he began to ask questions. "Where's Pete?" "How is Art?" He would ask again and again, and we would call on the men in the bivouac tent to tell him they were all right. Charlie's chest hurt and he thought we had used up all the oxygen in the tent. He kept pleading with us to let him cut a hole in the tent to get more air. His breathing would come faster and faster until he collapsed. Then his breathing would subside and he would sleep.

Somehow, to our utter amazement, the three in the other tent managed to light a stove and make some tea. There wasn't much, but it was a godsend. Our spirits revived and we began to learn what happened to each man in the fall. It seemed incredible that Pete had belayed Art Gilkey, and also held five of us who fell. Pete is the most modest of men, and he insisted he was lucky, but I doubt that any other member of the team could have done it. Fortunately, the strain came in a series of shocks, as Bell and Streather's rope crossed the one to Charlie and me, and then we all slammed into the rope to Gilkey that Molenaar had tied into. The nylon rope stretched and stretched, but the belay and the belayer saved us.

All night I held Charlie, whose chest hurt. The night seemed endless, but we were so huddled together that body heat was warming and we all nodded off occasionally. Dawn found us haggard, still exhausted, and amazed we were still alive. Bob Craig and Pete in the bivouac tent made tea again, but it was a slow process starting with ice. Afterward they made a little cereal in our only pot. The night before we had had two pots, but one, set down momentarily just outside the tent, had promptly slid off the mountain.

All of us agreed that as soon as we could, we should start down.

Charlie's injuries seemed the worst. He could move well, but his chest bothered him and his mind was confused. George Bell was perhaps a greater worry. His hands and feet had frostbite and he doubted his ability to get his swollen feet into his boots. Also, he could not see well without his glasses. Schoening, after holding the fall, had had a coughing spell, and his throat hurt, but during the night he seemed to improve.

We weren't hungry, but the tea was warming and we managed to spoon down some cereal. The wind had been quiet that night, but now it began rising and we were eager to move away from the avalanche slope above. George Bell had a painful time getting his frostbitten, swollen feet into his rubber insulated boots. (High-altitude double boots had not yet been invented.) After much pulling and some cutting of the rubber, he got them on. Putting on crampons—Charlie's especially—was hard too, for there was no flat place to put them on, and nothing is more dangerous than a loose crampon.

We had no idea how well Charlie would climb, though he understood that we were about to climb down. We roped him between Schoening and Craig, and they started. All seemed to go well, though occasionally Charlie sat down and looked out into space until roused to go on. Ahead of us the rock ridge, much of it now coated with snow and ice, dropped off steeply.

We watched them descend safely a rope length and then roped up ourselves: Streather first, then George Bell, who sorely missed his glasses—and because of his frostbitten hands and feet was climbing on sheer guts—then Molenaar, whose leg was bothering him, and me. Streather, Craig, and I had come through the fall in the best shape.

To get to Camp VI we had to descend 1,700 feet at the angle of a steep house roof. We had not gone far when we saw an ice axe stuck in a snow slope at an odd angle. It turned out to be Houston's axe, lost in the fall. Molenaar traversed to it and gave it to Bell, who desperately needed its support. He could use it to guide him to footholds he could not clearly see. Even so, watching George tap around with the tip of his axe for a foothold, while we were climbing on slippery snow-covered slabs, was hardly reassuring to the rest of us. He knew, and we knew, that nobody must slip, and we belayed as if our lives depended on it—as they did. Despite all his handicaps, George climbed steadily and showed magnificent poise.

In places the snow had firmed so much we could crampon down it, but on a tiny ledge at the top of the steepest slope we had to take off our crampons to descend the rock slabs below. A perfect maelstrom of wind and snow, whirling up from below, struck us here. With numb fingers we got George's crampons off and then our own. I have rarely been so cold. My hands and feet lost sensation before Molenaar yelled that he was on belay out of sight below. Fortunately some fixed ropes of ours were usable and that helped.

About 200 feet above Camp VI, Tony Streather, our lead man, started down the wrong way and had to come back 20 feet. That was almost more than he could do, but he managed, and soon we practically climbed down onto the tents at Camp VI.

The other three were already there and had even started a stove. They had found snow in both tents, one of them filled to the top, for a couple of small rocks had fallen and pierced one, and a tiny zipper closure opening was enough to drive snow into the other. That we were there with shelter, safe from the avalanche danger of the previous night, seemed impossible, almost a second miracle. Our morale soared. The finest moment came when George Bell saw a little cloth bag and asked where it came from. We told him that Tony had found it halfway down from Camp VII and thought it was probably something Art had had. It wasn't. It had been in George's pack. He opened it in great excitement and there, to the utter amazement of all of us, was his spare pair of glasses—loose but unbroken! The rest of his pack, with camera, film, and diary, were gone, but the vital item was there. I'm sure it made George feel that he was meant to get off the mountain.

Art Gilkey's body we never found.* About 1,000 feet below the icy gully, a tangle of ropes and a broken ice axe showed where the avalanche

---

*Art's remains were found in August 1993 on the Godwin-Austen Glacier, about four miles from where he initially fell.

had swept him off the ridge to what must have been his instant death. Our thoughts were with him then and have been ever since, for a more gallant friend and companion never lived. He would have given his life for us, but chance or God had done it instead.

That evening Charlie had recovered enough to use the walkie-talkie at Camp VI to call Colonel Ata-Ullah at base camp and tell him what had happened. Ata had listened continuously since we had failed to keep a schedule with him the day before. "Thank God," he said, and for some time could say little more.

That night we had a real dinner with a canned ham and all the tea we could drink, but we fell asleep almost before we had stopped eating. Charlie woke up in the night and didn't know where he was, but the next morning he seemed adjusted again.

That night the storm increased in violence. Thank God, it had diminished the night before! The wind was now so cold that we feared George would do further damage to his feet if he went down. During a lull in the storm, Schoening and Streather descended to Camp V to save supplies, but the rest of us remained at VI.

The next morning, August 13, though the wind was very cold, we had to go down. Our fuel was gone and we had had a cold supper the night before. Before starting, Charlie and I began to chop to free our iced-in tent in order to carry it down. For all we knew, the tents below had been destroyed. As soon as Craig and Molenaar left the other tent, the wind shredded it. Our hands became very numb as we pulled at the guy ropes and struggled with the wind. Then we added the tent to our packs and started down. To our delight, George, wearing his spare glasses (kept in the frame by pieces of a Band-Aid), climbed steadily. Charlie also climbed well and anchored the rope as needed, though he did sit down occasionally and stare at nothing.

At Camp V, which Craig and Molenaar had reached, we drank cup after cup of hot orange-juice-flavored tea, a wonderfully warming combination. Below was the House Chimney, the barrier between the lower and upper portions of the Abruzzi Ridge. It was now 2:30 on a gloomy afternoon. The wind had dropped a bit but might pick up at any time. We were still going on reserve energy but were eager to have this major barrier behind.

The top of the chimney was not far away, but we didn't realize how hard it would be to get there. Since all the rocks were glazed with ice, a slip was easy here and belaying was difficult. We had heavier loads now, and needed special care when chipping footholds among the icy rocks of this exposed part of the route.

When we reached the A-frame that Craig and Molenaar had set up to lower packs, it was getting late. After Pete, Bob, and George went down and their packs were lowered to Dee Molenaar, we began to lower Charlie's pack. Somehow a rope on it caught on a protruding rock, the pack pulled loose, and all in it—Charlie's sleeping bag, diary, and everything else—dropped into the snow gully below and fell thousands of feet off the mountain.

After the bag fell, I made a split-second decision, which at that moment seemed brilliant but turned out badly. To save valuable time, I decided to rappel down wearing my pack instead of lowering it. Pete Schoening held the other end of the belay rope, and I had no doubt of our ability to rappel down to him. Charlie had climbed down from Camp 5 perfectly, though occasionally he had sat down, moving only after I started. He sat down now, possibly shaken by the loss of his pack, but I felt sure that as soon as I started he would follow.

I rappelled quickly but Charlie did not follow. Five or 10 minutes passed, and we were all shouting to him to come down before he finally began. He had become confused about the ropes and it was getting dark. Once started, he came down fast. If anything had happened to him then, I wouldn't have cared whether I got off the mountain or not.

One of the tents at Camp IV was partly iced in, but we used it and another tent for shelter, and crawled into our wet sleeping bags, Charlie using half of mine. The wind was cold all night for we couldn't keep it entirely out, but it now lacked the deadly force and ferocity of the storm at Camp VIII. When another gray dawn broke, a gaunt, hollow-eyed group gathered to plan what to do. There was food at Camp IV but no decent shelter and we all had the feeling that we must keep moving down or we would never reach base camp again. As George Bell stated later, "K2 is a killer mountain—it tries to kill you."

This time Streather and I started ahead. We found powder snow masking loose rocks, making part of our normal route too dangerous to use. Most of our fixed ropes were buried, and we had to cut steps straight down, hard at the best of times, and to men in our condition completely exhausting. We checked a slip just after it started in one particularly bad place. Then Schoening led down to Camp III, which was well stocked with food. When we reached it, we ate like starving men: chocolate, biscuits, date bars with almonds, Gruyere cheese, and dried apricots. We opened a can of concentrated orange juice, mixed it with snow, and gulped it.

We desperately needed rest, but wanted to waste no time in getting George and his frozen feet as low as possible. When his feet began to thaw, despite his courage, he would need to be carried.

If ice coated the route from Camp III to II, as it had coming down from IV, we were in for a dangerous time now, for growing confidence and exhaustion do not go well together. In some places we could kick steps in the snow, in others escape onto rock or cut steps, but delicate moves were needed. The first rope of Schoening, Bell, and Houston was turning off the main slope into a more protected gully when a great rock, falling from very high, whizzed just over their heads and smashed to bits below.

We were approaching the final couloir leading to Camp II when we heard Hunzas shouting, and out on the steep slope emerged Ghulam, Vilyati, and Hidayat, roped together with pack rope, tears flowing down their faces. What an emotional gathering! How we all kept from falling down 1,500 feet to the glacier I don't know. They took our packs, brought us to camp, and spoiled us in every way they knew. We sat on sleeping bags as they brought us pot after pot of hot tea and rice cooked in milk and began to massage our legs. We couldn't believe it was really happening. Those moments were worth a thousand lesser arrivals. We were down and safe—all but one! Him we would never forget.

Then came the sleep of exhaustion. We slept late and the next morning ate second helpings of everything before starting for Camp I and base camp. Tony and I went ahead, meeting other porters who were on their way to Camp I. Walking stiffly, with numb toes, we finally reached base camp, where Colonel Ata-Ullah greeted us as if we had risen from the dead. "Thank God," Ata kept saying. "Thank God!"

Merely being at base camp seemed an unspeakable luxury. George, whose feet were painfully thawing, reached the glacier by his own willpower, and from there porters carried him on a folding cot to base camp. We had lost 10 to 20 pounds apiece since our climb began, but despite the battering of the storm we were all down again—*except for Art*. On a prominent rock outcrop at the juncture of the Savoia and Godwin-Austen Glaciers, Colonel Ata-Ullah had had the porters build a big, 10-foot cairn for Art Gilkey. Here the next day we gathered for a memorial service for our dear companion. We were still so exhausted that we were barely able to limp to the site of the cairn to pay tribute to that courageous, selfless man. (A few years later a large glacier in Alaska, where he once worked, was named for him.)

Since a lot of our normal strength had drained away, our descent from base camp to Askole seemed endless. George was carried on a lightweight canvas and steel cot brought for the purpose. Poles lashed to its sides were shouldered by four men at a time. In places along the river the track became too steep for the litter, and one-third of the time one of the Satpura porters carried George piggyback. Mohammed Hussain, the strongest porter, usually was the one, walking barefoot to get better purchase on small footholds, and briefly resting with George on his back about every 10 minutes. Whether he walked along cliffs, across sharp stones, or through glacier torrents, Mohammed Hussain never dropped George, and carried his 170 pounds as if the load were a perfectly normal one.

When a rope bridge had to be crossed, George sat on the central strand and pulled himself across. After 11 trying days, he was placed on a zhak, to float down the river the rest of the way to Skardu. From there he was flown to Rawalpindi, and on to Boston, where at the Massachusetts General Hospital doctors found he had the thickest blood they had ever seen. There, after several weeks of care, he lost only a small toe and part of a big one.

Ata-Ullah, Schoening, and I, with some porters, left George and the others at Askole and made a fast climb over the 16,644-foot Skoro La Pass, a shortcut, in order to make preliminary arrangements for George at Skardu. During our descent toward Shigar, a huge boulder, probably dislodged by a porter high above us, dropped down the trail in great bounces. Fortunately nobody was hurt. It was the mountain area's last salvo. A few days later we were all with our many friends in Rawalpindi, and not long afterward home again, sobered by our experience.

On our arrival home, despite our failure to reach the summit, we were deluged with requests from publishers who wanted us to do a book on the expedition. *The New York Times* and other papers had given us publicity, as had NBC, which helped our finances by presenting a half-hour television program to a national audience, using film taken by Charlie and George Bell. With Bob Craig's assistance, I also wrote two articles for the *Saturday Evening Post*. These also contributed to popular interest. In the fall, to help pay off the last of our debts, I used Charlie's films to give illustrated talks about the expedition, and later began coordinating work to be done on the book, for we decided that as many as possible of the expedition members should share in the writing. We finally settled on McGraw-Hill Book Co. to be our publisher because of its international network. They proved to be a sound choice, for after the book came out in the U.S., editions were printed in Japanese, Norwegian, Spanish, and German, as well as an English edition. A picture book with some text was also published in France.

Gail

Some guests at our wedding at Gail's home in Cleveland, Ohio: Peter Wood (left), Archibald MacIntosh, R.H.B., Walter Wood, John Case, Henry Hall. The three at right were former presidents of the American Alpine Club.

CHAPTER XVII

Marriage
1954

IN THE WINTER OF 1954 Gail Oberlin and I realized how many interests we enjoyed in common, how fond of each other we had become, and were engaged. We had met at an American Alpine Club meeting in Philadelphia a few years earlier, when she became the first secretary of the club. I had thought her especially good looking and interesting, but marriage was not on my mind. It was not until our return from K2 that I learned what a courageous, intelligent person she is, and she learned more about me.

Gail had grown up in Cleveland, attended Vassar College, and taken an M.A. in social work at Columbia University. She had climbed in the Alps, inspected tenements in Hell's Kitchen in New York, and spent nearly three years with the Red Cross in Europe during World War II. After the war, during a voyage to Brazil to visit an aunt whose husband was the Dutch ambassador, she was shipwrecked on a reef in the Bahamas—but that is another story.

Late May and June was a frantic scramble for me as I faced mountains of student papers and deadlines to finish our book, *K2—The Savage Mountain*, before driving to Cleveland for our wedding. Brother Bill was best man, Gail's cousin, Leslie Hogeboom, was matron of honor, and a whole planeload of friends flew from New York to the wedding, which Gail's father and brother managed, for her mother had died. John Case, Henry Hall, and Walter Wood, all former presidents of the American Alpine Club, were there, as well as the current president, Gail's brother, John.

The Cleveland Plain Dealer had announced our engagement with the headline, "Gail Oberlin to marry adventurer," a caption that annoyed and

After the wedding on the way to Italy.

amused Gail's father. Someone sent the headline to the *New Yorker*, and to the delight of our friends it was printed with the statement, "Just give us the news please."

Bill Saltonstall, the principal at Phillips Exeter, had given me a half-year sabbatical, and we decided to use it well. It was the first (and only) marriage for both of us, and we soon began a trip around the world we would never forget. It began by our taking an Italian ship to Genoa, a fine old city I never quite reached in World War II.

The boat stopped for a few hours in Barcelona, where Gail's aunt now lived. She whirled us off to a champagne luncheon with fried octopus followed by a fast tour of the city. We debarked at Genoa and took a train north to Switzerland, where we made some climbs before the weather turned bad and chased us to Austria. We were snowed in for a couple of nights at the Adler's Ruhe (a hut high on the Gross Glockner) but a spectacular sunrise returned and we were soon ringing the bell on the summit. Mail had been sent to us in Vienna, so we went there and found a cable from John Case stating, "Meet us Bombay November second. Permission received for Nepal."

For years I had dreamed of going to Nepal, and had chafed at being unable to accept Charlie and Oscar Houston's invitation to go there with them in 1950, when they discovered the route to Mt. Everest from the south. No passage to India by plane or boat was available in Vienna, and so we flew to London to solve the problem. Finally, at almost the last moment that would get us to Bombay on time, we acquired separate berths on the liner *Strathaird*, and arrived a day before the deadline.

John and Anne Case had managed to get permission to spend two weeks in Nepal (a closed country) because they and Nehru were taking part in the inauguration ceremonies for India's first oil refinery. When their official duties were over, we flew to Delhi with a man from Stanvac (the oil company), and continued by DC-3 to Kathmandu.

We landed at Gaucher Airport, an unpaved, dusty field with a small shelter serving as the airport building. When we went inside to present our passports, we were asked if we were from the American government. We answered "No." There were puzzled expressions and the question, "What are you then?" I thought a bit and said, "I suppose you could call us tourists." At this the smiling official called to a friend, "We have tourists. We have tourists." Then he turned to us and said pleasantly, "I knew we would have tourists *some* day."

There was no American embassy in Nepal, only two or three Americans, and a single representative of American AID. In Kathmandu, there were only 11 automobiles, most of them big touring cars with elaborate rubber bulb horns, autos carried in from India by coolies.

We lodged at the Royal Hotel, a section of the palace of the Third Prince consisting of three bedrooms and a small dining room. The prince had rented it and its large garden to Boris Lissanevitch, a former dancer with Diaghilev. Our room had two tiger skins on the floor, and Gail and I shared it with its previous owner, Panduchi, a beautiful ring-tailed Himalayan red panda, which still considered it home.

We enjoyed walking around Kathmandu, but what we really wanted was to go to the mountains. This Boris arranged, lending us his own cook and a man to go with us who spoke English. Anne Case preferred to stay in Kathmandu, but the rest of us, with food for eight days, flew to Pokhara in a DC-3, sitting in bucket seats and looking alternately out the windows at the mountains we were passing (such as Himalchuli or Manaslu) and at our fellow passengers, especially an old lady with nose ring and large gold earrings who sat across from us, her eyes tightly closed the whole way, praying loudly all the time.

Pokhara was delightful. A broad path was paved with flat stones and shaded by large shade trees. Small shops lined the street and occasional

Gail breaking camp on the ridge above the Pokhara Valley
across from Annapurna

small shrines, most very old, with garlands of marigolds and vermilion markings. Poinsettias gave color, and high in the distance, looking like clouds at first, rose the shining snows of Machhapuchhre (the fish's tail), a peak of the Annapurna Massif just short of 23,000 feet.

In Pokhara we hired a few men as porters and started to head north toward the mountains, but fortunately met botanists from a British Museum expedition who had stopped to make tea. They suggested that we climb onto a ridge, about 12 to 15 miles long, above Pokhara, where there should be splendid views of Annapurna. The botanists had heard there was a trail along it that went on to the Kali Gandaki River.

The walk along the ridge crest the next day was a delight. Everyone we met showed great surprise at seeing us. Many, we felt sure, had never seen a Westerner before, and Gail especially startled them. At first they would stare at us and then burst out laughing. Most had no idea what a camera was for. At the end of the ridge we had a grand view of Dhaulagiri before a steep trail descended to the village of Birethanti, where we spent the night. We continued on for a couple of days, seeing more and more surprised villagers, but did not have time to drop down to the Kali Gandaki, one of the great rivers of Nepal. John and I were eager to climb up to the snow level on Annapurna, but when we made a strong try, we were stopped by thick bamboo.

We returned to Kathmandu with memories of smiling people on the trail and camps shaded by 30-foot rhododendrons; as well as the morning when the cook was drunk and the other Nepalis cheerfully dunked him in the river.

We parted with the Cases in Kathmandu, flew to Calcutta, and on to Bangkok, where many of the klongs (canals) had not yet been filled in and we visited markets by boat. Bangkok was exotic, but we were heading for New Zealand and soon departed. Engine trouble delayed us in Singapore and we were put up at the legendary Raffles Hotel. With time on our hands, we went to a market where we bought tropical fruits that were new to us, including a durian. This fruit looks like a giant unhusked horse chestnut, has some of the sweetest, creamiest pulp in the world, and smells like the strongest sewer gas.

We flew on to steamy Darwin, Australia, and continued to Sydney, which struck us as far less colorful than Nepal, Thailand, and Singapore. We flew next to Auckland, New Zealand. We had exchanged letters with Ed Hillary, now Sir Edmund, who had arranged that we visit there the Roses, his delightful in-laws. John Rose was president of the New Zealand Alpine Club, and the Roses and Hillarys gave us our first taste of New Zealand's warm hospitality. After a morning with Ed, talking mountaineering as he moved his bees around, we traveled to Christchurch in the South Island.

Advice there from members of the Canterbury Mountaineering Club was to cross to Hokatika on the Tasman Sea and ask Peter Graham, a well-known mountain guide, about local climbing conditions. We did, and on his advice trekked through the tree-fern forest to the Alps, crossed the range near Mt. Cook, and descended the Tasman Glacier to the Hermitage, a famous mountain hotel. As Graham had pointed out, Mt. Cook was glittering with ice.

Since we had no crampons we did not linger in the Alps, but took a bus south to Te Anau, a beautiful lake, for some fishing. We caught several enormous trout, kept one, and the next day stopped at Dunedin to see our friend Noel Odell, the Everest climber, who was a visiting professor at the university. When he opened the door, we handed him a seven-pound trout. We had a fine visit with the Odells before heading back to the North Island, where we met my Harvard classmate Art Emmons, his wife, Evie, and his two daughters. Art was taking a short vacation from his post at the American embassy in Canberra, Australia.

Gail and Sir Edmund Hillary in Auckland, New Zealand.

We shared a rented car, did some fishing together, and on Christmas Day, Gail, Art, and I climbed Mt. Ruapehu, a 9,500-foot volcano, the highest peak on the North Island. In 1932 Art nearly climbed Minya Konka (Gongga Shan) in China, previously thought by some to be higher than Mt. Everest, but in doing it he had frozen his feet. Art climbed well going up Ruapehu, but lack of toes bothered him on the way down.

Our time with the Emmons family was a special treat, but now we must leave New Zealand. At Wellington we boarded the freighter *Brisbane Star* for the long trip across the Pacific. We saw no land the entire way, though we passed close to Pitcairn Island in cloudy weather. Huge royal albatrosses, birds with the world's largest wingspread, followed us, wheeling and soaring but hardly ever making a wing-beat. We made friends of the captain and crew, and thanks to Gail's arrangements with the cook, my birthday was celebrated with a suckling pig and huge birthday cake.

At the Pacific entrance to the Panama Canal, we saw a giant crocodile, but he did not go through the locks with us. The *Brisbane Star*'s agent, who now boarded, did, and he arranged passage to New Orleans for us on a United Fruit banana boat. Just outside the canal's eastern entrance, we went down a Jacob's ladder to a small boat and were transferred to the freighter. This was an American ship, run with less formality than the *Brisbane Star*, and we soon knew all the ship's officers.

Our voyage north seemed fast. We came up the Mississippi at night, joining the captain and the pilot as they watched the radar. New Orleans was getting ready for the Mardi Gras. After savoring a dinner at Antoine's, at Gail's suggestion I bought a fake gambler's moustache. A day later, when we arrived in Cleveland to be met by her father and brother, I put on the moustache. Unfortunately, I had no gold earrings. We had departed from Cleveland with the words, "Gail Oberlin to marry adventurer," and the least I could do was try to look like one.

At the Salar de Maricunga

CHAPTER XVIII

The Ojos del Salado
1956

O N OUR RETURN TO EXETER, we were just in time to take over George Bennett's classes and move into Porter House, where I had lived as a student. There were advantages to living in an academy house, but we were eager to have our own home, and spent much of the spring seeking a place we liked that we could afford. Mrs. Shute, a widow, wanted to sell her home, but we considered her price too high. Finally, late in the summer, we were awakened by a breathless phone call from Mrs. Shute saying that she agreed to our price. Shortly before school began in the fall, we moved into our new home, a large frame house on High Street at the top of a hill about a mile from school, with lots of space behind the house. There was plenty to do.

The following academic year went quickly, and in early spring of 1956 a phone call came from Adams Carter. The American Geographical Society had received letters from the geographical societies of both Argentina and Chile asking for a survey party to determine the height of the Ojos del Salado, a high peak in the Andean Cordillera that forms a disputed frontier between Chile and the Argentine about 400 miles north of Aconcagua. Since the mountain is in a high, poorly mapped area, there was much confusion and acrimonious accusation, for as we learned later Argentine and Chilean climbers who reported they had climbed the Ojos del Salado did not always climb the same mountain. Claims that the mountain was the highest in the Western Hemisphere so increased interest in it that four different expeditions went to climb it in January and February of 1956. Two of them, an Austrian and a Chilean team, reached the same summit. Captain René Gajardo, the leader of the expedition from Chile, reported an

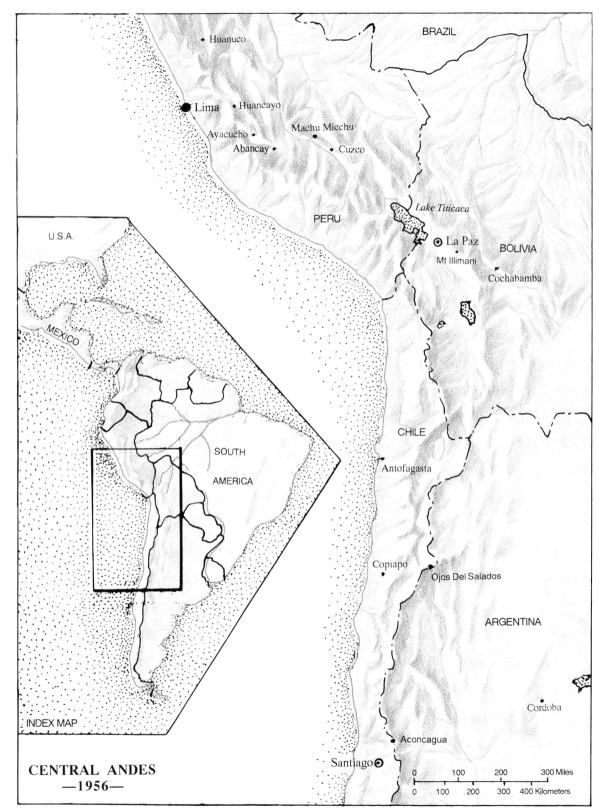

Huanuco

Lima • Huancayo

Ayacucho •   • Machu Micchu

Abancay •   • Cuzco

PERU

Lake Titicaca

⊙ La Paz   BOLIVIA

Mt Illimani

Cochabamba

U.S.A.

MEXICO

SOUTH

AMERICA

INDEX MAP

CHILE

• Antofagasta

• Copiapo   ● Ojos Del Salados

ARGENTINA

• Cordoba

• Aconcagua

Santiago ⊙

BRAZIL

CENTRAL ANDES
—1956—

| 0 | 100 | 200 | 300 Miles |
| 0 | 100 | 200 | 300 | 400 Kilometers |

aneroid reading at the summit of 23,241 feet, a figure quickly seized by the world press as showing that the mountain was higher than Aconcagua, the Argentine mountain long considered the Western Hemisphere's highest. Chileans, of course, were delighted and claimed the mountain as their own, to the extreme annoyance of the Argentines.

To help resolve this bitter dispute, the American Geographical Society asked Ad Carter to form a survey party. Ad spoke fluent Spanish, already had some surveying experience with Bradford Washburn, and immediately accepted, with a proviso that he must have with him an experienced survey- or whose work would be respected by the two countries. Ad immediately asked Gail and me to go with him and his wife, Ann, and added Peter Weaver, a surveyor well known in South America. Gail's brother was sup- posed to come with us, but John had various delays and was not available for the first part of the expedition.

Needed items for the climb and survey were quickly put together, and in June Gail and I left with them by freighter bound for Antofagasta, Chile. This was a grand trip for us. We sailed down the coast to Panama, where this time we got off at the Atlantic end, took the train to Panama City, and reboarded our ship before it headed into the Pacific. At Antofagasta, Ad and Ann Carter, John Wylde, Peter Weaver, and Captain Gajardo of the Chilean army met us. The latter, a brisk, decisive officer, had been leader of the Chilean expedition that had climbed the Ojos del Salado. We had hoped to meet at Antofagasta representatives of the Argentine Association Tucumana de Andinismo to accompany us. The Chilean Mapping Service had assigned to us two officers and six enlisted men and included the use of a two-and-one-half-ton truck. Ad told us that no Argentine climbers had come, and Captain Gajardo did not want them. Animosity between the two countries was obvious, but we did not learn until later that the Chileans had told the Argentines in threatening terms that they were not wanted, and if they came and got hurt it would be their own fault.

As soon as our gear was unloaded from the ship, Captain Gajardo had it loaded on the truck to take off immediately. He said we could leave notes for any fool Argentines who might show up, but *we should leave now*. We did, after arranging where and when to meet with Major Correa, who would be driving with Chilean enlisted men direct from the army base at Copiapo, while we would be coming from Potrerillos.

Ad and Gajardo rode in the front of the truck, while Gail, Ann, and I rode in the back. Through the dust that the army six-by-six kicked up, we could see mile after mile of arid land with nothing living or growing on it. Finally the truck stopped, and with surprising quickness we all pulled out our sleeping bags and collapsed by the side of the road.

Some hours later we reached Potrerillos, 150 miles from the Pacific, with a population of 10,000, mostly Indians, the headquarters of the Andes Copper Mining Company's big mine and smelter. We were hospitably welcomed, but we did not remain long in the dreary company town with its tame condor, for we heard that a storm was expected, and if it were a big one it could block our route to the International Highway for a good six weeks.

On July 21 we left Potrerillos on a track that traversed bare slopes with lots of switchbacks. These switchbacks ran down or up long slopes hundreds of feet high. Captain Gajardo loved daring driving, and sometimes would turn the truck straight downhill, missing an entire switchback, and then haul the truck, dangerously near to overturning, onto the next switchback below. To get around switchback corners where the truck needed to back up, he would quickly back to the very edge of the road, despite the long drop beyond. He seemed surprised at how often we decided to walk down some of the slopes rather than ride with him.

Mineralized soils colored the region but nothing grew on them. We crossed a 12,000-foot pass, continued to the salt flat at Pedernales, and in bright moonlight kept going through several inches of snow to the north edge of the Salar de Maricunga at 12,500 feet. We had reached the International Highway, where Major Correa and the survey party were to meet us, but they had not yet arrived. On the way we had coffee at a hut where a dead rhea hung on the gate. The job of the three men there was to keep from freezing a small stream that was piped 50 miles to the Potrerillos mine. Their hut was the closest habitation to the mountain.

The next morning we saw a sign that said Tinogasta (in Argentina) 357 (kilometers), and under it Potrerillos 133. The temperature was zero Fahrenheit and windy. The truck radiator was frozen because the motor had not been running while it was being drained, and the Chileans had no antifreeze. While waiting a day for Major Correa and thawing the radiator, we made a practice climb of a small mountain the height of Mont Blanc. On it were hundreds of tracks of guanaco and birds similar to ptarmigan.

The following day, leaving Gail and Ann to confer with Major Correa if he came, the rest of us drove along the International Highway to see if its passes were open. They were as far as we went, but on one we had some wild skidding. The water of the Colorado River had flowed out over the valley floor, coating the road with ice. There were no chains in the truck

ADAMS CARTER

Gail and our tent en route to the Ojos del Salado

and we had to use our ice axes to cut grooves in the ice to aid the truck's advance. We chopped ice for hours to get around one corner and over a pass. On the other side we saw nine guanacos, which seemed about the size of our mule deer. Ahead was a downgrade with two feet of drifted snow in it, and there we turned back to camp. We had gone only three miles despite hours of hard work.

The next day we built a cairn in the road and left a note in it for Major Correa. Then, after the radiator was thawed once more, we headed for Barrancas Blancas at the foot of the Ojos del Salado. We shoveled snow and bucked our way across the whole Colorado Pass and down onto the flat, snowy Campo de Piedra Pomez that led to the pampa below the mountain. Progress was sometimes measured foot by foot, since the wheels cut through the snow and pumice crust and churned on loose pebbles below, but at least we could see the sharp peak of the Ojos rising above us. By repeatedly shoveling in front of the truck, and with the major urging the truck on, we reached Barrancas Blancas at midnight.

The temperature had dropped and the wind had risen, so at first light we began to move to a more protected place. We hardly had the tent down and were stowing it when gusts reached almost hurricane force, pushing us

R.H.B. and Adams Carter in the truck we did not want
to abandon in the Atacama Desert

around and searing our faces with windblown bits of ice. Captain Gajardo
became very excited and yelled that a major storm was coming and we
would have to go back across the Colorado Pass. Every five or 10 years a
huge storm strikes this extremely dry area and blocks all roads for months.
Gajardo shouted that we must hurry or be stranded there for the winter. If
that happened, we would have to struggle through snow for 70 miles, aban-
doning the truck, which Gajardo told us was worth $50,000, a sum we
should have to pay if it were abandoned. Although we were wearing insulated boots and windproof clothing of the sort we had worn in the Yukon
in the winter, the windchill was grim. We jammed everything back into the
truck, climbed in, and hoped that we could get through Colorado Pass
before it became blocked.

Even the heavy American army truck felt the force of the 100-mile-
an-hour winds as we bucked through drifts on our way to Colorado Pass.
The gas line soon froze and Soto, the major's driver-mechanic, had to
uncouple it and blow it clear despite the subzero temperature and wind
velocity. In some places traction on the loose gravel of the road was so bad

that the truck had to back 20 or 30 feet and then hurl itself forward to gain a foot or two, repeating this maddening process again and again until firm ground was reached. Most of the time the road was blown clear, but the air was filled with icy particles blown horizontally. When drifts, hardened by the wind, stopped us, we all jumped out to shovel our way through, exhausting work at nearly 15,000 feet. By nightfall we had battled only as far as the top of the Piedra Pomez Pass, the intermediate one between Colorado Pass and our camp. It was doubtful we could crest the higher pass beyond, from which gravity could help us descend to the Salar de Maricunga.

A few hours later, as we ground along the next pampa salt flat, we glimpsed, through the blowing snow, what seemed like stars. It was Major Correa's party, coming from their headquarters at Copiapo, and now suffering from insufficient clothing and frostbite. They were bravely attempting to rescue us. With our backs to the wind to protect us from the driving storm, we made a half circle around Major Correa, who, with his hat pulled down and his chin in his collar, showed only a small part of his face. His eyes and mouth looked grim. He reached into the cab of his truck and pulled out a bottle of *aguardiente,* fiery Chilean brandy. He pulled out the cork with his teeth, took a big swig, and handed it to the man next him. It made the rounds and came back to Correa, who drained the bottle and tossed it aside.

"Now we must decide," he yelled over the roar of the storm. "Either we go on to mountain or back to Copiapo." Before anyone could say a word, he put a hand on his big revolver and shouted, "If you say go back to mountain, I go bang, bang, bang." As he yelled "bang," he pointed at each of us in turn. He had obviously had enough, more than enough, and he wanted that understood. "We are going out," we shouted, and quickly climbed into our truck to get out of the wind.

The rest of our retreat went better, for we had more manpower to battle the drifts, and finally crossed Colorado Pass. We had been doing exhausting work for more than 20 hours straight, and at what looked like a sheltered place on the far side began to set up camp. Ad and Ann were inside our four-man tent trying to raise a tent pole, and Gail and I were holding the corners of the tent, when a furious gust of wind struck. The corners were yanked from our hands as Gail and I were blown over, while the tent with the others inside rolled them head over heels across the rock-strewn pampa before we could catch it again and hold on. An air mattress that Ad had just blown up was inside the tent door when the gust struck. It shot up like a fighter plane and disappeared into the sky, never to be seen again. We waited for a lull, then crawled back into the rear of the truck with the collapsed tent, pulled on our sleeping bags, and sank among the gear.

Waking about 10:00 a.m., we found that the wind had diminished and Soto had started a fire with bits of wood and dead bushes to make some tea. Resting against the fire was our truck radiator, frozen again. Both truck radiators had frozen, but eventually they thawed and our battered party began the long drive to Copiapo. We saw no human beings for most of the drive to the coast, and when we did it was a group of drunken Indians who had just driven off the road and overturned their pickup truck. Fortunately, nobody was much hurt, and we were able to help them flip their car back onto its wheels. The incident made us aware that we could have good luck as well as bad. We reached the overturned truck just after emerging from a single-lane gorge. If the Indians had not overturned their car, we could well have met them head-on.

At Copiapo we were welcomed by officers of the Chilean army, to whom the officers were great heroes. We ate at the officers' mess and were given rooms without roofs, evidence that rain rarely falls there. The change from fighting a blizzard in subzero temperatures to warmth and a benign slothfulness was almost too much for us. The officers had limitless supplies of excellent Chilean wine, and they wasted no time trying to get us drunk. They sang romantic songs with a chorus of "Devolvarme el Amor Mío," and military songs with gestures, such as one where at the end of each stanza they pulled an imaginary lanyard to fire a big gun. We sang some songs with them and drank some wine, but took no part in their games of forcing someone to drink a goblet of wine fast to a chorus of "Chupo, Chupo, Chupo."

As soon as we could, we boarded a plane to Santiago. Ad and Ann hoped to regroup there, seek more help, and come back to do the survey, giving up climbing the mountain. On our arrival in the capital, we were met by officers who politely asked us if we wished to see the president of Chile. Knowing that we had achieved little, we said "No," whereupon we were asked if we wanted to see the minister of national defense. We said "No" again but were promptly told that he wanted to see us.

We learned later that he had expected us to declare that the highest peak in the Western Hemisphere is the Ojos del Salado of Chile. This would be a great victory over the Argentines, he thought, and would strengthen Chile's claim to the disputed area. When we came to Santiago with no such announcement, he was furious. He stormed at us, practically stamping his foot, "You foolish Nordamericanos," he said, "why do you come down here in the dead of winter when you get frozen and have to call on us for help? You are ignorant. You should have known better."

When he calmed down, we told him that we had plenty of warm clothing and had received no frostbite, nor had we asked for help. He muttered something about "Nordamericanos know nothing," and we parted.

We later learned that our "successful" return was to have been greeted by a great reception, with medals all around and speeches about the glory of Chile and its government. Fortunately we missed all that. Gail's brother, John, had now joined us, and we three, not having time for a second attempt to survey the mountain, now departed for La Paz, Bolivia. Ad, however, with his usual energy and six weeks' time we did not have, added an experienced Chilean climber to his survey team and returned to Colorado Pass once more. Eventually this group established that the height of the Ojos is 22,590 feet, making it the highest volcano in the world but 244 feet lower than the Argentine's Aconcagua. Whether the peak is in Chile or the Argentine, they did not try to decide, and they did not visit the ministry of defense again.

La Paz is generally considered the highest city in the world, but at the time of our arrival, the value of its currency, the boliviano, was probably the world's lowest. A few American dollars produced a suitcase of bolivianos, which nobody wanted. We took a car to the high Altiplano to see the ruins of Tiahuanaco, and looked longingly at 21,000-foot Mt. Illimani, which rises close to La Paz.

An Indian driver, who spoke only Quechua and broken German, drove us to Copacabana on Lake Titicaca, a huge lake roughly 140 miles by 70 that figures prominently in Inca legends. A couple of days later, on a worse road, a different driver took us to the Peru border and on to Puno, where the steamboats dock and the remarkable railroad to Cuzco begins. On the way we passed through a town where we saw only Indians and a festival was being held. Some people were dressed in their best clothes, and others as devils, demons, and caricatures of wealthy Spaniards. Many of the older men wore collars a foot or more wide covered with jaguar skins.

The train the next morning slowly crossed a 17,000-foot pass, but unlike a former Exeter colleague, we did not collapse from lack of oxygen. At Cuzco we admired the Inca walls, blocks of stone so carefully fitted that no penknife blade could pass between them. This skill was shown best on the outskirts of the town and in the ruins of Sacsahuaman, a fortress where massive boulders had been precisely fitted together.

Delighted with this introduction to Inca culture, we took the train to Urubamba and Ollantaytambo, where a bus took us up the switchbacked road to the stronghold of Machu Picchu. The site, high above the Urubamba River, was so impressive that we decided to spend the night. At sunset, we still had light long after it was dark in the jungles below. Contiguous to Machu Picchu is a higher mountain named Huayna Picchu, from which one looks almost directly down upon the ruined town. We climbed the steep trail to the top, where steps cut in the rocks start down on the far side, the last one seeming to step off into space.

Returning to Cuzco, we were about to leave for Lima by air when we met Fred Ayres, a mountaineering friend. Together we learned of a good driver who would take us on a three-day journey to the capital by a narrow, little-traveled mountain road. We were not surprised that few drivers would make the trip. On parts of the road on odd-numbered days, the single-tracked road, often hundreds of feet above a river, was open one way only, and on even days the opposite, while on Sundays it was open both ways. The cardinal rule for driving in the road was, we were told, "Never swerve. If need be, hit head-on."

Our car rounded corners continually, and the driver, especially on Sunday, blew the horn loudly most of the time. Sometimes we were higher than Cuzco, sometimes down in river valleys, then up again along narrow ridges or on tracks blasted from sheer canyon walls. Partially cleared land-slides sometimes made the track smaller, with the outer wheels less than a foot from the outer edge.

On the first section, to Abancay, the road was not bad, but farther it required the driver's complete attention. He would have preferred to stop at Abancay, but we persuaded him to push on to Andahuaylas. At times, we climbed to over 16,000 feet, but had little time to get out, stretch and look around. We were all tired from being constantly thrown about when, just before nightfall, we reached the town. What a disappointment. The town had an ominous, run-down air, and the hotel itself was the filthiest in our entire experience.

Our dirty, second-floor room, with half a windowpane broken away, was in the back. The room was on a balcony that contained at one end a faucet and wash basin, used by everyone in our part of the hotel. To get there all walked past our uncurtained windows. Dinner consisted of a soup that smelled and tasted unpleasant, with a rooster's head floating in it. After checking our bed for bugs, we lay down on the gray sheets and napped. If I had had a gun, I would have slept with it under my jacket, which I rolled up to use for a pillow. No wonder Andahuaylas became the center of the Shining Path guerrilla movement.

In the morning there was stale bread and coffee, a jet-black liquid poured from a bottle to which warm water was added. We were glad to be off, and soon there were splendid views of snowy mountains, for we were crossing the Cordillera Blanca. There were no villages in the higher parts but we did pass a bridge across a ravine like the famous one of San Luis Rey. Lima seemed impossibly far away. It was Sunday, a day when traffic moved both ways on the single track, but our driver was always alert for oncoming traffic. All went well, and at Ayacucho we had a better dinner and better room, lighted by a candle.

On the way to Huancayo (10,958 feet), we passed occasional ranches that raised marvelously sweet oranges as well as indigo. While we were eating lunch, our plans were changed, for the driver was offered a high price to return at once to Cuzco. He pointed out to us that this was a day when a train from Huancayo went to Lima. We could continue by train and we did. Despite the rough roadbed, the train seemed almost gentle after our rough travel in the car.

John left for the U.S. the next day and we flew to Panama, where we visited the natural island zoo of Barro Colorado in Gatun Lake, formed during the building of the Panama Canal. We loved being in the jungle for a night. Then off we flew to Boston and home.

CHAPTER XIX

Mt. Koven
and Glacier Peak

1957

THE FOLLOWING ACADEMIC YEAR was a busy one and by June I was ready for some climbing. John Oberlin wanted more climbing too, and we agreed to meet in the Wind Rivers. Gail and I drove to Wyoming together, taking with us Marco Einaudi, a leading member of the Exeter Mountaineering Club. With Fred Truslow, a classmate of Marco's, we made several climbs, including a new route on Mt. Koven. On that climb as we were nearing the top, an early afternoon thunderstorm swept in. Snow fell and the wind was cold. Afternoon thunderstorms are common in the Tetons and the Wind River Range, and we automatically pulled on parkas, made ourselves as comfortable as we could on a yard-wide ledge, and began to share chocolate and dried apricots. In 10 or 15 minutes the snow stopped, there was sunlight, and the storm seemed over.

I stood up to stretch, and John, who earlier had warned us not to lean against the mountain wall behind, stretched against it. Below our ledge there was empty space for a long way, while somewhere above, not far away, was the summit. Crash! Something struck me from behind like a giant kick in the pants. Gail grabbed me. John grunted, "I'm burned, hold me," and collapsed on the ledge. There was a strong smell of ozone and the tingling of electricity in the air. The boys called that they were all right, although one of them later had a lame shoulder for a while. John quickly came to and said he was unharmed. He had felt intense heat as the electricity passed along the metal zipper of his parka, but there were no burn marks on his skin. A hole in his hat, however, showed where the electricity had struck him as he momentarily leaned back against the rock. The lightning bolt apparently struck the summit, which we soon learned was only 150 feet above us, ran down the rock, shocking us all, and passed through John's hat and out his boots. After pulling ourselves together, we completed the climb.

The following summer (1958) we were in Europe again, taking a Dutch freighter to Amsterdam and traveling thence to Paris and the Lake of Geneva. There we had fine visits with Swiss climber René Dittert, and Gail's aunt and uncle, who had moved from Barcelona. John Oberlin met us in the Engadine, and at Pontresina we had good climbs of the Biancograt on the Piz Bernina, and the Disgrazia near Sondrio.

In December 1958 I became president of the American Alpine Club for the regular three-year term. I had been on the council for several years, editor of the *American Alpine Journal*, and vice-president, but to be president was still a surprise.

The summer of 1959 took us to Mexico, where we did some climbing, and the following June we were in Norway. That summer was unusually wet, with streams running high in the Jotunheimen. We had an exciting crossing of one named Pigg Gravi. During our return home in a small freighter, we ran into a hurricane south of Greenland and were the first ship to report it. Waves became huge and the surface of the ocean white from the bursts of tropical rain. Crockery smashed as we made a 90-degree turn toward the Azores. We reached port three days late, and Exeter the day school opened.

In the summer of 1961, Gail and I drove across the United States, seeing friends along the way. We climbed in Glacier Park, and in the Cascades with Dee Molenaar and George Senner, but most fun was the climb of Glacier Peak, an old volcano. It was important because through it I came to know Willi Unsoeld.

Pete Schoening had been teaching a class in mountaineering at the University of Washington, and he planned the climb of Glacier Peak as their graduation exercise. Pete thought it would be fun to assign this climb to his class and then sneak up the back side of the peak to watch them as they came up. Willi, Dee, and I were to join him.

There were immediate difficulties. Part of Pete's chemical plant caught fire and he couldn't come with us. Willi was seriously delayed by family problems, too, but the next day Dee, Gail, and I waited for him at the beginning of a path leading through woods that would take us to the back side of Glacier Peak. Finally, fearing Willi had been prevented from com-

Willi Unsoeld

ing at all, Dee and I started out on the 12-mile walk to where we would camp. Gail was not coming with us and would tell Willi what we were doing if he came. We reached high meadows on the back side of the peak in time to find a pleasant place for our sleeping bags, and were sitting eating the food Dee had brought, which accidentally included baby food, when we heard a whistle across the meadow and there saw Willi.

He was wearing shorts and had no pack or ice axe. "Hey, Willi," yelled Dee, "where's your ice axe?"

"Jolene wouldn't let me bring it," he yelled back. "She was afraid you guys would get me to stay. I've just come to tell you fellas that I can't come with ya; I've got to get back."

He sat down, a bit out of breath, for he had pushed hard to reach us before dark. We gave him some baby food, he shared some jerky, and we all began to talk. Willi had a headlight and sleeping bag but no warm clothes or climbing gear. Jolene was worrying about an important meeting the following afternoon that Willi couldn't afford to miss. She was making sure he would be there.

It wasn't hard to persuade Willi to spend the night with us in the heather, for at dawn, when we left to climb to the top, he could return to Jolene and his four children, who were camping at the road. We talked until way after dark before falling asleep, and hadn't been asleep long when Dee woke up and started talking, saying that his mattress was no good. He had blown it up three times and each time it gradually went flat. Dee talked so much that Willi and I couldn't sleep. A full moon was lighting everything.

"What size are your boots?" Dee asked Willi.

"Nines."

"Then you can wear this," said Dee, passing over a crampon. Willi looked at it and fitted it to his boot. The size was right.

"See if you can get these on your legs," said Dee, passing over a warm sweatshirt. Willi pulled hard and got the sweatshirt arms onto his legs. The sweatshirt wouldn't stay around his waist very well, but Dee solved that with an extra shoelace.

"I can't do it, fellas. I got to be back, and anyway I don't have an ice axe."

Before Willi's arrival, Dee and I had discovered a seven-foot wooden tent pole with a metal spike on the end. It probably had been there for many years, but when Dee pole-vaulted with it, he announced that it was strong. "How about this, Willi?"

"Okay, let's go. It's impossible to sleep with you yakking all night, Molenaar."

That was how we set off by moonlight, at first kicking steps up the snow slopes and then cutting a few steps to help our one-crampon men. I used my own crampons, too small for the others, and we all took turns using the long pole and our two ice axes. At the summit we huddled behind some rocks and watched dawn breaking. Soon the wind dropped, the sun warmed us, and we all fell asleep.

The next thing we knew, a voice that seemed to come from under our feet was shouting, "On belay." Instantly all of us were wide awake and peering over the edge. Fifty feet below us a man wearing snow glasses and all the latest mountaineering equipment was belaying two other men. Everything was being done by the numbers, both by this rope of three men and two similar ropes farther below.

Willi looked around frantically. "Gosh, I know that guy," Willi said. "Pete got me to talk to those fellas about having the right equipment." For a moment he stared at the sweatshirt on his legs and the big seven-foot tent pole and looked wildly for a place to hide. There was no place and no time. In a moment a head popped up some six feet from us and stared in open-mouthed wonder. Finally it spoke. "Aren't you Willi Unsoeld?" What happened can be imagined. Willi said he couldn't stay. His last words were, "If I miss that appointment, Jolene will kill me. I'll leave the crampon at the meadow." Dee and I considered the graduation exercise a great success.

CHAPTER XX

The Peace Corps and Kathmandu

1961-1963

IN NOVEMBER OF 1961, while watching an Exeter-Andover soccer game, I met Josh Miner, who quickly became a friend. Josh was the director of admissions at Andover and a great admirer of Kurt Hahn, then the headmaster of Gordonstoun School in Scotland and the founder of Outward Bound. Josh had been working to get an Outward Bound school funded and operating in the U.S. He was also working with William Sloane Coffin to help get the Peace Corps started.

Throughout the winter we kept in touch, and he and Coffin kept phoning me about personnel for the Peace Corps. Finally, in March, I had a call from the Peace Corps headquarters saying that Sargent Shriver wanted to see me. The caller didn't know why. I thought this was probably about getting people to work in the new Peace Corps training camp at Arecibo, Puerto Rico. I agreed to go to Washington during our spring vacation to see him. What a surprise! I liked Shriver immediately, we talked for an hour or more, and to my amazement he offered me the job of running the Peace Corps program in Afghanistan, Pakistan, or Nepal. The next morning, back in Exeter, after talking with Gail, I went to see Bill Saltonstall, the principal of Phillips Exeter, asking for a leave of absence to go to Nepal. He looked surprised, thought a little, and burst out, "That's just what I would like to do." (As a matter of fact he became the Peace Corps representative in Nigeria the year following.)

I had visited and liked all three of the countries Shriver offered, but Nepal was the most remote and I felt it would be most fun to be there.

Shriver approved the choice and told me to get a deputy to share responsibilities. It was then that I remembered Willi Unsoeld, our moonlight ascent of Glacier Peak, and his easy rapport with the young men who came over the top that day. I phoned Oregon from the Peace Corps office and reached Willi at breakfast. "Willi," I said, "this is Bob Bates. I'm calling from the Peace Corps office. How about coming to Nepal with the Peace Corps?" There was a slight pause before I heard Willi call, "Hey, Jolene, we're going to Nepal." That was how a great partnership started.

Shriver told me he wanted to try something new: to have Peace Corps staff for a country and their volunteers go through training together. We were to learn about Nepal and its language at George Washington University in Washington, DC, and then complete training by attending an Outward Bound school in Colorado. We would all begin together on June 15.

On that magic day, about 80 Peace Corps volunteers gathered at George Washington University to begin training. They were a very diverse group, ranging in age from 18 to 61, but mostly in their early twenties. Nearly all were college graduates and some had graduate degrees. What a cross-section of America at its best! They radiated optimism, hope, and determination to do their part in revising the image of the "ugly American," yet very few could be considered starry-eyed do-gooders. They were very individual, there for different reasons, but all were risk-takers, full of curiosity about other parts of the world, not knowing where they were going or what they would be doing, but ready to take part in something different, something challenging. Obviously the Peace Corps appealed to their idealism, but these were *doers*, men and women who had worked as ranch hands, welders, prune pickers, carpenters, commercial photographers, foresters, chemists, chicken farmers, teachers, oil field workers, boat builders, dairy farm managers, occupational therapists, museum curators, YWCA counselors, electricians, botanists, lubrication mechanics, painters, mail carriers, river guides, engineers, and professional puppeteers.

The best feature of training with our volunteers at George Washington University was that we began to know each other and developed a sense of being a team. Gail and I, and Willi and Jolene Unsoeld and their four children, all lived off campus, but we attended the programs and language studies of the whole group. None of the teachers had ever been in Nepal, as Gail and I had, and too often they would begin their talks with, "Now I've never been in Nepal, but I know Thailand well and I assume that in many ways the Thais are similar." What saved the program was four Nepalis sent from Nepal, who served as teachers; and Professor Randolph Carr, from the University of Pennsylvania, who directed the language program.

Professor Carr had never been in Nepal, but he was an excellent linguist and teacher who had been studying Nepali. Even he, however, was not prepared for the problems he faced when he brought together his four teachers from Nepal, plus the Nepal ambassador's daughter and two Nepali graduate students, with whom he tried to work out the correct Nepali terms for short English conversations. Sometimes the Nepalis had several different ways of saying the same things. Newari is the language of many of the people in Kathmandu, although Nepali is the official language, while in the hills different languages are spoken by the Gurungs, Tamangs, Rais, Limbus, and so forth. Carr finally decided that we would learn only Nepali, but even there differences existed in trying to translate English words. That Carr succeeded as well as he did owed a lot to his initiative, imagination, and determination.

I can learn languages fairly easily if I can read them, but I have a poor ear for learning by sound. I was starting to make progress when the head of the Peace Corps program in Sri Lanka (known as the representative or rep) left and had to be replaced immediately. The Peace Corps staff in Washington was very thin. Ollie Popenoe, who had been doing the staff work both for our program and Sri Lanka, was sent off in a hurry to Colombo. I took his place in Washington and thereafter had little time for language training. I attended all Shriver's staff meetings, at which policy for the entire Peace Corps was made. We discussed training, reasons for volunteers to be sent back, problems concerning illnesses, deaths, or pregnancies, and even whether to forward volunteers' junk mail to all parts of the world. I came to know Shriver well and admired his instant rapport with people at all levels. In these meetings I especially admired Bill Moyers, but Jay Rockefeller, Jack Vaughn, and Daniel Patrick Moynihan also stood out.

Before leaving for Nepal, Gail and I had lunch in Boston with Henry Stebbins, the American ambassador, and his wife, Barbara. We quickly recognized that our relationship with the embassy would be a happy one.

An advance man, Bruce Collard, had been sent to Nepal to make arrangements for housing our volunteers and ordering simple furniture. After a week he cabled that he could make no arrangements unless he had the title of Peace Corps Representative in Nepal. This was my position, but since I was not yet in Nepal and arrangements there were needed, I cabled him to take the position until I arrived.

For the second half of the training program our volunteers were to go to what was then the only Outward Bound school in the U.S. It had been set up recently in Marble, Colorado. The Unsoeld family was to go to Marble, while Gail and I, with Robin Bullard, a secretary selected for us by the Peace Corps, went ahead to Kathmandu. Robin, a recent graduate from Katherine Gibbs Secretarial School, was young, very pretty, idealistic, and dedicated to the idea that the Peace Corps treated all foreign people fairly, whereas the American embassy and the U.S. AID mission probably did not. She had never been out of the U.S.

At Kathmandu, we had a few days with Bruce Collard and dinners at the embassy before the volunteers and the Unsoelds arrived. Arrangements had been made for all of us to stay at the Royal Hotel, for Boris Lissanevitch had taken over the rest of the palace of the Third Prince and now had a real hotel with many rooms, turbaned waiters, and fancy menus. Our main concern was to keep the volunteers healthy during their indoctrination process, preventing stomach troubles and other ills as far as possible as their bodies gradually became accustomed to the food and water in Nepal. Their arrival was delayed by the total cancellation of India Airlines planes during the brief India-China War in northern Assam. Finally, however, a plane became available in India, and we and the Stebbinses greeted the Unsoelds and 69 tired volunteers who had survived the arduous training course and several days of waiting in New Delhi. Two other volunteers were to fly in later. In accordance with an agreement with Boris, we brought them all to the Royal Hotel, where they were to continue language training.

In an unexpected way, our Peace Corps group had become of great importance to all Westerners in Nepal. This was explained to me in great secrecy by Mr. Armstrong, the administrative officer at the American embassy. The problem started with Brigitte Bardot, the enormously popular French movie actress. She had been asked to take a major part in a movie about Marco Polo, to be filmed in Nepal. A French film director had visited Nepal and reached an agreement with Boris to supply 60 elephants and hundreds of Tamangs to be ready at a certain day to take part in shooting the film. On the agreed date, the Tamangs had given up the best part of the harvesting season to go to Butwal in the Terai, the jungle area in southern Nepal where the filming was to begin. Boris had promised the Tamangs high wages for taking part in the film, but at the appointed time nobody came from France and there was no message for Boris. Something had happened, though he did not know what. Meanwhile the elephants

Mac Odell and R.H.B. in the main street of Dhankuta

were chomping several hundred pounds of fodder a day, and the Tamangs were getting hungry. They wanted their money!

Nearly a month had passed since the farmers had been assembled. Now no tourists were coming to Kathmandu because of the India-China War in Assam, and so Boris had no money to pay the Tamangs. He was beginning to fear for his life.

Since Boris had become a British subject, the Tamangs considered the British embassy to be responsible for his actions. They sent an ultimatum to Boris and another to the British embassy, saying that if they were not paid by the following Monday they would burn down the British camp at Barawa, which happened to be handy. Nepalis are usually a very good-natured, mild people, but if aroused enough they can become wild and smash or kill anything in their way. If they burned the British camp, that action could easily fuel further violence, especially in Kathmandu, where both the British and American embassies would be in danger. Peace Corps volunteers might become involved, too, for the number of Westerners in Nepal at the time was very small, and all Westerners might be considered to blame.

The Peace Corps volunteers were scheduled to have three weeks' training in Kathmandu before going to their villages. Boris would take us all at a

PEACE CORPS PHOTO

Training with volunteers in Washington

much-reduced rate if we would pay in advance. Our government regulations stipulated that payment be made only after services had been rendered, and Boris' service had not yet been received. If I approved payment in advance, legally I would be spending funds for something not yet authorized by the American government, but both the head of U.S. AID, from whom the money would come, and our ambassador were eager to have me do it, though Armstrong made clear that they should in no way be officially involved in the transaction. The Tamangs were threatening to burn the camp the following day. Would I approve immediate payment to Boris three weeks in advance? I did.

The next morning early, two large burlap sacks were brought to our apartment. With the shades drawn, Boris, Colonel Wylie of the British embassy (member of the 1953 Everest expedition), and I sat around two tiger skins on the floor, and began counting out rhinos (100-rupee notes showing a rhino on the back). We counted the piles twice. In U.S. dollars, the amount wasn't so much, but to Nepalis it seemed a fortune. I signed for the money and gave it to Boris, who gave it to Wylie. A plane and pilot were waiting for him, and he immediately departed for the airport. Gail, Tsering (Wylie's favorite Lhasa apso), and a large and very smelly white goat that loved to lie by our side door were the only other observers.

Later that evening Colonel Wylie called to say all was well at Butwal, and at dinner in the British embassy at Kathmandu there had been an enthusiastic toast to "a certain friend."

Seventy-one volunteers from 28 different states, Hawaii, and the District of Columbia came to Nepal as members of Nepal I. We had 56 men and 15 women, including four married couples. They had attended nearly 60 different colleges, and only five had no college experience. Fourteen had graduate degrees. Many came from colleges I had never heard of, but six were from the University of New Hampshire, four from Harvard, and two each from Princeton, Dartmouth, Carleton, Western Michigan University, and Chico State. The states best represented were California and New Hampshire. One was still a Dutch national who lacked a couple of weeks to receive his American citizenship. During our 15 months in the Peace Corps (for I had only a year's leave of absence and a summer vacation), there were three marriages, while two volunteers were dropped, two resigned, and one was injured and flown home.

In Nepal Professor Carr made friends with local teachers, who helped him to improve the language training. Meanwhile the volunteers began to walk around Kathmandu and Patan to try to talk with Nepalis in their own language. Some Americans soon developed sore heads from not ducking low enough to enter doorways high enough for the small Nepali people, but very low for our tall volunteers. U.S. AID had become a big organization in Nepal, but most AID people stayed in their compound and rarely went out of Kathmandu. They predicted terrible health problems for the volunteers, especially those going to live in distant villages.

Our volunteers were to live in Kathmandu and a dozen different small towns and villages, most of which I could visit only by walking. They generally taught English, either in schools or colleges, but most officially or unofficially taught other things too. In 1962 Nepal had been visited by few Westerners, and the volunteers were the subject of considerable curiosity. It was not uncommon to find people who knew next to nothing about America, as I found when making a visit to a volunteer in a remote mountain town. As darkness was falling, I selected a well-kept house and asked if I could get some supper and a place to unroll my sleeping bag. As usual I was made very welcome and dal-bhat was served (rice with lentil sauce, the national dish).

While I was resting and eating, my host asked numerous questions, most of which I could not understand. He especially wanted to know where I had come from. That he had never heard of the Peace Corps did not sur-

PCVs Frame, Tuveson, and Fisher at Bhaktapur.
Note mountains in distance.

prise me, but that he had never heard of America did. I told him that it was a country farther away than England, and larger, too. That stopped our conversation, for he knew I was lying. England, he indicated, was the biggest country in the world and the farthest from Nepal. (For a long time the only Westerners in Nepal were British.) I also met people from remote districts who were accustomed to using flint and steel. To them I showed a marvelous invention: matches.

Some volunteers were to serve in the local colleges or secondary schools of Kathmandu. While driving two of them to their new home, Gail and I had an unpleasant experience. Political tension in Kathmandu was extreme at the time because of a threatened coup by members of a banned political party, whose leaders had recently been jailed. To get to the volunteers' house, I needed to drive around the corner of the jail, but by mistake drove around the wrong corner directly toward the front door. I stopped when I saw my mistake, but a soldier came forward and aimed his rifle directly at me from a few feet away. He was swaying from side to side, obviously very drunk and ready to shoot. We put up our hands and stayed still, not wanting to be shot while driving away. There were some long moments while I tried to tell him in Nepali that we meant no harm and had made a mistake. Finally an officer came out, brushed away the sentry's swaying rifle, and we went on.

Willi and I settled into an office on the main street, a good location close to the American embassy. Before long a Nepali came from U.S. AID to discuss a job with the Peace Corps. He was Dhruba Bhakta Mathema, who became our chief clerk, dear friend, and the most valuable asset the Nepal Peace Corps was to have for years to come. Dhruba was an extraordinary man. Born in Nepal, he had been in exile in India after the ruling Rana family hanged his uncle, one of the four "martyrs" whose busts are now prominently displayed in Kathmandu. Dhruba, when in India, had lived in Kalimpong. When the Chinese invaded Tibet, he had acted on the Tibetans' behalf as a "minister without portfolio," visiting the British and American ambassadors and Nehru himself, asking aid for the Tibetans that never came. We learned quickly that he was a man of great integrity and wise guidance. His sons were later to become distinguished, too, at Tribhuvan University, the World Bank, and UNICEF. Another became the top city planner in Nepal and a daughter received her Ph.D. at Stanford.

Getting to know Kathmandu, Dhruba, and our volunteers took time, and the weeks spent at the Royal Hotel were useful in more ways than language study. The volunteers were to be spread into a number of villages, all without telephones or reliable mail service, and the Peace Corps doctor, Mark Rhine, a former student of mine, had grave concerns over potential illness and how long it would take a sick person to return to Kathmandu.

One of our early duties was to get our volunteers to the villages where the Nepal government wanted them. Willi and I took turns accompanying them, but we considered getting them as comfortably settled as we could to be a primary responsibility. Naturally, some places were better than others, and some volunteers were more imaginative in turning big ideas about teaching or farming into useful work. What they were officially doing wasn't necessarily what they ended up doing, and usually what they did outside of their few hours of teaching was more useful to Nepal than their teaching.

The volunteers were to be paid at the same level as their counterpart teachers, but since the volunteers were not living at home, we increased their monthly stipend. Even so, they were paid only $46 a month, the lowest salary of any Peace Corps person. Of course there were no local supermarkets to shop in, and volunteers soon found that procuring food and water took a substantial amount of time. Indian peanut butter was available in Kathmandu. That was familiar, and many volunteers left Kathmandu for their villages with a good supply. Another group for the first month lived almost entirely on rice liberally doused with Indian ketchup, also bought in Kathmandu.

Merely living in Nepal taught the volunteers much about themselves and their abilities to solve problems and the numerous frustrations of their daily lives. Frequently, they would set out to bring about what they saw as needed changes, only to be frustrated by convention, the caste system, lack of communication, or problems common to all underdeveloped countries. The way they stuck to their jobs despite all sorts of problems was admirable.

For Willi and me, attending dinners of government officials was obligatory. Such duties probably seemed to the volunteers a waste of time, but in their way they contributed to our success as much as John White's increasing egg production at Parwanipur from 360 to 600 per week.

At first the people of Kathmandu could not believe that American teachers were shopping like ordinary Nepalis with baskets on their backs. "See," was the overheard remark, "now the Americans are bringing over their own coolies."

Volunteers frequently made, or had made, furniture to supplement the bulky items purchased by the Peace Corps through U.S. AID. When Les Gile, a New Hampshire farmer, had a simple kitchen table made, he estimated that the material cost 90 percent and the carpentry 10 percent, while at home the costs were just the opposite.

Most of the volunteers' successes were in building character—their own! What they would have considered success at home was not available. Practical successes were small, such as starting small lending libraries, building latrines (usually the Nepalis would not use them), and planting seeds of new vegetables; but they were clearly successful in teaching English and making friends for America. One such success was Ralph Goetze's work as an architect. He was a graduate of Harvard College and the Harvard School of Architecture. In Nepal, he found plenty of work, but his greatest accomplishment was in designing the first buildings for Prithni Narayan College in Pokhara. When he arrived in Nepal, students were studying in the open air with a tiny thatched roof over them. When he departed two years later, the brick buildings were up and students had moved in.

There was Barbara Wylie and her Happy Free School, which started with five low-caste children who did not go to school. Others wanted to come. Her success soon snowballed to 50 children, and the school's name was decided by the children themselves. It was so successful that the government eventually took it over.

Ron Elliott had a different success. He was supposed to be instructing in agriculture, but the tools he had expected to use were not available on the first day of school. There was a crude blackboard, and on this he drew pictures of the tools he did not have. At that the school's principal, who was observing from the back of the room, rushed forward crying, "Students, we have always wanted an art teacher and now we have one." Ron soon found that the Nepalis knew more about their particular agriculture problems than he did, but he found plenty of other ways to be useful.

Another volunteer saw that pairs of oxen had separate yokes and pulled separately. Accordingly, he painstakingly carved out an ox yoke of the sort his grandfather had used in New Hampshire. Only then he learned, as other volunteers did, that Nepalis had good reasons for most of the things they did. Nepali oxen are small, too small for the heavy yoke Les Gile carved, and they plow small terraces where oxen often fall off. Yoked to another ox, an ox falling off a terrace would probably break his neck.

Gail and I moved into a house with thick adobe walls on Putli Sadak (Butterfly Street), a busy thoroughfare in the area called Dilli Bajar. Across the street from us was a wall of Singha Durbar, the great Rana palace, where the royal band practiced every morning, starting very early, usually with "Britons Never Shall Be Slaves," or "Colonel Bogey," made famous by the *Bridge on the River Kwai*. Next door to us on one side stood a house with many Chinese, who played the radio loudly until late at night. Our neighbors on the other side were young ladies of leisure, who often borrowed our dahlias to put in their hair. Our house had peculiarities, too, such as a bathtub with a drain an inch above the bottom, so that after a bath it was nearly impossible to remove all the water. Water for all purposes had to be pumped to a tank on the roof. Another problem was that the wrong paint had been used on all the cement floors and it never dried, so that rugs put on the living room floor were glued on permanently. The house was airy, however, and large enough so that volunteers in town for a day or two could stay with us. On a normal morning it was hard to tell Santa, our man, how many would be having breakfast.

One of our visits to volunteers I remember especially. A jeep had been sent to Kathmandu for the use of volunteers in eastern Nepal, though the only road it could use there was from Biratnagar to Dharan. We had volunteers in both these towns and in the more distant mountain villages of Dhankuta and Bojpur. No road in Nepal then went from Kathmandu to eastern Nepal, but we believed it would be possible to get there by driving through India. We talked over this plan with Chandra, the wiry ex-Gurkha who took care of our jeeps, and on occasion served as our driver. Chandra was enthusiastic. He could drive us and serve as interpreter when needed.

Gail, Chandra, and I took food for ourselves and packages for the volunteers, and set off one morning down the road of a thousand switchbacks that links Kathmandu to the Indian border. As we swung around turn after turn, first climbing to get over the Mahabarat Range, descending, then climbing again to cross the Siwalik Hills, I was glad we had Chandra with us. The last time I had driven with him down the Rajpath, the jeep's gas tank had grazed a rock and the tank began to leak. Chandra had reacted immediately, taking soap from his old army toilet kit and sealing off the leak. It worked, and we were able to finish our business and get back to Kathmandu.

At Birgunj in the Terai (the southern district of Nepal), we had lunch with the volunteers posted there. Then we turned east along what was to become Nepal's East-West Highway. At this point it was less road than a track through dense jungle with thick underbrush. There were no houses on it and the road forced us to drive slowly.

Shadows were lengthening when we crossed the newly built bridge over a small river flowing south. On the eastern side stood a little temporary bamboo shelter about three feet high, open on one side, made by the bridge builders. We had seen nobody for some time. The stream, with big sal trees near it, was very beautiful; peacocks were crying and roosting for the night, and monkeys were moving around in the trees. Since the road was a bad one to travel after dark and the shelter looked like a better place to sleep than in the jeep, Gail and I decided to spend the night there. Chandra was dead against it.

"Why?" we asked.

"Tigers."

"Who is afraid of tigers?" Gail asked.

Chandra, a very polite man, looked at her sternly. "Memsahib, you speak like a child." He had never called her Memsahib before.

No better alternative appearing, we set about gathering dry wood for a fire and soon had a roaring blaze. We ate our supper around it. Chandra was going to sleep in the car, waking from time to time to put on more wood, but we ducked into the shelter, put down our sleeping bags, and were soon asleep. I didn't sleep well and was glad when daylight came, but it was accompanied by a sprinkle of rain. When this stopped, I got up and joined Chandra, who was working on the fire. He had had a sleepless night, too, and was anxious to move on.

We had tea with bread and cheese, and then Gail and I decided to walk ahead down the road for a hundred yards or so to see if we saw birds or animals. The air was fresh after the rain and we heard no animals, but we hadn't gone 50 feet when we came across the tracks of a big tiger, going in the direction we were going, and made since the rain. He had probably watched us eat breakfast. We followed the tracks, hoping we might see him down the road, but less than 100 feet farther on they turned abruptly off into thick brush. Gail started to go ahead to see where the tracks went, but we quickly came to our senses. When Chandra drove up, we got into the jeep. Our attitude toward tigers had changed.

A few miles farther on, we came out of the heavy jungle, and after a long, bumpy ride finally reached Janakpur, normally reached from other directions. Since we had talked previously about the possibility of stationing a volunteer in Janakpur, on our arrival I had a discussion with the head of the school. We were too late to start for India that day and slept on the floor of the schoolhouse.

No direct road led to India, but we were told we probably could work our way there through the remaining forest. Next morning we headed south and were soon winding around individual trees, following a track probably made by bullock carts. Ahead were flat, open fields where distant water buffalo rushed away in alarm. Finally we saw a man on a bicycle, and at this sign of civilization realized that we must have crossed the open border into India. Ahead of us a woman raced out of a house, grabbed a child who was playing in the track, and returned. Our jeep may have been the first motor vehicle she had ever seen. The track became a road, and we eventually reached the city of Darbhanga, where we found a restaurant that had some eggs and flat bread. People continually stared at us and even more at the jeep. All asked where we had come from. Headed south again, we passed other villages and finally reached the great bridge over the Ganges between Patna and Monghyr, where we had to show our passports. From there a long drive east on good roads brought us to the city of Bagalpur on the Ganges, where a dak bungalow offered a good night's sleep.

Not far away was a village of boatmen. After some difficulties, two boatman agreed to take us and the jeep down the great river to a village below the confluence of Nepal's Dudh Kosi River and the Ganges. We were to land at a place on the north bank where a road led north to our objective, Biratnagar.

In the morning the boatmen were not at all eager to take us. They kept talking about "dacoits" (pirates), which sounded to me like a ruse to get higher pay. Eventually they told us to drive the jeep up two boards and across the deck, although the boat's beam was so narrow that the jeep's bumpers overhung to port and starboard. Chandra did it, and we anchored the jeep strongly with chains and ropes. Thereafter the only way to go fore or aft on the boat was through the jeep or around the sides by holding on to it. Chandra whispered to me that he had persuaded them to take us by telling them, "Sahib has a gun."

The boat had no engine, but used a big steering oar and a sail of the sort used by Christopher Columbus. The boatmen were in no hurry to leave and went home to eat. When they returned, they let the current sweep them downstream to an island, where they took on supplies and idled about until midafternoon.

Finally we pried the boatmen loose and they cast off. Immediately the gray water seized us and we were swept downstream, one man steering with the oar. Almost at once he navigated an area with big whirlpools. Then, as the river broadened and the current slackened, the boatmen put up a sail, and when that began to flap they rowed, singing a song to keep their stroke as they pulled. Chandra went into the hold, where a fire was smoldering, boiled some rice, and made tea. (We never expected to be drinking tea made from the waters of the holy Ganges, the final resting place of the cremated bodies of countless faithful Hindus.)

As darkness came on, we suddenly anchored. The river had spread out, and the shores on either side seemed at least a mile away. Chandra could not understand much of the dialect spoken by the two boatmen and didn't know why they had anchored, but they mentioned dacoits again and insisted that we be absolutely quiet.

It was dark some hours later when we heard the sounds of paddling. A clouded moon gave little light as we stared upstream. A boat was coming down toward us. Our boatmen became very scared; their hands were shaking. One of them whispered to Chandra, "Sahib must get his gun." I had no gun, of course, and my only offensive weapons were a small jackknife and a flashlight, though sounding the jeep's horn might scare away robbers.

The noise of paddling increased and with it the sound of people talking animatedly. The boat seemed to be coming down with the current directly onto us. Gail and I waited, breathless. Suddenly our boatmen cried out as a smaller boat, filled with men, banged into us. Everyone was shouting. In a moment the current slid the boat past us and on downstream, but not before a man jumped onto our boat. He quickly sat down by the mast, pulling his cloak about him. I was gripping the heavy flashlight, but he made no threatening moves. Downstream we could hear receding shouts from the other boat. The new arrival said nothing. He merely sat there. If he had a knife under his cloak or planned to rob us, we couldn't tell, but since our boatmen showed no alarm, we relaxed, too.

Not long afterward we pulled up the anchor and started downstream, helped by a cloudless quarter moon. Gail and I dozed in the back of the jeep and Chandra in front. At first light the boatmen pulled into a harbor where we tied up to other boats. As the "passenger" quickly disappeared, Chandra and I staggered off to a Nepali office to make our return to Nepal legal. From the harbor to Biratnagar was a long but easy drive, and after visiting volunteers there and in Dharan, and leaving our jeep, we flew back to Kathmandu.

Visiting our volunteers in different parts of Nepal was so interesting that I felt we should be paying the Peace Corps for the privilege. Our official position also had its advantages. For instance when Birendra, the Crown Prince, returned to Nepal from Eton for his Sacred Thread Ceremony, we were one of only three American couples invited to it. The ceremony, which began at 8:00 in the morning, was a very formal affair, with all the generals wearing dress uniforms, medals, and tremendous plumed hats. The British ambassador wore formal knee breeches and a three-cornered hat like Admiral Nelson's.

The script for a Sacred Thread Ceremony seems to parallel to some extent the story of the Prodigal Son. What we saw was 16-year-old Birendra, dressed in rags, and with a bundle tied to a stick slung over his shoulder, going off to make his fortune. (Of course the rags and the bundle were made of gold cloth, since he was a prince.) His relatives pleaded with him to stay, but he walked out through the tall palace gates and disappeared. This brought a pause for refreshments. Soon after, the young man returned wearing princely clothes and riding on a richly decorated horse, followed by an elephant and a whole parade of dancers, jugglers, musicians, and marching troops.

After certain ceremonies with the priests, which we did not see, Birendra stood at the head of a long receiving line, where scores of people brought him gifts, mainly platters holding beautiful carvings made of fruits and coconuts, all decorated with flowers. These he received with a nod to each giver.

Only a small group of ambassadors, generals, Nepalese officials, members of the royal family, and a few others were invited to this fascinating affair. We were lucky to be invited, though officially I was the third-ranking American in the country. We went home, changed our clothes, and quickly left for a potluck supper with volunteers. Nobody could say our job was not a varied one.

For a couple of months Willi Unsoeld was away from the Peace Corps, with Shriver's permission, serving as climbing leader of the American Everest Expedition led by Norman Dyhrenfurth. We knew that Willi and Tom Hornbein had hopes of making a daring new route on Everest by climbing the West Ridge, and then completing the first traverse of the mountain by coming down to the South Col camp. Father Moran, a Jesuit priest who had started the best school in Nepal some years earlier, was an active ham radio operator who kept in daily communication with the expedition. One special evening he invited Gail and me, and Jolene Unsoeld and her children, to hear the expedition news. He told us it might be exciting.

Fortunately the weather was good, and at the appointed hour he sounded his call sign, "9NIMM Mickey Mouse." Men at base camp answered and added that there might be good news. They put us through to those at a higher camp who were trying to reach Tom and Willi on the mountain. We knew what a dangerous climb these two had contemplated, and had no idea what had happened to them since. Then Willi's voice came on from the top of Mt. Everest. One can imagine our excitement.

Jolene spoke to him, and Terris, their small daughter, told him she had "wode a pony." Willi's answer to Jolene was, "This is the last time, Jolene. I mean it. I really do." The hour was so late that we feared the two could not possibly get down to the South Col camp before dark. If they did not, they would have to spend the night on the steep upper snow slopes without hot food or shelter. Could they survive such a night at 28,000 feet? Willi knew they had to start down, and his last words were a quotation from Robert Frost: "'And miles to go before I sleep.'" A very worried and serious group left Father Moran and headed home.

A couple of hours later (as we learned afterward) Willi and Tom met Lute Jersted and Barry Bishop, who had reached the summit from the South Col the same day and were slowly descending. All four had to bivouac. That windless night in the snow Willi thought his own feet were all right, but he worked ceaselessly to warm Tom's cold feet. In the morning he found that his own feet had frozen. After a painful descent, he was brought by helicopter to Kathmandu, where Jolene, Gail, and I met him on his arrival. Later, after a long stay in the hospital, nine of his 10 toes were amputated.

Gail greatly enjoyed our life in Nepal, as I did, but she steadily lost weight and eventually energy. Since Doctor Rhine did not know the cause, he and I agreed it would be best if she returned to the U.S. in June, a few weeks before I would need to leave to get back to school in September. I flew with her to Delhi and saw her off. Not long afterward I learned that doctors in the U.S. found that she had no major health problem, though she had lost 35 pounds. Good food soon brought back her normal good health.

After her return, I sent her a Nepali basket full of orchids we had kept on the porch of our house. I had gathered them from downed trees during my visits to volunteers. They were sent dry with the proper certificates of health from Nepal and were brought through U.S. customs in the official way. None were outstandingly beautiful orchids, but some lovely ones have continued to bloom in our cool little greenhouse in Exeter ever since.

Willi was supposed to take over as Peace Corps representative when I returned to Exeter, and he was convinced that he could do it despite his toes. Accordingly I began gradually saying good-bye to friends and volunteers and planning my return to Exeter. Shriver had offered me posts in African countries but I had refused. I had also been asked to talk to volunteers of the next Nepal groups, who were training in Oregon and would be leaving in mid-September for Nepal. I could do this just in time to return to Exeter for my first classes. En route, I decided to take two weeks of vacation, for I had taken none since joining the Peace Corps.

From Calcutta I went to Rangoon, then to Bangkok, and on to Pnom Penh, the beautiful capital of Cambodia. At Angkor Wat, I spent a couple of days traveling to different ruins. The morning after my arrival, I was walking along the far side of the lake that separates the hotel area from the ruins, when I noticed a mahout riding an elephant that dragged a 50-foot chain behind. They had just crossed the lake and were headed for the jungle when the elephant's chain caught on a rock outcrop. The caught end of the chain was near me, and so I waved at the rider and released the chain. At that the mahout indicated I should come with him. Where, I had no idea, but I walked to a ruin to which he directed the elephant, climbed up 15 feet on it, and from there scrambled onto the elephant's bare back.

The mahout, who was sitting on the elephant's neck, indicated that I should get on close to him and put my arms around his waist, for we were about to go steeply uphill. I climbed on, grabbed the mahout, and sat with my legs spread out on the elephant's broad back, smooth except for occasional coarse hairs. There was nothing to hold onto except the mahout, and when we started uphill I was thankful he was there. We pushed our way through jungle, the mahout indicating that he had something to show me. Suddenly he stopped beside a wall with the most beautiful Khmer bas-relief I had seen. I could step off the elephant right at the base of the relief. He pointed the direction of a well-known temple from which I could return, and waved good-bye; he wouldn't take any money. The splendid carving was completely undamaged, and when I later asked about it at the hotel, the only answer I got was that it was in an area where they didn't go.

A week later I reported in at Peace Corps headquarters and soon was home.

Gail inspects a Nepalese swing; Machapuchre (the fishtail) in the background

CHAPTER XXI

Iceland and the Matterhorn Centennial

1964-1965

EXETER DID NOT SEEM very exciting after our life in Kathmandu, but Gail and I enjoyed being back in our own home together. It wasn't just the conveniences of life in Exeter, or not cooking with mustard seed oil on a kerosene stove. Shriver had offered us the job of "rep" in countries in both East and West Africa, but we didn't want to make a career of government work. My classmate Ernie Gillespie was now the acting principal of the academy, and I was glad I could be useful to him. I was also sure that a teacher could not hope to find better students than those at Exeter.

The following summer after a good school year, we decided to do something entirely different. Since our friend Dick Brinckerhoff had been telling us about Iceland, we went there. Our plan had been to rent a car to drive around Iceland, but none was available. We were told that many fords were too deep for anything smaller than a truck. We were, however, in luck, for Iceland was about to have its first tour, using two small buses with extra large wheels and a truck to solve fording problems. This experimental two-week tour, run by Icelanders, was about to cross the country from Reykjavik in the south to Akureyri in the north, and then return through the eastern central area. The tour had no other Americans. Most of the 30 people on it were Icelanders, with a few young Germans, older Dutch, and a Danish couple.

Though we saw some of the world's great waterfalls and a few geysers, locally pronounced "geezers," to me the most interesting sights were the old craters throughout the central lava fields, many holding water at their bottoms where the wild calls of nesting loons and swans echoed from rim to rim. Moss grew on many of these crater walls, and the contrast among the black lava walls, the flying swans, and the emerald green of the moss was enchanting. At one crater I nearly burned a hole in my trousers by sitting on a rock that had not entirely cooled.

On the east coast, we saw boys and girls of 16 working in a big fish-packing plant. Sixteen-year-old girls, like those we saw planting flowers in Reykjavik, were giving a month of service to their country. They didn't resent the requirement, and obviously were having a good time as well as doing useful work for society. If such a system could be carried out in the U.S., wouldn't it strengthen the fiber of our whole society!

When the two small tour buses stopped to eat, the young Germans always crowded in first. World War II had not been over long, and the aggressiveness of the young Germans was very annoying to the Dutch and Danes. Toward the end of the tour the Germans realized that they were not quite accepted by the others, but this all ended on a festival day. The Germans, shouting that there must be a bonfire, began holding hands and jumping over a small fire. Then they began grabbing our hands and jumping, and soon the old Dutch cavalryman whom they had most offended had his hand seized by a German nurse and they jumped over the bonfire together. That changed the whole atmosphere. We began to see our group as an indication of how Europe might develop in the future.

Before we left Iceland, we went to the Vestmannaeyjar, the southern-most part of the country, near where Iceland's most recent active volcano had appeared. This was Surtsey, a volcano that had risen from the sea a few miles south of the Vestmannaeyjar Peninsula and its nearby islands. A young fellow named Arne agreed to take us in his small boat to an island famous for puffins, if the sea wasn't too rough to land. It wasn't, and we climbed some 400 feet above the sea to a small plateau, where a tiny house had been built about 30 feet from the sheer cliff edge. A cross, marking where a man had slipped and fallen off, warned us to be careful. Puffins were flying along the cliff edge, many bringing back small fish to their nesting holes.

In the hut stood some 12-foot poles with small circular nets at the end. These were for catching puffins. Arne showed us how to tie ourselves to a rock and reach out with a net to snare puffins. Netting the birds was not too difficult, as we reached out from the cliff edge and looked straight down on surf hundreds of feet below. Of course we let the caught birds go. After dark we had grand views of Surtsey erupting from the ocean about a dozen miles away.

On our return from the island, Arne asked us to dinner at his home. Almost the first of his mother's words were, "Do you like chicken?" We said we did, supposing she would be giving us some for supper. Not at all. "We don't like chicken," she announced. "We don't think it has any flavor." That should have tipped us off. For dinner, we had puffin, and it did have flavor—a strong, gamey flavor, too. We could understand her estimate of chicken, but we were not converted.

· · ·

A year later, I was asked to represent the American Alpine Club at Zermatt, where the Swiss government was celebrating the hundredth anniversary of the ascent of the Matterhorn. It was a large celebration, with the Swiss government providing air tickets for guests and all expenses while the guests were in Switzerland.

When Gail and I arrived, we met several of the official guests at the railroad station. It didn't take us long to come to know them all, including Eric Shipton, whom we took to at once, and John and Joy Hunt. John Case and André Roch were there, both getting on in years but climbing together with the enthusiasm of 15-year-olds, and also Noel and Mona Odell, whom we had last seen in New Zealand. Several members of the successful British Everest team were there, as well as climbers from different countries of Europe, including a delightful Greek who had been married on top of Mt. Olympus. Eric and I came to know each other when we led ropes on some minor climbs such as the Rimpfischhorn. Most of us planned to climb the Matterhorn, and Eric and I decided to do it together.

To avoid the sun on the muggy afternoon before the climb, we were about the last to leave Zermatt to walk up to the Hörnli Hut for the celebration dinner. All climbers were to sleep at the hut that night and leave on the climb early in the morning. As Eric and I followed the path toward the hut, we noticed a heavyset man in a dark jacket, whom we had first seen far below us. He was climbing fast, as we were not, and reached the hut almost as soon as we did.

We were ushered into a place at the end of a little table and a moment later the heavyset man was placed opposite us. He stared fixedly at Eric and then said, "You're Shipton, aren't you?"

"Yes," Eric acknowledged.

"I'm Harrer," said the other man, "and I want to thank you. You got me out of jail."

Eric opened his mouth in astonishment, and then, looking most properly British, replied, "I'm sure I never got anybody out of jail in my life."

"Yes, you did," said Heinrich Harrer. "When Aufschnaiter [his climbing companion] and I were interned at Dehra Dun at the beginning of the war, the house where they put us had a small library, and in it was your book *Blank on the Map*. It had a small map, and since we had none to get us to Tibet, when we escaped we tore it out and took it with us, and that is how we managed to get there."

Good conversation followed that lasted into the small hours, for snow had begun to fall shortly after our arrival at the hut, and it continued to fall. We knew what that meant. The original plan was for five of us to climb the Zmutt Ridge—Eric and I on one rope, and John and Joy Hunt with a Swiss climber on the other—but in the morning there was two feet of snow outside, and of course no climbs were possible.

After a leisurely breakfast, Harrer, Eric, and I descended to Zermatt together. I hated missing the climb of the Zmutt Ridge, but at least we heard wonderful stories of Tibet and of Harrer's and Aufschnaiter's work there. (Aufschnaiter had been in Nepal working with the Swiss when we were with the Peace Corps, and we had met several times.)

CHAPTER XXII

Outward Bound
and Mt. Russell

1966

I N EXETER I BEGAN SEEING MORE of Josh Miner, now swamped by the successes of Outward Bound. Since he desperately needed help I was granted a half-year off from Exeter to help him.

Josh and I worked on a number of projects, but the one I found most interesting was at Trenton High School in New Jersey, where many high school students were dropping out. The school administration and the head of the Poverty Program in Trenton were eager to stop it. Our solution was to find something that would make students want to stay in school. With money from the Poverty Program, we hired several of the most popular and respected members of the senior class at the high school and set up a pilot program of rock climbing, overnight camping, and whitewater canoeing. The seniors we hired loved it, and the dropouts became jealous.

Finally, we agreed to let the dropouts take part if they would agree to the following program: go to school at least three days a week and spend at least one morning a week with a teacher, one-on-one, at the Trenton State Teachers College. An experienced outdoorsman led the weekend activities, while highly motivated teachers at Trenton State worked on the students' academic problems. Together they turned the students around. In fact, the program became so successful that Trenton High School developed a similar program of its own the next year and funded it.

During the summer of 1966, Ad Carter was planning an expedition to Alaska to attempt the second ascent of Mt. Russell in the Alaska Range.

Mt. Russell stands out among its neighbors.

Shipton on Mt. Russell

He asked me to join him, and when I told him that Eric Shipton was interested, he asked him too. Mt. Russell is only 11,670 feet high, but not an
easy climb. In addition, we planned to make a new route. Seven of us were
in the party, including Eric, Larry Carter (Ad's son), and Dr. Harry
McDade.

Eric flew to Anchorage direct from Europe, and two days after his
departure, thanks to Don Sheldon's plane, we were all camped on an 8,000-
foot plateau, deep in the Alaska Range, a couple of miles northeast of the
peak. From this base a direct route took us to nearly 10,000 feet, where we
set up three small tents and began to work out a traverse onto the northwest ridge. Here, while climbing a 60-degree slope, Ad fell into an apparently bottomless crevasse. From where we were belaying, we could not give
him much help, and it required tremendous effort for him to get himself
out. When we returned to our tents, however, we were sure that our route
would give us a good chance at the summit the next day.

The chance never occurred, for that night a storm struck with winds of
more than 100 miles an hour. Eric and I shared a small, Meade-style, two-
man tent, which blowing snow threatened to bury. Every half hour or less we

Mt. Russell from the east; our high camp

took turns opening the oval entrance to shovel snow away from the drifted sides. We did not realize that Ad Carter's tent was in worse shape than ours. To our astonishment, during the storm Ad suddenly arrived at the door of our tent, covered with snow and wearing only one boot. Almost as soon as we let him in, he disappeared, for the snow he brought in with him produced an immediate fog in the tent. Since the wind had shredded his tent, shelter was more important at that moment than finding his other boot.

The storm continued, though less violently, and after three days we fought our way down to base camp, where at first we found no sign of our large tent left there. (It had been blown down and completely covered by snow.) If we could not find this tent in that white expanse, our situation would be critical, for there was no possibility of walking out to civilization. Since we knew the approximate position of the tent, however, Ad by probing soon was able to locate it under a couple of feet of snow.

For the next 10 days, while the storm continued, Eric and I lived in the two-man mountain tent we had brought down from the camp above. Completely shut in, we shared all the stories we could think of, read, cleared away snow, and drank oceans of tea. It was here that Eric declared that if he were doing his life over again, he would not go six times to Mt. Everest. "That's too long for any mountain!" He also told of his great desire to go to a high, icy peak in Central Asia named the Great Ice Mountain, which had been surveyed by a British explorer in the 1890s as being over 25,000 feet high. I never had heard of this peak before. Eric said that when he was consul at Kashgar, he and Bill Tilman had hoped to reach it and climb it, but it was "too far."

During the storm, eight feet of snow fell, and we had to move the tent three times. Eric's ice axe disappeared in the snow and we never found it. When the storm cleared, we radioed Sheldon that we were ready to be picked up when he could do it. Our chance to climb Mt. Russell that summer had gone. A day or two later, Lowell Thomas, Jr., landed and flew us to Anchorage, from where Eric, Harry McDade, and I joined Gail at Camp Denali, with its stupendous views of Mt. McKinley. After a few days of wandering the McKinley lowlands and viewing caribou and Dall sheep, we reluctantly headed south.

The trustees at Outward Bound, apparently appreciating the work I had done to help Josh Miner, had asked Gail and me to visit the four main schools at their expense and report on our observations. This we did with great pleasure, starting with the Oregon Outward Bound School in deep forest, then going on to Marble, Colorado, where Joe Nolde and Jed Williamson showed us that the Colorado school had progressed immensely since our Peace Corps group had trained there in 1962. We continued east to visit the school at Ely, Minnesota, with its great waterways for canoeing, and found John Pieh and his father doing well with groups of both sexes. We flew home in time to visit the final exercises at Hurricane Island, the sailors' Outward Bound in Maine, run by the dynamic Peter Willauer. We had plenty of good moments at all of the camps, but one at Hurricane Island I especially remember. A black boy was being highly complimented for his leadership and all-around performance. He listened quietly, and then said simply, "It's the only time in my life I ever started even."

CHAPTER XXIII

Phoksumdo Tal and Sikkim

1967

I N 1967, WHEN I HAD a sabbatical leave, Gail and I decided to make good use of it. Since our Peace Corps days, many tourists had flocked to Nepal, but some regions were still off-limits or practically unseen by Westerners. One of these was Dolpo, a mountainous area of Tibetan-speaking people west of Mustang and south of the Tibetan border. Knowing that an English linguist interested in Buddhist religions had reached a Dolpo monastery on a lake in the Kanjirobi Himal, we decided to visit this lake, Phoksumdo Tal, if permitted, and asked Harry McDade to join us. Harry, a surgeon, had a limit on his time of 30 days plus two weekends, but we believed we could make the trek and return within this time limit.

During our Peace Corps service in Kathmandu, our friend Colonel Jimmy Roberts, British mountaineer and former military attaché, had trouble finding employment for Sherpas he had trained for expedition work. We, and probably others, suggested to him that he start a trekking service for them. Jimmy began with a few trips, but in no time his treks developed into an international trekking business. We now wrote to him, asking for help with permissions and porters, and these arrangements he made.

At the Kathmandu airport Willi Unsoeld met Gail and me and invited us to stay with him and Jolene at Lal Durbar, their old Peace Corps home. Harry McDade arrived shortly afterward. Jimmy Roberts had secured our permissions as well as the services of a top-notch sirdar, Nima Tenzing, with Phoo Dorji as cook. Neither had been to the area where we were going.

At Pokhara we picked up two Tamangs and two Tibetans as porters and headed west. Two days later, as we were walking east of the Kali Gandaki River, I noticed a large, dark brown snake, about 10 yards ahead on my right, that was crossing the sand and rocks at fast speed on a direct collision course with me. I kept on for a couple of steps, wanting to get a good look at him before he changed course and disappeared, but he didn't change course and began to hiss loudly. As I stopped, he crossed the path three feet in front of me. It was then I noticed his partly raised hood. He was far bigger and longer than I had realized, and I was mightily impressed. That snake acted as if he ruled the world. A Nepali, who was coming from the opposite direction, looked impressed too, but all he said was, "Hamadryad (King cobra), sahib."

The next day at Beni, where we saw two Peace Corps volunteers, we crossed the Kali Gandaki. They were the last Westerners we were to see for the next 23 days, except for three Swiss who were working with Tibetan refugees in Dhorpatan. We ascended the Mayagdi River, passing the sulphurous hot springs of Tatopani, which were not inviting, and continuing to the village of Darbang, where we bought potatoes. Rhododendron trees, some with trunks so large that two men with outstretched arms could not reach around them, were in full bloom in various colors of red and pink, and we sometimes passed noisy flocks of Himalayan laughing thrushes. We also occasionally came across collections of goat horns for Kali or tiny shrines made of a few sticks, flowers, feathers, and a drop or two of blood, while high above us through openings in the trees we glimpsed the crests of Dhaulagiri (26,810 feet) and the then-unclimbed southwest peak of Annapurna.

Finally we crossed the 11,000-foot Jaljala Ridge, where new prayer flags were fluttering near three ancient upright stones. We were now 8,000 feet above where we had seen the hamadryad, but we had to drop down nearly 1,000 feet to Dhorpatan, a broad valley without trees, formerly used as summer pasture by Magars but now used by some 250 resettled Tibetan refugees. There was no village center, but instead many individual Swiss-style houses with overhanging eaves and rocks on the roofs, all built with Swiss funds. Yaks and dzos dotted the valley, with red-cheeked Tibetan girls watching over them.

We had walked for a week to reach Dhorpatan, the jumping-off point for our five-day journey across the Dhaulagiri Hills and the Jang La (pass) to the Bheri River and the Tibetan-speaking area of Dolpo. We did not stop long at Dhorpatan but turned north toward the first high pass, the Phagune Dorji. That night we camped at 11,000 feet with a roaring fire, and before 10:00 the next morning crossed the 13,400-foot pass, with its vast views of Dhaulagiri, Putha Hiunchuli, and Churen Himal (24,158). From there we dropped down 4,000 feet to the Gustang Khola, full of meltwater from the slopes of Dhaulagiri, and went on to camp 2,000 feet lower than where we started early in the morning.

The next day, at our first rest stop, a porter pointed out to us a big man who was carrying a huge load, well over 100 pounds. He had a deep-seated cough and looked very ill. Harry examined him and stated that he had pneumonia and would be dead soon unless he had medicine and complete rest. He gave him a huge dose of penicillin, told him he must rest, and left him with another large dose to be taken the next day. That seemed the end of the incident, but two days later, at about 14,000 feet, we came across the same man and the other porters. He still had the tremendous load. Grinning at us, he indicated that he was all well now. He had rested a day, then caught up with his companions by making double marches.

We crossed a bridge guarded at each end by two dhauliyas, wooden votive statues of a man and a woman. Huge holly trees grew here. At a khami village three shepherds, two men with sickles and one with a kukri, were shearing about 60 sheep. Each sheep in turn was tied with its neck resting on a forked stick.

Between the Phagune Pass and the Jang La there were five main ridges. We were glad to cross the last of these and ascend to the 15,000-foot crest, marked by a sizable cairn, chortens, and the skulls of two bharal, the blue sheep. These were the sheep George Schaller was seeking when he and Peter Matthiessen made the same trek a few years later, going on beyond Phoksumdo Tal to Shey. Matthiessen's book, *The Snow Leopard*, relates their experiences.

South and to the east, we could trace our route of the past days. Ahead stretched the mountains of Dolpo, while to our right we had views of the rarely seen north side of the Dhaulagiri Range. Across the pass we found less snow than on the southern side, but the 7,000-foot descent to the Bheri River was arduous. We camped two-thirds of the way down, and the next day avoided Tarakot by climbing a small ridge, then dropped down to the west past enormous, solitary cedar trees, some with a shrine carved into the trunk. We camped under the largest cedar I have ever seen.

Reaching the Bheri River, we found a good trail, and 10 miles later stopped at the crossroads village of Dunyer (Dunahai), where there was an Indian checkpoint. Our passports were approved, but the officials insisted we have tea with them. Tea is usually safe anywhere, but this tea probably was not boiled, for later Gail had stomach problems.

At Dunyer several women with musk deer tusk necklaces watched us as we crossed a bridge over the Bheri and began to ascend the Suli Gad, a beautiful wild stream flowing from Phoksumdo Tal. Climbing steeply, in the afternoon we passed more crude wooden dhauliyas or dok-pas (effigies of protecting spirits) at the entrance to the medieval village of Rohagaon. Such protectors from evil spirits go back to eras before Buddhism and B'on-Po were competing for people's souls. There were also piles of goats' skulls, but what struck us especially as we entered the compact village, built into the hillside, was the exceptional ferocity of the big mastiffs chained by every door, and the ingrained dirt on the hands and faces of the villagers. The women wore black rags and made no attempt to welcome us. We mounted ladders from one roof to the next as we climbed up through the town, and furious barking accompanied us. We had planned to stop at Rohagaon for the night, but the town was so dirty that we kept on and camped in a somewhat flat place high above the Suli Gad.

The next day the river rose to meet us as we headed north, and at Murwa, a cleaner village, with B'on characters on a chorten, we camped on a harvested buckwheat field within sight of the spectacular waterfalls flowing from Phoksumdo Tal, nearly 2,000 feet above.

Harry's time was getting short, and we were up early the next morning to zigzag up the steep, juniper-covered slopes to the south end of the truly beautiful lake, three miles long and half a mile wide, formed by some ancient landslide. Its turquoise waters, with white birches fringing the shore, and the white peaks of the Kanjirobi Massif rising to nearly 23,000 feet at the head of the valley, nearly took our breath away. On the only part of the lake shore not surrounded by cliffs stood the old monastery. It had not been well kept up. The only lama in residence was not impressive, though the site was.

A boy was having great difficulty starting a fire with his flint and steel, and so we gave him some matches and showed him how to light one. He was openmouthed in astonishment.

We would have loved to continue around the lake and across another pass to the Shey Monastery, but Harry was worried about his plane connection in Kathmandu. Regretfully, we descended to Murwa and kept on downstream until dark. On the way we saw an amazing display by a golden eagle, which climbed almost out of sight and then folded both wings and dove at tremendous speed, pulling out just before he seemed about to crash.

He did Immelmann turns that showed his complete control of the air. I hope some potential mate was watching, for he (or she) was superb.

Two long days took us through Rohagaon and Dunyer to Tarakot. Harry was ahead coming into Rohagaon, where he was attacked by two fierce mastiffs. There was no time to pick up a stone. He kicked one in the face and held off the other with his ice axe until the owner arrived. Tarakot, the center of several smaller places and once the capital of the district of Tichu-Rong, was known locally as the dzong, or fortress. Here each stone house if need be could become a fort. Tibetan influence was strong in Tarakot, and some people spoke Tibetan, but most inhabitants were actually Magars. As at Dunyer, some women were wearing necklaces of tusks from the musk deer, now very rare in Nepal.

An early morning start took us two-thirds of the way to the Jang La, and when we reached the tents that Nima had pitched we had a surprise. Since it was Harry's birthday, Nima had baked him a cake, not helped by the altitude but much appreciated.

That night light snow fell. Nima was worried that a big storm was coming. If it did, it would be very hard on our porters, who had no extra food and a minimum of warm clothing. In the early morning we crossed the Jang La and stopped for lunch in an unroofed shelter for animals, where the wind whirled dirt and powder snow. From there we pushed on as fast as we could across the trackless snows ahead. The porters were so worried that whenever they stopped to rest, they wrote prayers in the snow. It was getting dark when we finally found the critical place where a steep, winding path led away from the windswept upland and down a cliff. The last ones to gain the path were aided by a porter with a lantern. At the bottom of the cliff, caves in a great rock wall were all full of Tibetans waiting out the storm. We had had only one stop for more than a minute or two in the past 13 hours.

The next day Harry was deathly ill, with no idea what hit him. He was so weak that he could walk only a few feet before sitting down. Being an experienced doctor and not knowing how to cure himself greatly upset him, but he dosed himself liberally with antibiotics and gradually improved. We camped that night lower down among very large trees. Phoo Dorji made soup, but Harry could eat nothing.

In a wild area the next day, I was waiting for the others when I noticed an animal like a large fisher crossing 100 feet of cliff. He moved fast, mostly in catlike bounds, crossed an open slope, and easily climbed 15 feet straight up a big oak. There, with great ease, he turned around on the side of the tree, arched his neck, and coolly observed me for half a minute. He then bounded off as if he hadn't a care in the world. From nose to tail he was about four feet long. I later identified him as a Himalayan palm civet, not a Binturong.

On March 17 we crossed the Phagune Dorji Pass in five inches of snow. The only tracks on the way were made by a large cat and by someone walking barefoot. We reached Dhorpatan in the afternoon and again talked to the Swiss advisor we had seen there before. It was our last day with Harry, who now felt well enough to go on at top speed with Nima in order to catch his plane at Kathmandu.

Gail and I made good time too, including a 16-mile day to reach Beni. Thousands of pink primroses were blooming in the snow near Jaljala Ridge. Going south from Beni to Kusma, we saw several huts made of branches with leaves, where families whose homes had been lost in a recent landslide were living. In one of the leaf huts a woman was singing sweetly and as contentedly as if she were in the home of her dreams. No wonder we like the Nepalese.

On our return from Dolpo we stayed for two or three days in Kathmandu with the Unsoelds. During that time Jolene introduced us to a very shy, attractive Tibetan woman who had escaped from Lhasa a month earlier. She was working at a Kathmandu hotel, and had entered a class where Jolene taught English to Fulbright scholarship hopefuls. Jolene told us that the young woman's English was better than her own. Obviously intelligent, she came from an important Tibetan family, and had gone to a good school in Kalimpong. She was at home during a school vacation when the Chinese invaded Tibet in 1959. Her house then was taken over by the Chinese, and her father and mother put to work on the roads, while she was sent to clean latrines. Since she was in danger of being forcibly married to a Chinese, her father and mother insisted that she leave Tibet, and finally she managed to get to Kathmandu. Her plan now was to go to Dharmsala in India to work for the Dalai Lama.

From Kathmandu we flew to Calcutta, where on the evening of our arrival we had just fallen asleep when the phone rang. "Is this Mr. Robert Bates?" I said it was.

"Number One wishes to speak to you. Please hold."

Number One, speaking with a pleasant English accent, came on the line. He was the king (chogyal) of Sikkim, who had learned from mutual Tibetan friends that we would be in Calcutta at this time and would like to visit Sikkim. An invitation for us had been sent to Kathmandu but returned by staff at the American embassy, who didn't know where we were. The chogyal wanted to meet us, though at the time we did not know why. "A car will meet you at Siliguri at 8:00 a.m. day after tomorrow," the voice said. We agreed to be there and the conversation ended.

Getting to Siliguri in time was not easy, but at the appointed hour we were there and met by a chauffeur in a well-upholstered car. As we drove up the Teesta River to Gangtok, the capital of the small, independent mountain state, we wondered what lay ahead. Driven directly to the palace, we were greeted by Manuel, a small, wiry Anglo-Indian, the private secretary of the king. He greeted us warmly and told us we were to stay at the Royal Guest House. We would be meeting the king and queen the following day. It was all too good to be true. The delightful guest house had an extraordinary view, while the furnishings inside were a combination of western beds and chairs with attractive Lepcha bedspreads and decorations. We couldn't help writing a couple of letters on paper for use by guests, embossed with a coat of arms and the words "The Royal Palace Gangtok."

Thus began a 10-day visit to mountainous Sikkim, a country with 4,000 flowering plants, 400 orchid species, 30 different rhododendrons, and more than 600 varieties of butterflies. The next morning we were shown the excellent Buddhist library, and that afternoon had tea in the garden with the chogyal and his queen, the former Hope Cooke of New York. Afterward, as the chogyal came to know us better, we dined in the family room of the palace, each of us eating off a small, brightly painted table decorated with a ring of carved skulls. The chogyal was an easy man to talk to. Over an excellent red wine at dinner, he told how he hoped to make English the basic language of Sikkim, so it would be easier to do business with Westerners and to take care of tourists, whom he hoped would come as soon as he could build attractive places for them to stay. He also had high hopes for exports to the West of carpets and cardamoms. It was obvious that the chogyal was feeling the heavy hand of India, and wished to deal with the Western world directly, for India, after the loss of Pakistan, had begun to put great pressure on this small, independent kingdom.

The chogyal wanted to see us for two reasons. The main one was to discuss getting Peace Corps volunteers to Sikkim to teach English. He wanted them because all his teachers were supplied through India, and so far they had had no success at all in teaching English. He was sure our Peace Corps teachers would do much better. In addition, he hoped to find one or two volunteers who shared his deep interest in ham radio.

To show the quality of English teaching, he led me down below the palace to a village where he had gone to school as a boy. On our way, as we scrambled down a slope, he yelled and fell back onto me. He had almost stepped on a snake. "Was it poisonous?" I asked. He had not stopped to find out. Classes at the school were not in session, but we met a few students. On our return he asked if we would like to go off for a week visiting schools in Sikkim and evaluating how English was being taught. We would stay at the Royal Guest House in Western Sikkim, with its splendid views of Kanchenjunga. Here he had spent his honeymoon. With us would go the minister of education, a driver, and a cook.

The next day, after great efforts, the five of us, together with our bags and food, somehow squeezed into the jeep and were off. The minister of education was a pleasant, educated man who spoke unhappily about the teachers sent to Sikkim from India. When we stopped at what was supposed to be the best school in the area, we could see why he was disturbed. We found the English spoken by the Indian teachers to be largely unintelligible. The textbooks students were using were a few copies of *Ivanhoe*. It was no wonder that Sikkimese students were unable to make progress learning the most useful language in the modern world. The minister of education was not surprised by what we saw. We suspected that the Indian government intentionally did not encourage Sikkimese students to become fluent in an international language.

We hated having to return. The chogyal had wanted us to see at firsthand what he knew was there, and thought our experience could serve as evidence for his need of better teachers. Before we left Sikkim, he introduced us to Mr. Coelho, the resident Indian political agent, who had the authority of the Indian army behind him. When World War II started, the king of Sikkim had put the kingdom's foreign affairs under British control, and when the British left India the Indian government took over this privilege. By now India had begun to treat Sikkim as a poor vassal state.

The day we left, we had a long lunch with the Coelhos. It was clear that they considered themselves the real rulers of Sikkim. Though we communicated with the chogyal for some months afterward and lined up ex-volunteers to serve in Sikkim, India never allowed him to select teachers for his schools.

CHAPTER XXIV

Southern India, Kenya, and the Ruwenzori

1967

I N SIKKIM WE HAD MET Mr. and Mrs. Gauba, Hindus prominent in Bombay, who invited us to visit them there, and strongly recommended that we see some of the wonders of southern India.
Accordingly, after our return to Calcutta, we visited some of the great
Orissa temples: impressive Bhubaneshwar, with the classic Hindu temples,
and Puri, with its images of Jagannath and the great Car of Jagannath (the
Juggernaut), 45 feet high and 35 feet square, with 16 seven-foot-diameter
wooden wheels to roll it. Each June, when the annual celebration is in
progress, 4,200 professionals pull the Juggernaut through the streets.
Nothing can stop it.

We continued on to Madras, where we rented a car to take us to see the
carvings at Mahabalipuram on the Coromandel Coast. Then, driving
south, we saw Madurai's magnificent temple, before turning west and south
to Cochin and tropical Kerala. The game park at Periyar with its teak and
rosewood trees delighted us, and also its variety of game, which included
gaur, with their striped legs, elephants, and huge squirrels, the largest in the
world. We then headed north to Mysore, for the maharaja's palace was
open to visitors, and on to the busy city of Bangalore, where murals show
General Cornwallis' victorious battles, for his forces were far more successful in India than in Virginia's Yorktown.

What surprised us most about southern India was how high it is, much
cooler than northern India, with granite everywhere. Even fence posts and

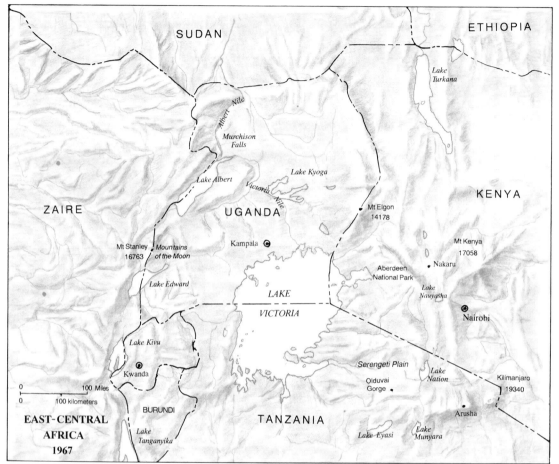

cow stalls are often made of granite. West of Bangalore, we visited the impressive temples of Belur and Halebid, very different in style from what we had seen before. On the way from Bangalore, we were startled by a colossal statue at the top of a hill. We climbed up 470 steep steps, carved in the rock, to reach the 70-foot-high nude statue of a Jain sage, still in perfect condition though carved before the year 1000 A.D. From the knees downward, the legs are carved into the rock in relief. Every 25 years, we were told, this statue is especially revered, with libations of milk, wine, and honey poured over the head. By pure luck we saw priests pouring the libations, while at the statue's feet a musician, garlanded with flowers, played a flute by blowing air through his nose.

From Bangalore we went by train to Muslim Hyderabad, then continued to Aurangabad to see the rightly famous frescoes of the Ajanta Caves. The richness of Indian art is almost overwhelming. At Bombay we visited the Gaubas, moving in a moment from ancient India to modern India and the sophisticated society of modern Indians of the upper classes. Then, heading west, we flew to Nairobi, where our Peace Corps friends, Bill and Jay Warren, insisted we stay with them, even though they had six children of their own and a couple of adopted ones, all living together in a large former army barracks.

The Warrens had been working hard in Nairobi and were eager to see more of Africa. First we went with Jay and one daughter to lakes Naivasha and Nakuru, with their flocks of flamingos and other water birds, then to a wild area near Aberdare National Park, where snarling leopards came out of the jungle after dark to tear off great chunks of meat tied to a stand.

On our return we took off in a Land Rover with Bill and three of his boys on a safari through game parks, eating our own cooking (basically Gail's) and sleeping in tents. Our first problem with animals occurred in the Masai Mara Reserve in Tanzania, as we were trying to get to a camping area before dark. A big elephant coming the other way disputed ownership of the road and made us back up again and again. It was dark by the time he disappeared. As we waited to make sure he had left the road, a group of hyenas formed around our jeep and we were surprised at how their eyes glowed in the dark.

We continued to the Serengeti, where as usual Gail and I camped in a small tent. In the morning when we emerged we saw no animals, but two lionesses rose out of brush 15 yards away, gave us a disgusted look, and walked off with dignity. The next night we pitched our tent on thick grass outside the park at the upper edge of the Ngorongoro Crater. This grass apparently was important to a wild buffalo, who waked us by his loud breathing as he cropped huge mouthfuls of it. He almost poked his head in the window of our tent before he decided that something was wrong and silently disappeared. In the morning, we saw that he had cropped to within a foot and a half of the tent. The crater was then a marvelous zoo, with lots of rhinos, black-maned lions, and thousands of gazelles.

Tanzania, Uganda, and Kenya had formed a union, and so we had no problems crossing their borders. In Lake Manyara, we saw much big game (lions, giraffes, hartebeest, topi, and migrating wildebeest), but were most intrigued by lions that avoided flies by roosting in trees, their legs and tails drooping from the branches.

We stopped at Olduvai, made famous by the Leakeys, and drove on to Arusha, having great views of Kilimanjaro on the way. Later, on the way north, we had some moments of concern. It was getting dark. Our tents were pitched in a wooded area, and we were hungrily gathered around our stove, which sat on a box, as Gail cooked macaroni for supper. The boys had gathered firewood, and we were planning to have a good fire after dinner.

As we stood near the box, I happened to look down at my feet and saw, to my surprise, that a timid-looking, very thin, long green snake, coming from behind me, was moving forward between my legs, heading toward the box. When he was all the way through, I announced his presence, causing an immediate commotion. The snake quickly slithered into the small twigs of a branch that was part of our gathered firewood. One of the boys grabbed the other end of the branch and gave a great heave, but the branch was so dry it broke, with fragments raining down on top of us. Outside the small circle of light by the stove, it was too dark to see anything clearly, and where the snake dropped nobody could tell. No one dared move. Fortunately the snake didn't go into either of our tents, for later at a museum we learned that he was a very poisonous viper.

Back in Nairobi, we again met a friend of the Warrens, Norman Myers, who became a lifelong friend. Norman, after graduating from Oxford, had gone to Nairobi to serve as a magistrate. After Uhuru (Independence), an African had replaced him as magistrate, but Dorothy, his wife, was able to retain her job as a city planner. She supported Norman as he became a top animal photographer, who supplemented their income with his pictures. He asked us if we would meet him in Uganda, where he wished to take pictures in Queen Elizabeth National Park. We grabbed the opportunity and set off.

One evening we were awakened by a small herd of elephants feeding on the tree under which our tent was pitched. They fed on the far side, but Gail and I, fearing they would move around the tree and trample our tent, sneaked out and got behind the Land Rover. In a few minutes the elephants left the far side of the tree and paraded, single-file, around the tree to our side. There were several adult females and three or four half-grown or smaller young ones. As each elephant neared us, she would stop, raise her trunk to sniff, pause, and then go on. Each, in turn, did exactly the same thing, even the smallest. After feeding on our side of the tree, they moved on.

Before we left the U.S. we had corresponded with Steve Jervis, a friend in the American Alpine Club who was about to leave for a year in Nigeria. We hoped to go together to the Mountains of the Moon, now known as the Ruwenzori, which lie between Uganda and Zaire (the Congo). Before

With our Bakonjo porters in the Ruwenzori

setting out from Nairobi with Norman, we sent Steve an urgent message telling him where and when to join us, but we did not know if he had received it.

After a stop at Fort Portal, Norman dropped us off at the railhead at Kasese. From there we went by train to Kampala, where we bought food and learned more about the Ruwenzori area. Our old friend Henry Stebbins was now ambassador to Uganda, and he and Mrs. Stebbins greeted us warmly. We promised to stay with them on our return.

We loaded expedition supplies on the night train to Kasese, and the next morning drove from there to Ibanda, where we managed to locate Peter, a tall, very black African of the Bakonjo tribe, whom Norman knew. Peter, who was willing to act as our sirdar, agreed to the food and wage scale that Norman suggested. Peter quickly found three young, strong-looking men as porters. They immediately went to a grove of bananas to tear off strips of fiber to use as pack ropes, a variant of the goat-hair ropes porters use in the Karakoram and Nepal. To our great pleasure, Steve joined us before we began our trek to the first of the metal huts that the Uganda Mountain Club has strategically placed on the route to the Ruwenzori.

The trip in to the Bujuku Huts at Stuhlmann Pass took us three days, for everything had been soaked with rain, including Bigo Bog. When we

Gail crossing the Nile

could, we jumped from tussock to tussock (not buttock to buttock, as I once heard someone describe it).

We were impressed by the extraordinary gigantism of this wet area near the equator. Giant groundsel 20 to 30 feet high and blooming lobelia plants standing higher than our heads gave the impression we were walking through a science fiction landscape. All the way in to the mountains, we saw nobody except briefly three native hunters with bows and spears and not much clothing except monkey-skin pouches. Hyrax droppings and leopard tracks were everywhere. As soon as we stopped for the day, our porters began hunting hyraxes, kin to the elephant though the size of a woodchuck. Since the porters speared several, Gail used an onion and some potatoes to cook up a delicious hyrax-liver hash.

At Bujuku Lake we finally stepped across a stream that is probably the true source of the Nile, and kept on to Stuhlmann Pass and the Bujuku Huts at about 13,000 feet. Around us were the 16,000-foot peaks of Mts. Stanley, Speke, and Baker.

We waited a day for better weather, then climbed to the Irene Lakes Hut at 14,700 feet, a small A-frame better for two than three. Despite the weather the next day, we climbed the east ridge of Margherita, one of the Stanley peaks, to where it leveled off near the height of the summit. Clouds enveloped us there, and finally, after waiting some time for them to lift, we were forced to descend, reaching the foot of the ridge just at dark, with no time to reach the Irene Hut. Having no headlights, we bivouacked, with hyraxes screaming off and on all night. Their shrieks were startling, but in a way comforting, for we knew leopards wouldn't bother us when there were hyraxes to eat.

The next day we were at the Bujuku Huts when three Peace Corps volunteers from Somaliland arrived. These and the three hunters were the only people we saw between leaving Ibanda and returning. Though continued wet weather and clouds limited our climbing, we gained the feeling of the Ruwenzori, at least from Bigo Bog to the ice of the Stanley Plateau.

After memorable baths at the home of the Stebbinses in Kampala and a splendid dinner with their friends, we returned to Nairobi, thanked the hospitable Warrens, and headed north to Addis Ababa in Ethiopia. Addis, then still under the rule of Haile Selassie, was a city with quiet dignity and pleasant people. After a few days there we returned to the U.S.

CHAPTER XXV

Shah Dev

1967-1968

W E HAD NOT BEEN BACK in Exeter long before a telephone call from the State Department asked us to take on an unusual assignment connected with our Peace Corps experience in Nepal four years earlier. A discussion with Ambassador Stebbins had prepared us that it might happen. King Mahendra of Nepal had sent his older son, Birendra, to Eton, where he had been a student for seven years. (Birendra was the young man whose Sacred Thread Ceremony we had been invited to witness in Kathmandu.) Now, Birendra was being sent to extend his education internationally by spending a month at the University of Tokyo in Japan, an academic year at Harvard University, and a month in Israel before returning home. He was to arrive in Boston from Japan at the beginning of Harvard's fall term.

There in September Gail and I met him, along with Nepal's ambassador to the United Nations, State Department officials, and the master of Quincy House (the Harvard dormitory where he would live as a special student). With him was his tutor secretary, a young professor at Tribhuvan University in Kathmandu named Narayan Prasad Shrestha.

We felt on good terms with both men at once and looked forward to showing them something beyond the academic experiences of college life. Both spoke good English and eagerly accepted the idea of meeting Americans where there was no diplomatic protocol. Since nobody at Harvard was supposed to know who the prince was, he was registered as Mr. Shah Dev, as if Shah was his first name. Shah Dev actually means "King God," though probably few if any at Harvard realized that. His real name is Birendra Bir Bikram Shah Dev.

*The Crown Prince of Nepal (center) and his secretary Narayan Shrestha (at left)
during a weekend at Martha's Vineyard*

Shah Dev and Narayan lived in Quincy House in regular college rooms.
We would drive from Exeter and pick them up there or find them waiting
for us on the sidewalk at the appointed hour. On the first weekend after our
meeting, we drove them to the Carters' house in Jefferson, New Hampshire,
where they were surprised to find that a man wearing very old blue jeans,
who was picking apples when they arrived, was their host.

From then on we frequently introduced them to friends and took them
to events such as Harvard football games, plays, the Boston Museum of
Science (where Brad Washburn was the director and showed them around),
and even to a World Series game, which Shah Dev much enjoyed. Boston
doesn't often get into the World Series, and we were able to go only
because the State Department sent us tickets. Since the game was played
on a weekday, I had to miss a class in order to go. When a friend agreed to
take the class for me, I told him only that I had to go to Boston on an
important matter. That afternoon, however, he watched the ball game on
TV and saw us all sitting in the commissioner's box.

We had parked our car at the Harvard Club and, like thousands of
Bostonians, walked to Fenway Park. Seeing vendors selling banners and
Red Sox buttons, the prince made a point of buying a big button and wear-

ing it. He enjoyed being part of the crowd, and as we walked along asked, "Why do they call it the World Series? What other countries are playing?" He seemed surprised at my answer. Birendra carefully watched the game that followed, cheering the home team's victory.

Our most interesting experience with Shah Dev came during Christmas vacation when we met the prince and Narayan in Miami and drove to Key West. The prince enjoyed being free from protocol and took pains to talk to strangers we met casually, such as people in a motel swimming pool or someone sitting on a stool next to him at a cafe coffee counter. He kept telling us, "I may never be able to do this again." On his 21st birthday the four of us had a quiet dinner together. None of us knew at the time that a year later, following his father's death, he would be literally a King God, and that day would become a national holiday.

In Charleston, West Virginia, where we stopped on the way north, he welcomed a visit to a Vista volunteer rural program and also to a federally funded Job Corps Center. He especially liked the give-and-take at the Vista meeting. Later, at the Charleston Airport, where we began our flight to Washington, Shah Dev helped to carry the bags, but on our arrival in Washington we were met by the entire staff of the Nepal embassy and he couldn't lift a finger. We were back in the world of protocol again. We felt sorry for Shah Dev.

CHAPTER XXVI

Mexico, Tsering, Eastern Europe, and Mt. Ararat

1968-1970

A
T THE TIME WE WERE INTRODUCING the crown prince to American ways, I was urged to become the executive director of Outward Bound, but turned down the idea. I believed in what Outward Bound was doing but preferred to stay at Exeter. In former years when asked to consider headmasterships, I had always given the same response.

Gail and I had bought a 200-year-old farm two miles from our house, with about 100 acres of land (mostly woods), because there was a threat to make it into a racetrack. The barn was the most immediate problem, but the previous owner, an old Vermonter with a great sense of humor, worked on it with me and we put it back in good condition. The house took longer, but the combination of a former student who was an architect, and another who had been a Peace Corps volunteer, did wonders. We eventually decided not to move there, but the farm has been a joy to us and also to the tenants who since have lived there.

At the end of the summer in 1968, we flew to Yucatan and visited several of the great Mayan temples, such as Uxmal, Chichen Itza, and Tulum. The Spanish quality of Merida, our base, was especially pleasing. From there, we flew to Cozumel and Isla Mujeres in Quintana Roo, where we strolled along miles of empty beaches marked only by flotsam and turtle

Mt. Ararat rises above the Turkish town of Dogubayazit.

tracks. Our best experience in Yucatan, however, came after entering a recently discovered limestone cave. Deep inside it, a shallow pool two-thirds surrounded by beautiful stalactite columns made the space inside seem like the altar of a temple. Small gifts of pots and grinding stones, placed around the pool by worshippers hundreds of years earlier, lay untouched. As we stood there in silence, flashlights bringing to life the beauty of the pool, the gifts, and the surrounding stalactites, one could not help sharing a religious experience with those who had brought the gifts so many centuries earlier.

On our return we found a letter from Tsering Yangdon. In the years since we first met her in Kathmandu, we had corresponded with her. She had found no future in Dharmsala and wished to come to the U.S. Her letters showed wisdom beyond her years, and we became increasingly interested in helping her. Since Tibetans then were considered by the U.S. government to be Chinese, however, she had no chance for legal immigration to the U.S. Our solution came through the inspiration of the Admissions Department of the University of New Hampshire. We had thought of applying for her entry to the summer session there, but the authorities were so impressed by her command of English and the maturity of her letters to us that they admitted her to the university on part scholarship. We wanted

Camp on Mt. Ararat

her to arrive in time for the beginning of the 1968 college academic year, but she was held back by Indian red tape and did not arrive until November.

Tsering stayed with us until there was a place for her in International House at the University of New Hampshire. Meanwhile she began sitting in on courses. When the second term began, she became a full-fledged student. Soon she was helping fellow students with their English. She was graduated in three years and went to Johns Hopkins University on scholarship, where she took a master's degree in health and nutrition, a field that she believed would be useful to her on her return to Tibet. Returning to Tibet, however, was not then possible, and so she took a job working for the State of New Hampshire. Later she married a college classmate at our home, beginning a very happy marriage, and has been practically a member of our family ever since.

In the summer of 1969 we traveled to Eastern Europe. At Trieste, a fine old city where East and West had come to terms, we took a train to Ljubljana, the attractive capital of Slovenia, then continued to Bled, and on to the fine trail-hut complex in the Seven Lakes Region of the Slovenian Alps. Wildflowers were everywhere. We spent five or six days trekking from hut to hut and climbing Triglav, Yugoslavia's highest mountain, by the normal route.

Leaving the lakes and mountains, we took a train to Belgrade, and a day later a night train to Bucharest. A Romanian advertisement in the *New York Times* had stated that anyone with an American passport needed no visa to enter Romania. It was true. In the Bucharest railway station, when Gail thanked someone for carrying her bag, he kissed her hand, the last action we expected in a communist country.

We saw no Americans at all. Since hotels were full, we were sent to a bed-and-breakfast place, a room in an apartment occupied by a snaggle-toothed old battle-axe who must have been born a party member. She fingered Gail's sweater and asked if she wanted to sell it, but we were well treated. Though the bathroom was a disaster, our room, the master bedroom, had a television that worked. Here, to our delight, we were able to see Armstrong's splashdown into the ocean after returning from the moon walk. A dozen people crowded around as we watched it, all cheering the astronauts.

In Bucharest we wandered into a large store to see what was being sold there and indicated to a salesgirl that we were just looking. Speaking French, she asked if we were Danes. We denied it. Then she tried the other Scandinavian countries, and finally all the countries in Europe, with the same result. Frustrated, she finally blurted out "What are you then?" We answered, "Americans." She looked amazed. That thought had never crossed her mind. She turned around and announced loudly so everyone could hear her, "They are Americans."

From Bucharest we went to Tulcea on the great Delta of the Danube to see the rich bird life in the waterways. On the way, the two-car train stopped in the middle of an orchard. We saw the engineer take a small bag to one of the plum trees, which were full of ripe plums, and begin to fill it. At once the conductor stepped out and began to fill his cap. Then most of the people in the car piled out and began filling their arms or pockets. Everyone returned in high spirits and the train moved gaily on. A man sharing a seat with us dropped several plums in Gail's lap. Laughing, he announced, "They are ours; they belong to us."

We went on to Constantsa and began a slow, 12-hour train trip to Bourgas in Bulgaria, discovering en route that neither Romania nor Bulgaria would change or accept any of the other country's money. At the border we had a long wait. Plowed fields, watchtowers, and lots of barbed wire showed that relations between East European countries were not always cordial. Two customs guards eagerly looked at every advertisement in our copy of *Time* magazine before returning it.

The train went slower and slower and did not reach Bourgas until several hours after dark, but a friendly brakeman assured us in broken German that he would take care of us. He took us to the chief train dispatcher in the station, who made phone calls and then indicated in sign language that we should stay in the waiting room and he would do something. It was after 11 p.m. and we had had no dinner, but fortunately a small restaurant in the station still had some goulash, and when you are hungry enough you can eat anything. Just before midnight a man who spoke only Bulgarian appeared from the train office and beckoned us to follow him. We took a streetcar. After a 15-minute ride we stopped at a big apartment house and went up several flights of stairs. There the man banged again and again on a door, which a red-cheeked woman in a nightgown finally opened. Obviously she had been asleep. She was the train dispatcher's wife, and since the apartment had no phone she did not know we were coming. When the man who had brought us left, she set out two glasses of slivovitz for us and, using sign language, excused herself. Soon she returned in a dressing gown. She apparently had remade the bed where she had been sleeping and now turned it over to us.

The next day her son, who spoke some English, explained that his father could not find lodging for us anywhere the night before. After finding a room for us at an official bed-and-breakfast place, the family insisted that we have dinner together at their home that evening. It turned out to be a jolly affair, with the son interpreting whenever he could. Since the beach near Bourgas is famous, we spent a day there enjoying the sun and the chance to speak with some of the many East German tourists. We were quickly asked in German who had killed Kennedy. The Germans were sure he was the victim of a Russian plot, though they did not dare say so directly. A couple of them said they would spend their vacations in Afghanistan if the roads getting there through Russia were not so bad.

At Bourgas, we boarded a fast Bulgarian boat to go on to Varna. We had just boarded her and were watching loading activities when the first mate joined us. Speaking good English, he introduced himself as Michael Georgi. We found that he liked the works of Somerset Maugham and the humorist Art Buchwald (whom he said was "very popular in Bulgaria"). When I asked if he had read Conrad, he answered, "Of course," and mentioned several of his novels. Inviting us to his cabin to see a few books he had with him, he declared that the cabin was ours to use as long as we were on the ship. Then he said, "You must have a Michael cocktail." Taking two small glasses, he filled them with one-third vodka, one-third cognac, and one-third Bulgarian red wine. Then he departed. We saw little of him until we landed at Varna, but not because of the effect of the Michael cocktail. At Varna he instructed a friendly Pole, who was disembarking, to find us a lodging, then gave us a warm good-bye.

We did not stay long in Varna but took one of the country's best trains to the old city of Tornovo. It was here, as we were sneaking pictures of Russian tourists, that we saw Russians sneaking pictures of us. As we had found throughout Eastern Europe, the restaurants in Tornovo had live music with their meals. This music often was played so loudly that conversation was impossible with anyone except the person seated next. This situation encouraged people who wanted to talk to move where nobody else could hear the conversation. At one attractive restaurant a man moved in beside us and gradually introduced himself as a doctor. He told us what long hours he worked, saying that he and a streetcar conductor at the opposite end of the table received the same wages. When we asked if the system could not be changed, he looked around and then with a frown replied, "Grosse Fische kleine Fische essen." (Big fish eat little fish.)

One other experience in Bulgaria struck us. We were strolling along a path toward a monastery when we met a man who asked where we had come from. No other people were in the area. He had a pocket full of bitter rowanberries, which he was eating, and offered us some. When we finally told him we were Americans, he stated firmly "Luna (referring to the moon)—America dobre (good)—Nixon." He raised his thumb and gave a little cheer when he said "Nixon." Next he said "Brezhnev, Kosygin," and pretended to vomit. We were sure that many Bulgarians felt the same way.

During the spring of 1970, Bob and Robbie Dodson again urged us to visit them in Istanbul, this time with a plan to take a ship to Sochi on the Black Sea, and from there drive to Elbrus, the highest peak in Europe, and climb it. Afterward, we were to travel to Yerevan, cross into Turkey near Kars, and climb Mt. Ararat. Although we applied far in advance, no visas came from the Soviet Union until it was too late to get to Sochi. Instead we drove in two cars from Istanbul across Turkey to Ararat, in company with five members of the Dodson family and three others.

Just before we left the U.S., at the Arctic Institute of North America office we were shown pieces of shaped wood from an ice-covered structure that exists on the upper slopes of Mt. Ararat. It partially emerges in summers after a snowless winter. Since the top of Mt. Ararat is the legendary landing place of the Ark, this structure excites the imagination of fundamentalists, who are positive it is actually Noah's Ark. One such fundamentalist living in Texas was paying for an Arctic Institute expedition to go to the mountain and explore the iced-in structure.

In the late 19th century, Lord Bryce had climbed Mt. Ararat and brought back a piece of the wood, which he had given to the British Museum. When he was asked what it was, he had replied, "Gopher wood," for, according to the Old Testament, that is the wood the Ark was made of. Nobody in modern times knows what gopher wood actually was. The bit of wood Bryce brought back was determined by forest experts to be yellow oak, a species now growing no closer than 300 miles from Mt. Ararat. In recent years small pieces of the wood on Ararat were carbon-dated in France and the U.S. A French report gave a date of 5000 B.C., but Americans had interpreted the readings as 500 A.D. At least, the wooden structure was very old.

We were eager to see the mysterious construction, but when we arrived in Turkey we learned that Russia had denounced the Arctic Institute Expedition, claiming its purpose was to spy on the Soviet Union and plant nuclear devices in the snow. The Turks therefore had rescinded permission. We were in no way part of the expedition, though we had been invited to join it on the mountain.

Setting out in a van and a station wagon, we drove across the great Anatolian Plateau to Ankara, then to Cappadocia and the honeycomb caves of Goreme, before reaching Erciyas, one of Turkey's highest mountains, which we climbed.

We drove east through rural country, where people were threshing in front of their homes. Piles of dung cakes for cooking often towered 15 feet high. We went through Erzurum and were headed toward Dogubayazit, when we stopped just before dark at a comfortable hotel for dinner. The younger generation insisted we should drive on at night, but we refused. It was lucky we did, for Turkish roads are not always well marked. The next morning we drove down a straight road to where a bridge over a river had been removed. A warning sign was lying flat where wind had blown it. It was with difficulty that we stopped in time; at night we would have driven straight into the river.

At Dogubayazit, the nearest village to Ararat, we went into the single hotel to register. When we handed in our passports, I noticed that the clerk smiled and nodded at a middle-aged man who had been reading a newspaper nearby. He stepped forward, introduced himself, and said he would take care of our passports. He added that he had climbed Ararat, had read about our expedition in the newspapers, and had come to guide us on the mountain. This was a subterfuge, but it was the Turkish way of making sure we did nothing on the mountain that could offend the Russians. The man insisted on joining us, and two days later climbed with us to Ararat's summit (16,915 feet). He made sure also that we did not reach the wooden structure that we had hoped to see high on the opposite side of the mountain. At first we did not know he was a colonel in the Turkish Secret Service, but that came out later.

Ararat stood out magnificently above the plain. From the summit in the early morning we had a fine view of the Caucasus, and of Ararat's dark shadow stretching 100 miles or more across the flat terrain to the west. On top stood flags left by many European climbing clubs, but we did not do what a friend had suggested: almost completely bury in the snow a worn life preserver with faded letters reading "ARK."

As we descended the mountain to where young Kurd shepherds were controlling their sheep by throwing stones with slings of the type David must have used when he killed Goliath, the colonel had an altercation. Why people yelled at him we didn't know, but we all knew what he meant when he drew his pistol and threatened them.

We drove on to Lake Van, a large lake with much soda in it and an intriguing Armenian church etched with stories from the Old Testament. Keeping on to the Mediterranean, we passed through Tarsus, made famous by St. Paul, to Antalya. Here we rented a fishing boat for a few days and in it putt-putted along the coast, looking into small harbors where we could see through clear water broken amphoras and pieces of marble inscriptions carved before the time of Christ.

One of the greatest stories of Ancient Greece told how Bellerophon, riding the flying white horse Pegasus, saved the world from the Chimaera, a three-headed monster breathing fire, who threatened to destroy it. What scared the ancient Greeks 4,000 years ago still exists in a desolate area of southern Turkey a mile or more from the coast. Nobody lives near the site, but from the Mediterranean at night one can still glimpse the Chimaera's fire.

We landed from our fishing boat and trudged across sandy soil to where a blackened area, 100 yards or more square, showed that it had been burned over. Within this uneven ground, a few remains of Greek temples were standing at crazy angles, for the ground had sunk under them. Their inscriptions were still clear, but in this wasteland nobody was in sight. In one part of the burned area, when we looked carefully, we could detect a few small, flickering flames. When I touched a piece of dry grass to one, a fire immediately sprang up. Apparently a seep of methane gas had been burning in this area for thousands of years. The flames we saw were not high and possibly never were, but the burned area obviously at one time had led to the rumor that a terrible demon was loose here, intent on destroying the world. The Pegasus story of course tells of the first attack from the air.

It seemed amazing to us that nobody was here and that the world was taking so little notice of an object that once appeared to threaten its survival. One might call the Chimaera the atom bomb of ancient times, the difference being that the atom bomb is real while the Chimaera was never a danger.

In no time we were back in the Dodsons' house in Bebek (Istanbul) with its sweeping view of the Bosphorus, watching modern tankers that know a great deal about methane gas.

In the summer of 1971 we were again in Europe, wishing to visit countries behind the Iron Curtain that we had not seen before. We started by going from England to Sweden by boat, working our way to Malmo in the south of Sweden and taking a boat to Poland, which seemed very crowded. As in the countries farther east, however, we found friendly people as soon as they learned we were Americans. We visited beautiful Cracow, and since we wanted to see Eastern Europe's main mountain-climbing area, the Tatra, took a train to Zakopane, close to the Czechoslovakia border. It was jammed with workers. Since all huts were overrun, we left Poland and crossed into Czechoslovakia, where the crowding was nearly as bad. In both these countries, practically nobody could speak English. We now had visited all Eastern European countries ruled by communism and confirmed how unpopular it was.

R.H.B. and Gail on the Godwin–Austen Glacier, K2 behind

CHAPTER XXVII

The Memsahib Expedition and the Coronation

1974-1975

GAIL AND I HAD LONG HOPED that when the Karakoram, closed for several years by Pakistan, became open to visitors, we could go there together. In early 1974, when friends in Lahore wrote that a change was in the offing, we went at once to the Pakistan embassy to make an application to visit K2 in June. We also phoned the Carters to see if they would go with us if permission were granted. As we expected, they were enthusiastic, though Ann had some concern about whether her bad back would hold us up. Finally our application to enter Azad (Free) Kashmir was approved.

Pakistan Airways flew us to Karachi, and then on to Rawalpindi, where our friend Maj. Gen. Safdar Butt introduced the liaison officer he had found for us, Maj. Manzoor Hussain. With him, for the next few days, we rose at four every morning to go to the airport for our flight to Skardu, but each day, after waiting for hours, we were told that bad weather in the mountains would prevent our flight. One morning while waiting I took a picture of a sign saying Islamabad. Unfortunately, in the background a piece of the airport was showing, and I was quickly arrested. Manzoor soon freed me, but the experience showed how suspicious the Pakistanis had become about India's future actions toward them.

Much had changed in Skardu since our expedition of 1953, but we were able to find some Satpura men to be our porters, while big

A porter and Paiju Peak

Mohammed Hussain, who carried George Bell so many miles on his back, became our sirdar. Gail and Ann impressed these Baltis so much that we were promptly named the "Memsahib Expedition." Since bridges had been built across the Indus, "Alexander's barge" now lay abandoned, while jeeps and small trucks drove across the river, on to Shigar, and almost halfway to Askole. It seemed effete not to walk the whole way, but we were glad to reach a point near Dassu before load carrying became necessary. We all negotiated the slabs on the long, hot walk to Chongo, and in Askole were welcomed by the lambadar and his wife. Askole had not changed much, but there was talk of extensive change "when the road comes."

Nick Clinch and Tom Hornbein were ahead of us with another family party, their objective being to climb Paiju, an unusually beautiful mountain. Three days after leaving Askole, I climbed to Nick's base camp on Paiju, where I met them at a very tragic moment. A Pakistani member of the party, who had refused to use a rope, had just fallen from near the summit and been instantly killed. It was a somber meeting.

Our journey up the Baltoro went well. We met some young French climbers who were out to climb one of the steep pinnacles near the Trango Towers, and two days later, as we came over a rise and entered the huge amphitheater of Concordia, we saw tents ahead. As we reached one, a head popped out and said, "Will you have tea or coffee?" I had never seen other climbers in the area before, and despite the friendliness of a Japanese party couldn't help selfishly regretting that "our mountains" were ours no longer.

We pitched tents near our old campsite, and after a day's reconnaissance, Ad and I, with two of our best porters, worked out a tricky route through crevasses and ascended halfway up the Savoia Glacier, where we camped. Clouds interfered with our view at first, but in late afternoon they cleared, and we had the view we wanted. Our conclusion was that if snow conditions were right, a couloir northeast of Savoia Pass could be climbed to what appeared to be the west ridge. It was a harder route than the Abruzzi Ridge, dangerous in certain snow conditions, but a way to move high quickly. We recommended that Jim Whittaker, who was to lead an American expedition to K2 the next year, should take a look at it from the air, for beyond the couloir a route might be possible slightly around to the north in an area we could not see.

Back in Rawalpindi, we promptly set off to see General Butt, who had had much to do with our getting permission for the Memsahib Expedition. He was working with the Chinese, who were building the road from Hunza to Kashgar. As the Pakistan engineering officer in charge, he was

ADAMS CARTER

Camp on the Baltoro Glacier

with the road builders much of the time, and he spoke highly of the Chinese officers and engineer troops. I spoke to him about my hopes of someday getting to the Ulugh Muztagh. He was much interested.

We had been unable to attend the wedding of Birendra, now the king of Nepal, because it came in the middle of the school year. By good fortune, however, the coronation came in February 1975, when we had a leave of absence. It was a glorious occasion, the result of two years of planning and the expenditure of many rupees. Official guests, such as Prince Charles and Ed Hillary (now Sir Edmund), came from all over the world, but we were personal guests of the king—something also special. The Shankar Hotel, beautifully upgraded and decorated since we had seen it last, was where we stayed for a week, together with half a dozen of Birendra's Eton classmates and their wives, two Jesuit teachers whom he had known in Darjeeling, a Japanese professor from Tokyo University, a Frenchman, a Harvard professor, the Carters, and us.

We were honored guests everywhere, and enjoyed lots of free time between the various ceremonies for the king and performances by groups of

ADAMS CARTER

Crossing the rising Punmah River

Nepalis. We saw local temples we had not had time to visit when we were working in Nepal, and although protocol prevented our seeing the precise moment of the crowning, we had excellent seats for all events. According to Narayan, who was much in evidence, at one time it was planned that we and the other personal guests should ride on elephants in the procession after the parade, but the expense of keeping elephants in Kathmandu was so high that this idea was dropped. Six or eight elephants were used just for the relatives of the king.

Thanks to former Ambassador Stebbins, the U.S. gave the perfect wedding present. Kings of Nepal traditionally wore great sprays of feathers in their crowns. For this purpose they wanted bird of paradise plumes, but could find none anywhere. Luckily, however, just before a decision had to be made about America's present to the king, a set of the rare feathers was seized by customs agents while being illegally smuggled into our country. It was the ideal present and much appreciated.

We enjoyed the glitter of the coronation, with the red-jacketed lancers, the painted and caparisoned elephants with their elaborate howdahs, the bagpipe bands, and parades of Gurkhas. Best of all, after the official guests had gone, we went to a dinner and dance in the Royal Palace for the king's personal guests. After living in the same hotel together for a week, we were all friends. A fine buffet was served, followed by a dance, with a small Nepali orchestra pounding out the beat on madels (Nepali drums). We all

*The coronation of Birendra Bir Bikram Shah Dev, King of Nepal
(note the plumes in his crown)*

were dancing the twist or something vaguely like it, with the Japanese professor and the French businessman blending into a swirl of His Majesty's Eton friends and their wives. Tiger-skin rugs with heads mounted had been pulled back from the floor, and, as the space became crowded, we all began to trip over the tiger heads. Meanwhile, His Majesty watched with a delighted smile on his face. At midnight our departure was announced, and like Cinderella we entered our buses. Our modern fairy story was over.

After the coronation we spent a week trekking in the Langtang, the mountain region northeast of Kathmandu, visiting Kyangjin, where great wheels of yak cheese were being made. Five feet of snow in the passes prevented us from making the long climb to Gosainkund.

On our return to Kathmandu, we flew to Tehran, where we at last saw the Peacock Throne, together with captured crowns crusted with jewels, and baskets of cut and glittering emeralds, rubies, and diamonds. We visited Isfahan also, and near Shiraz marveled at the remaining reliefs of Persepolis, one of the wonders of the ancient world. Iran seemed to us very unhappy about its recent Westernization. Some Iranians showed distinct hostility to Americans, especially in Tehran. In retrospect, we were fortunate to visit the country when we did.

CHAPTER XXVIII

Manzoor's Wedding, Tigers, and the Triple Expedition

1975-1976

THE FOLLOWING ACADEMIC YEAR, 1975-76, was my final one at Exeter, for the school then had mandatory retirement at age 65. During the year the academy executive committee and other duties kept me busy, as well as parties honoring four of us who were retiring.

That fall at an American Alpine Club meeting, I learned from Nick Clinch that Eric Shipton had also talked to him about the Great Ice Mountain in Central Asia. Nick, a lawyer from California, and an old friend, was a distinguished leader of mountain expeditions. His parties had made the first ascents of Masherbrum and Gasherbrum 1, the latter being the only American first ascent of an 8,000-meter (26,247-foot) peak. (He had also led the expedition making the first ascent of the highest peak in Antarctica.) We decided to work together to get permission to go to the Great Ice Mountain, listed for nearly 100 years under the name Muztagh on the world's great maps, with an elevation of 25,339 feet. If this height were accurate, it was certainly one of the highest unclimbed mountains in the world—and one of the most difficult to approach. A major problem for us was that the Chinese were allowing no Americans to go to China.

Nick and I had good connections with General Butt and other Pakistani climbers, and knew that Chinese and Pakistani engineers were working together on the Karakoram Road. Perhaps a joint effort with Pakistani and Chinese climbers could be forged.

Gail and I had just received a letter from Manzoor Hussain, telling of his spring wedding and urging us to come. If we went, in Pakistan we could discuss with General Butt the idea of having an expedition to the Great Ice Mountain with climbers from China and Pakistan. Through Nick the previous fall, Gail and I had met in Yosemite Nalni Jayal, from Garhwal, also a mountain climber, who had worked his way up in the Indian Civil Service to become head of all forests and game parks in India. He had invited us to visit him and see what was being done in India to save tigers. If we went to Pakistan and India, we could join him too.

When we arrived in Rawalpindi in April, we promptly phoned General Butt. As the top-ranking engineer officer in Pakistan, Butt had been working closely with Chinese engineers who were building a road from Kashgar in the Xinjiang to the Hunza Valley of Pakistan. He told us that he and his men got along well with the Chinese, and that the Chinese would like to be on good terms with the Americans too.

The idea I presented to him was to organize a "Triple Expedition," where members of the three countries would share as equals, each having a special part to play in climbing the mountain. Americans would provide climbing equipment and technical skills, the Pakistanis trucks to take personnel and supplies to the mountain, and the Chinese porters to carry loads on the nontechnical parts of the climb. General Butt would be the leader of the expedition.

As we hoped, General Butt was enthusiastic. The first move, he said, was to discuss this plan with General Mirza, president of the Pakistan Mountaineering Association, and we did. He also liked the idea and asked me to discuss it with the American embassy to get their permission to go ahead.

The American ambassador was away from Islamabad for a week and so we now turned our attention to Manzoor's wedding, which was to be held partly in the old Sikh city of Hassan Abdal and partly in Peshawar, for Manzoor's bride was a Pathan. Manzoor's brother-in-law, Fazal Hussain, who worked for a big German pump company, put us up at the company guest house in Hassan Abdal, and since we were considered honorary members of Manzoor's family, soon after our arrival Gail had her left hand beautifully decorated with henna (the designs not to be washed off until the wedding was over).

Out in front of the house rented for the occasion, wood fires were already burning under tremendous cauldrons of rice. Gradually all

Manzoor's beautiful sisters and cousins appeared in bright silk dresses with ornaments. Then the professional dancers came and began to sway their hips and undulate in front of each man in turn to the wild drumming of a big madel. The dancers looked as if they came from a primitive race. They had big frames, with large hooked noses, large heads, and big hips and breasts. People would hold a rupee note or two behind someone's head, and these professionals would dance up, bouncing and raising one hip at a time, then take the notes.

More wild drumming and dancing went on, and a feeling of expectation as Manzoor appeared wearing a beautiful blue-gray suit. Finally, a bus from Peshawar arrived, filled to the brim with ladies from the bride's family. A kaleidoscope of color surged into the house. Rose petals showered on the Pathan ladies as they entered the women's part of the house, carrying high over their heads a huge flat cake topped with lighted candles.

Gail told me afterward that the Pathan ladies danced holding the cake over their heads. Then the ladies from Manzoor's side and the bride's side took turns at some very fast whirling dances, arms thrown out in back, with legs stomping suddenly and reversing.

Manzoor now was captured by the women, and when we saw him next he looked tired and very disheveled. He had henna spots all over his new clothes, with one slight tear, and his leg was bloody where he had struck a chair while trying to escape, but he wore lots of rupees. Obviously the ladies, especially Razia (Fazal's wife) who arranged the match, and his new mother-in-law, were absolutely delighted by it all.

Pathans are jealous of having their women marry outsiders. Major Humayan, Manzoor's best friend, told me that when he and his family came to get his own Pathan bride, nobody was there to receive them. They waited an hour and then went home. The bride's four brothers had driven her to Humayan's home and placed her in a dandy on the floor. Humayan had never seen her before, and when he came home and found her there, he gently lifted the golden headdress that concealed her face and asked, "Are you my wife?" She said, "Yes." "From then on," he told us, "everything was okay."

I had last seen Peshawar 39 years earlier, when it was surrounded by triple strands of barbed wire, with sentries patrolling to protect it from raids by the Faquir of Ipi. All was peaceful now as we stopped at a large house to be greeted by flaring torches, bagpipes, and drums. Flower decorations were placed around our necks and I was quickly escorted to join a quiet group of men, while Gail disappeared into an atmosphere of the Thousand

and One Nights. A delicious dinner
was served as I sat with the men, talking occasionally with someone who
spoke English. It was clear that the
men had a very small part in the celebration. Though the dancing and bagpipes were to go on until 4:00 a.m., a
doctor from the pump company was
leaving earlier, and we drove back
with him.

The following afternoon we paid
our respects to the married couple, but
the ceremonies were not over. We
were driven to a huge, open area
beside a temple sacred to the Sikhs.
The setting, with the white shrine,
the colorful tents and 350 people
milling around, the women in brilliant
colors, and the bagpipe band with

*Manzoor Hussain on his
wedding day*

their leopard skins and drums parading at full volume, was unforgettable.
No other Westerners were there. This was a feast given by Manzoor's family and his father's friends, and we ate of the best. Pilaus, kabobs, curries,
several kinds of rice and eggplant, all kinds of sweetmeats, fruits, and soft
drinks were served until everyone was stuffed. Even the children, who
before the feast had climbed mulberry trees to reach the sticky white fruit,
had lost all desire to eat more.

After the banquet there was a ceremony in which Manzoor untied,
with difficulty, bright wool tassels tied about Nimi's wrists, and she did the
same for him. The day ended with a reception for Manzoor at the Officer's
Club in Rawalpindi.

The American ambassador was still away, but we had a fine meeting
with Mr. Constable, his deputy, who was especially interested in the proposed expedition's Chinese connection. He stressed the fact that the U.S.
had no official relations with China, and therefore the U.S. position on our
proposal was "no position." We could climb in China just as we could in
Pakistan or Switzerland if the Chinese did not object. He told me that personally he liked what we were doing and wished us luck, but it was obvious
that he doubted we could persuade the Chinese to work with Americans.

Afterward I met with Butt and Mirza, and the generals agreed to ask the foreign minister to present the idea of the Triple Expedition to the proper Chinese authorities. We all realized that if the Chinese were interested in improving relations with Americans, this was an opportunity for them to begin.

Getting an answer from the Chinese would take time, and accordingly, I phoned our old K2 friend, Ata-Ullah, in Lahore. His first words were, "Where are you? Come and stay 5,000 years!" He wanted to send his son with a car to drive us to his home, but despite disturbances trains were still running and we were soon on our way.

Ata met us at the station and gave us a tremendous welcome. We had not seen him since Harper's had published *Citizen of Two Worlds*, his fine book on his own experiences, with special insight into East-West relations. He had begun writing the book in our living room in Exeter. Nobody could provide more generous hospitality than Ata and the Begum (his wife), and we had plenty of time to talk with them and others in the family because a curfew had been declared for all Pakistan.

Two weeks later, after a short visit to see friends in India, Butt told us that Pakistan's foreign minister had approved our plan for the Triple Expedition and formally asked the Chinese Foreign Office to invite the Chinese Mountaineering Association to take part. The Chinese answer had just arrived. It was a refusal, saying in effect, "If the Americans wish to work with us, they must deal with us directly." If at this point the American government had seen an opening to deal with the Chinese directly about the expedition, good relations between the governments might have developed considerably sooner than they did.

When I returned to the American embassy in Islamabad to report, both the ambassador and Mr. Constable were out of the country, and the staff apparently had no interest in probing what seemed to me to be a diplomatic opening. There would be no Triple Expedition, that seemed sure.

Our last discussion before departing for London was with Yoshizawa, leader of a large Japanese K2 expedition. I encouraged him but not his plan to make a new route up one of the rock ribs on the southeast side of K2, for we had seen it overwhelmed by avalanches in 1938.

When we unlocked our front door in Exeter a few days later, I was still convinced there must be some way to get to the Ulugh Muztagh.

Statue of Buddha at Bamiyan

CHAPTER XXIX

Afghanistan and the Minaret of Jam

1977-1978

A T HARVARD I HAD ROOMED in Dunster House with Waldo Holcombe, a physics major and member of the championship crew, who became a lifelong friend. Waldo's oldest son, Arthur, who was now a career staffer of the United Nations, came naturally to international relations, for Waldo's father, a prominent professor of government at Harvard, years earlier had helped write the constitution of China for Sun Yat-sen. Arthur, now deputy head of UNDP in Afghanistan, during the Christmas holidays in 1977 said to me, "Though I have had some exotic assignments, I have never been able to get Dad and Mother to visit us in East Africa or anywhere else. In Afghanistan, we have some unusual projects coming up, and if you and Gail will go with us perhaps I can persuade Dad and Mother to come too."

Would we go? Would a fish swim? In the next weeks, we worked out a plan. Gail and I, with Waldo and Ruth Holcombe, and our classmate Bob Saltonstall and his wife, Nancy, would meet Arthur and Sue Holcombe in Kabul the following spring and accompany him and his family on a special UNDP reconnaissance for the projected East-West Road across Afghanistan. Herat could be reached from Kabul only by going a long way south through Kandahar or a long way north through Mazar-i-Sharif. The UN project was to build a far more direct road, using the existing road from Kabul to Bamiyan as a starting point, then improving the narrow track through Chagcharan, and somehow continuing due west through mountain valleys to Herat, passing the amazing Minaret of Jam on the way.

The Minaret of Jam, 172 feet high,
built 1193–1202 A.D.

Arthur was involved in assessing the difficulties and advantages of building the projected road, with special reference to the development of the country's livestock, and also the attraction for tourists.

We six had planned to leave Boston for Afghanistan in May, but in April a coup overthrew the Afghan government, and tank battles raged briefly through Kabul. Gradually things settled somewhat, however, and Arthur wired us that we should come. We flew from Boston on June 10, and after a couple of days in London arrived at 6,900-foot Kabul on July 12. When our Ariana Airways plane landed, we would not have been allowed to stay in Afghanistan if Arthur had not been there to meet us. All foreigners had been told to leave Kabul and no more were being allowed in.

En route Waldo Holcombe had picked up what seemed to be some sort of flu, and the day after our arrival in Kabul he developed a high fever and apparently pneumonia. A doctor used by the American embassy told him he should rest for a week at least and not depart on the journey west with the rest of us. If he recovered enough, the doctor said he could fly to Chagcharan and join us there.

Kabul amazed me by the tremendous changes that had occurred since 1938. I felt like Rip Van Winkle. No longer was there only one American in the whole country. The city had grown tremendously, and there were now modern roads, shops, and buildings. We were told, however, that modern Afghanistan would disappear as soon as we left Kabul, and it did.

We drove away in two Land Rovers, one owned by the UNDP and one that we rented, both full of supplies. With us was Abdul Gafur, former deputy minister of agriculture in the Afghan government, and now working for the UNDP. The ancient road from Balkh to India had been modernized, probably by an influx of Russian money, and we were able to head north swiftly toward the Salang Pass. Before reaching it, however, at the Panshir River we turned west on the road to Ghorband and crossed the Shibar Pass (the watershed between the Oxus and the Indus). Winding through narrow mountain valleys, we finally passed the high cliff castle Shahr-i-Zohak, where Genghis Khan's grandson was killed 750 years earlier, leading to the massacre of the people of Bamiyan. Ahead lay the lovely Bamiyan valley, with its fertile fields tilled by Hazara people (probably descendants of Bamiyan's conquerors, for many Afghans are Pathans). An agricultural research farm, where we camped, gave us beautiful views of the Bamiyan cliffs and the snowy Koh-i-Baba Range beyond.

Bamiyan is famous for the thousands of Buddhas, big and small, carved into grottoes that honeycomb a soft reddish rock escarpment stretching along one side of the valley. The grottoes vary greatly. Some are Buddhist chapels with saintly figures, but from afar the eye focuses immediately on two great standing Buddhas carved into niches in the cliffs, the highest standing more than 173 feet high. To see them more closely, we climbed up tunnels carved in the rock to windows over the head of each, and afterward visited many of the smoke-darkened grottoes, some with hundreds of small Buddhas carved in the walls.

The next day we continued on a fair dirt road and reached the Band-i-Amir lakes and the tiny village near them, where we spent the night. These two beautiful lakes suddenly appeared as we drove down off the high, dry plateau we had been crossing. The water in each was of an incredibly beautiful shade of transparent blue. One sat in a giant overflowing bathtub made of calcified deposits; the other, longer and deeper, had fish in it. Across this bigger lake we could see a small mosque tucked into a cliff. No other sign of human beings appeared along the shores, but nearby two very simple, so-called hotels had been built, neither with tourist prices. One cost 25 cents per night and the other 50 cents. At that price, we could afford to go first class. Our room was a small, windowless box, where we put down our sleeping bags on mattresses with sheets. A lighted lantern gave some illumination. Outside, an open-air latrine was available.

Arthur's two young daughters and younger son put on bathing suits and had a swim. I am sure they were in no danger, though later we learned that previously a French woman who swam in the bigger lake had been considered indecent and shot—hardly an inducement to tourism. At our small hotel we had a good pilau in the evening, and in the morning a good breakfast before heading west.

As we drove toward Panjao, crossing more passes, we continued to see pockets of Hazara farmers whose farms held huge mounds of shrubs collected for forage. Men were carrying bundles of them, which had been slid down from high up on the hillsides. Finally, at a meteorological station where camels were grazing on the hill across from us, we stopped and pitched our tents.

During the following day we crossed pass after pass and occasional watchtowers or mud brick houses. Frequently we saw shepherds moving large flocks along the road, all brilliantly marked, and occasionally a lone horseman passed, always with a rifle slung over the shoulder, and sometimes with belts of cartridges across his chest.

Fine dust blew in our faces as we entered the flat Chagcharan valley, the capital of Ghor. Several thousand sheep were there, including hundreds being bargained for at the bazaar. The Hari Rud River runs through town, and from the only hotel, where we stayed, we had good views of sheep being forced to swim the Hari Rud, which we were more or less to follow to Herat.

The morning after our arrival at Chagcharan, we eagerly awaited the arrival of the Kabul plane. Waldo and Sue were on it, but he did not look himself. Waldo had insisted that he was well enough to travel and would improve as we went along, but we were all uneasy about his appearance.

We crossed the Hari Rud at Chagcharan in the morning and followed the northern bank of the river on a rudimentary road built by the Ford Foundation's Food For Work Program. Our eagerness to reach the Minaret of Jam was increasing. This incredible 13th-century monument was rediscovered in 1957 in a remote mountain ravine between Chagcharan and Herat.

The next day we began seeing the black yurts of Kuchis, nomads who travel between central Afghanistan and the northeast provinces of Pakistan. Their movable tents, never pitched beside a road, were always protected by large dogs. The Kuchis sometimes ran toward us, waving and inviting us to visit them. We were asked into one large yurt, where plenty of fine rugs lay on the floor. The owners were obviously well-to-do people who enjoyed

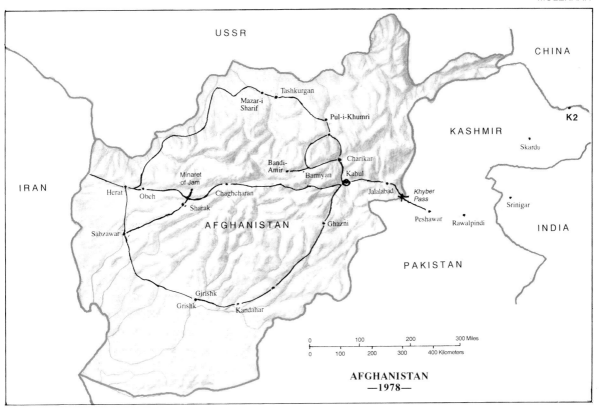

AFGHANISTAN
—1978—

their free life of moving with the sheep. Two young women, who did not cover their faces, had ropes of small silver coins hanging down around their faces. At another yurt, everyone in the family was involved in cheese making. Some were milking, others boiling the milk or making yogurt by rocking a sheepskin full of boiled milk hanging from the tent roof. An old lady with bad teeth asked for matches, but they seemed very self-sufficient. Lots of children and puppies were playing, and an old man waved a big knife and pointed at a baby boy to indicate that a circumcision was coming.

Late in the afternoon, after bumping along a fairly dry brookbed that became steeper and steeper, we reached the Hari Rud again and crossed it on a newly built, rickety, cantilevered bridge. Just downstream, standing on a gravel bar above the Hari Rud at the point where it is joined by the Jam River, rose the remarkable Minaret of Jam. This nearly 200-foot minaret, rediscovered so recently, was built in sections like the Kutab Minar at Delhi, the only tower in Asia to exceed it in height. (Which was built first is not clear.) Each of three sections was smaller than the one below. At the top, a small pavilion served as a watchtower. The tower was built of mud brick over a wooden scaffolding and was handsomely ornamented with formal patterns and inscriptions, two said to be from the Koran and two longer ones glorifying King Ghizathuddin of Ghor, who built the minaret, starting in 1193 and finishing it nine years later. Little is known of the kings of Ghor, except that in the days before the Mongol invasion of India, they regularly invaded and plundered that country.

Near the base of the tower we found a small roadhouse with bare rooms, where a government guard was stationed to protect the tower. He greeted us warmly. A few apricot trees were growing but nothing else.

Reaching the tower was the high point of our reconnaissance. The next day, with great difficulty, we climbed inside it and worked our way to the top of the second section. The wooden steps required great care. From there the house below looked tiny, but even the minaret looked small when we climbed up to a ruined fort high above and looked down. Nature had protected the minaret well. The gorge to the east that we had driven through would have been easy to defend, and major natural obstacles protected the valley on all sides. It must have been, however, more of a hideaway than a developed capital of a country.

Our pleasure at being there increased in the afternoon when we went for a swim in the fast-flowing Hari Rud. After a second night at Jam, we left by a road to the south that met the Shahrak-Herat Road, where we turned west. Then came the most difficult part of the route we were reconnoitering. We worked our way over to the Hari Rud on a rudimentary road that almost dropped one Land Rover into the river. A ford was supposed to exist but just where was vague, and we all waded into the water to try to find the best place. When the Holcombe girls located it, our lead vehicle, with great uncertainty, drove into the river. Water flowed over the headlights, and in one place was somewhat deeper than the engine's exhaust, but, since the river bottom was solid, rapid driving kept the engine from stalling. The second Land Rover also managed to cross.

After slowly negotiating a very poor road, we reached arable land, where irrigation ditches again and again cut a better road, causing a great jolt at each crossing, hard on both machines and riders. Late in the afternoon we reached Obeh. Since Obeh was famous for its baths, we eagerly joined Bob and Nancy Saltonstall and several dirty Afghans who were waiting their turn. When ours came, Gail and I entered an almost pitch-dark room, where an enormous flow of water rushed loudly in and out of a huge bathtub that constantly overflowed. We took off our clothes in a little dimly lighted cubicle and climbed in. The water in the tub was warm and wonderfully refreshing, but the almost complete darkness and the force of the rushing water made the bath less soothing than we had hoped.

Afterward, greatly refreshed, we pitched our tent on the roof of a nearby restaurant, where we had a fine dinner.

The next morning we reached Herat, a city existing at least since the ninth century B.C. Its castle, the symbol of Afghanistan, stands on a mound built by Alexander the Great about 300 B.C. Italian archaeologists, who were working in the castle, later showed us some of its huge underground chambers and tunnels, which they were restoring. While Arthur met with officials, the rest of us visited the covered bazaars, the great minarets, and the ruins of splendid 15th-century buildings decorated with lovely turquoise, indigo, and yellow-brown tiles. The heat was savage, but we refreshed ourselves with Afghan "beer," made of yogurt, mint, cucumbers, and water.

Our main reconnaissance had now ended, but we drove southeast to Bost to see what was left of the old summer palace of the kings of Ghazni and what must have been once a large city. Then we began our return to Kabul by the southern route, spending a night on the way at Kandahar ("Alexander" in Arabic). This route was much the same as the one we had taken across Afghanistan in the opposite direction 40 years earlier, but now there was a good road the whole way, built by both Russians and Americans. Groups of Kuchi tents were still visible once or twice, but the traffic of cars and trucks made them seem in a different world.

The Land Rover we were in was halfway to Ghazni the following morning when we stopped to wait for the other one to catch up. When it did not come, we drove back and found our companions sitting disconsolately by the side of the road, looking very subdued. A small crowd of Afghans was angrily facing them. Apparently a schoolboy had suddenly swerved into the road in front of their car, and the driver could not stop in time. The car had knocked the boy down and broken his leg. Arthur, leaving the others at the scene to make room in the car for the boy, dashed with him to the hospital in Kandahar, where he also reported the accident to the police. When he returned, he brought with him a policeman, who permitted us to go on to Kabul that night. (Weeks later, after the boy's leg healed perfectly, and all hospital bills had been paid, a cash settlement was made to the boy's family.) We were very glad to get Waldo back to Kabul where he could again see the doctor. His condition had become worse than when he arrived at Chagcharan.

Since the doctor wanted Waldo to get complete rest for several days, Gail and I and the Saltonstalls decided to take a few days for a visit to Mazar-i-Sharif, the biggest city in northern Afghanistan, not far from the River Oxus (now known as the Amu Darya), the border with the Soviet

Union. While we were arranging for a car to take us, we thought over what we had learned from our reconnaissance with the UN.

First of all, the route we had taken could be developed into a good road from Kabul to Herat. It would need at least one bridge over the Hari Rud, but the resulting road would be quicker and far more interesting to tourists, an important consideration to the UN. We also confirmed the fact that all across the country people disliked and feared the Russians. Lots of Afghans told us that in the fall fighting would begin to eliminate the Russian influence in the new government. What they didn't know, nor we, was that soon there would be another coup, leading to the Russians moving in in force, beginning the Russian-Afghan war. We also didn't realize that we would be the last Westerners to travel across central Afghanistan for at least a dozen years; that is, until the end of the war.

With the Saltonstalls, we headed north on a good road built by the Russians, passing through the Salang Tunnel, which rises to more than 12,000 feet as it crosses under the snowy Salang Pass. This tunnel later became the most important link in the whole Russian supply line to Kabul. The tunnel looked so modern that it seemed strange to see camel caravans and donkeys among the trucks, buses, and autos. We came out of the tunnel in beautiful hill country and dropped down to Pul-i-Khumri, where there was supposed to be a good hotel. We found it, but it had been taken over by "the military" for a meeting of some kind. When the ladies asked if they could use the restroom, they were escorted to it by men carrying tommy guns. Everywhere we went, people seemed jumpy and suspicious.

After a quick lunch at a roadside restaurant, we drove on to Surkh Kotal, a hill of archaeological significance, where we saw separate ruins of second century A.D. Greek-Kushan columns and a fourth century Buddhist stupa carved down 40 feet into solid rock. These cultures later came together in other areas to provide the masterpieces of Gandara art.

The weather was very hot, and after a stop in Tashkurghan we were glad to drive on rapidly to Mazar-i-Sharif, whose central axis is the tomb of Ali with its beautiful blue domes (a shrine of special significance to Shia Muslims). Mazar, we found, had a small, modern business section, together with open shops selling fruit, hardware, and carpets of many kinds. We stayed at an Afghan hotel, bare and empty except for some Russians, who kept very much to themselves. The hotel was so stiflingly hot, well over 100 degrees Fahrenheit, that we had a big Japanese fan brought into our room. Even so, at night we took three showers apiece.

After each, we were cool enough to sleep for a couple of hours until the heat wakened us again.

In the morning we admired Ali's tomb and the clouds of white pigeons living in its grounds. As they flew past the blue domes of the tomb, they made a constantly changing kaleidoscope of blue and white patterns. When we stepped into the airlines office, at our appearance a picture of the murdered head of the Daoud regime was quickly covered by a picture of Taraki, the man who had overthrown him, and who soon was to be murdered in turn by the more ruthless Amin.

One reason for coming to Mazar was to visit the ruins of Balkh, the great rich Bactrian city conquered by Alexander in 329 B.C. and completely devastated by Genghis Khan's 100,000 horsemen in 1220. Years later Tamburlaine was crowned there, and his son rebuilt this merchant city in the late 1300s, but little remains. The inner walls of the city at one time extended a mile across. Arrowheads are still found within them from the terrible Mongol invasion more than 700 years ago. Our visit over, we said farewell to the long Bactrian camel trains, each led by a donkey, that were carrying heavy loads along the northern route toward Herat, and returned to our dreary hotel. Mazar, and Balkh before it, had been centers for the lapis lazuli trade, and we were pounced upon by small boys who hoped to sell us pieces.

After a second hot night in the grim hotel, we flew back to Kabul, where Waldo had not improved. We were advised to get him back to the U.S. as soon as possible. He probably did not remember much of the flight back, with a short stop at an airport hotel in London. At the Massachusetts General Hospital in Boston, they found that he had developed a serious bone marrow problem that apparently had nothing to do with our trip to Afghanistan. In a couple of weeks, he was able to return home, but he never fully regained his strength.

Poster in Shanghai for a performance of Much Ado About Nothing *in 1979*

CHAPTER XXX

China

1979

DESPITE OUR FAILURE IN 1977 to receive permission for the "Triple Expedition" to the Great Ice Mountain, Nick Clinch and I had not given up, and when Gail and I were invited to be members of a small American Geographical Society trip to Beijing in February 1979, we were delighted to go. (A friend and former student, Ed Bernbaum, had visited China the previous fall, and at my suggestion had been able to discover the name of the head of the Chinese Mountaineering Association.) Our group was led by a man who had grown up in a missionary family in China and had good relations with Chinese working at the UN. The group was very small, consisting of the leader, two assistants, a woman from the American Geographical Society, and eight tourists. Of the latter, three were especially interested in what had happened to the Christian religion in China, and one was an "adventurer," who thought of the publicity he could get if he could follow Marco Polo's travels through China; two others, like us, were travelers interested in whatever we could see.

We met at the Kennedy International Airport in New York and took a Pakistan Airlines plane to Karachi, where we spent the night. The next morning we flew to Peshawar, where we were driven to the Afghan frontier and shown rifles being made. All sorts of military gear seemed in high demand.

Leaving the others in Peshawar, we engaged a car to drive us to Swat, where we saw Churchill's Picket, a small fort at the entrance to the Swat Valley, which he had built early in his career. A few fields of opium poppies were interspersed with wheat fields and areas where wild tulips bloomed in this beautiful, fertile valley, whose name had intrigued me ever since I first heard Edward Lear's verse,

"Who, or Why, or Which, or *What* is the Ahkond of Swat?"

We didn't meet the Ahkond, or Wali, as he is known today, but we did see his home and garden before driving to Islamabad, where we had been invited to have drinks with Mr. Hartman, the American ambassador, who impressed us very favorably. He spoke frankly of the fact that embassy warnings before the revolt against the Shah of Iran had been ignored in Washington.

The following afternoon our group took off for Beijing, also flown by Pakistan Airlines. As we headed north, I spoke to a stewardess about my interest in K2, which lay ahead, and as we approached Nanga Parbat I was summoned to the cockpit. Unfortunately clouds came in, Nanga Parbat was partially obscured, and to my deep regret K2 and the big Baltoro and Concordia peaks farther ahead were smothered.

Our route continued north, flying well east of the Russian border, though we had grand views of one big Tien Shan peak, probably Pobeda, dark against a red sunset. Below us all was black until lights indicated we were passing Urumchi, where we turned farther east. For hours we flew over long areas of blackness, until just before dawn we saw lights in the flight path and landed at the Beijing Airport. After some delay we were driven into the city, passing miles of poplar trees, many recently planted along the road. Along the streets people were just waking up and doing their morning tai chi chuan. We were to be in the old wing of the Beijing Hotel, with its huge red and gold columns at the entrance hall and bonsai trees at each elevator landing. From our room on the third floor, we could look out on the Forbidden City and see part of huge Tiananmen Square.

The next morning a woman guide asked all of us what we would like to do in Beijing. My number-one request was to meet with the head of the Chinese Mountaineering Association (CMA), Mr. Zhi Zhan Zhun, but during our five days in Beijing we were unable to meet anyone from the CMA. We were supposed to visit Nanjing and Shanghai afterward, and then spend our last three days in China at Mukden (now known as Shenyang). Our group learned, however, that the Mukden region was suffering from an extreme cold spell, and so voted to return to Beijing for our final days in China, giving up Shenyang. Such change was not easy to arrange, but it was made, permitting us extra time for me to locate Mr. Zhi Zhan Zhun.

Gail climbing on China's Great Wall. (Note the lack of visitors.)

During our days in Beijing, we visited places that tourists regularly see now, such as the Forbidden City, the beautiful Temple of Heaven, the Summer Palace, the Ming Tombs, and the Great Wall, to which we traveled by train. One morning we were taken into a dry-goods shop, where we met the manager. He took us behind the counter, raised a concealed trap door, and led us downstairs to a brightly lighted tunnel, which we walked down. He told us that similar air-raid shelters were built under most of Beijing, each constructed by the residents of the area. We walked for half a mile, passing occasional storerooms, and finally came up in a former temple, where we were served the ubiquitous green tea while our questions were being answered.

From Beijing, the old North Capital (Bei means north), we flew to Nanjing, the South Capital. Here we saw the ancient royal roadway lined with statues of animals, real and imaginary, that was later copied at the Ming Tombs near Beijing. The Chinese also took us proudly to see the big bridge over the Yangtze River. Russians had agreed to build it, but when the split between the two countries came, the Russians left, sure that the Chinese would never be able to build it alone. To do it, the Chinese had to produce steel they had never made before and redo the engineering, but they built the bridge themselves.

We went on to Shanghai and were assigned to the hotel where Nixon had stayed when he made the agreement restoring American-Chinese relations. In a theater nearby, *Much Ado About Nothing* was playing to sellout crowds. Shanghai seemed much more Western and less ideological than Beijing. The Bund and the Park Hotel reminded us of European seaports. We were allowed to cruise down the Huangpu River to the sea. En route we saw big freighters that had anchored and lots of working junks, many with threadbare sails. A strong impression struck us that Chinese industry was ready to take off as soon as government regulations allowed.

Our overnight train journey to Beijing was basically comfortable. On our arrival, we found someone calling loudly for Mr. Robert. He was looking for us, saying that we must be at the Beijing Hotel at 11:30 the next day, for Mr. Zhi Zhan Zhun was coming to see us. He did. Mr. Zhi turned out to be a stocky, self-assured Chinese, who spoke no English but had with him an interpreter. When I asked about the Great Ice Mountain, hoping to get a picture of it, he said he had never heard of the mountain. He made several phone calls and then said, "China has many mountains. We don't even know all their names." He asked in return what mountains American climbers would like to visit in China. I mentioned several peaks but did not put Everest at the top of the list. I did, however, make a formal request for permission for an expedition to climb the mountain that the Chinese now name the Ulugh Muztagh if the area became open in the future.

After our return from Beijing, Nick and I continued our efforts to learn more about our mountain and the area around it. Through Dee Molenaar's friend Bob Krimmel of the Geological Survey, who was working on satellite interpretation of glaciers, I received three different heights for a mountain named Mu Tzu T'Aki Shan, whose map coordinates seemed to be those of our mountain. All altitudes were lower than those on current world maps for [Ulugh] Muztagh. Through Krimmel, I was able to purchase satellite color photographs of this area of the great Kunlun Range. One showed a patch of ice approximately 30 to 35 miles across that appeared to be the "Great Ice Mountain" of our dreams. Of course there was no way to tell the shape of the mountain or its height.

To break through the Chinese roadblock it seemed essential to get scientific support, and at Nick's suggestion I went first to Phil Smith, American Alpine Club (AAC) member and deputy director of the executive office of the president. We had luncheon in the White House dining room with Peggy Finarelli, who had responsibility for dealing with China. Both were very interested in what I told them, and they worked out the names of persons I should meet. All of them showed considerable interest, though nobody knew how to persuade the Chinese to open for us the area of our mountain. If we gained permission—and funding as well—all would then be happy to take part in plans for any expedition to the Kunlun.

Another name mentioned was that of Professor Peter Molnar of the Massachusetts Institute of Technology, a geologist concerned with earthquakes, plate tectonics, and the origin of mountains. Nick and I went to see him in Boston and were at once impressed by his ability and his enthusiasm.

Nick and I had searched the climbing literature for information about our mountain without success. When Nick told our problems to his wife, Betsy, a former researcher for the National Geographic Society, it took her no time to find an article in the May 1896 issue of the Royal Geographical Society's *Geographical Journal* that showed a route to our mountain from the village of Cherchen on the southern Silk Road. It also described how the Littledale party, in trying to reach Lhasa from the north, had passed near the "Great Ice Mountain." Nick was astonished and asked what magic Betsy had used. "It was easy," she said. "I looked it up in the index." Knowing the right index helped. The first paragraph of the article titled, "A

Journey Across Tibet from North to South and West to Ladakh" especially attracted us. It was written by St. George R. Littledale, and read:

"We left England on November 10, 1894, the same party as usual: Mrs. Littledale, myself, and our dog, accompanied in addition by my nephew, Mr. W. A. L. Fletcher, of Oxford University boating renown, who proved himself to be in every respect an admirable traveling companion. My scheme was to strain every nerve to reach Tibet, and, if possible, Lhasa, with plenty of food and animals to carry it. Most of the other expeditions had failed owing to their arriving in a more or less destitute condition, and then, of course, the Tibetans could dictate their own terms. We also relied upon bribery, and went well prepared with the sinews of war for wholesale corruption."

The Great Ice Mountain, we later found, also had been approached by the French explorer Dutreuil De Rhin in 1893 and measured to be 7,340 meters high (24,081 feet), while Littledale's survey gave it 7,723 meters (25,340 feet), the figure that has been on world maps for nearly a century. Sven Hedin also saw the peak in 1900, but we could learn of no Westerner who had seen it from the ground since then. No pictures or detailed descriptions of the mountain existed, though maps showed it to be the second highest unclimbed peak in the world.

Some months later Nick and I went to see John Service, who had been an admirable and effective member of the American embassy in Beijing before the McCarthy people falsely claimed that he was a communist and used political force to have him removed from the State Department. Speaking for the American Alpine Club, we asked him how we could persuade the Chinese government to open China to mountaineering expeditions from the West. We also told him of our interest in going to the Great Ice Mountain. He gave us good advice and the name of an official at the Chinese embassy in Washington, with whom we had an important discussion. Shortly thereafter China began accepting requests for a few climbing expeditions. Unfortunately, as explained to us later, the Great Ice Mountain was in an area kept strictly off-limits to all foreigners. In other areas, however, mountains began to be opened up to foreign expeditions. One of these was Minya Konka, or Gongga Shan, as the Chinese now call it.

This high peak, once thought to be possibly higher than Everest, had been climbed by our friends Terris Moore and Dick Burdsall, members of the brilliant and daring Sikong Expedition in 1932. Twenty-five years later, a Chinese Mountaineering Association team under Zhi Zhan Zhun climbed the peak, believing they were making the first ascent, for all records in China of the American climb had long since been destroyed. To our surprise we learned that Lance Owens, a Los Angeles surgeon whom we did not know, had applied for permission to climb this mountain. Apparently his application arrived just after the order came to permit some foreign climbing, and since the Chinese had already climbed the mountain, they granted Dr. Owens' request. They also told him that when he came to China the following spring to negotiate arrangements for the climb, he could bring someone else with him.

When Dr. Owens asked me to accompany him to China in the spring of 1980, the AAC voted to pay my expenses as the AAC official dealing with the Chinese about mountain permissions in general and the costs of mountain expeditions in China. We left by Braniff Airlines in April 1980, making the long flight to Seoul, Korea, from Los Angeles before continuing on to Beijing.

Zhi Zhan Zhun was a tough bargainer. Everything had to be spelled out. On our second meeting with him, we had a surprise. Lance and I had both imagined that no other expedition would be given permission to climb Gongga Shan at the same time. The China Tourist Agency, however, had invited the tour group called Mountain Travel to send a representative to negotiate a climb on the same mountain at the same time. Fortunately, the man they sent was a friend and a very fair person, Al Read, a first-rate climber who had been running the tour group's activities in Nepal. Zhi Zhan Zhun and the three of us bargained together. Lance was eager to keep expenses low, but that was of secondary importance to Read. Mountain Travel wanted to be on excellent terms with Zhi Zhan Zhun, and Al naturally was accommodating. We considered all expenses, including clothing for Chinese climbers, as well as the cost of food for them and for the horses and horsemen who would bring the climbers to the mountain and back. We considered the cost of fodder, what would happen if a horse died on the way, and how many handlers for the horses and cooks would be needed. Insurance was to be paid, too. The Chinese were not missing a thing.

When Zhi Zhan Zhun told us that the expedition must pay for the horses for eight days—two days to round them up, two days to go to base camp, two days to return, and two days to go back to pasture—Lance asked if it wouldn't be cheaper to buy horses and resell them at the end of the expedition.

At this, Zhi Zhan Zhun became furious, or pretended to be, giving a speech about the poverty of people in the Gongga Shan area, and about how any Westerner wanting to come to such an area must pay a lot to help these poor people. We strongly suspected that none of what was to be paid would ever get to people in the local area, but we were not in a position to argue. When we finally agreed and signed a formal contract, Al Read said, "One other thing. We would like to have a trek to the mountain at the same time."

Zhi Zhan Zhun looked puzzled, but asked, "Do they pay?"

"Of course."

"Then there is no problem."

As we were leaving, Zhi Zhan Zhun stopped me and let Al Read go out. When Al was beyond earshot, he said, "What is a trek?" We told him.

"People pay to walk?" he said, with openmouthed astonishment.

"Yes."

"In China nobody pays to walk," he muttered, shaking his head as if the world had gone crazy.

That evening the Chinese gave a banquet for us, with Mr. Jin Shu, chairman of the International Sports Section of the All China Sports Federation, as the most honored guest. In 1972 he had brought to the U.S. the table tennis team that opened Chinese-American relations. Mr. Jin, who spoke English, obviously considered mountaineering to be a minor sport. Zhi Zhan Zhun sat on my left and an interpreter on my right. Across the table sat wiry Jin Shu. Halfway through the banquet, Jin Shu made a speech, saying how fine it was that we had with us at the table Zhi Zhan Zhun, who had made the first ascent of Gongga Shan, the mountain of our expedition. At this Lance Owens quickly stated that we enjoyed having Mr. Zhi Zhan Zhun with us, but he had not made the first ascent of Gongga Shan, since Americans had climbed the mountain many years earlier.

Complete silence was followed by an explosion of Chinese from Zhi Zhan Zhun, who before had been feeding me special tidbits. The interpreter on my right whispered, "He says the Americans never did it."

Obviously, this was not the time for a drag-out fight, and I quickly asked Zhi Zhan Zhun about the climbers who were with him on Gongga Shan and the equipment they used, but during the rest of the banquet the atmosphere was strained.

Throughout the visit I had been trying to make progress on getting to the Ulugh Muztagh. Finally, by using the names of Shi Ya Feng, whom I had met through Brad Washburn, and others I had met at the Chinese embassy in Washington, a meeting was arranged for me with Mr. Sun

Hong Li of the Academia Sinica. Mr. Sun had led many scientific expeditions to Tibet but could give me no information about the Ulugh Muztagh. He told me that Chinese scientists were interested in the Kunlun, but did not consider work there a high priority. If American funds for research were available, Academia Sinica interest would increase, but all science in high mountains had to be done in conjunction with the Chinese Mountaineering Association.

Dr. Sun was about to lead an expedition of foreign scientists across Tibet to Lhasa, and then south along the recently completed road to Kathmandu. He asked if I had scientific credentials of any kind, saying that if I had I would be welcome to join the group. Of course I wanted to go, but I was in no way a scientist and told him I deeply regretted my lack of a proper scientific background. Mr. Sun was a pleasant, highly educated man, whom we were to meet again.

Before departing from Beijing we had to make another sad refusal. Zhi Zhan Zhun told Lance and me that we had permission to go to Gongga Shan to reconnoiter the mountain at once if we wished. We both wished, but Lance had to return now or lose his job. I had only city clothes and, like Lance, had commitments back home. If only we had known a month or two earlier that such a reconnaissance was possible, we could have done it. Lance wanted to make a new route if possible, and we both realized that a reconnaissance to investigate such a route should be done before he went in with his expedition. It would take up to two weeks.

Weeks later, Lance's expedition, and the one Read was interested in, went to Gongga Shan, but neither succeeded in reaching the top. Lance's party was unable to climb a new route. The other group, with very strong climbers, were following Moore's route when they started an avalanche. One man was killed and several others were injured.

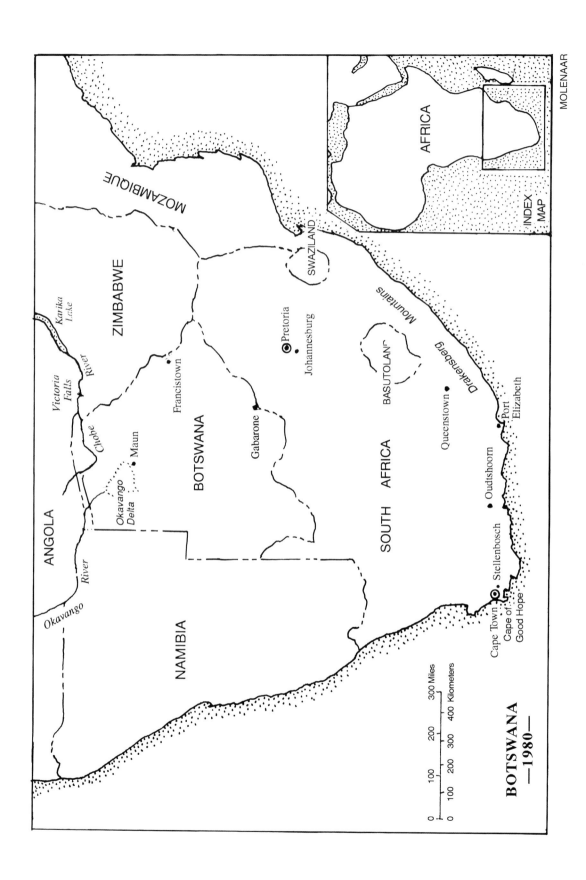

BOTSWANA
—1980—

MOLENAAR

CHAPTER XXXI

Botswana
1980

ONE OF OUR MOST ACTIVE and imaginative Peace Corps
volunteers in Nepal was a young Princeton graduate named Mac
Odell. We liked him, kept in touch, and later became very fond
of his father and mother, who some years later moved to Amesbury,
Massachusetts, near Exeter, and took over the country's oldest boat house
for the building of wooden boats. Mac and his wife Marcia both took their
Ph.D.s at Cornell and thereafter went to Botswana to work in country
development for the government. They kept after the senior Odells and
Gail and me to come to visit them, and finally, in August 1980, when they
were spending their third year in Botswana, we figured we never would
have such an opportunity again, and went.

We flew to Johannesburg, then on to Gaborone, the capital, where Mac
and Marcia spoke Tswana and were on excellent terms with local people.
After a couple of days in Gaborone, we left on a safari to the game parks in
the Maun area, seven of us traveling in a light truck, including two-year-old
Jamie, and Mac's father and mother, Jim and Peggy Odell, who had come
from the U.S. also. Mac had developed ingenious plans for the truck. A
huge piece of plywood the size of the floor was secured over it halfway to the
roof. Stores for our trucks were stacked under the plywood; and on the plywood, lying on sleeping bags and propped up, three adults and Jamie could
rest fairly comfortably, with views through the side windows.

We drove to Francistown, spent the night there, then drove west to
Maun, a small village but the main center in northwest Botswana. It had
a hospital, a post office, a hotel, and not much more. On the way we saw
ostriches, impala, and other antelope, but in the game parks at Chobe,

Gail beside an anthill in the Okavango area of Botswana

At the base of a baobab tree in Botswana

where we took with us each day a government guide, we saw lots of other animals. Giraffes sometimes seemed to be everywhere, and from warthogs to elephants there was great diversity. Jamie's first intelligible words were "ippo" and "graffe." We were near the great Kalahari Desert, where only bushmen can live off the land, and a few of these small people worked in Maun.

Late one afternoon we pitched our tents near a giant fig tree. Suddenly a tremendous, angry scream from the opposite side of the tree made our hair stand on end. It came from a hippo on whose grounds we were camping, though we did not realize it. No other animal noise can be more startling. Hippos are probably the most dangerous animals in Africa, especially if you are between them and water, as fortunately we then were not. One night we were awakened by human screaming; a South African tourist, who had gone to a latrine, had been charged by a hippo. The man had run right through the spikes of a thorn tree to get away, and, though he escaped, the next day he was a lacerated, bloody sight from the thorns.

One evening as we were cooking our supper over a wood fire beside the Savuti Channel, I was admiring three huge trees, beautifully silhouetted against the evening sky, when I noticed one of the great trees begin to sway until it toppled with an enormous crash. An elephant was getting his supper too.

That night, very tired and more than half asleep, I heard the tread of an animal and then the swish as it brushed past the side of the tent. In a moment it was gone. I was too tired to investigate, but in the morning a fresh elephant footprint was found two feet from where my head had rested. We hadn't realized that we were camped on the edge of a game trail.

After some effort we had good views of the great sable antelope with their long curved horns, and one day we came across a pack of wild dogs stalking a family of waterbuck.

The Okavango is a 10,000-square-kilometer wilderness, caused by geologic uplift that blocks the normal flow of the Okavango River. From Maun we flew across the islands and waterways of the Okavango Delta to Xaxaba on Chief's Island, a camp on the edge of the Moremi Wildlife Reserve. From here we made forays by dugout along clear water channels lined with papyrus. On the firmer ground, we found occasional baobab trees and huge termite mounds, some rising well above our heads. We saw kudus, lechwe, situtunga, and other antelope, and were impressed by the long snake skins hanging in bushes where they had been shed. This part of Botswana is well known for its black mambas, very poisonous snakes. The father of the woman who with her husband ran the rustic camp had been killed by a 12-foot black mamba, but we never saw a snake there.

The morning after our return to Maun, however, a woman suddenly realized that a Russell's viper had entered her room and was on the floor near her chair. Fortunately, she kept cool, and not moving her feet, called to someone, who came in and dispatched the snake. Russell's vipers are fat, ugly, and very poisonous.

On our return to Gaborone, we left the Odells with warm good-byes, departing for Johannesburg to begin travels in South Africa. Botswana seemed to be a country where blacks and whites worked well together. We wanted to see if race relations in South Africa were as hopeless as the Odells told us they were.

After a day in modern Johannesburg, we went by bus to nearby Pretoria, the capital. People told us we must see the Voortrekker Monument, the holy of holies of Afrikaners. It was open to whites every day, but to anyone, meaning blacks, only on Tuesdays. With difficulty, we secured tickets for a Tuesday. The monument is a huge, domed building, made of granite and circled by a frieze of ox wagons of the sort used by the Boers in their great trek in the 1830s. Inside, a frieze shows heroic actions in the country's history, especially scenes from Voortrekker wars with the Zulus and other tribes. A light shining on an open book symbolizes the covenant that formed the Union of South Africa. It is a monument both to the history of South Africa and to white supremacy.

The day we went there, several bus loads of black schoolchildren had been brought in, to the annoyance of the man in charge of the museum, for they kept shouting to one another. South Africa's praise of her heroes shows some parallels to the U.S., as we remarked to the man in charge. His sour reply was, "You did it right. You killed off your Indians. We should have finished ours off too."

Angry, we left, stopping to say hello to some of the neatly dressed black schoolchildren outside who were waiting to get in. Gail spoke to a girl and asked, "Where do you come from?"

"Soweto. Where do you come from?"

We said, "America." Her face lit up and she quickly demanded, "Can you help us? Give us arms." We had already felt the racial tension in South Africa, and it continued as long as we were in the country.

From Johannesburg, we flew to Port Elizabeth on the southern coast and picked up a rented car to be turned in at Capetown. That began traveling we have never forgotten, for South Africa is the California of Africa, one of the most beautiful countries in the world. Driving west along the Garden Coast, with views of the brilliant sea and empty beaches, we finally stopped at Plettenberg Bay. There, after a stroll on the beach and a dip, we spent the night at one of my three favorite hotels in the world. The others are in Darjeeling (India) and Ecuador.

The Cape of Good Hope was beckoning now, a place I once thought of as being at the end of the world. When a child, the triangular postage stamp from there had been the prize in my collection. We found the Cape flowers astonishing, especially the giant proteas, famous across the world. We spent the night halfway between Capetown and the end of the Cape itself, which next day we found absorbing. As one looks down on its swirling foam, there extends to the horizon an immense expanse of water where the Indian and Pacific Oceans meet. At the Cape itself on a windy day, we saw whitecaps rising, a few gulls swooping with the wind, and a couple of big oil tankers rolling in the swells.

In Capetown, relations between blacks and whites seemed better than in Johannesburg. The National Botanical Garden at Kirstenbosch attracted us, and we enjoyed taking the cable car to the top of Table Mountain and looking down on the city. We would have preferred to climb there, but time was short.

Starting our trip home, we went to the airport the next morning to fly to London en route to the U.S., but we never got to London. In fact, we almost never came home at all. We boarded a fully loaded, two-engine

Airbus for a scheduled South African Airways flight. Taking off after a normal run, we must have been up about 600 feet when the plane struck something. There was a terrible screech of tearing metal and the plane shuddered. Nobody said a word. Everyone was too scared to move. The plane dipped slightly but kept on toward some hills. Gradually we began to turn and a voice announced, "We have had a bird strike and are returning to base to assess damage."

Still no one spoke. Gail and I were squeezing hands and looking out the window. We seemed to be holding our altitude as the plane slowly turned in a wide arc out over the bay. Still nobody spoke. The plane kept turning very, very gradually until finally, minutes later, another announcement stated, "We are over the field and preparing to land." The landing was smooth. Nobody cheered, as one might expect. The passengers lined up and filed out, saying little, but they knew how close we had come. Then we saw the pilot climb down wearily. He was pale as his white uniform. We looked through huge holes torn in the metal of the jet engine. Blood streaked the forward part of the plane. As we entered the airport building, a passenger who was also a pilot was saying, "They said an Airbus with a full load of passengers and fuel could fly with one engine, but I never believed it till now."

After several hours of waiting, we were all flown to Johannesburg, where by chance we met the Odells, who had left Gaborone an hour earlier. Jim and Peg Odell left soon, but we had a long wait before a flight for us was arranged. It went via the Ivory Coast and Madrid. By the time we finally arrived in New York, Boston, and Exeter's High Street, our home looked better than ever.

CHAPTER XXXII

Efforts to Reach the Great Ice Mountain

1980–1983

W E HAD KEPT IN TOUCH with Professor Molnar, who in October 1980 wrote me a letter saying why an expedition to the Ulugh Muztagh would produce valuable scientific information. In part it said, "Geologically, the Tibetan plateau is probably the least known large area in the world. . . . The Altyn Tagh Fault [close to the Ulugh Muztagh] . . . apparently is the longest and most important strike-slip fault on earth. . . . It is one of the earth's spectacular features and we know next to nothing about it."

He continued, "The second peculiarity of the Ulugh Muztagh region is the volcanism. . . . Volcanism in northern Tibet is simply not what most earth scientists expect. Most are shocked to hear of it, and some flatly disbelieve it without looking at the evidence."

Later he added, "In the long run our study of the Kunlun holds the key not only to the origins of one of Asia's highest and most remote peaks, but also the key to an understanding of how the Tibetan plateau, by far the highest and most extensive of all continental plateaus, formed."

David Challinor, the Smithsonian's secretary of science, was also excited about our plan and sent Nick Clinch a fine letter in January 1981 confirming Smithsonian interest in exploring the Kunlun.

At this point Nick wrote a detailed letter to James Lilley, who was to become the American ambassador to China. It proposed a letter from Vice-President Bush to Vice-Premier Fang Yi. This letter was not sent, but in April 1981, when Jack Mendelsohn, the science advisor to the president, was in Beijing, a cable was sent to him signed Haig, asking him to discuss with Wu Yikang, director of the State Scientific and Technological Commission Dealing with U.S. Affairs, our request to come to Beijing to consider a Chinese-American expedition to the Kunlun. He was informed that the request expressed the interest of the vice-president. Later Nick had a brief chat with Mr. Bush at a dinner and was told that Chace Untermeyer (the executive assistant to the vice-president) knew our problem and was doing what he could.

That fall through friends I met Christopher Wren, top foreign correspondent of the *New York Times*, who was soon to begin work in Beijing. He was very interested in what I told him about the Ulugh Muztagh and said he would like to go too if that were possible. Chris, whom I had heard of previously as a mountain climber as well as foreign correspondent, insisted I come to New York to meet the managing editor of the *Times* to consider what part the *Times* could play in our potential expedition. I met with Mr. Rosenthal, the executive editor, and several members of the staff. He said that the *Times* would like to send someone with us if that were possible, but had no influence in China to help us get permission and could not make a financial grant to the expedition. Possibly the *Times* might pay for articles on the expedition, but this practice, which yielded us revenue on K2 in 1938, was now rare.

When Nick returned to Beijing after an Everest trek, he did his best through the American embassy to find why the Ulugh Muztagh area was off limits, and how to get the restriction removed, but got nowhere. Since no movement seemed likely on our application to go there, in October we went to Kathmandu with Brad Washburn to help him fulfill his lifelong ambition to make the best map ever made of Mt. Everest. We introduced him to several people, especially Dhruba Bhakta, with his extensive experience in getting things done in Nepal.

While Brad was struggling with bureaucrats who were scared to make decisions, we were visiting in Kathmandu with Tsering Yangdon, her husband, Art Taylor, their young son, Nima, and Tsering's mother, who spoke only Tibetan. Art was working on a rehabilitation program for Nepal.

Shortly before our departure for the U.S. we had an informal meeting with the king, who lit his pipe, put his feet up, and talked like an old friend. He was trying to get his ministers to take responsibility, and therefore told us that Brad must work through channels to get permissions to make his Everest map. Brad did, but it was slow work.

In December 1981, Zhi Zhan Zhun, the real authority in the Chinese Mountaineering Association (CMA), came to the U.S. to receive an honorary membership in the American Alpine Club, but he had no news of any change in the restrictions barring foreigners from entering the area of the Ulugh Muztagh. We tried again in April 1982, when Jin Shu and Wang Fuzhou, climbing leader of the successful Chinese ascent of Mt. Everest, visited the U.S.

Nick Clinch gave Wang and Jin a tour of the West Coast, while Gail and I did the honors on the Atlantic side. Jin, head of the international branch of the All China Sports Federation, was interested in American sports. We took him to see the facilities at the University of New Hampshire, and later Harvard gave a luncheon for him with all the Harvard athletic coaches. Jin suggested that the next Harvard-Yale football game be played in China, but admitted to difficulties in arranging it.

Both Wang and Jin were very interested in meeting Terris Moore, who had become a legend in Chinese climbing circles. The Chinese did not believe that an American expedition could have climbed the great Gongga Shan in 1932. When Gail and I took them to the Moores' house in Cambridge, where they saw many pictures of the successful Sikong Expedition, they were tremendously impressed. Though we drove them to New York and showed them the Empire State Building and other points of interest, nothing impressed them so much as meeting the Moores. At the airport, as we were seeing them off, Jin Shu turned and made a sort of apology by saying, "We simply didn't know." What he meant was that records of what happened in the pre-Mao era had been largely destroyed and they had no way of knowing that Americans had climbed Gongga Shan 50 years earlier.

Since one can often do more to influence decisions by appearing in person, Gail and I decided to go to Urumchi to see if that would help us gain permission to enter the forbidden area in the southern part of Xinjiang Province. Lance and Jackie Owens joined us for our flight to Beijing, and we went on together by overnight train as far as Xian, a city Gail and I particularly wanted to see.

As is well known now, it contains one of the archaeological wonders of the world, the great underground terracotta army of the first emperor of Qin, who unified China in 221 B.C. The lifelike, life-size soldiers, with their horses and chariots, were not discovered until 1974. They were very impressive.

With the Ulugh Muztagh in mind, we continued west, again by train, but Lance and Jackie were no longer with us when we entered our soft-berth compartment. There we quickly met our two new companions. One was a solid, moon-faced Chinese man in military uniform, who had many packages stowed for him by a younger man also in uniform. The other person turned out to be an American teacher from a Connecticut school, who had just had an unpleasant divorce and was getting away from his part of the world.

The affable Chinese man offered us tea immediately, for a Thermos of hot water and tea is always available in first-class coaches. We didn't know the rank of the Chinese man, who spoke no English, and we, his three companions, spoke only a dozen words of Chinese. He first indicated that we should decide who was the oldest. When I said in Chinese what I thought was my age, he roared with laughter. I had told him I was 92.

When the train stopped several hours later and passengers poured out to check the local melons, we met a Chinese woman who spoke some English and was reading a Hemingway novel. We asked her how we could discover the rank of our Chinese companion. She said, "How many pockets does he have?"

"Four."

"Then he is a general."

The general's greatest reaction came when the Connecticut man produced a copy of *Time* he had bought in Hong Kong. On the cover was a picture of Castro. As the amiable general looked at the picture, his face became ferocious. "Castro, Cuba," he grunted out, each word accompanied with a downward thrust of his thumb, then loudly, "Russki!" and at that he stabbed his back with his thumb. Nothing could have been more emphatic.

The trip was slow. Our departure from Xian had been late, and it wasn't until the third night that we arrived near Turfan, nine hours late. We enjoyed the ancient oasis, though our guide had no local knowledge and not much English. The Turfan Depression is almost 500 feet below sea level, one of the deepest areas in the world, but its grapes are world famous, and its melons rival even Hami melons. We climbed the tower of Emin Minaret, and later, for the first time, heard Uigur music coming from instruments we had never seen before.

From Turfan we drove to Urumchi, a city of more than a million people, where much steel is made. There we tried to reach a geologist with whom we had corresponded about the Ulugh Muztagh. Unfortunately, he had left the city for parts unknown and could not be reached by phone. At the Xinjiang Institute of Geography and everywhere else, we were told the same thing: the area you are interested in is off limits to foreigners. It was all very disappointing.

We were offered a chance to go to Kashgar, but the route southeast from there to Hunza and Pakistan was not open.

After we flew back to Beijing, we were offered different places to visit. We selected Chengde, the old summer capital of the Manchus, about four hours by train from Beijing. The palace area, named the Mountain Area for Escaping the Summer Heat, surrounded by six miles of walls, is about double the size of the Forbidden City in Beijing. It is a place of extraordinary rock formations (one of which I climbed), dozens of gardens, pagodas, moon gates, and copies of famous Buddhist temples, all built in the 18th century.

Very few Westerners recently had gone to Chengde, but we met two people there. One, to our surprise, was the Turkish ambassador to China, who had just come from the Xinjiang, where he found he could understand the Uigurs, whose language is an old form of Turkish. The other was a woman of about 40, who looked Chinese, but dressed, talked, and acted like a well-to-do American or Canadian. After becoming acquainted, she told us that as a young girl her mother had been sold to a prosperous Chinese merchant living in Vancouver, who had bought her sight unseen. She had been sent by boat to Vancouver without knowing a word of English.

After our four-hour return trip to Beijing, we said good-bye to friends and flew to Tokyo. We were supposed to stay there three days and then fly to Russia for 10 days in Leningrad and Moscow before returning to the U.S., but again something happened. A Korean plane flying from Anchorage, Alaska, was shot down by the Russians, and all flights to the Soviet Union were canceled. This meant that we did not go to Russia but stayed for a week in Tokyo. Our flight home via Paris crossed the Arctic, with views of large masses of icebergs.

CHAPTER XXXIII

The White House

1983

T HAT FALL WE LEARNED that King Birendra was finally coming to Washington. A stream of invitations followed, including gilt-edged invitations to a formal luncheon given by the State Department and a formal dinner at the White House.

When we flew to Washington, John Twiss, the marine mammal commissioner and a former student, met us at the airport and took us home for a delicious dinner. In the morning, we drove to the State Department luncheon in the Jefferson Room, where Vice-President Bush officiated. Birendra noticed us at once. He stepped forward with the remark, "Well, Bob, we made it." I spoke with him for a minute, then thanked the vice-president for trying to help us get to the Ulugh Muztagh.

The Jefferson Room is beautiful, an ideal place for a small luncheon. I sat next to a royal princess who said little and had on her other side an assistant secretary of state who didn't know much about Nepal. After the watercress mousse, the quail with herb dressing, and dessert, there were short, courteous remarks by the vice-president and the king, and the luncheon was over.

That evening, after being turned away at the normal driveway to the White House, since barriers were being erected to prevent terrorist attacks, we drove in a side entrance, where our invitations were checked. We were escorted first into an anteroom, where a cheery fire blazed. Our coats were immediately taken, and, while Gail went to the ladies' room, I sat down in a comfortable chair to listen to two women in marine uniforms who were playing lovely duets on a harp and flute. Another man came in at almost the same time and sat down beside me while he waited for his wife. I said,

"Bates," and he said, "Yeager." Yeager at that moment didn't mean any more to me than Bates did to him. We chatted briefly, but it was some minutes before I realized that this was Chuck Yeager, the man who first broke the sound barrier.

We entered the big room on the main floor, where other couples were arriving too, most with important titles, until about 100 were there. Brad and Barbara Washburn greeted us enthusiastically, as did Jim Whittaker and Dianne Roberts. Nepal's ambassador and his wife also joined us.

When everyone was there, President and Mrs. Reagan, with the king and queen of Nepal, entered and formed a receiving line. As we approached the head of the line, a State Department aide asked our connection with Nepal. I told him, and he whispered this to the president, who nodded, gave me a warm handshake, and patted my shoulder. Nobody stopped to chat.

After drinks and hors d'oeuvres we went to assigned tables. I sat next to a man who whispered that he had given directly or indirectly a couple of million dollars to the last presidential campaign. On my other side sat Mrs. Donovan, wife of the secretary of labor, and beyond her Senator Nunn. Gail sat near Barbara Bush at another table but there the Marine Band practically drowned out conversation.

At the appropriate moment, President Reagan took on his favorite role of master of ceremonies. He made a welcoming speech, greeting the king cordially, and sat down. Birendra, I knew, had been working his head off over his speech, in which he presented Nepal as a small country between big neighbors, a region of peace that needed financial help to develop jobs. The audience applauded the king politely, but many guests hardly knew where Nepal was and certainly had no serious interest in its future problems.

Coffee and liqueurs, and also cigarettes and cigars, were passed, and shortly afterward we all moved to the East Room. People kept nodding to us. Everyone was outgoing, as if we were all old friends enjoying together a superlative party. One jolly man and his wife who sat down beside us began to joke about when he did and did not wear a wig. He turned out to be Willard Scott, the weatherman.

When we were all seated, two pianists, Ferrante and Teicher, who looked and dressed alike, played duets on two pianos. They started with "Yankee Doodle" and then a special potpourri of patriotic songs put together for the occasion. After they had finished, the president rose and, in his master-of-ceremonies manner, told two funny stories that brought down the house.

As we walked out of the East Room, we were invited to stay and dance in a smaller room where the Marine Band was playing dance tunes of the 1930s. That was too good to miss, and Gail and I began dancing, only to find ourselves soon between the Reagans and the band, whose trombones were a threat if we moved to give the first couple more space. They looked as if they were enjoying themselves, as we were.

That was the end. Our borrowed Volkswagen was driven to the door for us and off we drove.

CHAPTER XXXIV

Egypt
1984

I N FEBRUARY 1984, one of our former Peace Corps volunteers, Flemming Heegaard, asked us to visit him in Cairo and later make a trip down the Nile in a felucca. Flemming, who spoke Arabic and was living in Cairo, had charge of a vast number of AID projects in Egypt. The year before, his program had trained over 25,000 people, including the rural development officers of 830 villages. He asked us to stay with him and his daughter in their rented house in Maadi, a Cairo suburb.

Exeter is not at its best in the spring mud season, and since Flemming is an imaginative friend, in March, as he suggested, we flew to Cairo. There Maria, his housekeeper, fed us fish soufflés and a variety of Egyptian dishes. Flemming had arranged a car and driver for us, and we made good use of them.

One weekend with Flemming we visited Alexandria, a city still with the flavor of the 19th century, and then took an overnight train to Luxor (the ancient Thebes), where we were fortunate in our hotel and guide. Tourists were few. No temple in the world can compare in size with Karnak, a true wonder of the world.

Of course we spent the better part of a day at the Valley of the Kings and Valley of the Queens across the Nile, viewing the tombs of Tutankhamen and Ramses VI, as well as the beautiful mortuary temple of Queen Hatshepsut. Reliefs on the latter, showing every kind of fish found in the Mediterranean (87, I think), caught our fancy. No new ones have been found since.

From Luxor we drove to Aswan with its great modern Russian dam, then flew south to Abu Simbel, where we admired the colossal statues of

Gail at Abu Simbel

HEEGAARD PHOTO

Sailing down the Nile in a felucca.

Ramses II and his wife, saved from the waters of the dam by an international campaign. Flemming met us on our return to Aswan and we boarded a felucca owned by Jamal, a boatman Flemming knew. It had a tall mast and long lateen sail and also a canvas screen that could be raised or lowered to cut off wind or sun. Flemming already had placed in it sleeping bags, water, and food. Jamal's uncle was going with us.

For the next couple of days we sailed or drifted, landing at night on sand islands where there were no footsteps and only the tracks of big, harmless monitor lizards. The temples we passed were most impressive when seen from a felucca. We were comfortable and soon absorbed the tranquility of this ancient form of travel. Feeling refreshed, we sailed into Luxor, paid Jamal, and took the night train to Cairo. With many thanks to Flemming, we left Egypt. What a grand way to escape the mud season in New Hampshire.

Looking for tigers in the Nepal Terai

CHAPTER XXXV

India, Nepal, and Bhutan

1985

THE FOLLOWING SUMMER (1984) I had my first real illness since I was seven. Something gave me a stiff neck, and stiffness gradually spread to most of my muscles. When I could hardly turn over in bed, I was sent to Dr. Shearman, an arthritis specialist, who gave me a shot of cortisone. Hours later I went upstairs two steps at a time. Apparently I had developed a form of rheumatoid arthritis that could be controlled by using a small amount of prednisone.

Through the years I had kept in touch with George Russell, a close friend ever since he entered Phillips Exeter Academy in the late 1940s. In the intervening years, George and his spunky wife, Jane, had developed a small mutual fund into an internationally famous pension business, the Frank Russell Company, but they had never taken a long vacation. George now proposed that Gail and I plan travels in interesting mountain areas for the four of us. That sounded delightful and it was.

During the summer Gail and I worked out plans for travels in India, Nepal, and Bhutan, while George and Jane adjusted their schedules to permit our departing for a glorious 40 days the following February and March. The opening of the Ulugh Muztagh region to foreigners was still on my mind, of course, as it had been since Nick Clinch and I had started our work to get there, but since the vice-president had had no success in helping us, the chance of an immediate opening seemed very small.

421

A few days before Gail and I were to leave for India, however, an unexpected phone caller from California asked if we had just received permission to go to the Ulugh Muztagh. When I said, "No," I was told that an American had permission and the speaker thought he might be involved with us. What a shock! I phoned Nick at once but he had heard nothing. Then, with the help of a friend who speaks Chinese, I phoned the office of the Chinese Mountaineering Association (CMA) in Beijing. The answer at the other end was confused. Yes, the permission had been given to another American, but his plans were uncertain. There was still a chance for us.

I talked to Nick again and we fired off the following telegram to Wang Fuzhou and Zhi Zhan Zhun:

> We understand that mountains in Tibet are being opened to climbers. We would like to renew our request for a joint Chinese-American Expedition in 1985 to Ulugh Muztagh. We would like to come to China to discuss this expedition with you as previously outlined. We are sending you immediately a detailed proposal by letter.
>
> Robert H. Bates and Nicholas B. Clinch.

The CMA replied that we should come, and even though Nick had been in bed with the flu when the first bombshell arrived, he flew to China at once to negotiate if that were possible.

Before we left for India the following message came from Nick in Beijing: "This has been wild. Nothing is absolute yet as there have been more ups and downs than a roller coaster, but I think you had better start dragging out your long underwear and start practicing your Mandarin."

That was enough for me. I had great confidence in Nick. We could go to India with the feeling that the problems of getting to the Ulugh Muztagh were being resolved.

After a day in London, Gail and I flew on to the Indian capital, reaching it some hours ahead of George and Jane. That began their first visit to Southeast Asia and our fun in sharing travels together. As we suspected, they were superb traveling companions. We met at the old Imperial Hotel on the Janpath, and during their first day in Delhi went by tongas to the Red Fort. Before we knew it, George and Jane were thoroughly enjoying India, getting their own tongas and three-wheeled rickshaws and even plunging into the traffic at Chandni Chowk. One day we dined in Old Delhi with our friend Jogindar Singh, and on another occasion with Nalni Jayal, who took us to the Delhi Zoo, part of his domain.

A long day took us to Agra to see the Taj Mahal, which was breathtaking as ever. At a distance it appeared to be so fragile that a puff of wind would blow it away. We saw it first from the Agra Fort, behind whose exquisite marble screens Shah Jehan, after he was deposed, sat for years looking at his creation across the Jumna River, but unable to visit it. In any light, with people or without, it seems the most beautiful building in the world.

We also visited Fatehpur Sikri, Akbar's impressive capital that was used for only nine years because of lack of water. The world should take note that this sort of disaster can happen again.

After a week in India, we flew to Kathmandu and were driven to the Shankar Hotel. I had made a date with Sir Edmund Hillary, and he and George Lowe joined us for lunch the next day. I gave Ed, from Brad Washburn, a picture of Everest taken from 39,000 feet, and also a just-completed part of Brad's Everest map, which showed the contours of the summit.

The next day we flew to Tiger Tops (a camp in the wildlife protection area) in the Terai, where elephants met us at the airstrip. On the way, we saw several Asian rhino and a sloth bear, and in the evening a shoeless walk took us to where a tiger was tearing chunks of meat from a kill.

Back in Kathmandu, we had a great dinner at Dhruba Bhakta Mathema's home. Then we were off to Pokhara by plane to begin a trek. Before leaving Pokhara, we had time to visit our former Peace Corps volunteer Dorothy Mierouw, who had continued to live in Nepal. She had built, at her own expense, a unique Nepalese museum. We also visited Prithni Narayan College, which when we first saw it in 1962 had only 31 students in an open shed covered with a grass roof. Partly thanks to Peace Corps help, it had developed, and now consisted of a dozen or more buildings serving 3,500 students.

In the afternoon, with a cook and several porters, we began our long walk to Ghorapani, pitching our tents the first night near a Tibetan camp. Gail and I remembered our 1954 trek along the ridge that runs west from Pokhara, with grand views of the Annapurna peaks, especially Machhapuchhre (the fish tail), and also Dhaulagiri. All of the villages on the ridge had grown since we first saw them in 1954 and more terraces had been built by farmers. We passed Lumle, and at the end of the ridge dropped down nearly 2,000 feet to cross the Mahdi Khola near Birethanti at 3,400 feet. Our trek from there to Ghorapani (9,300 feet) showed that much of the forest recently had been cut.

On a cold, cloudy morning, George and I were up early to climb Poon Hill to see the sunrise touch the highest points of Dhaulagiri, Annapurna,

Nilgiri, and the whole Annapurna Range. It was like watching a tableau. Then, in what was almost a spiritual experience, the rich sunrise glow touched to life one summit and ridge after another, until the whole world seemed a land of hope and promise.

That day the route from Ghorapani to Ghandrung (6,400 feet), a fine Gurung town, led up and down several thousand feet through woods of blooming primroses and daphne, but the trails were treacherous with melting snow, ice, and mud. More ups and downs were followed by a long climb toward Dhanpus, where many orchids bloomed along the trail. Later we pitched tents on a terrace with many rhododendron trees in full bloom. We hated to leave the exhilarating mountain air the next day as we dropped down to the dusty trail to Pokhara.

Our permission to visit Bhutan required our being in Siliguri (near the airport of Bagdogra) on the morning of March 1. To be there at the right time, we flew to Patna to spend the night. Patna, along the Ganges River, was sizzling hot, and the lower altitude brought lassitude, but George grabbed the opportunity to take a bicycle rickshaw and visit the Ganges.

After waiting two hours in Siliguri, we noticed a wild-looking young man with a scarf around his head, one end hanging down behind, who seemed to be looking for someone. He was Singh, who had come in a small bus, our Bhutan guide, and his use of good English belied his appearance. We asked him many questions as we drove east for three hours across flat country to the Bhutanese frontier, which begins where the hills and mountains of Bhutan first rise from the plains.

Ahead was Drukyul, "Dragon Land," the true name of Bhutan, a country Gail and I had long wished to enter. Beyond Phuntsholing, where we went through customs, we drove a few kilometers up wooded slopes to a modern hotel run by the Bhutan government, which fortunately was limiting the number of tourists entering the little kingdom. Practically everyone was wearing Bhutanese dress, the kho, a sort of knee-length, wraparound garment that looks very practical, at least in mild weather.

The next day we lunched near a great hydroelectric plant under construction and continued on to Paro, Bhutan's second city. Bhutanese houses are very attractive, mud or brick below and wood or plaster above, with carved windows, painted wall decorations, and big eaves as in Switzerland.

Singh, we found, wanted to become a climber and would be traveling to Japan for mountaineering training in the fall. He showed us our first dzongs—great, strongly constructed, medieval monastery forts. One, the Kyichu Dzong, had a fine museum inside. Afterward we went with Singh to his mother's house, where a snow lion and a tiger were painted on opposite sides of the front door. Singh's mother, a handsome but worn-looking woman, showed us the house, including the family lakhang (the Buddhist word for temple), where there were elephant tusks, thankas (religious paintings), and silver bowls. She said she had paid to educate all her sons, but now they had left her to run the family farm herself.

In the morning we were off to the Tiger's Nest, a landmark temple built into a pocket of rock near the top of a sheer cliff. After three hours of climbing or riding we reached a small teahouse below and across a gully from the three small Tiger's Nest buildings. Jane had arranged to have a "messenger" arrive there breathless with a fake telegram for George from the acting head of the Frank Russell Company. It said that the business was falling apart and George must immediately return. That shook him for a minute or two, and then we all had a good laugh.

We climbed to the level of the Tiger's Nest, crossed the narrowing gully on a small bridge, and reached the ledge where Padma Sambhava supposedly had landed when he flew from Tibet on the back of a tigress and gave orders to build a temple there. Big beams had been carved to fit into the rock at the edge of the cliff, as well as into huge boulders lying in the pocket. Like any great cathedral, the little buildings showed what faith can do. The only monk there showed us everything. Prominent among the thankas were an old and a new statue of the Guru and the Tigress. An imposing altar possessed huge elephant tusks, gleaming silver bowls, and the biggest butter lamp in Bhutan. The whole Tiger's Nest was a place to savor.

At Thimphu, the capital, to which we drove the next day, we met Dhruba's bright nephew, Amanda Pradhan, who was the minister of electricity. Thimphu had fewer than 10,000 people, but its main building was impressive. This was the huge Tashichhodzong, finished in 1970, which housed both the central government and Bhutan's most holy monastery. As the Drukyul flag indicates, religion serves with the government equally in the running of the country. The building showed the basic style of Bhutanese dzongs: fortress shape, thick walls, and an inner court.

In Thimphu we learned that Bhutan did not wish to strip away its forests as Nepal had done, having instead a policy of strict obtainable yield. We were told also that King Jigme Singh Wanchuk, who had become king in 1974 when he was 18, was not only popular but a strong ruler. He was determined to have the current Bhutanese culture and environment remain.

We were headed farther east to the Bumthang Valley and on the way the next day, stopped at ancient Punakha, where 500 monks lived in a

The national sport of Bhutan: archery

dzong-like monastery. Old thankas and drawings of the Wheel of Life were everywhere, with depictions of taras, Padma Sambhavas, and tigers. The sounds of prayers and trumpets alternated during our visit.

At Tongsa, the most important town in central Bhutan, its old dzong is rightfully famous. We were in the lakhang there, admiring the huge butter lamps, when the weekly ceremony of the "Lament for the Dead" began. Some 30 monks were reading from books of prayers, blowing long and medium-sized trumpets, and sounding bells, rattles, and cymbals. The service was done with precision, the music rising and falling, always controlled, as in a symphony, with each monk having a personal part, depending on the score. Two boys held two big drums for older men, who banged them at intervals. The eight-foot trumpets kept a background tone, and at special moments an eight-year-old boy rang a bell.

The Tongsa dzong is only half a religious building. The other half, traditionally, is run by the crown prince of Bhutan with the title of penlop (governor).

Leaving Tongsa, we continued east, crossing an 11,000-foot pass on the way and dropping to 9,000 feet at Jakar in the Bumthang Valley. The hotel there was only half built, but a privy was dug for us in the yard with a piece of cloth draped around it. We learned that we were in what was to

George Russell examines a Bhutanese bow.

become a luxury hotel. To prove that, dinner started off with a hot Bhutanese cocktail, made of arak and butter, with scrambled eggs topped into every glass. The dried yak meat and pakorhas that followed were barely edible, but I smuggled some out to a dog, which loved them. One room had a fairly modern convenience that we enjoyed, a little potbellied stove, which kept off the chill night air when we were going to bed or getting up.

The Bumthang Valley is dotted with temples. The first we saw dated to the seventh century, and supposedly was founded by Padma Sambhava, but surely it was a holy place long before him. It suggested the extraordinary wealth accumulated in Bumthang's old dzongs.

Here we saw our first contest of Bumthang archery, the national sport. Since money had been bet on the outcome, yells of approval or groans swelled at every shot at the foot-wide target, which was more than 120 yards away. If an arrow struck near the target, members of the shooter's team danced on one foot, waving the other in the air, with arms thrown up. If an arrow struck the target, a rare moment, wild cries erupted from the bowman's team, whose members bowed again and again like courting cranes. When the winning hit came, the triumphant team held hands in a circle and danced, first on one foot then on the other. Local spectators, except the losers and their families, loved it all.

Our next temple contained a weight of chain links weighing 50 or 60 pounds. Singh put the links on his back, went down on his knees and prayed. George did likewise and stood up. The monastery had weird paintings of imaginary demons with eyes on stalks and long necks ending in evil, grinning faces.

A three-day trek with porters and a cook began the next day. We visited more temples and crossed an 11,000-foot pass, the highest Jane had climbed up to that time. On the far side, we met an old woman who was carrying a dog the size of a large terrier. She and others stuck out their tongues at us in the old Tibetan greeting, to show that their tongues were not black and so they were not demons. Most passers-by said, "Kusuzumbola" (How do you do, sir?), as we proceeded down into the Tang Valley.

We were surprised by the size and opulence of the Ugyenchoeding, a huge gompa whose owner lives like a medieval lord of the manor. At another big farm in the upper Tang Valley, we were shown the farm's private temple, with a huge prayer wheel, big sculpted figures, and large lighted butter lamps with paper prayer flags twirling in the hot air above them. After a long descent we reached a school where we were invited to visit classrooms. In each, we were greeted with, "Good afternoon, sir." The school had many UNICEF books, and all students were studying English.

The Tang Valley, with its astringent mountain air and smell of pines, was exhilarating, and we hated to leave it. At last, when we reached the road where our little bus was to meet us, we found one more holy place, where a river had cut a gorge and a deep pool. Hundreds of new prayer flags fluttered, and modern carvings and clay votive figures had been left among the rocks. We were told that if we could squeeze through a tight rock crevice there, we would lose all our sins. We squeezed. Worship here probably predates Buddha by many centuries. A fine, 40-mile drive on a road that is an engineering triumph brought us back to Tongsa. Our trek had been a great success.

The last days had been exceedingly windy, with fresh snow close to Thimphu, and on our drive back to Phuntsholing, we saw where trees had blown down and several roofs blown off. Fruit trees were blooming everywhere as we continued toward the Indian plains. We were ready for a climate change and welcomed the drive to Siliguri, where a car met us and drove us up the winding road to Darjeeling. Here we introduced Jane and George to our old friend Mary Tenduf La, at our favorite hotel, the

George and Jane Russell with Phurpa (Mary) Tenduf La at Darjeeling

Gail and R.H.B. with Phurpa (Mary) Tenduf La

Windamere. We had first stayed there in 1954, and the staff greeted us as old friends.

After visiting a Tibetan refugee center and the Happy Valley Tea Estate, we went to the home of Tenzing Norgay, who with Sir Edmund Hillary first climbed Mt. Everest. We had brought a razor for him from his son Norbu (then a student at the University of New Hampshire). Tenzing seemed much recovered from his serious illness, and he and Daku were eager to see us. We appreciated their warm hospitality. The best part of our visit to Tenzing was to hear what he said about his Mt. Everest companions. He respected John Hunt, but really loved Eric Shipton, who he said "brought him up." He showed us many pictures in his trophy room and spoke highly of Pasang Kikuli and the two other Sherpas lost on K2 in 1939 while trying to rescue Dudley Wolfe.

The weather had been cold and raw in Darjeeling, but in Delhi it was warmer. After a night at the Imperial, we were off to Srinagar and a handsome houseboat on Dal Lake. We arrived on a mild, sunny day, hoping to get the chill of Darjeeling out of our bones. Kashmir and Dal Lake were now cool and damp, however, but we enjoyed shikara travel and seeing the old Mogul Gardens, strong in form but lacking their summer colors. The huge chenar trees still seemed ageless, but when Gail and I stopped at Nedou's Hotel, where our K2 expedition had stayed in 1938, we found nobody in the hotel staff who had been there so long ago.

We had a good visit with Suffering Moses II, the papier-maché artist, but since bad weather persisted, we were not sorry the next day to return to Delhi, where on our last day in India the temperature was in the 80s. The big surprise was the amount of mail for us at the Imperial. For me, the best news came in two letters from Nick Clinch, who had been in China again working out an agreement for us to go to the Ulugh Muztagh. Nick's latest letter told that he would soon leave for Urumchi again to firm up details about the expedition.

Wakened at 3:00 a.m for the flight to London, we put our last odds and ends of rupees into the expectant hands of waiters and porters, with just enough left to pay the taxi and airport departure tax. At Heathrow, where we separated, we weren't looking our best, but what fun we had had! Jakar, and the dzongs and lakhangs of the Tongsa Valley now seemed in another world. As we parted, Gail and I looked at one another in complete agreement—George and Jane were the best ever of our travel companions.

In London we went to the Alpine Club and the Royal Geographical Society to try to learn more about the Ulugh Muztagh, but could find nothing written about it or the Arkatagh Range. In a way, this was good. If we ever reached the mountain, what we found wouldn't be old hat. Finally, we located a 1967 map that listed the Mu-Tzu-Taki Shan (23,697 feet) in the exact place where the Ulugh Muztagh should be. There was also a 1980 map listing the altitude of the same peak as 21,510 feet. Those heights were depressingly under St. George R. Littledale's figure of 25,339. Obviously, there was confusion, about both the height and the name of our mountain.

Nick Clinch, the co-leader

CHAPTER XXXVI

The Great
Ice Mountain at Last

1985

ANOTHER LETTER FROM NICK CLINCH, sent from
Urumchi, was the first one I opened on our arrival in Exeter. In it
he told that he had been welcomed warmly by the Chinese and
was negotiating. That was encouraging, but it was not until he phoned
from Palo Alto a few days later that I felt sure we were going, though even
then the formal protocol agreement had not been signed. We had worked
so long to get permission that it seemed too good to be true.

We must move fast, for the Chinese planned to leave on September 25
from Urumchi and return in 40 days. Also, we must try to raise funds,
select personnel, and order equipment. It would not be the small reconnaissance party walking or riding horses in from Cherchen that we had originally planned. Nick had learned that in the fall of 1984 a Chinese team had
driven trucks almost to the base of the mountain. They had tried to climb
it but two of the climbers had fallen off, ending the attempt. In the area of
the mountain they had seen lots of game, including wild yaks, wild asses,
Orongo antelope, dog-faced bears, and snow leopards. To get to the mountain from Urumchi would require a 1,100-mile drive by truck or jeep, with
the last 500 kilometers completely off any road.

It was not until the end of May 1985 that Nick made a final trip to
China and signed the protocol agreement at Urumchi. The Chinese were
agreeing to their first joint Chinese-American mountaineering expedition.
We were to provide equipment, tents, and climbing gear for all climbers; in

Pete Schoening

addition the Chinese also wanted us to provide trucks and jeeps needed to take the party to the mountain. The Chinese made it clear that we were getting a very special permission. All foreigners had been kept out of the southern two-thirds of the Xinjiang Province for the previous 30 years—the reason why our efforts to go there, though pressed at the highest levels, had been refused. In October, the Xinjiang would be celebrating 30 years of becoming part of the People's Republic of China. This celebration was part of the reason we were going now, for the Chinese had had trouble climbing the mountain in 1984 and they needed help. The climb of the Ulugh Muztagh, together with the completion of the Great Hall of the People in Urumchi, were to be the big celebrations of the event. It was very important to the Xinjiang government that our climb be successful.

Our venture would be no small investigation by three or four climbers. It was to be a fully mechanized, high-power attack, with 16 Chinese climbers, an interpreter, scientists, movie and still photographers, a radioman, and reporters. Nick made a valiant effort to get vehicles from one of our big automobile companies with an office in Beijing, but the shortness of time before our departure was against us. Eventually, seven huge army trucks (previously bought from the French), three Land Rovers, and two jeeps were assembled by the Chinese, with one or two of the trucks to carry loads of fuel. The Chinese told Nick that 50 foreign expeditions had asked permission to go where we were going and that traveling across the desert was very hard on all vehicles, as they had found the previous fall.

Eight Americans were to come, and the Chinese wanted all of them to be climbers. Finally, however, they accepted our demand for two scientists. One was Peter Molnar, who had been a member of our proposed team for years, while the other was rugged Clark Burchfiel (Schlumberger Professor of Geology at the Massachusetts Institute of Technology (MIT), member of the National Academy of Sciences, former football player at the University of Illinois, and a Molnar colleague). Thanks to Recreation Equipment in Seattle and Patagonia, sporting goods firms, most of our clothing and equipment needs were easily met. Each of us contributed to the expedition cost, while Nick Clinch, the treasurer and basic leader of the expedition, must have paid far more than his share.

Though at age 74 I was not much of a climber, I was listed as one. Nick, who had climbed Masherbrum and led the successful Gasherbrum 1 (Hidden Peak) Expedition, was still a good climber. Our climbing leader was to be Tom Hornbein, from Seattle, an anesthesiologist, and though 54, like Nick, still one of America's outstanding expedition men. He and Willi Unsoeld had astonished the climbing world in 1963 by their bold traverse of Mt. Everest, with a bivouac at 28,000 feet on their descent. Pete Schoening, who had saved my life on K2, and later made the first ascent of Gasherbrum 1 with Nick's expedition, though 60, was also still a strong climber. We wanted a crack photographer and found him in Jeff Foott, 42, who had made documentary films for many years for the BBC. Jeff gave up making a documentary film in Manchuria to come with us to film the reported wildlife we were to find. Finally, the youngest member of the party was Dennis Hennek, 39, photographer and experienced mountaineer, who in recent years had made the first ascent of Great Trango Tower in the Karakoram and Gaurishankar.

A major object of the expedition was to find the true height of our mountain. Through Brad Washburn, we gained help from the U.S. Army Map Service, which recommended taking a geoceiver, a computer that can focus on navigation satellites to establish latitude, longitude, and altitude as well. If we did not know the altitude at points from which we made our observations, there was no way we could establish the height of our mountain. How Littledale had established the height at which he had begun his observations was, and still is, a mystery.

The U.S. Army Map Service could not lend us a geoceiver, but when Clark Burchfiel and I flew to Washington and went to their research section, we were given a cram course on the use of a machine; later they also gave us tape cassettes with the calculated orbits of five navigation satellites we could reach from the Ulugh Muztagh. This meant that we would know when to turn on our machine to start searching for each satellite. Our battery would be used in cold weather, and it was necessary to conserve its use as far as possible.

The geoceiver, or Doppler as we called it, was only part of the survey equipment. We were to use a theodolite to get angles to the summit from positions where the geoceiver established our altitude. To ensure that we could get theodolite readings from different points, Bradford Washburn again helped us by lending me a Uniranger Laser Ranging System, which could instantly report exact distances up to several miles. Using this machine and the theodolite, we could establish distances between survey points, and the height of each. I was also able to borrow a Kern theodolite from a friend at the University of New Hampshire, but we finally had to rent a geoceiver at a high price.

While everyone was working on his own project, cables began coming in from China asking the name of our honorary leader. Of course, we had no such person and had never thought of having one. At first we didn't pay much attention to the request, but it seemed of great importance to the Chinese, who said they must know his name. Nick and I talked about it and agreed that although nobody had been able to help us, Vice-President Bush had tried, and we should ask him if he would be our honorary leader. Nick wrote to him and received no answer. More urgent cables came from the Chinese in the Xinjiang.

After two weeks without hearing from the vice-president, we agreed that Nick should call his office. He did, and the office told us that Bush knew about our letter. If he had not answered it, it probably meant that he wasn't interested. The Chinese wanted a name *now* and so, believing Bush to be uninterested, we agreed to try someone else in our government. Senator Evans of Washington State had been interested in mountain climbing for many years, and he knew of our attempts to get to the Ulugh Muztagh. We asked him and received an immediate and enthusiastic acceptance.

That problem we thought was settled, but a couple of days later a letter arrived from the vice-president saying that he would be very pleased to be our honorary leader. What to do? Under the circumstances it would be awkward to ask the two to be joint honorary leaders. What other title could we use? The Chinese love the word chairman, and so we upped Vice-President Bush to be our honorary chairman. The reaction in China was instantaneous. Governor Tehmer Devamette of the Xinjiang was immediately elevated to honorary chairman of the Chinese half of the expedition, and Lu Ming, head of the Xinjiang Sports Federation, became their honorary leader.

On September 9, I said good-bye to Gail at the airport, sad she would not be coming too. Except for Peter Molnar and Clark Burchfiel, we all met in Palo Alto at Nick's house on the day before we were to fly to China. Molnar and Burchfiel were already in Tibet with a British geology expedition traveling from Lhasa to Golmud in Qinhai Province. We would meet them in Urumchi. Jeff Foott and Dennis Hennek, whom I had not met before, I liked at once. Dennis seemed strong, powerful, and direct. Jeff was tall, lean, and handsome, a man who loved his work. After I had gone to bed, Pete Schoening arrived, and in the morning we had a warm reunion.

There was much to do that first day, including trying on our purple Kolasch boots and other clothes while getting our baggage organized. While we were working, Tom Hornbein finally arrived, with his bald head, prominent nose, and beard. His charm, intelligence, and energy we all felt at once.

We wanted to be sure that Chinese climbers realized we were giving them the same clothing and equipment we had for ourselves. Since we had the names of individual Chinese climbers and some evidence of their sizes, we filled packs for each just as we did for ourselves, and stenciled individual names on each pack. What we failed to realize was the completely centralized, authoritarian style of Chinese climbing. Later, when we arrived in Urumchi, all bags for the Chinese were immediately emptied and their contents placed in the general storehouse. None of the items would be kept by individual climbers.

Urumchi was a long way off at the moment, and it took a lot of listing, packing, and checking the next day to get all of our equipment together and finally moved at the proper time to the airport. When we checked in there, I was astonished to see a large paper banner marked Bates Expedition, showing the outline of a mountain with a figure on top identified as Bates. Then, George and Jane Russell jumped out yelling, "Surprise!" I have never been more surprised in my life. They had flown from Tacoma to see us off.

My mouth must have been still open in surprise when I entered the plane, carrying a long tube of satellite pictures for the Chinese and the theodolite in a blue shoulder bag. At Tokyo, where we were to change planes, we met a French climber whom I had last seen on the Baltoro Glacier. He was returning from Everest. We also met Barry Bishop, an old friend from the *National Geographic*, who was about to leave for Bhutan.

We flew on to Shanghai, then to Beijing, where at the airport we met Wang Fuzhou and Lu Ming. She was a large, awkward, moon-faced woman, with small eyes that almost closed when she smiled, as she did frequently. Wang Zenghua was there, too, the leader of the Chinese climbers going to the Ulugh Muztagh. We also met Professor Zhou Zheng, a close friend of Wang Fuzhou, who spoke good English and was going with us.

During the next two days, expedition members were taken to the normal tourist places, and on the second evening a magnificent banquet at the Peking Duck Restaurant was hosted for us by the CMA. Xinjiang Governor Tehmer Devamette and Lu Ming, our official Chinese honorary leaders, were there. In fact, Lu Ming had brought for the banquet some of Xinjiang's famous Hami melons. Through an interpreter, Governor Tehmer gave me information about the Xinjiang (the fastest growing part of China) and let me know that he loved Uigur dancing. At intervals during the dinner, Nick, the governor, and I made short speeches. There were many toasts and calls of "Gombey!" (Bottoms up!). Many of the toasts were made in fiery maotai, which I avoided. Governor Tehmer kept adding delicacies to my plate, so that I was well filled when we reached the soup and ice cream that marked the end of the meal. As we departed, the governor told me that after the expedition he would have a whole sheep roasted for us in Urumchi.

Urumchi is a modern industrial city with more than a million inhabitants, about half Uigurs and half Han Chinese. Pushing the railway across China was one of Mao's greatest achievements, for near Urumchi there is coal and iron ore. These he exploited, sending half a million Chinese from South China willy-nilly to do it.

At Urumchi the next day, Peter Molnar, his future wife Sarah Neustadtal, and Clark Burchfiel met us at the airport. We were surprised to find Peter's use of Chinese to be so good, but of course this was his eighth trip to China. All of us were billeted at the Sport Hotel, where Nick and I piled the Doppler, tripod, Uniranger, and our own baggage into a small room. We all ate at a training table for athletes.

In the afternoon, when we met with Lu Ming, Wang Zenghua, and other government officials to discuss the objectives of the expedition, we ran suddenly into hardline right-wingers and tough bargaining. We Americans agreed that climbing the mountain, finding its height, and whether or not it was a volcano was our mission, but we also wanted to work on the area's geology and to take pictures of animals. Government hardliners in charge of science in the Xinjiang did not want us to investigate *anything* during our trip. They indicated that if anything were to be discovered, they would do it, even if it took 100 years or more.

Our signed agreement listed two geologists in our party, but the Chinese right-wingers wanted to restrict their actions to within 100 yards of the road during our travels to the mountain and back, and to our camp at the Ulugh Muztagh massif itself. These restrictions were also to apply to our wildlife photographers, Foott and Hennek. They would not be permitted to go off taking pictures on their own.

This was a far cry from what Nick and I believed we had permission to do. We had expected the geologists and photographers to have wide-open opportunities to examine geologic features of interest and to photograph wildlife. We were told instead, however, that we would be the first foreigners to be allowed south of Urumchi and Turfan, and we should consider ourselves lucky to be going at all. The hardliners would not budge.

We had been permitted to come to the Ulugh Muztagh because climbing the mountain was to be part of the celebration of the 30th anniversary of the time when the Xinjiang became part of the People's Republic of China. That accounted for the publicity about our expedition. We were also expected to give interviews and talk on television. Tailors in Urumchi made two suits for every member of the expedition: There was a hat, jacket, and trousers to wear during our 2,200 miles of jeep, truck, and Land Rover travel to the mountain and back, 1,000 kilometers of it off roads. A light green shirt, carefully fitted black suit, and scarlet tie were also prepared for each of us, to be worn at a banquet in Urumchi's Great Hall of the People on our return.

On the morning of September 18, a problem seized our attention. The key element in our survey of the height of the Ulugh Muztagh was our geoceiver computer, rented from Magnavox at a high price. We had been promised that on the day before we flew to China the computer would be delivered to Nick's house in two boxes, one containing the antenna. A few small spare components were to come, too, though the Magnavox people

Peter Molnar

were sure we would not need them. The two boxes, beautifully packed (one listed as the computer, the other the antenna) arrived as agreed in Palo Alto. They were so strongly secured that we decided not to open them then. In Urumchi, however, we did open them. The geoceiver was in perfect condition, but the long, light package, whose bill of lading said it contained the antenna, held only a few spare parts. The antenna itself had been left out.

Our whole expedition, now 53 men in all, was to depart for the mountain at dawn on September 21. Without the antenna, we probably could not contact the satellites needed to find our elevation at base camp, thereby causing one of the major purposes of the expedition to fail.

Peter Molnar reacted fast. He grabbed a telephone and by stretching his Chinese vocabulary got through to the Chinese Mountaineering Association office in Beijing, where he explained the problem. The CMA promised that if an antenna were sent from San Francisco, they would meet the plane and send the box on to Urumchi. Flights to Beijing from San Francisco we knew left regularly each morning. If we could get an antenna on the next plane, it could be sent on to Urumchi, and thence be taken by jeep to catch us before we reached the desert and were out of reach of any jeep chasing us.

Pushing his luck, Peter tried to call Magnavox near Los Angeles, and finally got through. We figured that it must be about 5:30 p.m. their time, but it was worth trying. The phone rang and rang, but Peter held on and finally someone said, "Nobody here. Everyone gone home." Peter was attempting, with no result, to get the home phone number of Vice-President Fernandez, when the voice said, "Wait a moment." A female voice took over, "What is it you want? I'm on my way home."

"This is an emergency. This is an emergency," Peter kept saying. "We're calling from Central Asia." Finally he made the woman understand that the company had made a terrible error, and that all sorts of problems would occur if something were not done to rectify it right away. The person at the other end of the line didn't know Mr. Fernandez, but she promised she would try to reach his boss, Mr. Quintana, and get him to call us back right away. We made sure she had our correct number, but since we didn't know her name and might want to call her back to see if she had succeeded in reaching someone responsible, Peter asked for her name and telephone number. There was a pause. Then she said abruptly, "No, I won't give you my name and telephone number. My husband might not like it." She put down the receiver.

Whoever she was, she had promised to speak to somebody in charge. She had the basic information and our phone number, and so we decided to wait to see if anything happened. Meanwhile, we would investigate Pete Schoening's idea of trying to put together an antenna that would serve. Some hours later, we were awakened by a call from an official of the company. He had quickly taken in the situation and promised to have an antenna for us on the morning flight from San Francisco to Beijing. Amazingly enough, although the man called from Los Angeles, he got an antenna to San Francisco in time for it to be sent on to Beijing by the morning plane. Though a Sunday intervened, slowing getting the antenna out of Beijing, it arrived in Urumchi only two days after our departure.

On September 19, the Xinjiang authorities put on a splendid banquet in our honor, with much photographing of the Chinese and American teams. Commemorative medals were presented to us, and as the Chinese team filed by, we shook hands with each man. That night several Chinese geologists came to our room to tell Nick and me how angry they were at the restrictions placed on our scientific work by the hardliners.

The next day, the day before we were to leave, Lu Ming took us to a grandstand where we could join the big brass in watching a colorful practice parade for the big one to be held on the actual day celebrating 30 years of union with the People's Republic. Army groups were turned out for this practice event, as individual groups of Mongols, Kazakhs, Uigurs, Tajiks, Kirghiz, and other minority groups paraded past. Children in a rainbow of colors were dressed as rabbits or butterflies, and there were many floats and old-style Chinese paper dragons. Unfortunately we had to leave before the end of the parade, and missed a float showing our mountaineering party.

The Chinese members of our joint expedition now numbered 45: 16 climbers, 12 drivers, a cook, an interpreter, four geologists, a radioman, someone to run the camp generator, photographers, and reporters (and a doctor added on the way to the mountain). At dawn on the day we were to depart, all 52 of us, dressed in identical uniforms, formed a line to hear several speeches. Behind us, in military formation, stood our seven huge army trucks, three Land Rovers, and two jeeps, all freshly polished and with a flag flying from each. A small crowd heard Lu Ming and an enormous Uigur give speeches, hers in Chinese and his in Uigur. Wang Zenghua, the Chinese leader, gave the final talk. As he finished, he dramatically shouted something, then fired a pistol in the air to signal our departure. Everyone ran to his assigned vehicle. Motors roared, firecrackers and torpedoes exploded, and as drummers pounded three large drums brought in for the occasion, we boarded our vehicles for departure.

We were glad to be off, and glad, too, to find that the first part of our trip south would be on a paved road. Now my main concern was whether the antenna would catch us. It had reached Beijing safely we knew. At Urumchi we had tested the uniceiver and theodolite, so we knew they should arrive at the mountain ready for use. Our geologists and photographers, however, were worried that they would not be allowed to move off the road because of the political dispute between the CMA and the Chinese Environmental Protection Association. Lu Ming had told us that this problem went much higher than her authority, though she would do what she could to help.

Our jeep was the last vehicle to leave. It held Lu Ming, Zhou Zheng, Guo (the interpreter), and Nick and me. We drove for a couple of hours through dry, sparsely inhabited country. When we stopped for a rest, the American geologists asked if a Chinese geologist could come in their jeep. This was arranged to everybody's pleasure, especially since we stopped later at an abandoned asbestos mine, where our geologists found serpentine rock, formed from scraps of ancient sea bottom that had been pushed up eons ago.

Vines of the clematis family were blooming along the road as we headed south. We crossed three lines of hills and later passed several military farms near Bosten Lake, whose waters we were told held large fish. At 4:00 p.m. we stopped for biscuits and soft drinks, but did not reach Korla, our first destination, 500 kilometers from Urumchi, until 9:30 in the evening. Before driving into Korla, we waited on the outskirts until all vehicles could parade in together.

Everyone was tired and ready for a meal. I expected Korla to be a large village of more than 500 people. To our amazement, we entered a city of more than 100,000, with a very modern hotel, 14 hospitals, a tire factory, a washing machine factory, and so forth. At the hotel we were warmly greeted by the party secretary and the governor of the district, then taken straight to our rooms. Here we found modern bathtubs, hot water, toilet paper, and even bathrobes and slippers, together with a huge bowl of sweet pear-apples, grapes, figs, and dried apricots. We couldn't believe it.

We had hardly had a chance to wash when we were summoned to a reception given by the Party secretary and the local governor. Here we were offered more delicious fruit, but soon were escorted to the dining room, where we were served a 20-course banquet at least as fine as the one in Urumchi. A handsome rooster made of vegetables graced the center of our table. Obviously the first foreign visitors to the area in 30 years were to be highly honored. Finally, stuffed, sleepy, and full of toasts in beer, we retired to our modern hotel rooms. Primitive, lonely Central Asia, hah!

The next day was a rest day for the vehicles. They needed it and we weren't sorry to have it, too. It gave an extra chance for the antenna to catch up with us. A big Party conference was being held on the hotel grounds and we were told not to photograph it. We were more or less confined to the hotel, for when two of us started to look around town, we were quickly picked up by the police and brought back with a scolding. Pete Schoening, however, wearing an expedition T-shirt the Chinese had given us, walked around with the conference visitors without being stopped. We were still learning the great differences in attitude between liberal Chinese and the hardliners.

Late that evening a big delegation, with the local governor, mayor, Lu Ming, and others came to say good-bye and to wish us well. After the others had left, Lu Ming and the interpreter lingered and we told her of our concerns about the antenna and the need for our scientists and photographers to have their own transportation. She promised we would get the antenna, and said she would see what she could do about our freedom of movement, but she did not look confident about the latter.

When Lu Ming left we quickly turned in and were sound asleep when Nick's call to Betsy and mine to Gail (placed earlier) came through. When I told Gail that we were in Korla, where there were 110,000 people, she remarked, "You're 50 years too late." Probably true. It was a thrill in this remote place to hear Gail's natural, cheerful voice.

The next day, after many handshakes, we were on our way before 8:00 a.m. Red flags marked Chinese-American Muztaga Expedition in gold lettering flew from our front mudguards. Pete had a roll of one-inch sponge rubber against the middle of his back, for he had strained it in car-

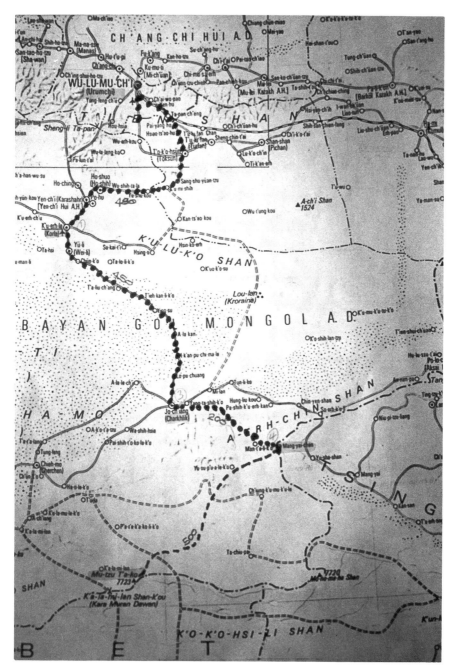

*Map of the route from Urumchi to the Ulugh Muztagh. The underlined places
from N. to S. are Wulumuchi (Urumchi), Korla, Ro-Jeng (Ro-Chiang),
Mangyai Chen, and the Ulugh Muztagh (Mu-Tzu-Taki Shan).*

rying the Doppler computer. For the day's provisions, we each had been issued a plastic bag with three slightly sweet rolls (one with meat baked into it), and a glass jar of apricot sections. From the hotel we had also brought grapes, pear-apples, and melons. After about 10 kilometers the macadam road changed to gravel. Not long afterward, the long straight road turned and here we found the lead jeep, which had failed to make the turn and crashed into an irrigation ditch. The windshield was smashed and a Chinese geologist had blood on his face. Another had small cuts, but nobody had serious injuries. With 10 men pushing, we rolled the jeep back onto the road. It still ran, and with the injured men in it was sent back to Korla for repairs.

We kept on, following the Tarim River and traveling at high speed on a rough road. Someone commented that the Chinese drivers had little "feel" for machinery. Near Korla there had been some sagebrush, but farther south we entered the real Takla Makan, a sandy desert with big dunes up to 200 feet high, formed into a crescent shape by the wind. Small ones were creeping across the road, though a few wretched people with brooms were trying to keep the worst stretches free. The dust kicked up by our vehicles became so bad that we all put on surgical masks Tom had thoughtfully brought. We were now reaching an area of military farms, each stretching along the road for a mile or more, with fields of cotton, sunflowers, and some tomatoes. Occasional small houses usually had strips of melon drying. In some places we saw prisoners working with armed guards near them. Other workers, with no place to run away to, were unguarded. At Military Farm 34 we stopped. Some of our Chinese companions complained about lunch not being ready there, but that didn't bother us. We went off under some trees to eat our rolls and apricots, happy to stop.

After a considerable wait, we learned that truck number seven had struck some other vehicle and Wang Zenghua had gone back to investigate. Our vehicles were supposed to continue along a yellow brick road, standing six to 10 feet above the countryside, which stretched straight to the horizon. If we kept on it long enough, Tom remarked, maybe we would come to the land of Oz, which Dorothy had reached at the end of her long yellow brick road. Some parts of the road were very rough, for each section was maintained by the people in the district it passed through, and some had done little work on it for a long time.

Nothing could have been more desolate than the emptiness we were passing through, with flat, dry ground from horizon to horizon, where continuous wisps of dust blew across the road. Occasionally we would pass a road mender's simple hut, but mile after mile there was only desolation until we noticed in the far distance a line of trees. Just before we reached it, the jeep ahead of us ran out of gas, but we were waved on because a truck with fuel was coming behind. We kept on until the trees became poplars as we drove into Ro-Jeng (Ro-Chiang), the former Charkhlik, an old, mud-walled town of 16,000 people. Here Marco Polo had stayed and bargained and Sven Hedin had wintered. In no time we were steered into a serai-hotel protected by iron gates. Again pear-apples were in our room and this time a Thermos of hot water. After a late dinner in a large mess hall, we turned in.

The next day, another rest day to work on the vehicles, we conferred with Wang Zenghua and Guo about how to give the geologists and Foott and Hennek more freedom of movement. Being in convoy, Foott, for instance, could not stop to photograph the huge hawks and various ducks we saw along the Tarim River. He had given up a $14,000 job to photograph Siberian tigers and another one documenting Manchurian cranes to be with us, and he was afraid he would get no pictures. Wang agreed to let him and Dennis Hennek leave the mountain early to go to Acchikul Lake for animal pictures. He also agreed to help Molnar and Burchfiel to have free time to spend on geology work on the way to the mountain.

After this helpful conference, Pete Schoening and I strolled around the bazaar. When Pete used Nick's Polaroid camera to photograph some children, a crowd quickly gathered. The bazaar had no local crafts to sell— Marco Polo would have been disappointed—but the local melons were very good. A doctor and dentist were plying their trades, sitting at tables in the open air. The dentist, who had a drill operated by a foot treadle, had a sign, in Chinese of course, that boasted, "My work is long lasting, aesthetic, and of superb quality."

In the evening, after another reception and dinner with local officials, we were summoned to an open-air auditorium to see a music and dance troupe that had come from Cherchen, west of us, a place where Littledale nearly a century earlier had left the Southern Silk Road to go south past the Ulugh Muztagh, hoping to reach Lhasa. Anyone who could afford the small admission fee was in the audience. To our surprise we saw good dancers, athletes, and pretty girls, together with clowns and an orchestra using stringed instruments none of us had seen before. The drummer was especially good. Small plays were put on, apparently half in Chinese and half in Uigur, some of it propaganda. One skit where a country girl showed herself too smart to be taken in by a city slicker had members of the crowd stamping their feet with pleasure.

Molnar and Burchfiel finally got away the next morning about 11:30 on their drive to learn about the Altyn Tagh Fault, the least-known major fault in the world, but they were not given the Chinese maps they had been promised. The head geologist of our party, also named Wang, did not want them to go at all, and did all he could to obstruct them, but Peter's Chinese and Clark's insistence this time won the day. We learned something that morning. In China a driver is a person of authority, whose sole job is to look after the welfare of his vehicle. He therefore is not interested in driving unless he is absolutely required to do so. Our drivers, all army personnel on loan, were independent. Their usual excuse for not doing something was that their vehicles had not been fueled.

Shortly after Peter and Clark left, we had the electrifying news that the antenna had arrived. The "giant," a huge, amiable seven-foot Chinese we had met in Urumchi, and two others had driven 17 hours straight from Urumchi to get it to us before we crossed the Altyn Tagh Range. The box was identical to the one containing spare parts, but this one did have the antenna in it. Pete quickly put it together.

Ro-Jeng had a few small, modern stores, reminding me of smaller Shigar and Skardu in Baltistan. The air was dry, poplars were giving shade, and new mud walls were being built as houses pushed out into the desert, helped by irrigation.

The following morning (September 26), we left early, driving across an arid plain close to the Altyn Tagh outer range, which comes down abruptly to the level desert floor. A few miles beyond, we turned into a canyon that cut through a huge outwash plain and began a corkscrew climb across the range on a road produced by a fine bit of engineering. Higher, we reached a small coal mine that was being worked, then continued to the top of the pass at 12,400 feet, where snowy mountains in the distance gave us all a psychological lift. The trucks were having trouble with the long climb and we had several waits.

After descending on the far side, we met two Chinese geologists who had left the previous day with Molnar and Burchfiel. The Americans had gone off on foot, but they soon joined us, too. They were happy about a very successful trip despite the obstructions by geologist Wang, a very regressive Party hack whom the other Chinese geologists considered an ignorant man. A few miles from where we met them, at about 10,500 feet, we reached a barracks used by workers at a large mining complex called Mangyai Chen. Here we were in Qinhai Province, close to the Tibetan border. The trucks again needed work and we spent an extra day.

After breakfast, several of us went for a walk. Someone had heard that the area was restricted, and when I asked the interpreter whether that meant we shouldn't go for a walk, he said, "If you ask them, they will refuse. If you don't ask them, they can't do anything about it." We needed exercise and climbed a couple of small hills to get a view of the roadless desert we were about to enter. A few small furzes were growing and there were tracks of a pika. Across the valley we could see the tailings of the big asbestos mine. After lunch, on our return, I was met by Wang Zenghua and the geologist Wang (whom we named the Mudhen, though Ostrich would have been better). They were angry about our walking away from the barracks and said we must limit our walks to the yard. First they said this was because we were near the Tibetan border, and then changed the reason to the possibility that bad criminals in the hills would rob and kill us. We believe that the Mudhen was scared to death for fear Peter Molnar might discover something of geologic importance that the Chinese did not know about. Our walk was good for our legs and we were glad that we had gone.

In the afternoon we were told we could make telephone calls to the U.S. Three of us did. Nick reached Betsy, who told him she was worried about their daughter at Wellesley because a huge hurricane was about to hammer the East Coast. When I reached Gail—at 4:00 a.m. her time—I asked about the hurricane, which had not yet reached Exeter. Of course, I couldn't help thinking how astonished Littledale and Sven Hedin would have been to see how easy it is now to talk to someone on the other side of the world—even from the heart of Central Asia.

We repacked in the afternoon and were away by 7:30 the next morning. After leaving the barracks, we passed through the main mine area, the most godforsaken place I have ever seen. Had Dante seen it, he would have placed it among his worst hells. Asbestos debris and asbestos dust covered everything. The few workers, who were wearing dust masks and goggles, were dust-covered, too. They watched us drearily as if waiting without help for life to end. We passed the track that runs east to Golmud, then plunged into the desert.

In no time at all trucks began to get stuck in the soft sand. So much black smoke poured out as they strained that we thought one of them had caught fire. Already one truck had had radiator trouble before getting to Mangyai Chen and been left behind. What was in it had been placed in the other trucks, but we didn't know where our Doppler and antenna were now and could only hope that they were all right.

After hours of charging ahead, making 10 yards, backing, and charging on for another small gain, sometimes using the help of eight or 10 men to push, we reached a small hill of wind-etched stones, and later a small oasis about 300 yards wide, where a small stream emerged from the gravel. A few flowers bordered the water and some voles lived there.

Ahead was a long, empty quarter where the sand was firmer. Across this we pushed until just before dark, when we reached a small wardens' cabin, for the area ahead was officially a national wildlife preserve. Since the temperature was well below freezing, with a raw wind blowing, we were glad to enter the bare room where we were to sleep. We each took a few cookies from a broken box in the truck, and this kept us going until 10:00 p.m., when we were given a very piquant soup with sliced boiled potatoes, peppers, and noodles.

At first light we were awakened to receive bowls of coffee, with bread and jam, a breakfast we much preferred to the normal Chinese breakfasts of steamed bread, peppery vegetables, and rice gruel. Foott and Hennek drove away first in an attempt to get extra time to photograph animals in the Acchikul Lake area, but as we learned later, their truck kept getting stuck and they had to return to the wardens' building to follow the route we took. As far as we could tell, the three wardens were responsible for protecting an area larger than the state of Texas. We soon saw skeletons of various animals that probably had been shot the year before—possibly by the first Chinese party to go to the Ulugh Muztagh.

As we drove along, two wild yaks—black, handsome creatures—suddenly charged downhill toward us. The truck behind us sounded its horn and increased its speed, passing us, but the yaks showed their speed, too, and crossed in front of the forward truck. Next, eight wild horses, beautiful creatures, with manes and tails flying, raced past us; and moments later, eight Orongo antelope, some of the loveliest animals I have ever seen, passed very near. The antelope were fawn-colored with white rumps and legs, and one had tremendous horns. All these animals seemed to consider us rivals who were showing off our speed. Two kiang, the wild asses for whom the Xinjiang is named, also ran alongside us. I had never before seen animals run so strongly and gracefully.

One truck was having so much trouble that we finally left it and went on to where the lead jeeps had stopped for the night. We had had a day without much food as we crossed rough country that pitched us around inside our Land Rover. Tom and I had agreed to take turns on the back seat, but Tom had not gone far when a bump banged his head against the ceiling so hard that it left blood on the roof and streams of blood running down his face. We stopped at once to wash his head and patch it. The blow gave him a bad headache, but fortunately did not crack his skull. From then on I wore my down jacket with the hood up when I rode in the third tier of seats. Pete's back also was hurting, and we were all glad to stop. We had traveled about 200 kilometers without roads since breakfast.

The truck left behind was carrying our sleeping bags and extra clothing. This was unfortunate, because the temperature dropped and the wind became bitter. Six of us crowded into one Land Rover for warmth, but we had a long wait. About 10:30 p.m. we shared some pieces of chocolate and bread, and at midnight visited the cook tent and had some tea. Afterward, Wang Zenghua insisted that Nick and I lie down on two sleeping bags in the cook tent. Half an hour later our sleeping bags and tents arrived.

The following day the Chinese went back to try to free all of their trucks and get them together. The temperature was about zero when we awoke, but the wind had dropped. We were to remain at the camp all day, and so Pete and I went for a five-mile walk, seeing at least 60 antelope in various small groups. Six came within about 80 yards of us.

On October 1, the day of the big celebration in the Xinjiang, the whole party lined up after breakfast, with minority members in front. Wang Zenghua made a speech about the celebration day and what it meant. When we started on again, we saw more antelope, kiang, and two bears. The lead jeep reached the bears in flat country and chased one of them for 15 or 20 minutes in a very cruel way until the bear, foaming at the mouth, finally escaped up a hill to safety. We Americans were cheering the bear and damning the "environmental protection" wardens, who kept right behind him, driving him as fast as he could run all the way. When we reached the long-awaited shore of 40-mile Acchikul Lake, we got out to look at some big ducks and small, brown-headed seagulls. Since hundreds of birds were massed offshore, I told the driver to move to where the view of them was better. Chinese photographers were already taking pictures there. Jeff and Dennis jumped out and joined them.

Apparently the lake was all right for the Chinese to photograph but not for us. The "environmental protection" jeep, which had come with us from the wardens' house, rushed up and one of the men in it jumped out and tried to grab Dennis' camera. Both men were angry. I would bet on Dennis against any two ordinary men, but this was not the time for battle. I ran over to try to prevent it. Our driver began honking the horn loudly just as Wang Zenghua drove up and yelled at us to get back into our Land Rover.

The Great Ice Mountain on the Xinjiang-Tibet border

The Ulugh Muztagh. Base camp was in the foothills in the valley rising from lower right.

Base camp

At that we returned, very annoyed by what we considered inexcusable treatment. Chang (the number two Chinese) came over and scolded our driver. At that point I stormed over to see Wang Zenghua. He made it clear that we must drive on quickly and leave everything to him. At lunchtime he and Guo, the interpreter, told us that the environmental protection agency (EPA) men were very ignorant, that China is not a free country, and in China everyone has to obey the rules. The EPA men were apparently angry that they were not being paid to let us go through their "domain." Politics exists everywhere and we were in the middle of a Chinese problem. Dennis and Jeff Foott, who had come to China mainly to photograph the wildlife, naturally were furious. Later we had a good look at a black and tan bear and also at a reddish wolf, which didn't seem at all scared.

Twice we climbed to more than 16,000 feet, finally camping within view of the peak we had worked so hard to reach, the Ulugh Muztagh. It is a handsome double peak, the two separate peaks seeming from our angle to be close to the same height. From 50 miles away, it looked like a major mountain, but we did not believe it could be as high as Littledale had figured.

At dinner we learned that one truck, was badly mired to its mudguards and would have to be left during the expedition. One truck unloaded its

Tom Hornbein, climbing leader

fuel, returned to the mired truck and brought back the tents and food it had been carrying. We were now camped at more than 15,000 feet, where even putting up the tents was beginning to be tiring. Putting on boots in the morning had become a cold process, too.

That morning we drove onto a plain filled with loess, crossed it to a broad canyon, and went up that as far as we could drive. The place where the truck stopped became base camp. We believed we were not much higher than 16,500 feet, but later measurements with the Doppler showed base camp to be at more than 17,400 feet.

The Chinese worked hard to set up their big tents army-style in a straight line, while we Americans set up our light, four-man tents in separate flat or protected positions nearby. In the morning Molnar and Burchfiel started a 24-hour warm-up of the Doppler computer. To our great relief, it seemed to be working well. Meanwhile, the Chinese had erected a 25-foot radio mast for communication with Urumchi. It was assembled as if it were a giant erector set.

The Chinese wanted a big flag-raising ceremony. Their radio mast could be climbed by two men at the same time, and the photographers clearly thought this fact presented a great "photo opportunity." First, we were arranged in a mixed Chinese-American half-circle. I was given a huge Chinese flag to hold and Wang Zenghua held the American flag that Senator Evans had given us (a flag flown over the White House on the Fourth of July). Zhou Zheng, from the CMA in Beijing, began the ceremony with a fine speech. Then I passed the Chinese flag to an active young Chinese climber and Wang Zenghua passed the American flag to Pete Schoening. They held the flag poles together and marched jointly uphill to where the giant antenna had been raised. They climbed to the top, where they affixed the flags. The Chinese flag bearer was in his early twenties and Pete Schoening was nearly 60, but despite our altitude Pete kept step manfully with the Chinese and the two reached the top of the radio antenna together. Nick and I shook hands with Wang Zenghua to end the ceremony. At once—probably for the broadcast on Chinese radio—three Chinese with packs started up the mountain immediately to scout out a route to Camp I.

We had not expected the attack on the mountain to start so soon. In Urumchi we had stated that we wanted several days at the base to become acclimatized, to get to know each other better, and to learn jointly certain words; also to establish the climbing skills of individuals on the two teams. We Americans certainly needed time to acclimatize. For one thing, our age was against us. We were 39, 42, 42, 51, 55, 55, 58, and 74, while the Chinese climbers were all in their twenties. We had the experience, while they were in better physical condition, and they had been training hard at an altitude of 15,000 feet for a month prior to our arrival.

Our understanding with the Chinese had been that they would do most of the backpacking, at least until we became acclimatized, but that did not happen. The Chinese on the mountain believed that every man should carry an equal amount, including the heavy canned food, rock pitons, and other unnecessary items they had brought. Wang Zenghua's main interest seemed to be to get as many Chinese to the top as possible, and he didn't want to wait for any acclimatization. This put our climbers in a very unfavorable position, for the Chinese began to notice at once that they were starting off with heavier loads than the Americans. There was no time to share common mountaineering terms or to give the inexperienced Chinese climbers practice in the use of ice screws and belaying on steep ice.

At almost 75, I couldn't carry much on the mountain, and so the best thing for me to do was to help establish the mountain's height. Peter Molnar and Clark Burchfiel, the geologists from MIT, already had carried the Doppler to their tent, from which the top of the mountain was visible. It was our hope to carry a prism to the summit and shoot it with Brad's laser-ranging device to establish its height above base camp. If we could not find the height of the mountain in this way, we would need to set up a triangulation network with measured baseline in the flat valley that we had crossed to the foot of our canyon.

On our first day in camp, Nick, Tom, Pete, and I spent a lot of time with Wang Zenghua, talking about where camps should be placed, when they should be occupied, how many stoves would be needed, what tents and climbing gear would be needed where, and so on. I also spent time with Molnar and Burchfiel, who had now charged the Doppler. It was a thrill to turn it on and watch as it contacted satellites as they came over the horizon, measuring the small change in the signals as the navigation satellites advanced or receded. The Doppler established the height of our camp gradually, starting at 5,245 meters, and settling at 5,268. This information would be vital if a prism were carried to the top of the Ulugh Muztagh and we could shoot it from our base. Base camp itself was shut in, with no area broad enough to measure a baseline for theodolite readings.

To set up our triangulation, Molnar, Burchfiel, and I, with two Chinese geologists, drove down the canyon in two jeeps and out onto the flat valley to points where we could see both summits, as well as set up a long baseline to be measured by Washburn's Uniranger. No drivers wanted to take their vehicles down the rough canyon, but a Chinese geologist offered to drive one jeep, and another man said he would drive the other.

Though the alluvial plain looked flat, it had cutbacks, draws, and many small streams. We left Clark and the geologist jeep with the prisms and drove about three miles to a point where we set up the Uniranger. After solving the problem of getting power under cold conditions, we took 11 theodolite readings, then returned to Clark, who traded his position with Peter. We then drove even farther in the opposite direction and there repeated our sightings, finishing about 6:00 p.m.

A high wind and driver reluctance the next day kept us from returning to the alluvial plain. Instead I climbed to the top of a small hill in the morning and went off with Peter in the afternoon. He and Clark had spent a month between Lhasa and Golmud just before the start of our expedition, and both were well acclimatized. They were excited by finding tourmaline granite, which suggested volcanism, on glaciers originating on the Ulugh Muztagh, and also layers of volcanic rock just above base camp.

R.H.B. surveying with a theodolite

We were having trouble getting back to the alluvial plain to finish work at our survey points. The Chinese climbers had no interest in the survey, and the drivers wanted to protect their vehicles. I also tried to get permission for Clark and Peter to go 20 kilometers to the east next day to see the volcanism there, but again was refused. Wang Zenghua stated that the vehicles were involved only in the precise route to the mountain and return.

During our survey attempts, all other Americans and the Chinese climbers and drivers carried loads to Camp I. The next day three Chinese, who were ill, were sent back to Acchikul Lake. In the morning Nick and I climbed up to the cache above Camp I, but the weather turned very cold and windy. Accordingly I returned to base. Meanwhile, Clark and Peter somehow managed to get the Doppler to one of our three survey stations in the valley. They left it running, and thanks to Zhou Zheng got permission to leave next day after breakfast to complete the survey.

In the morning, however, we heard, "The truck is frozen"; "The jeep isn't gassed up"; "The clutch is gone on this jeep"; and excuse after excuse. The morning was ideal for surveying, but we couldn't get a vehicle. Finally, Zhou Zheng, whom we were learning to admire, ordered a truck and Land Rover to take us at once. As the vehicles were slowly being gassed, we watched a lenticular cloud forming. At 12:40 p.m., we finally started out.

By now the wind was blowing dust, and while we were surveying and reading the theodolite, I developed great eyestrain from the buffeting of the wind. Peter's eyes and mine focused differently, and this meant adjusting each sighting slightly. We had done both takes in the central station and were trying to see the small cairn of the farthest theodolite station, when I found that I couldn't see figures any more. All I could see came through a thick haze. I remembered what my doctor in Exeter had told me: People with PMR (polymyalgia rheumatica) using prednisone can go blind from eye pressure. At that point I told Peter I was through for the day and would wait for him in the Land Rover.

The truck with Clark was already on the way back, and I kept my eyes shut on the return trip. At camp, I soon crawled into my sleeping bag, where Pete Schoening brought me tea and momos (meat-filled dumplings). I still had a haze in front of my eyes, but in the morning, to my great relief, the haze had gone, though my eyes felt very tired. Before I left Exeter, I had had an eye exam. I remembered the doctor saying, "You're one of the lucky ones."

The lenticular cloud we had seen developed into a furious snowstorm, with violent gusts that brought hail. During the morning, Chinese climbers brought a note from Tom at Camp I asking for the other small tents, food, and some medical supplies. I moved at once into a big tent, and Clark, Peter Molnar, and Pete Schoening agreed to carry our small tents to Camp I and return. They had tough going but accomplished it. Clark stayed at Camp I, and the others returned with requests for more food. Direct radio contact between Camp I and base camp was not possible because a hill stood in the way, but when Camp II was set up, we had communication with it.

On October 11, Zhou Zheng, now in charge of the Chinese at base camp, ordered a truck to take us to the valley to finish the survey (I wore dark glasses and used eye drops). The main peaks were clouded over, but we surveyed the middle station easily and then the far station, with Peter Molnar observing and me recording. Afterward we picked up the Doppler, whose battery had gone dead after recording many satellite passes. Finally the clouds opened briefly to reveal both peaks, and Peter shot them, working with one hand bare all the time. I don't know how he stood the cold. Later computation showed the sea-level height of the Ulugh Muztagh to be 6,985, plus or minus seven meters (22,917 feet). The geoid height was 46 meters lower (or 22,716 feet). Obviously it was a major disappointment to discover that the Great Ice Mountain was so much lower than the elevation of 25,339 feet indicated in Littledale's survey in 1885.

With the survey now finished, Pete Schoening moved up to Camp I. I missed him, for he is not only a very good friend but he does the work of three men. On October 13 I heard that Nick was returning with his pack, and went up to meet him. A bad cold, almost pneumonia, had settled in his chest, and he had been barely able to move from Camp I to base. He arrived exhausted. By nightfall everybody at Camp I and Camp II was snowed in (Camp II was dug in at the foot of the great ice slope that leads to the summit ridge).

Two days later, Nick was better. In the evening we learned that Pete and Tom Hornbein had moved a cache to 6,200 meters, perhaps within a day of reaching the summit. The radio forecast from Urumchi predicted two days of good weather, followed by five days of bad. Climbing to a point where we could reach Camp II clearly by walkie-talkie, we learned that they had a meter of fresh snow with a temperature of -25 degrees Celsius (-10 degrees Fahrenheit) and a rising wind. Even at base camp, gusts of wind blew snow into the tents, so we could imagine the force of the wind at Camp II. At base our travel between tents became a stagger against blowing snow. Despite the snow, or because of it, a fox appeared in camp.

A furious wind that night struck the tents at base, and on the morning of October 17 we were eager to make radio contact with Camp 2. At 10:00 a.m., we learned that their tents had survived, but conditions were as bad as the day before and no travel was possible. If conditions improved, men from Camp I would come to base to get more food. Meanwhile at base the cook tried to raise our spirits by serving us five-perfume eggs—eggs basted with ginger and four other condiments. The shells were very soft and said to be edible, too, but I didn't eat them.

Jeff and Dennis returned on October 17, telling of big drifts at Camp II and lots of snow on the mountain, with potentially dangerous wind-slab conditions developing. They believed that the men at Camp II should move to Camp I to save food. It blew hard all day. In the evening we had a song contest in the big cook tent. The Chinese, who knew several American songs, sang better than we did, their favorite being the "Red River Valley." My biggest success came when I blew the whistle for the "Wreck of the Old 97." When we left the cook tent to go to bed, we noticed that stars were out and the wind had dropped. Maybe the weather was changing.

Our time on the mountain was now running out. I told Liang, one of the Chinese geologists, who spoke some English and French, that if bad weather continued we might not climb the mountain. His face fell and he said sadly, "Then it will be very bad for us." Exactly what he meant I never learned.

The weather was better next morning, not only at base but at Camps I and II, where Chinese and Americans had been snowed in under crowded circumstances. Tom Hornbein had been making logistic plans for the attack on the mountain, and leading the climbing as well. Pete Schoening, now over his heavy cold, was ready to share the leads. In a major advance to our plans, Tom and Pete secured fixed ropes and led Molnar, Burchfiel, and five Chinese up the steep ice slopes to set up Camp III at the top of a long scree slope at about 6,250 meters. Here Americans also built tent platforms and set up small tents. Burchfiel and Molnar, from the rock they found on the ridge, established quickly that the Ulugh Muztagh is not a true volcano. They returned to Camp II, taking one of the Chinese climbers with them.

The next day, October 19, was the critical one of the expedition, though I didn't realize that in the morning, when Zhou Zheng, two Chinese geologists, and I drove 25 kilometers to where Peter Molnar had found a striking contact between oolite, old sea bottom, and heavily metamorphosed rock. Exposed near the end of a big glacier, this contact is in a dramatic place.

In the afternoon, Dennis Hennek and Jeff Foott appeared at base with their packs. According to plan, they were to be the summit team with two Chinese. Something was wrong.

They quickly moved into my tent, where I heard their story. The plan all Americans thought had been agreed to was for Dennis and Jeff to lead four Chinese to Camp III, and next day, with two of the Chinese, go on to the summit. In the morning, as they were ready to head up to Camp III, Wang Zenghua, the Chinese leader, told them to take 10 Chinese with them. They said that was too many to lead safely, and there were neither tents nor food for them at Camp III. Wang Zenghua was obstinate. Apparently the Chinese consider the number of climbers reaching a summit to be very important. Dennis, who had led 10 of 11 expeditions he had been on, knew what he was saying when he declared that it wasn't safe to take 10 Chinese, and he wouldn't do it. Jeff, also an experienced climber, fully agreed.

The Chinese system is built on central command, and Wang did not appreciate that he lacked authority to order Americans to do something. Apparently he told Hennek and Foott that if they wouldn't follow his orders, they could take a jeep and go back to Korla. At this point they reached Tom Hornbein by walkie-talkie at Camp III, and he and Pete Schoening said they would come down to Camp II to straighten things out. Dennis and Jeff, feeling that they were being badly treated, descended to base camp with their sleeping bags.

Nick and I had realized from the start the complete difference in the way Chinese and American expeditions are run. Chinese climbers are paid to take part in expeditions, and their actions are tightly controlled by their leader. Americans have a very loose leadership, with many decisions made by individual climbers. Up to this time on the mountain, the two sides had done fairly well in understanding the other side's peculiarities, but what had now happened was serious. It could split the expedition in two and certainly would not help to broaden Chinese-American relations.

I had come to know Zhou Zheng and appreciated him as a man of intelligence and judgment. He was in charge at the base camp, and I sought him out, together with Liang, the best Chinese geologist, both of whom had a fair knowledge of English. I asked them to join me in the tent with Dennis and Jeff to hear their story. We five had a long talk, a good talk. Nothing was held back. Dennis and Jeff told how helpful and friendly most of the Chinese climbers were, but insisted that their leadership was using unsafe practices. If Chinese without sufficient tents or food were sent to Camp III, they could be wiped out by a storm. Similarly, the Chinese were not experienced in ice climbing, though our climbers had shown some of them how to use ice screws. Zhou Zheng and Liang were very disturbed by the conversation and by what they spoke of as an insult to Jeff and Dennis. After our meeting, Zhou sent a radio message to Urumchi to report that the Chinese were using unsafe practices. He did not mention what had happened.

Before we separated, we learned that the drivers were getting very worried about the cold and the difficulties of getting the vehicles out if heavier snows came. We agreed that someone should get up the mountain as soon as possible or our whole party would be in trouble.

Hornbein and Schoening at Camp III were very disturbed by Hennek's radio message and started down to Camp II to find out why Wang had changed the plans. Clinch arrived from Camp I about the same time the others reached Camp III, and the three had a long discussion with Wang Zenghua. Meanwhile, six Chinese ascended the fixed rope Tom had put in up to Camp III. Right or wrong, no Americans were now in position for a summit climb next day. Tom was feeling ill, and after a rest day and more discussions with Wang, he descended to base to prevent pneumonia.

That day Pete Schoening led Molnar, Burchfiel, and four Chinese to Camp III. They found that the Chinese who had been there had taken *all* the climbing equipment at Camp 3 and established a Camp IV two hundred meters higher, leaving no ropes, ice screws, or jumars at Camp III.

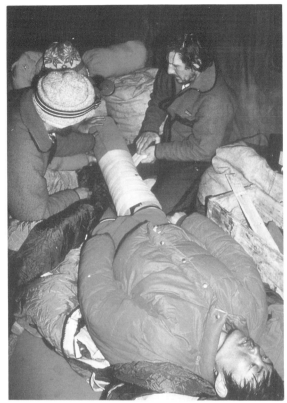

*Tom Hornbein and
Dennis Hennek
caring for injured
Zhang Baohua*

Pete was on the radio to get climbing gear brought down to them, when a joyous call broke in from the summit. Five Chinese had reached the top. This news we heard at the same time at base camp, where it caused pandemonium.

The next morning Pete Schoening and the others at Camp III were eating an early breakfast when an excited call from Camp II announced that the five summit climbers had tried to descend directly to Camp II from the summit, and two of them had had long falls. Looking down, Pete and the others saw three men at the base of the ice sheet. One seemed to be dead and another seriously hurt. Pete acted without hesitation, saying that he and those with him immediately were going down to help. He had been active in mountain rescue efforts many times before and was not going to stop now.

At the bottom, they found Hu Fengling, the leader of the summit climb, who had been lying unconscious all night. Near him was Zhang Baohua, who had fallen several hundred meters, too. He had an injured leg and a bloody face, but he could hobble. Apparently the successful climbers had not liked the thought of coming down the way they went up and had

tried to descend the unfamiliar southeast slope from the summit individually. Mahmud reached Camp II safely at 2:00 a.m, Wu Qianxin at 4:00 a.m.,
and a third, Ardash, using several ice screws, reached the bottom in time to
help the rescuers.

Nick and Guo, the interpreter, both coming from Camp II, helped the
Americans and Chinese coming from Camp III to put together a makeshift
stretcher to bring Hu to Camp II. Carrying him was not easy, requiring
three hours just to get him up a small grade below Camp II. Working at
5,850 meters required frequent rests.

Meanwhile at base camp we kept getting confused reports of what was
happening. Several Chinese and the Chinese doctor were sent to Camp I to
help bring down the injured men, while the camp cook began his most
intensive cooking of the expedition. The weather fortunately continued
good. If the bad weather we had had earlier had moved in while the many
Chinese were high on the mountain, their retreat would have been blocked,
and several might well have perished.

Late that night we learned that Hu had survived three falls of about 500
meters each, but his worst injury was badly frostbitten feet. He was being
carried toward base camp. The wind had now risen and the night had
become desperately cold. We hoped that as many of those coming from
Camp II as possible would stop at Camp I and not try to push on to base
camp, but people gradually staggered in, including Zhang Baohua, who had
been banged around and was absolutely exhausted. He said everything hurt.
His right kneecap, he thought, was broken, his chest hurt, and he had a sore
ankle. Tom and Dennis Hennek did a marvelous job of splinting his leg and
checking him all over. Guo was so impressed by their care of Zhang that he
kept repeating to me, "Americans must be the kindest people in the world."

The Chinese climbers on the mountain had had little food and practically nothing to eat for the previous 24 hours. Their descent from the summit had been one of "every man for himself." It was a wonder there were no
more injuries. Zhang said his crampons had broken, but that we could not
confirm. They were the best crampons money can buy, but it was possible
the metal had been damaged earlier by the Chinese pounding it to make it
fit a particular pair of boots.

At base camp we were all waiting up to care for Hu and those bringing
him down, but by 3:15 a.m., there was still no sign of him and I turned in.
He arrived about seven. Except for his feet, he was in better shape than
Zhang and a third Chinese who had also fallen. Wang Zenghua and the rest
of the climbers came in about the same time, all very tired. There was no

talk of Americans going back to reach the summit. Food was low, it was bitterly cold, and everyone was eager to pack up and head back to Urumchi.

The following morning (October 25 as scheduled), the tents came down, duffels were packed, and trash was burned. I felt sad that the garbage dump was not left to the foxes, which would have had some good mouthfuls there. About 1:00 p.m., we started off for Acchikul Lake, arriving just before dark. On the way, we saw antelope and many of the extraordinarily beautiful kiang. Again they took great delight in racing parallel to our convoy for a mile or more, and then, putting on a burst of speed, passing directly in front of us. Groups did this again and again, running hard at 15,000 feet.

At the lake a small tent was pitched, a huge pressure cooker was started, and soon all of us, very cold from the wind, were warming our hands on mugs of tea. Package after package of corkscrew noodles was then thrown into a large pot. Normally I am not fond of noodles, but nothing ever tasted better. After two helpings, I climbed back into truck number 6 with Tom. The night was clear, with good moonlight, and nearly everybody favored our using the clear weather to go on. Another foot of snow falling in the area we were about to cross would have stopped us cold—in more ways than one—and made the situation of everybody precarious.

Tom and I will never forget that night in truck number 6, as, leaning together for warmth, we drove across the seemingly endless expanses of snowy landscape that the moonlight made more dream than real. Mile after mile we jounced on, sometimes dozing, sometimes awake, until just before dawn we reached the small house of the game wardens. We were given hot water to drink, but nothing else, and after resting for an hour, drove on. Before leaving, we shared any biscuits or granola bars in our pockets, and Tom again produced some precious chocolate, which was carefully broken into small pieces and shared.

We drove all that day (October 26) until midafternoon, when we reached the outskirts of Mangyai Chen and began working our way through the depressing tailings of the asbestos mine to the building where we had stayed before. Tea, hot water, and then a nap readied us for another all-hands evening banquet, with toasts and praise for the expedition.

The drivers and machines had done marvelously well on our return journey, and they needed a day of rest and repair. We all relaxed, ate pearapples, talked, and tried unsuccessfully to make phone calls home. My toes, cold from lack of food and exercise the last couple of days, remained cold. Two or three others had the same problem, but none had frostbite.

The second night in Mangyai Chen, we had an even better banquet, but were not sad to leave early the next morning. The drive to Ro-Jeng was bumpy, but what a reception when we arrived! We didn't know that Governor Tehmer had ordered all the towns we stopped at on the way to Urumchi to celebrate our arrival. We waited at the edge of town until all vehicles were together, then paraded in on foot. Wang Zenghua and I were placed in front, with eight pretty dancing girls prancing before us as we walked into town. Schoolchildren and townspeople lined the streets, for a holiday had been proclaimed and practically everyone in town was enjoying the day off. We learned that some people had been waiting in the streets to see us for three hours.

Slogans, printed in English and Chinese, stretched across the main street, exhorting the populace to "be like the climbers." A reception at the town's main building came next, with various fruits set before us as officials made speeches in Chinese. Then we were ushered in to what, at the time, was the finest Chinese banquet I had ever tasted.

Our hospitable hosts expected us to stay overnight, but the expedition now was as eager to get to Urumchi as any horse headed for the barn. We took off early in the afternoon, bumping along the rough yellow brick road toward Korla, with Tom and me still riding in old number 6. About 10:00 p.m., we reached Military Farm 34, the one where we did not have lunch on our way south because of a mixup. They made up for it now, and at 1:00 a.m., with an eclipse of the moon outside, we sat down to a splendid dinner featuring large fish caught in a local reservoir. An hour later, still groggy from lack of sleep, we turned in, to be wakened at 7:30 a.m. for a Chinese breakfast and a quick departure for Korla.

About 20 miles south of Korla, Lu Ming was waiting for us. She was very emotional and tears kept running down her cheeks. She hugged and hugged Nick and me and kept exclaiming, "Oh, I was so worried about you." She took Nick, Wang Zenghua, and me into her small limousine for the drive to Korla, where, she told us, 3,000 to 5,000 people had been in the streets awaiting our arrival for several hours.

At the outskirts, we were met by officials and photographers. Pretty girls began pinning paper rosettes on us, while others presented us with bouquets of artificial flowers. Flashbulbs popped. Amateur and professional photographers swarmed around us as we began a march through streets lined with people. Drums banged a welcome, torpedoes and firecrackers exploded, and small girls danced as we went by. Schoolchildren, who were having a vacation, obviously thought we were the best thing that had happened in Korla for years. Banners across the road exhorted the citizenry to "Follow Example of the Jaint Expedition." If they followed our example, they went as soon as possible to take a bath, for that was what we did as soon as we reached the splendid hotel. The bathwater changed color appreciably, and soon afterward we were summoned to another splendid banquet. Speeches were given, and we had to say a few words. Later, to our delight, our phone calls to the U.S. came through loud and clear.

Our breakneck rush to return had now slowed down, and about 10:00 we were driven 40 miles to see Bosten Lake—the largest lake in the Xinjiang—the first foreigners to see it, we were told. The boat that was to take us out into the lake became stuck in the mud for a long time, because so many Chinese climbed onto it, but eventually we chugged out into the lake, where we saw a dull shoreline and little else. At least we appreciated the thought behind the excursion. That evening, we saw a wild movie about the Xinjiang, created as part of the 30-year celebration. It had a camel caravan, beautiful girls, a balalaika hiding secret maps, spies, brigands, and a handsome hero who did some fancy riding.

The next day (October 31), we eight Americans had a critique of the expedition with Lu Ming, Guo interpreting, and she took copious notes. Then we were asked to sit for a group photograph, taken with a camera that turned automatically. At 7:30, we dressed as best we could for the Korla banquet. That dinner is probably still talked about in Korla. We listened to many speeches and made some short ones ourselves, thanking the Xinjiang officials for all they had done for us. The mayor presented us with big felt hats (five-gallon size) and briefcases made in Korla, and finally, after many toasts in beer and soft drinks, we went off with our loot and were soon in bed.

On November 1 we departed at 6:00 a.m., before breakfast, each of us having been given a plastic bag with fruit, bread, and hardboiled eggs. Since the cabbage crop had just come in, many trucks were headed toward Urumchi crammed with factory orders for a year's supply. Nick and I rode with Lu Ming, who kept changing the tapes as we rolled along. "Que Sera, Sera" will always remind me of that ride. In the afternoon we ran into snow, which did not help the drivers of the cabbage trucks. We saw several that had slid off the road. As we were nearing Urumchi, a parked car belonging to the Xinjiang Mountaineering Association greeted us enthusiastically with cymbals and drums. At the gate of the Friendship Hotel in Urumchi, we stepped out into the snow to be welcomed by girls who pinned huge red sashes across our chests and escorted us to Governor Tehmer and other high officials who were waiting in the snow to greet us.

The next morning, after I shaved off my white beard, we again had an expedition critique with Lu Ming, Tom explaining where the "joint expedition" was not joint, from our point of view, and where Wang Zenghua had made mistakes. Peter Molnar was extremely critical of the geologist Wang, whom he rightfully called Do Nothing, and full of praise for our interpreter Guo. Peter also asked for permission to bring back rock samples for analysis and dating, something opposed by his nemesis, Do Nothing. Lu Ming listened carefully, occasionally shaking her head and always taking notes.

That night we were to have our big banquet in the Great Hall of the People, the Parliament building of the Xinjiang, finished just in time for the celebrations on October 1. It was a stunning modern building with more marble, glass, and glittery decoration than we expected in a communist society. Upon our arrival we were met in an impressive anteroom by Governor Tehmer, a Uigur, and the secretary of the Communist Party, a Han Chinese. The latter, in a welcoming speech, told us how important we were in opening the Xinjiang to foreign mountaineering. He was pleasant to us, though somewhat distant, and Governor Tehmer, who was older, treated him with respect.

All expedition members were dressed for the occasion in the individually tailored black suits for which we had been measured before our departure for the mountain. Nick and I sat at a table for 12 that was almost buried in flowers. Huge banners proclaimed our victory as the joint success of Chinese and Americans. Immediately after a toast was made, all glasses were refilled.

After several courses, a whole roasted sheep was wheeled in by the chef, and Governor Tehmer insisted I make the first cut. My cut was too high and there was laughter. Nick tried a little lower and there was laughter again. Then Tom, our doctor, stepped forward and cut a fine slice from the leg. Applause. It seemed the most delicious meat I had ever tasted. We had slices at first and then delicious small pieces on skewers. Nick made a gracious speech recalling various moments on the mountain and mentioning favorably all the individual Chinese he could think of. We then followed the Chinese custom of leaving the head table and visiting the other tables, "gombeying" at each with expressions of individual esteem and friendship. All 53 of us were at the dinner, together with guests from the Xinjiang

Mountaineering Association and the All-China Sports Federation, whose chief was Lu Ming. She was master of ceremonies and ran things well. The top people in the government were also at the dinner, including generals, leaders of the Communist Party, and visiting dignitaries.

During a slight pause, two splendid carpets, with the expedition insignia worked into them, were unrolled. They were presented to me for our honorary leaders, George Bush and Senator Evans, and I promised we would get the rugs to them. (We did, but what happened to them later I never knew.)

After the "gombeying" at separate tables, the party really started. The orchestra, which had played well for us during dinner, took center stage. A player with two spoons beat them exuberantly, and then others performed on strange instruments while entertainers danced. The drummer was sensational. Several stringed instruments, whose existence we had not known before, were played, and the governor, a lover of both music and dance, kept pointing out one musician to me, saying that he was the best player in the world on his particular instrument—one probably completely unknown in the U.S. The singers were good, too, but the dancers knew of the governor's love of dancing, and after their performance they decoyed him out on the floor. He danced, then returned to our table, took my arm, and led me onto the dance floor. I did my best to imitate him and received applause. Soon we were all throwing ourselves into Uigur dancing.

When we returned to our tables, the leader of the orchestra spoke to the governor. The next moment the interpreter spoke to Nick and me, "He says we have performed for you. Now it is the Americans' turn." Nick and I gave each other a surprised glance, then looked for a team member who could perform. All seemed amused. "That's your problem," they told us.

As Nick and I walked onto the floor, Nick said, "What should we sing?"

I said, "Let's try 'The Wreck of the Old '97.' They liked that at base camp." So, without adjusting our Uigur hats, we started in. "They gave him his orders at Monroe, Virginia, saying, Pete, you're way behind time. . . . "

When we reached . . . "his whistle broke into a scream," we launched into an imitation of an American freight train calling before a crossing, "Woo, Woo, Woo-Woo." It brought down the house. They clapped and clapped.

Guo, the interpreter, rushed up to us, panting. "They all want to know what the song is about."

"A train wreck," we answered together.

*Wang Zenghua, Nick Clinch, and Pete Schoening celebrating
in the Great Hall of the People in Urumchi*

He walked away slowly, shaking his head, puzzling no doubt about whether the song was somehow symbolic.

The dance went on. Space became too small, and the rugs were rolled back so everybody could dance. An attractive female dancer seized Dennis' hand, and soon he was doing Uigur dancing, too. Then came fox-trots for us Americans.

The governor had one last Uigur dance, moving gracefully and sedately, and then the music ended. He shook hands with the musicians and also with the waiters and waitresses. We shook hands, too, and went outside to our cars. The evening had been overwhelming. We felt that the Xinjiang was ours!

The following night, thanks to Nick, we held our return banquet for the Chinese, again in the Great Hall of the People. The governor, our guests, and the entertainers joined us with all of the enthusiasm of old friends meeting after a long absence, and the party was a tremendous success. I told the story from the Koran about how to know who is your real friend (if you have lived next door to him or have gone on a long journey with him—as we had done). After the entertainment, the rugs were pulled back again and gradually almost everybody began to dance. A Chinese girl asked me to dance, and though I stepped on her toes a couple of times, I was encouraged enough to ask Lu Ming to dance. Alas, she was not the dancing type, but she bravely tried. Built like a battleship, she turned like a supertanker. We were both happy when our dance ended. The feeling of friendliness and companionship on both sides, however, was exhilarating. Younger dancers, Chinese and American, were still having fun when Nick and I turned in before midnight.

Our departure for Beijing was delayed. Zhou Zheng was at the airport with us, happy to be returning to his home, and Lu Ming was there too to see us off. When we stopped on the steps to wave at nearly 50 companions who were together in the distance, they roared a good-bye. In the evening, we landed at Beijing in time for a last banquet.

We regretted having to make a quick departure from the capital next morning, for there were pleasant engagements we could not keep. By now, however, Beijing seemed almost next door to home, while Urumchi already seemed distant, and the Ulugh Muztagh as remote as the moon. Early the next morning Wang Fuzhou and Zhou Zheng went with us to the airport. Zheng had become a dear friend, and as a parting gift he insisted I take his own teacup and cover, along with a copy of his book printed in Japanese. In the plane, as we were winging our way to San Francisco, there was a moment when Nick and I looked at each other and raised a silent toast to Eric Shipton.

At San Francisco Betsy Clinch met us and drove us to Palo Alto for a lunch of cheeseburgers, milk, and cookies that tasted delicious, for we had had our fill of banquets. I phoned Gail, caught up a bit on things at home, and told her the time my plane should arrive in Boston the next day. A short night followed, for we were up at 4:00 a.m. for an early flight east. Though eager to be home, I was sad that this was the end of my partnership with Nick on our great quest. When I stepped off the plane in Boston, wearing for the occasion my five-gallon, Tibetan-style hat from Korla, Gail was at the gate wearing my favorite green dress, and it was so good to be home again.

· · ·

For 10 years Nick Clinch and I had worked to be the first Westerners in nearly 100 years to visit the Great Ice Mountain, a peak too remote for even Shipton and Tilman. Our Chinese-American expedition, however, was not the informal exploration by three or four friends that Nick and I had imagined when we first joined forces. Our problems in getting there at

R.H.B. after returning from the Ulugh Muztagh

all illustrate the sort of effort required when attempting to do something difficult for the first time.

Our expedition climbed the Ulugh Muztagh and found its true height to be just under 23,000 feet, a reduction from the 25,339-foot altitude that has stood out boldly on world maps for nearly a century. Thanks to professors Molnar and Burchfiel, the expedition made geologic history by examining the important Altyn Tagh Fault and finding that the mountain is not a true volcano. More important, they learned that crustal thickening is still occurring on the northern edge of the Tibetan Plateau as India continues to thrust northward. During the expedition we made new friends, and despite problems we broadened Chinese and American good relations.

·　·　·

In the following year Zhou Zheng came to the U.S., enabling Nick and me to give him tours of our East and West Coasts. Partly as a thank you for these visits and especially for our part in the expedition, Zhou and Wang Fuzhou in 1988 invited several of us to visit parts of Yunnan off limits to foreigners where a high peak on the Yunnan-Tibet border was unclimbed. Of course we accepted.

At Dechen, an old Tibetan city high above the Mekong River, Nick, Pete Schoening, Tom Hornbein, and four others crossed the river and headed for the unclimbed peak, while Gail and I, the Carters, and three others, under Zhou's guidance, visited Yi's, Nashi's, and indigenous tribes in Yunnan, but that is another story. This one ends here.

*Schoening, Molenaar, and R.H.B: three members of the
1953 K2 expedition 40 years later*

Ad Carter, R.H.B., and Brad Washburn discuss mountaineering matters.

In Retrospect

THIS BOOK SAYS LITTLE about my home life or my interest in improving the lives of others. It concentrates instead on the rare experiences and diversity of friends that the love of mountains has brought me. I have enjoyed the unmentioned small mountains as much as the big ones. Friends have been of great importance and I have done my best to reciprocate their kindness and companionship. Former students and faculty members, Peace Corps Volunteers, and companions in World War II are good friends, but shared mountain days have brought my closest friends, such as Brad Washburn, Charlie Houston, and Adams Carter, with whom I first shared a rope on Mt. Crillon in Alaska in 1933. Others stand out too, such as Nick Clinch, George Russell, Bill House, and the members of our expedition to K2 twenty years later. These men have enriched my life, for I have learned from them all.

Like me, they love mountains, and they also agree that in mountains, as in life, being first to do or discover something is twice the fun of being second.

INDEX

A

Abancay (Peru), 308
Aberdare National Park (Kenya), 353
Abruzzi Ridge (K2), 130, 136, 256 (ill.), 269, 271, 273, 286, 373; maps, 268, 272. *See also* Duke of the Abruzzi
Abu Simbel (Egypt), 417, 418 (ill.)
Academia Sinica, 401
Acchikul Lake (China), 446, 449-50, 456, 463
Acciarella (Italy), 221, 223
Aconcagua (Argentina), 299, 301, 307
Aden, 106
Afghanistan, 145-50, 151 (ill.), 152 (ill.), 382 (ill.), 384-91; East-West Road, 383; map, 387; Russians in, 390. *See also* Herat; Kabul; Kandahar; Minaret of Jam
Africa (east-central): map, 352. *See also* Kenya; Ruwenzori
Agra (India), 423
Ahdoo (K2 Expedition cook), 110, 113, 117
Aiguille Verte (France), 8
Air Transport Command, 211
Airdrops: during World War II, 168; during Wood Yukon Expedition, 170
Ajanta Caves (India), 352
Akureyri (Iceland), 333
Alaska Range, 337, 340. *See also* Mt. Russell
Alaska, 214; maps, 10, 17, 194. *See also* Alaskan Test Expedition; Aleutian Islands; Anchorage; Mt. Crillon, Mt. Fairweather, Mt. McKinley; other specific mountains
Alaskan Test Expedition, U.S. Army (1942), 164, 192 (ill.), 193
Aleppo (Syria), 155
Aleutian Islands, 214; Japanese in, 213
Alexander the Great, 389, 391
Alexander's barge (Indus River ferry), 116 (ill.), 119, 264, 373
Alexandria (Egypt), 417
Algiers (Algeria), 225-26
Algiers Hotel (Algiers), 225
Ali, Muslim prophet: tomb of, 390-91
All China Sports Federation, 400, 411, 466. *See also* Lu Ming
Allain, Pierre, 105, 260

Alpine Club (London), 260, 430
Alps, French, 8, 9, 69. *See also* Chamonix; Mont Blanc
Alsek River (AK/Canada), 42-43, 46-47, 51-52, 55-56, 57 (ill.), 58, 65, 254
Altels (Switzerland), 161
Altiplano (Bolivia), 307
Altyn Tagh Fault (China), 409, 446-47, 470; Altyn Tagh Range, 447
American Alpine Club, 101, 104, 124, 164, 167, 189, 193, 241, 257, 290-91, 311, 335, 354, 377, 397-99, 411
American Alpine Journal, 311
American Everest Expedition (1963), 329. *See also* Hornbein, Tom; Mt. Everest; Unsoeld, Willi
American Geographical Society, 171, 299, 301, 393
American Journal of Archaeology, 3
American Museum of Natural History (New York), 208
American School of Classical Studies (Athens), 156
Ames, Knight, 211
Among the Alps with Bradford (Washburn), 8
Amu Darya (Oxus River, Afghanistan), 389
Anchorage (AK), 95-96, 192-93, 214-15, 342
Andahuaylas (Peru), 308-9
Andes Copper Mining Company, 302
Andes, 299; map, 300. *See also* Aconcagua; Ojos del Salado
Andover. *See* Phillips Andover Academy
Angkor Wat (Cambodia), 330
Annapurna, 344, 423; Annapurna Massif, 294, 424
Antarctic, 183-84, 377. *See also* Byrd Antarctic Expedition; Siple, Paul; Wilkins, Sir Hubert
Antofagasta (Chile), 301
Anzio (Italy), 218-21, 226
Appalachian Mountain Club, 3, 8
Archery, in Bhutan, 426 (ill.), 427
Arctic Institute of North America, 245, 366-67; expedition to Turkey (1970), 367
Ardash (Chinese climber), 461
Arecibo (Puerto Rico), 314

Argentina: geographical society, 299; map, 300

Ariana Airways, 384

Arkatagh Range (Central Asia), 431

Armstrong, Mr., 317, 319

Armstrong, Neil, 364

Army War College, 188

Arnold, Gen. Henry ("Hap"), 212

Arusha (Tanzania), 353

Askole (Baltistan), 101, 120-21, 123-24, 140, 265-66, 269, 288, 373

Aslam, Dr., 265

Association Tucumana de Andinismo (Argentina), 301

Aswan (Egypt), 417, 419

Ata-Ullah, Col. ("Ata"), 258 (ill.), 260, 262-63, 279, 286, 288-89, 381

Atacama Desert (Chile), 304

Athens (Greece), 156

Aubrey, John, 36, 68-69, 107, 159, 241

Auckland (New Zealand), 295. *See also* Hillary, Sir Edmund; New Zealand; Odell, Noel

Aufschnaiter, Peter, 335-36

Aurangabad (India), 352

Australia, 295; Australian Antarctic Expedition, 107

Austria, 292

Ayacucho (Peru), 309

Ayres, Fred, 308

Azad Kashmir, 262, 371

B

Bad Tolz (Germany), 235

Bagalpur (India), 326

Bagdad (Iraq), 154

Baird, Pat, 238

Bakewell, Anderson ("Andy"), 168, 170-71, 172 (ill.)

Bakonjo people (Uganda), 355 (ill.)

Balkh (Afghanistan), 385, 391

Balmat, Jacques, 100

Balmhorn (Switzerland), 161

Baltistan, 112, 447; wazir of, 114-16; local traditions, 119, 373. *See also* Askole; Ladakh

Baltoro Glacier, 106, 123, 248, 267-68, 373, 374 (ill.), 438; map, 122

Baltoro peaks, 138-39, 394

Bamiyan (Afghanistan), 382 (ill.), 383, 385

Band-i-Amir (Afghanistan), 385

Bangalore (India), 351-52

Bangkok (Thailand), 295

Barawa (Nepal), 318

Barclay, Brigadier, 212; Barclay Mission, 212

Bardumal (Baltistan), 266

Barr, Mr. (Yukon bush pilot), 61, 65

Barrancas Blancas (Andes), 303

Barro Colorado (Panama), 309

Bates Lake (Canada), 52-53, 57-59, 61

Bates, Edith Richardson (author's mother), 2 (ill.); death of (1925), 4

Bates, Gail Oberlin 290 (ill.), 298 (ill.), 301-2, 303 (ill.), 305, 312, 319, 321, 324-30, 342, 411, 437, 443, 448, 469, 473; on honeymoon trip (1954), 292 (ill.), 294 (ill.), 295, 296 (ill.), 297; traveling in South America (1956), 301-9; climbing in Wyoming (1957), 310-11; traveling in Mexico (1959), 311; traveling in Norway (1960), 311; climbing in Glacier Park and Cascades (1961), 311; during Peace Corps training (1962), 315-17; living in Nepal (1962-63), 317-30; traveling in Iceland (1964), 333-35; traveling in Switzerland (1965), 335-36; trekking in Himalaya (1967), 343-48; traveling in Sikkim (1967), 348-50; traveling in southern India (1967), 351-53; traveling in East Africa (1967), 353-55, 356 (ill.), 357; traveling in Mexico (1968), 361-62; traveling in Eastern Europe (1969), 363-66; traveling in Turkey (1970), 366-69; traveling in Europe (1971), 369; climbing in the Himalaya (1974), 370 (ill.), 371-73; at coronation in Nepal (1975), 374-75; traveling in Iran (1975), 376; attending Manzoor Hussain's wedding (1976), 378-80; traveling in Afghanistan (1978), 383-91; traveling in China (1979), 393-94, 395 (ill.), 396-97; traveling in southern Africa (1980), 403, 404 (ill.), 405 (ill.), 406-8; traveling in Nepal (1981), 410; traveling in China (1983), 411-13; traveling in Egypt (1984), 417, 418 (ill.), 419 (ill.); trekking in Nepal (1985), 423-24; traveling in Bhutan (1985), 424-28; traveling in India (1985), 422-23, 428, 429 (ill.), 430; traveling in China (1988), 470-71

Bates, Robert Hicks, 19 (ill.), 31 (ill.), 32 (ill.), 33 (ill.), 55 (ill.), 62 (ill.), 63 (ill.), 66 (ill.), 70 (ill.), 72 (ill.), 85 (ill.), 87 (ill.), 142 (ill.), 158 (ill.), 182 (ill.), 207 (ill.), 211 (ill.), 259 (ill.), 263 (ill.), 292 (ill.), 298 (ill.), 304 (ill.), 359 (ill.), 470 (ill.), 472 (ills.); as child, 1-4; Maine vacations, 1, 3, 4, 65; first climbing experiences, 3-4; loss of mother (1925), 4; as student at Phillips Exeter Academy, 5; climbing in White Mountains (NH), 8, 9, 23, 165, 169; as Harvard undergraduate (class of 1933), 5, 7-8, 22-23; climbing in Alaska (1932, 1933), 15-16, 18-20, 24-34; as Harvard graduate student (1933-34), 36; as Penn graduate student (1934-36), 37, 67-68, 159; climbing in Yukon Territory, Canada (1935), 39-65; as visiting scholar at Oxford (1936), 68; teaching at University of Pennsylvania, 67-68, 99; climbing in French Alps, 69; climbing Mt. Lucania, Canada, (1937), 71-97; climbing K2 (Pakistan/China) (1938), 100-141; traveling in India and Afghanistan (1938), 143-50; traveling in Iran and Iraq (1938), 151-55; traveling in Turkey and Greece (1938), 155-56; traveling in Eastern Europe and Germany (1938), 156-57; climbing in Switzerland (1939), 161-62; teaching at Exeter, 163 (ill.), 165; climbing in Canadian Rockies (1940), 164; climbing in Wyoming, 164; climbing in Canadian Yukon, 167-70, 171 (ill.), 172-81; on summit of Mt. Walsh (Canada), 180 (ill.); promoted to captain in Quartermaster Corps, 189; testing army survival gear in Alaska, 192-206; on summit of Mt. McKinley (1942), 203 (ill.); testing high-altitude paper underwear, 204 (ill.), 205; promoted to major in Quartermaster Corps, 212; in Yugoslavia during World War II (1944), 218-19; at Anzio (Italy), 222 (ill.); awarded Legion of Merit, 229; in Italy during World War II (1944), 217-30, 232-36; in Quartermaster Corps after European duty, 236-37; returns to Exeter after wartime duty (1946), 241-43; receives Ph.D. (University of Pennsylvania,

1947), 243; loss of father (1948), 244; climbing in Saint Elias Mountains (1951), 245-55; on summit of Mt. Hubbard (1951), 249; traveling in Europe and Egypt (1953), 260; climbing K2 (1953), 262-89; articles in *Saturday Evening Post*, 289; marriage to Gail Oberlin (1954), 290 (ill.); on honeymoon trip (1954), 292 (ill.), 293-97; traveling in South America (1956), 301-9; climbing in Wyoming (1957), 310-11; named president of American Alpine Club (1958), 311; traveling in Mexico (1959), 311; traveling in Norway (1960), 311; climbing in Glacier Park and Cascades (1961), 311; during Peace Corps training, 315-17, 319 (ill.); as Peace Corps representative in Nepal (1962-63), 317, 318 (ill.), 319-30; traveling in Southeast Asia, 330-31; traveling in Iceland (1964), 333-35; traveling in Switzerland (1965), 335-36; climbing Mt. Russell (1966), 340-42; trekking in Himalaya (1967), 343-48; traveling in Sikkim (1967), 348-50; traveling in southern India (1967), 351-53; traveling in East Africa (1967), 353-57; traveling in Mexico (1968), 361-62; traveling in Eastern Europe (1969), 363-66; traveling in Turkey (1970), 366-69; traveling in Europe (1971), 369; climbing in the Himalaya (1974), 370 (ill.), 371-73; at coronation in Nepal (1975), 374-75; traveling in Iran (1975), 376; retirement from Exeter (1976), 377; attending Manzoor Hussain's wedding (1976), 378-80; traveling in Afghanistan (1978), 383-91; traveling in China (1979), 392 (ill.), 393-97; traveling in southern Africa (1980), 403, 405 (ill.), 406-8; traveling in Nepal (1981), 410; traveling in China (1983), 411-13; traveling in Egypt (1984), 417-18, 419 (ill.); trekking in Nepal (1985), 423-24; traveling in Bhutan (1985), 424-28; traveling in India (1985), 422-23, 428, 429 (ill.), 430; on Ulugh Muztagh expedition (1985), 433-55, 456 (ill.), 457-70; traveling in China (1988), 470-71

Bates, William Nickerson (author's father), 1, 2 (ill.), 3, 182 (ill.); loss of wife (1925), 4, 10; death of (1948), 244

Bates, William Nickerson, Jr. (author's brother), 2-3, 5, 7, 10, 22, 159-60, 163-65, 182 (ill.), 188, 242, 291

Battle of Britain, 161

Bean, L.L., 208, 223

Beardsley, Hartness ("Harty"), 40, 42, 44, 50, 51, 60

Bechtold, Fritz, 107, 136. *See also* Nanga Parbat

Bée, François ("Frank"), 170, 181

Beijing Hotel (Beijing), 394, 396

Beijing, 393-94, 396, 399, 410-13, 438, 440-41, 454, 469

Bell, George, 257, 259 (ill.), 270 (ill.), 271, 273-74, 276-77, 279-80, 282-89, 373

Beltsville (MD), 185

Belur (India), 352

Bengal Mountain Battery, 101

Beni (Nepal), 344, 348

Bennett, George, 299

Bernbaum, Ed, 393

Bhakta, Dhruba, 410. *See also* Mathema, Dhruba Bhakta

Bhaktapur (Nepal), 321 (ill.)

Bhang, 114, 117, 118

Bheri River, 344-46

Bhubaneshwar (India), 351

Bhutan, 421, 424-28, 438

Biafo Glacier, 121

Biancograt (Switzerland), 311

Bigo Bog (Uganda), 355, 357

Biratnagar (Nepal), 324, 326, 328

Bird, Tom, 161-62

Birendra Bir Bikram Shah Dev, 374-76, 410, 414; as Crown Prince of Nepal, 328; as student in U.S., 358, 359 (ill.), 360; crowned King of Nepal (1975), 360, 374-75, 376 (ill.). *See also* Kathmandu; Nepal; Sacred Thread Ceremony

Birethanti (Nepal), 294, 423

Birgunj (Nepal), 325

Bishop, Barry, 329, 438

Black Pyramid (Abruzzi Ridge), 273

Black Sea, 366

Blank on the Map (Shipton), 336

Bojpur (Nepal), 324

Bolivia: map, 300

Bollerud, Capt. Jack, 192 (ill.), 193, 197-99, 203

Bolling Field, 211-12

Bombay (India), 107, 351-52

Bost (Afghanistan), 389

Bosten Lake (China), 442, 465

Boston Museum of Science, 208, 359. *See also* Washburn, Bradford

Botswana, 403, 404 (ill.), 405-6; map, 402. *See also* Okavango

Bourgas (Bulgaria), 364-65

Bradburn, Maj., 254

Brady Glacier (AK), 34

Braldu River, 138, 140, 264-66, 268

Bremen (ship), 157, 162

Bride Peak (Chogolisa), 100

Bright, Norman, 72 (ill.), 74, 77

Brinckerhoff, Dick, 333

Brisbane Star (ship), 296-97

British Museum (London), 294, 367

British-American Himalayan Expedition, 101

Broad Peak, 124, 277

Browne Tower (AK), 195 (ill.), 197, 204

Browne, Belmore, 164, 204, 213; Mt. McKinley climbs, 164; 1912 McKinley expedition, 202-3

Brownie (sled dog), 56

Bryant's Store (Prince Rupert, Canada), 40-41

Bryce, Lord, 367

Bucharest (Romania), 364

Budapest (Hungary), 156

Buhl, Herman, 138

Bujuku Huts (Uganda), 355, 357; Bujuku Lake, 357

Bulgaria, 364-66

Bullard, Robin, 317

Bumthang Valley (Bhutan), 425-27

Bund, Shanghai, 396

Burchfiel, Clark, 435-38, 446-47, 453-57, 459-60, 470

Burdsall, Dick, 101, 104, 105 (ill.), 106, 110, 112-13, 125, 127, 139, 141, 143, 148, 153-54, 160-61, 163, 398

Burwash: Creek, 94; Landing (Canada), 71, 82, 89, 95, 171; Trading Post, 95

Bush, Barbara, 415

Bush, Vice-President George, 409-10, 414, 421, 436-37, 467

Butt, Maj. Gen. Safdar, 371, 373-74, 377-78, 380-81

Butwal (Nepal)
Byrd, Admiral Richard, 35; Antarctic Expedition, 183
Byroade, 261

C

Cache Creek (AK), 193, 205
Calcutta (India), 348, 351
California Institute of Technology, 245
Cambodia, 330
Camp Carson, 213
Camp Denali (AK), 342
Camp Hale (CO), 212-13. *See also* 10th Mountain Division
Campo de Piedra Pomez, 303
Campobello Island (ME/NB), 5
Canada, 164. *See also* Carcross; Mt. Logan; Mt. Lucania; Saint Elias Mountains; Yukon Territory
Canadian Defense Research Board, 248
Canadian Rockies, 164
Cannon, Vice-Marshal, 260, 261
Canterbury Mountaineering Club (New Zealand), 295
Cape of Good Hope (South Africa), 407
Capetown (South Africa), 407
Cappadocia (Turkey), 367
Car of Jagannath (India), 351
Carcross (Caribou Crossing, Canada), 41, 44-46, 60, 65
Carpé, Allen, 14, 77, 205-6
Carr, Prof. Randolph (University of Pennsylvania), 316, 320
Carter, Adams ("Ad"), 19 (ill.), 25, 28, 31, 32 (ill.), 36, 40-42, 47, 51, 52, 60, 161-63, 167, 169, 186-87, 189, 208, 235, 299, 301, 304 (ill.), 305-7, 337, 340-41, 359, 371, 373-74, 471, 472 (ill.), 473
Carter, Ann, 301-2, 305-6, 371, 373-74, 471
Carter, Larry, 340
Case, Anne, 293, 295
Case, John, 104, 248-49, 290 (ill.), 291-95, 335
Caserta (Italy), 218, 222, 223
Caspar's Cutthroats, 214
Cassino (Italy), 225
Casualties. *See* Mountain-climbing casualties
Cenotaph Island (AK), 12-15, 19, 20
Central Asia, 448; map, 444. *See also* Chinese Turkestan; Great Ice

Mountain; Ulugh Muztagh; Urumchi; Xinjiang Province
Central Hotel, Prince Rupert, Canada, 170
Chagcharan (Afghanistan), 383-84, 386
Challinor, David, 409
Chambers, George, 64
Chamonix (France), 8, 69; Aiguilles, 8. *See also* Dent du Requin
Champagne (Canada), 61, 64
Chandra, 324-28
Chapman, Spencer, 101
Charkhlik. *See* Ro-Jeng
Charles, Prince of Wales, 374
Chasseurs Alpins (French mountain troups), 187
Chengde (China), 412-13
Cherchen (China), 397, 433, 446
Child, Bill, 19 (ill.), 25, 31, 67, 160
Chile: geographical society, 299; map, 300. *See also* Ojos del Salado
Chilean Mapping Service, 301
Chimaera (southern Turkey), 368-69
China Tourist Agency (CITS), 399
China, 393-401; mountaineering in, 380-81, 396-99, 401, 411, 431, 433-70; Russians in, 396. *See also* Chinese Mountaineering Association; Chinese Turkestan; Kashgar; Minya Konka; Tibet; Triple Expedition; Turfan; Ulugh Muztagh; Urumchi; Xinjiang Mountaineering Association; Xinjiang Province
Chinese Environmental Protection Association, 442, 450, 452
Chinese Mountaineering Association, 381, 393-94, 398, 401, 411, 422, 438, 440, 454
Chinese Turkestan, 100, 115. *See also* Central Asia; Xinjiang Province
Chinese-American Muztagh Expedition, 443, 464, 466, 469. *See also* Chinese Mountaineering Association
Chobe (Botswana), 403-4
Chogolisa (Bride Peak), 100, 123-24, 138
Chogyal (king) of Sikkim, 348-50
Chongo, 266, 373
Chota Burzil Pass, 141
Christchurch (New Zealand), 295
Chukchi Sea, 210
Churchill (Canada), 209-10, 237-40
Churchill's Picket (Pakistan), 393

Churen Himal, 345

Cisterna (Italy), 227

Citizen of Two Worlds (Ata-Ullah), 381

City of Carlisle (ship), 260

Clark, Gen. Mark, 225, 230

Clement, Jack, 229

Cleveland Plain Dealer, 291

Clifford, Nicholas, 248-49, 251-52

Climbing gear: for K2, 103-4. *See also* Survival gear

Clinch, Betsy, 397, 443, 448, 469

Clinch, Nicholas B. ("Nick"), 373, 377-78, 393, 397, 409-11, 421-22, 430, 432 (ill.), 433-39, 441-43, 446, 448, 450, 454-57, 459-60, 462, 464-65, 466-67, 468 (ill.), 469-70, 473

Cochin (India), 351

Coelho, Mr., 350

Coffin, William Sloane, 314

Cold-weather testing. *See* Alaskan Test Expedition; Mountain troops; Office of the Quartermaster General; Survival gear

Collard, Bruce, 316-17

Colorado Outward Bound School, 342

Colorado Pass (Chile), 303-5, 307; Colorado River, 302

Comorin (ship), 104, 106, 107

Conant, James Bryant (Harvard president), 165; climbing in White Mountains, 165

Conant, Jim, 165

Concordia (Karakoram), 123-24, 138, 248, 268, 373, 394

Constable, Mr., 380-81

Cooke, Hope (Queen of Sikkim), 349

Copiapo (Chile), 301, 305-6

Cordillera Blanca (Andes), 309

Coromandel Coast (India), 351

Correa, Maj., 301-3, 305

Cowles, Betsy, 164

Cracker (sled dog), 56

Craig, Bob, 257, 259 (ill.), 272-74, 276-80, 282, 284, 286-87, 289

Credidio, Lt. Pete, 227

Crillon Glacier (AK), 15, 20, 35; Crillon Lake, 20, 24-25, 34-35; Crillon Plateau, 33 (ill.). *See also* Mt. Crillon

Crimson Project, 209

Crockett, Bill, 260-62

Crosby family, 156

Crosson, Joe, 95

Cuzco (Peru), 307-9

Czechoslovakia, 156-57, 369

D

Daiber, Ome, 40-42, 51-54, 56-61, 63 (ill.), 64-65

Daigneault, Alec, 232

Dal Lake (Kashmir), 110, 430

Dal-bhat (Nepali national dish), 320

Dalai Lama, 348

Darbang (Himalaya), 344

Darbhanga (India), 326

Darjeeling (India), 428-30

Dassu, 373

De Rhin, Dutreuil, 398

De Segogne, Henri, 105

Dechen (China), 471

Dehra Dun (India), 335-36

Delhi (India), 422, 430

Denali Pass (AK), 201 (ill.)

Denali. *See* Mt. McKinley

Dent du Requin (French Alps), 69

Deosai Plateau (Himalaya), 141

Devil's Lake (WY), 210; Devil's Tower, 208

Dezdeash Lake (Canada), 61

Dhankuta (Nepal), 318 (ill.), 324

Dhanpus (Nepal), 424

Dharan (Nepal), 324, 328

Dharmsala (India), 348, 362. *See also* Dalai Lama; Tibetan refugees

Dhaulagiri (Himalaya), 294, 344-45, 423

Dhorpatan (Nepal), 344, 348

Dill, Bruce, 210

Dittert, René, 260, 311

Dodge, Joe, 8

Dodson, Bob, 263, 366, 369

Dodson, Robbie, 366, 369

Dogubayazit (Turkey), 362 (ill.), 367

Dolpo (Himalaya), 343-45, 348

Donjek River (Canada), 71, 77, 82, 87, 89-91, 92 (ill.), 95, 171; Donjek Glacier, 91, 92 (ill.)

Doppler (geoceiver), in mountaineering, 436, 438, 443, 448, 453-57

Doriot, Col. (later Gen.) George, 207-8, 210, 213, 215-16, 218-19, 224, 226, 229, 231-32, 237

Doron, body armor for military gear, 232-33, 236

Dow, Russell ("Russ"), 25, 35, 72 (ill.), 73-74, 77, 80, 90, 93

Dras, 113; Dras River, 112-13
Dudh Kosi River (India), 326
Duke of Spoleto, 267-68
Duke of the Abruzzi (K2 expedition, 1909), 71, 100, 120, 123, 125, 138, 267-68
Duke River, 77
Dulles, Allen, 261
Dulles, John Foster, 261, 262
Dumordo River, 121
Dunedin (New Zealand), 295
Dunster House (Harvard), 22, 383
Dunyer (Dunahai), 345-47
Dusty Glacier (Yukon), 47-48
Dyhrenfurth, Norman, 329
Dzos, 112-13, 344

E

East Hubbard. *See* Mt. Kennedy
East Lucania. *See* Mt. Lucania
East-West Express, 10
Eastern Europe. *See* Bulgaria; Czechoslovakia; Romania; Yugoslavia
Eckmann, Ansel, 12, 14, 20, 24
Education, in Bhutan, 428
Edwards, Al, 69
Egypt, 417-19
88th Division, U.S. Army, 226
Einaudi, Marco, 310
Elliott, Ron, 324
Ellis, Bob, 24
Elmer, Lt. Waldo, 193
Ely (MN), 342
Emerson, John, 260
Emerson, Ralph, 36
Emin Minaret, Turfan (China), 412
Emmons, Art, 295-96
Emmons, Evie, 295
Erbil (Iraq), 155
Eskimo Pie Company, as testing site, 209
Essex Hotel, Boston, 183
Ethiopia, 357
Europa (ship), 104
Evans, Hugh, 230
Evans, Senator Daniel, 436, 454, 467
Everett, Walt, 7-8, 9, 19 (ill.), 24, 25 (ill.), 33 (ill.), 34
Exeter (*See* Phillips Exeter Academy) Mountaineering Club, 242-43, 310
Exeter (*See* Phillips Exeter Academy) Social Service Organization, 473

Exeter Clinic, 243. *See also* Houston, Dr. Charles
Exeter. *See* Phillips Exeter Academy
Exum, Glen, 164

F

Fairbanks (AK), 95
Fairweather Peninsula, 205. *See also* Mt. Fairweather
Fang Yi, 409
Fanny (sled dog), 51, 60
Fascist Museum, Rome, 227-28
Fatehpur Sikri (India), 423
Ferdozi Hotel, Tehran, 153
Fernandez, Mr., 440
Ferrante and Teicher, 415
Fetcher, John, 7
Fifth Army, 216, 226, 228-29, 231-32; Headquarters (Caserta, Italy), 218
Finarelli, Peggy, 397
Finch, George, 104
Finks, Lt. Col. Jack, 225, 226
First Armored Division, U.S. Army, 220
Fisher Glacier (Canada), 53
Fisher, Jim, 321 (ill.)
Five Miles High, 159-61
Foott, Jeff, 435, 437, 439, 446, 449-50, 452, 458-60
Forbes, Dr., 210
Forbidden City, Beijing, 394, 396
Ford Foundation, 386
Ford, Jim, 208, 209, 214
Fort Myer (Virginia), 185
Fort Portal (Uganda), 355
45th Division, U.S. Army, 220
Fourth Army, 229
Frame, Mike, 321 (ill.)
Frank Russell Company, 421, 425
Fraze, Franz, 184
French Alpine Club, 105
French Alps. *See* Alps, French; Chamonix
Friendship Hotel, Urumchi, 465
Frontier Mail (railway line, India), 107, 143
Fuhrer, Hans, 65
Fuller, Robert, 1

G

Gaborone (Botswana), 403, 406, 408
Gabriel, Sgt. Peter, 192 (ill.), 193, 203
Gafur, Abdul, 385

Gajardo, Capt. (later Maj.) René, 299, 301-2, 304

Ganges River (India), 326-27, 424

Gangtok (Sikkim), 349. *See also* Chogyal; Sikkim

Garhwal (India), 378

Gasherbrum 1 (Hidden Peak), 101, 123, 268, 377, 435. *See also* Hidden Peak

Gatun Lake (Panama), 309

Gauba, Mr. and Mrs., 351, 353

Gaul, Jim, 104

Gaurishankar (Karakoram), 435

Gebirgejäger (German mountain troops), 187

Genghis Khan, 385, 391

Geographical Journal, 397

George Washington University (Washington, DC), 315

Georgi, Michael, 365-66

Germany, 157; end of World War II in, 235

Ghandrung (Nepal), 424

Ghazni (Afghanistan), 148, 389

Ghizathuddin, King of Ghor, 388

Ghor (Afghanistan), 386, 388

Ghorapani (Nepal), 423-24

Ghulam (Hunza porter), 288

Gibson, Capt. E.R. ("Rex"), 164, 193, 195, 197 (ill.), 198-99

Gilbert, Dr., 243

Gile, Les, 323-24

Gilgit (India), 141, 260

Gilkey, Art, 257, 270, 273-74, 276-77, 278 (ill.), 279-80, 284-86, 288; loss of (1953), 282-83; discovery of remains (1993), 285; Gilkey Glacier (AK), 288

Gillespie, Ernie (Phillips Exeter acting principal), 333

Girishk, 150

Glacier Park (U.S./Canada), 311

Glacier Peak (WA), 311-14

Glaciological research. *See* Arctic Institute of North America

Glen House (NH), 9

Goddard, Pvt. William, 193

Godwin-Austen, Henry Haversham, 113

Godwin-Austen Glacier, 124-25, 127, 128 (ill.), 130, 137 (ill.), 138-39, 268-70, 273, 277, 288

Goetze, Ralph, 323

Golden Throne, 123

Goldthwait, Dick, 24, 35

Golmud (China), 448, 455

Gongga Shan (China), 399-401, 411. *See also* Chinese Mountaineering Association; Minya Konka

Goodwin, Maj., 221, 223, 260

Gordonstoun School (Scotland), 314

Gosainkund (Himalaya), 376

Graham, Peter, 295

Grand Teton (WY), 164

Gray Herbarium (Harvard), 10, 35-36

Great Gorge (AK), 191 (ill.)

Great Hall of the People (Urumchi), 434, 439, 466, 468

Great Ice Mountain (Central Asia), 342, 377-78, 397, 451 (ill.), 457, 469. *See also* Ulugh Muztagh

Great Trango Tower (Karakoram), 435. *See also* Trango Towers

Great Wall (China), 395 (ill.), 396

Greece, 156

Gregory, Gen. (quartermaster general), 203, 207

Grice, Lt. Col. (later Col.) L.O., 183-86, 189, 193

Grosvenor, Gilbert, 67; Grosvenor Glacier (Canada), 46

Gruenther, Gen. Alfred M., 225

Guillarmod-Eckenstein Expedition (1902), 127

Gulf of Gaeta (Italy), 225

Guo (Chinese interpreter), 442, 446, 452, 462, 465-67

Gurkhas, 375

Gurung people (Nepal), 316

Gustang Khola, 345

Gyalmo (Queen) of Sikkim. *See* Cooke, Hope

H

Hahn, Kurt, 314

Halebid (India), 352

Hall, Henry, 290 (ill.), 291

Hamadan (Iran), 154

Hamid, Gen. Sha, 262, 263

Hampton Roads (VA), 217

Hansen, 2nd Lt. Paul, 193

Happy Free School (Nepal), 323

Happy Valley Tea Estate (India), 430

Harbage, Prof., 241

Hari Rud River (Afghanistan), 386-88, 390

Haroun al-Raschid, shrine of, 152-53

Harper, Walter, 203; Harper Glacier (AK), 193, 196-97, 199 (ill.), 201
Harrer, Heinrich, 335-36
Hartman, Ambassador Arthur, 394
Harvard Fatigue Laboratories, 210
Harvard Mountaineering Club, 257
Harvard University, 22-23, 358-59, 383, 411. *See also* Dunster House; Lowell; Quincy House
Hassan Abdal (Pakistan), 378
Hattersley-Smith, Geoffrey, 248
Haydon, John ("Johnny"), 40, 42, 47-48, 52-54, 56-61, 62 (ill.), 63 (ill.), 64; snow-blindness, 49-51
Hazara people, 385-86
Hedin, Sven, 398, 446, 448
Heegaard, Flemming, 417, 419
Helmand River (Afghanistan), 150, 151 (ill.)
Henderson, Dr., 41
Henderson, Kenneth, 167
Hendricks, Sterling B., 192 (ill.), 195-99, 203-4
Hennek, Dennis, 435, 437, 439, 446, 449-50, 452, 458-60, 462, 467-68
Herat (Afghanistan), 146, 150-51, 383, 386, 389-90
Herkenrath, Dr., 41-42, 45
Hermitage Hotel, South Island, New Zealand, 295
Heron, Rand, 2
Hicks, John, 1
Hidayat (Hunza porter), 288
Hidden Peak (Gasherbrum 1), 101, 105, 108, 435; Hidden Peak Expedition, 136
Hildreth, Ambassador Horace, 260-62
Hillary, Sir Edmund, 295, 296 (ill.), 374, 423, 430
Himalayan Club (Rawalpindi), 260
Himalchuli (Himalaya), 293
Hitler, Adolf, 234
Hogeboom, Leslie, 291
Hokatika (New Zealand), 295
Holcombe, Arthur (son of Waldo), 383-84, 386, 389
Holcombe, Col., 220-22
Holcombe, Prof. Arthur (father of Waldo), 22-23, 383
Holcombe, Ruth, 243, 383
Holcombe, Sue, 383, 386
Holcombe, Waldo ("Wac"), 22-23, 36, 243, 383-84, 386, 389, 391

Holmes, Burton, 8
Horlicks Company, 102
Hornbein, Dr. Tom, 329, 373, 435, 437, 445, 449-50, 453 (ill.), 455, 457-60, 462-64, 466
Hörnli Hut (Matterhorn), 335
Hoto (Balti village), 120
House Chimney (Abruzzi Ridge), 271, 286; map, 272. *See also* K2
House, Bill, 101, 104, 105 (ill.), 107, 117, 125, 127, 130, 132-133, 135-39, 142-43, 154, 161, 164, 167, 185, 206, 208, 231, 237-41, 473
Houston, Dr. Charles ("Charlie"), 19 (ill.), 25, 28-30, 31 (ill.), 32 (ill.), 34-36, 99, 101, 106, 108-9, 120-21, 123-25, 127, 130, 132-33, 135-40, 142 (ill.), 143, 150-51, 153-54, 156-57, 159, 161, 163, 167, 241, 243, 257, 258 (ill.), 263 (ill.), 264, 265 (ill.), 266-68, 270-74, 276-80, 282-89, 292-93, 473; opens clinic in Exeter (NH), 243; provides medical aid to Baltis, 120, 140
Houston, Oscar, 104, 292-93
Hu Fengling, 461-62
Huancayo (Peru), 309
Huangpu River (China), 396
Huayna Picchu (Peru), 308
Hubbard Glacier, 44, 179; Hubbard-Alverstone Plateau, 249. *See also* Mt. Hubbard
Humayan, Maj., 379
Hungary, 156
Hunsaker, Peter, 161-62, 163
Hunt, John, 335-36, 430
Hunt, Joy, 335-36
Hunza, 378; porters from, 264, 266-67, 269, 271-72, 288
Hurdis, Lt. Col., 168
Hurricane Island (ME) Outward Bound School, 342
Huscroft, Jim, 12, 13-15, 20, 24, 35, 91
Hussain, Akhtar, 261
Hussain, Fazal, 378
Hussain, Maj. Manzoor, 371, 378-79; wedding of (1976), 378-79, 380 (ill.)
Hussain, Mohammed (porter), 289, 373
Hyderabad (India), 352

I

Ibachs, Joe, 21
Ibanda (Uganda), 355, 357

Iceland, 333-35

Ile de France (ship), 163

Imperial Hotel, Delhi, 422, 430

India, 421-22, 430. *See also* Bombay; Calcutta; Dharmsala; Delhi; Ganges River

India-China War (Assam, 1962), 317-18

Indian Aluminum Company, 263

Indus River, 112-14, 116 (ill.), 118-19, 140, 264, 373

International Boundary Commission, 39

International Highway (Chile/Argentina), 302

International House (University of New Hampshire), 363

Iran, 146, 151-54, 376. *See also* Meshed; Persepolis; Tehran

Iraq, 142 (ill.). *See also* Bagdad; Kirkuk; Mosul

Irene Lakes Hut (Uganda), 357

Irvine, Andrew, 125

Isfahan (Iran), 376

Islamabad (Pakistan), 371, 381, 394

Ismailia College (Afghanistan), 146

Isonzo River (Yugoslavia), 187; World War I campaign, 228

Istanbul (Turkey), 154-56, 366, 369

Italy: World War II in, 234. *See also* Anzio; Fifth Army; Naples

J

Jackman, Capt. Albert H. ("Jack"), 169-72, 174-77, 180-81, 186-89, 192 (ill.), 193, 197-98, 201, 203-4, 230

Jacobson, Earl, 170

Jacquot, Gene, 95

Jakar (Bhutan), 426, 430

Jalalabad (Afghanistan), 146

Jaljala Ridge (Himalaya), 344, 348

Jam (Afghanistan), 388; Minaret of, 386-88; Jam River, 387

Jamal (boatman), 419

Janakpur (Nepal), 326

Jang La (pass), 344-45, 347

Japan: end of World War II, 237; troops in Aleutian Islands, 213

Jayal, Nalni, 378, 422

Jersted, Lute, 329

Jervis, Steve, 354-55

Jhelum River, 109

Jigme Singh Wanchuk (King of Bhutan), 425. *See also* Bhutan; Thimphu

Jin Shu, 400, 411

Job Corps, 360

Johannesburg (South Africa), 406-8

Jotunheimen (Norway), 311

Jumna River, 423

K

K2 ("Karakoram 2," Pakistan/China), 98 (ill.), 99-101, 115, 116 (ill.), 121, 123-24, 131 (ill.) 134 (ill.), 135 (ill.), 137 (ill.), 241, 256 (ill.), 261, 269-70, 275 (ill.), 371, 373, 381, 394, 410, 430, 435; 1953 expedition, 257, 472; Japanese expedition (1976), 381; maps, 122, 126; Northeast Ridge, 127, 130; outfitting for, 103; provisioning for, 102-3; Southeast Ridge, 127. *See also* Abruzzi Ridge; Godwin-Austen Glacier; House Chimney

K2—The Savage Mountain, 289, 291

Kabul (Afghanistan), 146, 148, 383-85, 389, 391

Kalahari Desert (southern Africa), 405

Kalat (Pakistan), 149

Kali Gandaki River (Nepal), 294, 344

Kalimpong (India), 348

Kamchatka Peninsula (Russia), 210

Kampala (Uganda), 355, 357

Kanchenjunga (Himalaya), 125, 350. *See also* Sikkim

Kandahar (Afghanistan), 150, 389

Kandersteg (Switzerland), 161

Kanjirobi Himal, 343; Kanjirobi Massif, 346

Kantishna River (AK), 193

Karachi (Pakistan), 260-61, 263

Karakoram Range, 101, 109, 136, 371; map, 111. *See also* K2; Gasherbrum; Masherbrum

Karakoram Road (Hunza to Kashgar), 373, 377-78

Kargil River, 113

Karnak Temple (Egypt), 417

Kars (Turkey), 366

Karstens Ridge (AK), 196-97, 199 (ill.), 200 (ill.)

Karstens, Harry (1913 McKinley expedition), 202

Kasese (Uganda), 355

Kashgar (China), 342, 378

Kashmir, 102, 109, 430; status of, 264. *See also* Azad Kashmir; Dal Lake; Srinagar

Kathmandu, 293, 295, 316-19, 322, 343, 348, 374-76, 410, 423; political tension in, 321. *See also* Nepal; Peace Corps
Kenya, 353
Kerala (India), 351
Kermanshah, 154
Khan, Maj., 263
Khanaqin (Iraq), 142 (ill.), 154
Kharal, 113
Khyber Pass, 145
King Peak, 248
King, Maurice ("Maury"), 248-51, 254; search for, 254-55
Kirkuk (Iraq), 154
Kitar: disappearance of (1939), 273
Kluane Lake (Canada), 39, 40, 42, 64, 71, 77, 80, 82, 87-89, 171
Kochumal, 264-65, 268
Koh-i-Baba Range (Afghanistan), 385
Kolyma River (Russia), 210
Korla (China), 442-43, 445, 459, 464-65, 469
Korophon, 266
Koven, Theodore, 77, 205-6
Krimmel, Bob, 397
Kuchi people, 386-87, 389
Kunlun Shan (China), 397, 401, 409-10
Kusma (Nepal), 348
Kutab Minar (Delhi), 387
Kyangjin (Nepal), 376
Kyichu Dzong (Bhutan), 424

L

La Paz (Bolivia), 307
La Pérouse Glacier (AK), 12
La Pérouse, Comte de (Jean-François de Galaup), 13
Ladakh, 112. *See also* Leh
Lake Bennett (Canada), 41
Lake Garda (Italy), 233-34, 236
Lake Manyara (Tanzania), 353
Lake Naivasha (Kenya), 353
Lake Nakuru (Kenya), 353
Lake Titicaca (Bolivia/Peru), 307
Lake Van (Turkey), 368
Lal Durbar, 343
Land o'Lakes (WI), 210
Langtang (Nepal), 376
Lantern Club (Phillips Exeter Academy), 165, 242
LaVoy, Merle, 202-3, 206
Lawrie, Rob, 260

Lear, Edward, 394
Lee, Howard, 67, 160
Leghorn (Livorno, Italy), 229
Leh (Ladakh), 113-14, 141
Lemesurier Island (AK), 21, 30
Lena River, 210
Lent, Harold, 206
Leonard, Dick, 208
Lewis, Maj. Richard, 225
Lhasa (Tibet), 397-98, 401, 437, 446, 455. *See also* Tibet
Liang (Chinese geologist), 458, 460
Liligo, 267
Lilley, Ambassador James, 409
Lima (Peru), 308-9
Limbu people (Nepal), 316
Lindley-Liek Expedition, Mt. McKinley (1932), 203-6
Link, Capt. Edward, 229
Lissanevitch, Boris, 293, 317-19
Littledale, St. George R., 397-98, 431, 435, 446, 448, 452, 457
Lituya Bay (AK), 12-13, 19, 24, 35
Livermore, Bob, 234
Lloyd, Dr., 159
Logan Plateau (Canada), 40
Loomis, Farnsworth ("Farnie"), 102
Lovat Scouts, British, 212
Lowe, George, 423
Lowell Glacier (Canada), 23, 42-43, 45, 51
Lowell, A. Lawrence (Harvard president), 23
Lu Ming, 437-38, 441-43, 464-66, 468-69
Lumle (Nepal), 423
Lund, Capt. Harold, 192 (ill.), 193
Luxor (Egypt), 417, 419
Lyons, Lt. Col., 211 (ill.)

M

MacArthur, Gen. Douglas, 261
Machhapuchhre (Nepal), 293, 423
Machoi, 112
Machu Picchu (Peru), 308
MacIntosh, Archibald, 290 (ill.)
Madison Hut (Appalachian Mountain Club), 3
Madurai (India), 351
Magar people, 344, 347
Magnavox, 439-40
Mahabalipuram (India), 351

Mahabarat Range (Nepal), 325

Mahdi Khola (Nepal), 423

Mahendra (King of Nepal), 358

Mahmud, 461

Malaspina Glacier (AK/Canada), 245, 248

Mallory, George Leigh, 4, 125

Manaslu (Himalaya), 293

Mangyai Chen (China), 447-48, 463; map: 444

Marchman, Lt. Col. Frank G., 189, 192 (ill.), 193, 196

Marshall, Gen. George, 165

Mary Tenduf La. *See* Phurpa Tenduf La

Masai Mara Reserve (Tanzania), 353

Masherbrum (K1), 100, 123, 138-39, 267 (ill.), 268, 377, 435

Massachusetts Institute of Technology, 397, 435, 454

Matayan (Baltistan), 113

Mathema, Dhruba Bhakta, 322, 423, 425

Matterhorn (Switzerland/Italy), 28; centennial, 335-36

Matthiessen, Peter, 345

Maun (Botswana), 403, 405-6

Mayagdi River (Himalaya), 344

Mazar-i-Sharif (Afghanistan), 383, 389-91

McAnn, Maj., 146

McCarthy (AK), 74, 77

McDade, Dr. Harry, 340, 342-43, 345-48

McGonagall Pass (AK), 193, 205, 206

McGraw-Hill Book Co., 289

McLean, Bill, 208

Mead, Margaret, 2

Mekong River (China), 471

Memorial Hall, Harvard University, 22

Memsahib Expedition (1974), 373

Mendelsohn, Jack, 410

Merton College (Oxford University), 68

Meshed (Iran), 152-54

Metropole Hotel, Karachi, 260

Mexico, 311

Middleswart, Gen., 225-26

Mierouw, Dorothy, 423

Military gear, testing of, 222-30, 232-33, 245, 248. *See also* Doron

Minaret of Jam (Afghanistan), 383, 384 (ill.), 386-88

Miner, Josh, 314, 337, 342. *See also* Outward Bound

Ming Tombs, Beijing, 396

Minnesota Outward Bound School, 342

Minya Konka (Gongga Shan, China), 101, 125, 208, 296, 398

Mirza, Gen., 378, 380

Mitre, 123

Mogul Gardens (India), 430

Mohammed Ali (Hunza porter), 272

Molenaar, Dee, 257, 259 (ill.), 271-72, 274, 279-80, 283-87, 311-13, 397, 472 (ill.)

Molnar, Prof. Peter, 397, 409, 435, 437-38, 440 (ill.), 441, 446-48, 453-57, 459-60, 466, 470 (*See maps*)

Monahan, Bob, 9, 10, 12, 14, 16, 18

Mongols: in India, 388; in Afghanistan, 391

Monkey (sled dog), 51, 54, 56, 61

Mont Blanc, 8-9; conquest of, 100

Monte Rosa (Switzerland), 69

Montecatini (Italy), 229, 231

Moore, Terris ("Terry"), 14, 101, 192 (ill.), 195, 196 (ill.), 197-98, 201, 202 (ill.), 203 (ill.), 205, 208, 254-55, 398, 401, 411

Moran, Father, 329

Moremi Wildlife Reserve (Botswana), 406

Morrison, Clinton, 215, 232

Mosul (Iraq), 155

Mountain Travel, 399-400

Mountain troops, 206, 212; in World War I, 187; in World War II, 188; rope for, 206-7. *See also* Camp Hale; 10th Mountain Division

Mountain warfare, preparation for. *See* Alaskan Test Expedition; Mountain troops; Survival gear, testing of; 10th Mountain Division

Mountain-climbing casualties, 124-25. *See also* Gilkey, Art; Mallory, George; Pasang Kikuli; Wolfe, Dudley

Mountaineering in China. *See* China

Mountains of the Moon. *See* Ruwenzori

Moyers, Bill, 316

Moynihan, Daniel Patrick, 316

Mt. Adams (NH), 3

Mt. Alverstone (Canada), 44, 50, 86, 178 (ill.), 180, 246 (ill.), 249, 250

Mt. Ararat (Turkey), 362 (ill.), 366-68

Mt. Augusta (Canada), 44, 248

Mt. Baker (Ruwenzori), 357

Mt. Bona (AK), 86

Mt. Chomolhari (Himalaya), 101

Mt. Cook (Canada), 248
Mt. Cook (New Zealand), 295
Mt. Crillon (AK), 13-16, 18, 19 (ill.), 20, 24, 26-27 (ill.), 28, 30-31, 33-34, 36, 40, 180, 473
Mt. Dagelet (AK), 33 (ill.), 34
Mt. Elbrus (Russia), 366
Mt. Erciyas (Turkey), 367
Mt. Everest (Himalaya), 100-101, 124, 293, 296, 329, 342, 398, 410-11, 430, 435; 1922 expedition, 100. *See also* American Everest Expedition; Hillary, Sir Edmund; Hornbein, Dr. Tom; Tenzing Norgay; Unsoeld, Willi
Mt. Fairweather (AK), 9, 13-14, 86, 180, 250; map, 17; 1931 expedition, 205
Mt. Foraker (AK), 36, 101, 201
Mt. Gasherbrum. *See* Gasherbrum
Mt. Godwin-Austen. *See* K2
Mt. Hubbard (AK/Canada), 44, 47, 49, 53, 58, 81, 86, 178 (ill.), 180, 245, 246-47 (ill.), 249
Mt. Illimani (Bolivia), 307
Mt. Jette (AK/Canada), 51
Mt. Katahdin (ME), 5
Mt. Kennedy (Canada), 38 (ill.), 50 (ill.), 178 (ill.), 249
Mt. Kilimanjaro (Tanzania), 353
Mt. King George (AK), 45, 65, 179
Mt. Koven (WY), 310
Mt. La Pérouse (AK), 30
Mt. Logan (Canada), 44-45, 65, 86, 170, 248, 250; Mt. Logan Expedition, 16, 40
Mt. Lucania (Canada), 65, 70-71, 72 (ill.), 77-79 (ill.), 81-83, 84 (ill.), 85 (ill.), 96, 103, 171, 178 (ill.), 180, 248
Mt. Madison (NH), 3
Mt. Margherita. *See* Mt. Stanley
Mt. Masherbrum. *See* Masherbrum
Mt. McKinley (Denali) (AK), 164, 190 (ill.), 192, 202 (ill.), 205, 342; map, 194; Mt. McKinley Museum, 205
Mt. McKinley Cosmic Ray Expedition (1932), 205-6
Mt. Moran (WY), 158, 164
Mt. Owen (WY), 164
Mt. Queen Mary (AK), 45, 65, 178 (ill.)
Mt. Ruapehu (New Zealand), 296
Mt. Russell (AK), 337, 338-39 (ill.), 340 (ill.), 342
Mt. Saint Elias (AK/Canada), 19, 37, 45, 71, 86, 248, 250

Mt. Speke (Ruwenzori), 357
Mt. Stanley (Ruwenzori), 357
Mt. Steele (Canada), 65, 71, 77, 80, 86, 87 (ill.), 88 (ill.), 177, 180
Mt. Vancouver (Canada), 44, 81, 178 (ill.), 179, 248, 250
Mt. Waddington (Canada), 101, 208
Mt. Walsh, 174, 177, 178 (ill.), 179, 180 (ill.)
Mt. Washington (NH), 8, 9, 23, 161, 165, 189, 214
Mt. Wood (Canada), 166 (ill.), 171, 172 (ill.), 173 (ill.), 178 (ill.), 180
Mu-Tzu-Taki Shan (Central Asia), 397, 431, 444. *See also* Great Ice Mountain; Ulugh Muztagh
Mueneddin, Mr., 260
Muldrow Glacier (AK), 77, 193, 195 (ill.), 196, 198, 201, 205-6
Murphy, Audie, 222
Murwa, 346
Mush Lake (Canada), 58, 61
Musser, Sgt. Wilbur, 192 (ill.), 193, 205
Mussolini, Benito, death of, 234. *See also* Fascist Museum
Mustang, 343
Muztagh Tower, 123
Myers, Dorothy, 354
Myers, Norman, 354-55
Mysore (India), 351

N
Nairobi (Kenya), 353-55, 357
Nanda Devi (Himalaya), 101, 102, 103, 125
Nanga Parbat (Himalaya), 3, 109, 125, 141, 263, 394; German expedition (1931), 107, 136; 1934 expedition, 279
Nanjing (China), 394, 396
Naples (Italy), 217, 224-25
Narvik (Norway), 187
National Academy of Sciences, 435
National Botanical Garden, Capetown, 407
National Geographic Society, 37, 41, 45-46, 67, 96, 397
National Geographic, 438
Nedou's Hotel, Srinagar, 109, 430
Nehru, Jawaharlal, 293
Nepal I (Peace Corps group), 320
Nepal, 292, 314-15, 317-30, 358, 374-75, 414-15, 421. *See also* Kathmandu; Mt. Everest; Peace Corps

Nepali (language), 316

Nettuno (Italy), 218, 220, 227

Neustadtal, Sarah, 438

New Orleans (LA), 297

New York Times, The, 289, 364, 410

New Yorker, The, 292

New Zealand Alpine Club, 295

New Zealand, 295. *See also* Auckland; Hillary, Sir Edmund

Newari (Nepalese dialect), 316

Nez Perce (WY), 164

Ngorongoro Crater (Tanzania), 353

Nickerson, Al, 24

Niebling, Dick, 184

Nile River (Egypt), 417, 419; source of, 357

Nilgiri (Nepal), 424

Nilsson, Einar, 192 (ill.), 195, 196 (ill.), 197-98, 201 (ill.), 202, 203 (ill.), 208

Nima Tenzing (Sherpa), 343, 347-48

Nimi (wife of Manzoor Hussain), 380

Nimla (Afghanistan), 146

Nishapur (Iran), 153

Nixon, President Richard, 396

Noah's Ark, 366-68. *See also* Mt. Ararat

Nolde, Joe, 342

Nome (AK), 214

Nord Deutscher Lloyd, 157, 162

Normandie (ship), 161

Northeast Ridge (K2). *See* K2

Norway, 311. *See also* Jotunheimen

Nunatak Fiord (Canada), 51

Nunn, Senator Sam, 415

O

O'Daniel, Gen. "Iron Mike," 221, 224

Obeh (Afghanistan), 388

Oberlin, Gail, 163, 290 (ill.), 291, 297; marriage to Robert H. Bates (1954), 290-92. *See also* Bates, Gail Oberlin

Oberlin, John, 301, 307, 310-11

Odell, Jamie, 403, 405-6

Odell, Jim, 403, 406, 408

Odell, Mac, 318, 403, 406

Odell, Marcia, 403, 406

Odell, Mona, 335

Odell, Noel, 295, 335

Odell, Peggy, 403, 406, 408

Office of Strategic Services, 216

Office of the Quartermaster General (OQMG), U.S. Army, 169, 183-184, 186-187, 189, 227-28, 231, 235

Oggi, Kilian, 161

Ogunquit (ME), 65, 211

Ojos del Salado (Chile/Argentina), 299, 301, 303, 306-7; map, 300

Okavango Delta (Botswana), 406; Okavango River, 406

Olduvai Gorge (Tanzania), 353

Operation Muskox (U.S./Canada), 237-39

Oran (Algeria), 225-26

Oregon Outward Bound School, 342

Orissa (India), 351

Orr, Bob, 213

Outward Bound, 314, 337, 361, 473; at Hurricane Island, ME, 342; in Ely, MN, 342; in Marble, CO, 315, 317, 342; in Oregon, 342

Owens, Dr. Lance, 399-401, 411

Owens, Jackie, 411

Oxford University, 68, 107, 159

Oxus River. *See* Amu Darya

P

Paccard, Dr. Michel-Gabriel, 100

Padma Sambhava, 425-27

Paiju (Himalaya), 123, 267-68, 372 (ill.), 373

Pakistan Airlines, 394

Pakistan Mountaineering Association, 378

Pakistan, 260, 381; government of, 257; mountaineering in, 378-81. *See also* Islamabad; K2; Rawalpindi; Triple Expedition

Palestrina (Italy), 227

Palmer-Thompkinson, Peter ("Tony"), 161

Pan American Airways, 42, 95

Panama, 301, 309; Panama Canal, 296, 309

Panjao (Afghanistan), 386

Panshir River (Afghanistan), 385

Paris: at onset of World War II, 162; during World War II, 231-32; France et Choiseul Hotel, 260

Park Hotel, Shanghai, 396

Parker Pass (AK), 197, 204

Parker, Prof., 202-3

Paro (Bhutan), 424

Parwanipur (Nepal), 323

Pasang Kikuli (K2 Sherpa), 117, 123, 135-36, 138-39, 430; disappearance of (1939), 273, 430

Patagonia (sporting goods), 435

Patna (India), 424

Paumgarten, Harald, 9, 12, 16

Peace Corps, 314-15, 349, 353, 357, 473; importance in Nepal, 317-18; in Nepal, 317-30, 403,423; local reactions to, 320-21; volunteers, 315, 320, 321 (ill.), 322-23

Pearl Harbor, bombing of, 188-89

Pearson, Grant, 206

Pedernales (Chile), 302

Pegasus myth, 368-69

Penn Charter (private school, PA), 5, 37

People's Republic of China. *See* China

Periyar game park (India), 351

Perry, Dr. Lewis (Phillips Exeter principal), 184, 159-60, 184, 257

Perry, Prof. Bliss, 7

Persepolis (Iran), 376

Peru, 307; map, 300. *See also* Cuzco; Lima; Machu Picchu

Peshawar (Pakistan), 143-44, 378-80, 393

Petzoldt's Overhang (Abruzzi Ridge), 271

Petzoldt, Paul K., 102, 104-5, 107, 109-10, 115, 117, 120-21, 123, 125, 127, 130, 132-33, 135-39, 144, 159-60, 164

Phagune Dorji, 344, 348

Phagune Pass, 345

Phillips Andover Academy, 314

Phillips Exeter Academy (private school, NH), 5, 67, 159-60, 227, 237, 240-41, 248, 257, 261, 299, 311, 314, 330, 333, 337, 358, 421, 473. *See also* Exeter (NH) Mountaineering Club; Lantern Club; Perry, Dr. Lewis; Saltonstall, Bill

Phinsoo (K2 Sherpa), 110, 117; disappearance of (1939), 273

Phoksumdo Tal (Himalaya), 343, 345-46

Phoo Dorji (Sherpa), 343, 347

Phuntsholing (Bhutan), 424g, 428

Phurpa (Mary) Tenduf La, 428, 429 (ills.)

Piedra Pomez Pass, 305

Pieh, John, 342

Pinkham Notch (NH), 8, 9

Pinnacle Gully (NH), 9

Pir Panjal Range, 109

Pitcairn Island, 296

Platts, Howard ("Hugo"), 25

Plettenberg Bay (South Africa), 407

Pnom Penh (Cambodia), 330

Po River (Italy), 233

Pobeda (China), 394

Pointed Peak. *See* Mt. Kennedy

Pokhara (Nepal), 293, 294 (ill.), 323, 344, 423-24

Poland, 369; invasion of (World War II), 162

Polo, Marco, 446

Poon Hill (Nepal), 423

Popenoe, Ollie, 316

Porter House, Phillips Exeter Academy, 299

Porters. *See* Hunza; Satpura; Sherpas

Potrerillos (Chile), 301-2

Pradhan, Amanda, 425

Pretoria, 406-7

Prince Rupert (Canada), 12, 65, 170

Princess Charlotte (ship), 170

Prithni Narayan College (Nepal), 323, 423

Pul-i-Khumri (Afghanistan), 390

Punakha (Bhutan), 425-26

Punmah Glacier, 121; Punmah River, 266, 375 (ill.)

Puri (India), 351

Putha Hiunchuli, 345

Q

Qinhai Province (China), 437, 447

Quartermaster Corps, U.S. Army, 193, 216, 221, 236, 240, 248. *See also* Office of the Quartermaster General

Quartermaster General. *See* Office of the Quartermaster General

Queen Elizabeth National Park (Uganda), 354

Queen Mary (ship), 109

Quincy House (Harvard University), 358-59

Quintana, Mr., 441

R

Raffles Hotel, Singapore, 295

Rai people (Nepal), 316

Randall, Bob, 42-43, 44 (ill.), 45-46, 64

Randolph (NH) Mountain Club, 4

Rawalpindi (Pakistan), 107-9, 260, 262, 289, 371, 373, 378, 380

Read, Al, 399-401

Reagan, Nancy, 414

Reagan, President Ronald, 414

Recreation Equipment (REI), Seattle, 435

Reeve Airways, 74, 75 (ill.). *See also* Reeve, Bob

Reeve, Bob, 72 (ill.), 73-74, 75-77, 97
Reykjavik (Iceland), 333-34
Rhine, Dr. Mark, 322, 330
Richardson Highway (AK), 95, 96
Richardson, Edith Newell, 1. *See also* Bates, Edith Richardson
Riley, Dick, 9, 11-12, 16
Rimpfischhorn (Switzerland), 335
Ro-Jeng (China), 446-47, 463; map, 444
Roberts, Col. Jimmy, 343
Roberts, Dianne, 414
Robertson, David A., 66 (ill.), 68-69, 104
Robinson, Bestor, 171, 174, 184, 186, 208, 231, 235
Robinson, Gen., 188
Roch, André, 335
Rockefeller, Jay, 316
Rognan, Ernie, 13
Rohagaon (Nepal), 346-47
Romania, 364
Rome (Italy), 226-27, 228
Roosevelt, President Franklin D., death of, 232
Rose, John, 295
Rosenthal, A.M. ("Abe"), 410
Royal Afghan Mail, 146
Royal Geographical Society (London), 397, 430
Royal Guest House (Sikkim), 348, 350
Royal Hotel, Kathmandu, 293, 317, 322. *See also* Lissanevitch, Boris
Russell Fiord (Yukon), 45-46
Russell, George, 243, 248, 421-25, 427 (ill.), 428, 429 (ill.), 430, 437, 473
Russell, Jane, 421-22, 425, 428, 429 (ill.), 430, 437
Russians, in Afghanistan, 390
Ruwenzori (Uganda/Zaire), 354-57
Rymill, John, 106-7

S

Sabzawar (Iran), 153
Sacred Thread Ceremony (Nepal), 328, 358
Saint Elias Mountains (AK/Canada), 51, 65, 95, 168, 178 (ill.), 245
Salang Pass (Afghanistan), 385, 390; Salang Tunnel, 390
Salar de Maricunga (Chile), 302, 305
Saltonstall, Bill (Phillips Exeter principal), 261, 292, 314
Saltonstall, Bob, 383, 388-89

Saltonstall, Dr. Henry, 243
Saltonstall, Nancy, 383, 388-89
Santa, 324
Santiago (Chile), 306
Satpura (Balti village), 119, 121; porters from, 124, 289, 371, 372 (ill.), 373
Saturday Evening Post, 289
Savoia Col, 125, 127; Savoia Glacier, 100, 124, 125, 127, 138, 288, 373; Savoia Pass, 100, 373. *See also* K2
Savuti Channel (Botswana), 405-6
Schaller, George, 345
Schmaderer, Ludwig, 107
Schoening, Pete, 257, 258 (ill.), 263, 273-74, 276-80, 282-84, 286-89, 311, 313, 434 (ill.), 435, 437, 441, 443, 446, 450, 454-55, 457-61, 468 (ill.), 471, 472 (ill.)
Scott, Willard, 415
Scrambles in the Alps (Whymper), 3-4, 28
Second Division, U.S. Army, 210
Sella, Vittorio (photographer), 101, 124, 125
Senner, George, 311
Serengeti Plain (Tanzania), 353
Service, John, 398
Seven Lakes Region (Slovenia), 363
Seventh Infantry, U.S. Army, 227
Seward Glacier (AK/Canada), 44, 245, 248, 254
Shah Dev. *See* Birendra
Shah Jehan, 423. *See also* Taj Mahal
Shahr-i-Zohak (Afghanistan), 385
Shaksgam, 140
Shanghai (China), 394, 396
Shankar Hotel, Kathmandu, 374, 423
Sharp, Dr. Robert, 171, 181, 245, 248, 254
Sheep Glacier, 174
Sheldon, Don, 340, 342
Shelley, Prof., 99
Sherpas, 115, 117-19, 121, 125, 127 (ill.), 130, 132, 135, 136, 138, 141, 343; on 1938 K2 Expedition, 108-10. *See also* Pasang Kikuli; Tse Tendrup
Shey (Nepal, Himalaya), 345-46
Shi Ya Feng, 400
Shibar Pass (Afghanistan), 385
Shigar (Baltistan), 114, 116, 119, 140, 264, 289, 447; rajah of, 114, 116-17, 264, 373; Shigar River, 140
Shipton, Eric, 335-36, 340 (ill.), 341-42, 430, 469

Shrestha, Narayan Prasad, 358, 359 (ill.), 360, 375
Shriver, Sargent, 314-16, 329-30, 333
Shute, Mrs., 299
Sierra Club, 171
Sikkim, 348-50; Chogyal of, 348-50; schools in, 349-50
Sikong Expedition (1932), 398-400, 411. *See also* Minya Konka
Siliguri (India), 349, 424, 428
Silk Road, 397, 446. *See also* China; Kashgar; Urumchi; Xinjiang Province
Sind Desert (Pakistan), 102, 107, 262-63
Singh (Bhutanese guide), 424-25, 428
Singh, Jogindar, 422
Singha Durbar (Kathmandu), 324
Siple, Paul, 183-84, 186, 211
Siwalik Hills (Nepal), 325
Skagway (AK), 41, 65, 170
Skardu (Baltistan), 110, 114-18, 140-41, 261, 263-64, 269, 289, 447; rajah of, 114, 264, 371; valley of, 114
Ski troops. *See* Mountain troops; 10th Mountain Division
Skoro La (pass), 140, 289
Skyang Kangri, 138
Slauta, Michael, 216-19, 221-24, 226-29, 231, 235; in rodeo at Acciarella, 223-24
Slovenia, 363
Smith, Macauley, 164
Smith, Phil, 397
Smith, Tom, 12, 20-21, 35
Smithsonian Institution, 214, 409
Smythe, Frank, 212
Snow Leopard, The (Matthiessen), 345
Sochi (Russia), 366
Soto, 304, 306
South Africa, 406-7
South African Airways, 408
Southern Lights (Rymill), 106
Special Forces section, QMC, U.S. Army, 208, 212-13, 226, 231, 236
"Specter of the brocken," 28
Sport Hotel, Urumchi, 438
Srinagar, 109, 115, 124, 141, 143, 264, 430
Standardization branch, Office of the Quartermaster General, 184-85
Stanley Plateau (Uganda), 357
Stanvac, 293
Stassen, Gov. Harold, 261-62
State Department, U.S., 358-59, 398, 414

Stebbins, Ambassador Henry, 316-17, 355, 357-58, 375
Stebbins, Barbara, 316-17, 355, 357
Steele Cirque, 180. *See also* Mt. Steele
Steele Glacier. *See* Wolf Creek Glacier
Steele-Lucania Plateau, 77, 80, 82, 83 (ill.), 90
Stefansson, Vilhjalmur, 208
Strathaird (ship), 293
Streatfeild, Capt. Norman, 101, 108 (ill.), 124, 125, 130, 139, 140, 143-44, 162-63
Streather, Capt. Tony, 258 (ill.), 262-63, 266, 267 (ill.), 268, 272, 274, 276-77, 279-80, 282, 284-88
Stuck expedition, Mt. McKinley (1913), 203
Stuck, Archdeacon Hudson, 202, 204
Studebaker Company, 237
Stuhlmann Pass (Uganda), 355, 357
Suez Canal, 106
Suffering Moses II, 430
Suli Gad, 346
Sullivan, Gen., 218-19, 223, 225, 229-30, 232-35
Summer Palace, Beijing, 396
Sun Hong Li, 400-401
Sun Yat-sen, 383
Surkh Kotal (Afghanistan), 390
Surtsey (Iceland), 334
Survival gear, development of, 186-88; testing of, 180, 185-86, 189, 193-206, 208-14. *See also* Alaskan Test Expedition; Military gear; 10th Mountain Division
Survival rations, army, testing of, 174, 176, 197-98
Svanetia (ship), 156
Swat (Pakistan), 393; Akhond (Wali) of, 394
Sweden, 369
Switzerland, 311
Syria, 155

T

Table Mountain, Capetown, 407
Taj Mahal (India), 423
Takla Makan (China), 445
Tamang people (Nepal), 316-19, 344
Tang Valley (Bhutan), 428
Tanzania, 353
Tarakot (Nepal), 345, 347

Tarim River (China), 445-46
Tashichhodzong (Bhutan), 425
Tashkurghan (Afghanistan), 390
Tasman Glacier (New Zealand), 295
Tatopani (Himalaya), 344
Tatra Mountains (now Slovakia), 369
Taylor, Andy, 39-42, 46-47, 49, 51-52, 206
Taylor, Art, 410. *See also* Tsering Yangdon
Taylor, Miss, 146, 148-49, 151, 153, 160
Taylor, Nima, 410
Te Anau (New Zealand), 295
Teesta River (Nepal), 349
Tehmer Devamette, Xinjiang Governor, 437-38, 463, 465-68
Tehran (Iran), 153, 376
Tel Kochek (Syria), 155
Temple of Heaven, Beijing, 396
10th Mountain Division, U.S. Army, 212, 226, 228-30, 233-34
Tenzing Norbu, 430
Tenzing Norgay, 430
Terai (Nepal), 317, 325, 420 (ill.), 423
Tetons (WY), 158, 164
Tex (sled dog), 56
The Pas (Canada), 209
Thimphu (Bhutan), 425, 428
Third Division, U.S. Army, 220-23, 226-28
30th Infantry Regiment, U.S. Army, 222, 224, 227-28
34th Division, U.S. Army, 220, 232
Thomas, Lowell, Jr., 342
Thorington, Dr. James Monroe, 164
Tiananmen Square, Beijing, 394
Tibet, 363, 397-98, 401, 422, 437, 451, 471; invasion by China (1959), 348; Tibetan Plateau, 409, 470. *See also* Dalai Lama; Tibetan refugees
Tibetan refugees, 344, 348, 362, 430. *See also* Dalai Lama; Darjeeling; Dharmsala; Tsering Yangdon
Tichu-Rong, 347
Tien Shan (Kirghizia/China), 394
Tiger Tops (Nepal Terai), 423
Tiger's Nest (Bhutan), 425
Tigris River, 155
Tilman, H.W. ("Bill"), 108, 342, 469
Time magazine, 412
Times, The (London), 115, 155
Tinogasta (Argentina), 302

Tip (sled dog), 61
Tito, Marshal, 218-19
Toffey, Lt. Col., 227
Tolson, Mr., FBI official, 236
Tolti, 119; rajah of, 114
Tongsa (Bhutan), 426, 428; Valley, 430
Tornovo (Bulgaria), 366
Towers of Silence (Bombay), 107
Townsend, Paul, 248
Tragbal Pass, 141
Trango Towers (Karakoram), 123, 373. *See also* Great Trango Tower
Trenton (NJ) State Teachers College, 337
Tribhuvan University (Nepal), 358
Trieste, 363
Triglav (Yugoslavia), 363
Triple Expedition, 378, 380-81, 393
Truscott, Gen., 221, 224; "Truscott trot," 221
Truslow, Fred, 310
Tse Tendrup (K2 Sherpa), 140
Tsering Yangdon, 348, 362-63, 410
Tucker, Don, 5
Tuckerman Ravine (NH), 189
Tulcea (Romania), 364
Turfan (China), 412, 439; Turfan Depression, 412
Turkey, 155-56, 366-69. *See also* Chimaera; Dogubayazit; Istanbul; Mt. Ararat
Tuveson, Lee, 321 (ill.)
Twaddle, Col. (later Brig. Gen.) Harry L., 167-70
Tweedsmuir Glacier (Yukon), 46
Twiss, John, 414

U

U-boats, 217
U.S. AID, 417; in Nepal, 317, 319-20, 322-23
U.S. Army Map Service, 435-36
U.S. Geological Survey, 397
Uganda Mountain Club, 355
Uganda, 353-54
Ugyenchoeding (Bhutan), 428
Uigur people. *See* Tehmer Devamette; Urumchi; Xinjiang Province
Ulugh Muztagh (Central Asia), 374, 381, 393, 396-401, 409-12, 414, 421-22, 430-31, 434, 436, 438-39, 446, 449, 451 (ill.), 452, 455, 457, 459, 469; dispute over altitude, 398; map, 444.*See*

also Chinese Mountaineering
  Association; Great Ice Mountain;
  Triple Expedition
UNICEF, 428
Uniranger Laser Ranging System, 436,
  438, 454-55
University of New Hampshire, 362-63,
  411, 436
University of Pennsylvania, 2, 4, 36-37,
  67, 99, 159-60, 241, 316
Unsoeld family, 315, 317
Unsoeld, Jolene, 312, 314-15, 329, 343,
  348
Unsoeld, Terris, 329
Unsoeld, Willi, 311-15, 322, 329-30, 343,
  348, 435
Untermeyer, Chace, 410
Urdukas, 123, 267-68
Urumchi (China), 394, 411, 412, 430,
  433, 437-43, 447, 453-54, 458, 460,
  462, 464-65, 469; map, 444. *See also*
  Great Hall of the People; Xinjiang
  Province

V

Valdez (AK), 73 (ill.), 74
Vale of Kashmir, 109
Valiant Glacier, 174
Varna (Bulgaria), 365-66
Vaughn, Jack, 316
Vestmannaeyjar (Iceland), 334
Victoria Island (Canada), 239
Vilyati (Hunza porter), 288
Vis (Yugoslavia), 218-19
Vista Program, 360
Voortrekker Monument (Pretoria), 406-7

W

Walker, Col., 168
Waller, James, 123
Wang (geologist, also "Mudhen"), 447-
  48, 466
Wang Fuzhou, 411, 422, 438, 469-70
Wang Zenghua, 438, 442, 445-46, 448,
  450, 452-56, 459-60, 462, 464, 466,
  468 (ill.)
War Department, U.S., 184. *See also*
  Special Forces; Survival gear; World
  War II
War Production Board, 186
Warren, Bill, 353-54, 357
Warren, Jay, 353-54, 357

Washburn, Barbara, 414
Washburn, Bradford ("Brad"), 6 (ill.), 8,
  9, 14, 16, 18, 19 (ill.), 23-25, 28-31,
  33-34, 36-37, 39-47, 49-51, 53, 60-61,
  64-65, 71, 72 (ill.), 74-77, 80-83, 85
  (ill.), 86, 87 (ill.), 90-95, 102-3, 171,
  177, 189, 192 (ill.), 193, 195-98, 199
  (ill.), 201, 202-3, 205, 208, 301, 400,
  410, 414, 423, 435, 454, 472 (ill.), 473;
  as Boston Museum of Science director,
  208, 359; Everest map, 410, 423; snow-
  blindness, 30-31
Washburn, Sherry, 8, 9
Washington (ship), 162-63
Washington, DC, 414. *See also* Special
  Forces; State Department; White
  House
Wasson, Everett, 42, 44-45
Weasels (all-terrain vehicles), 237-39
Weaver, Peter, 301
Webb, Flt. Lt. Peter, 192 (ill.), 193, 197,
  203
Wells, Dick, 7, 8, 11
Whirlwind Glacier, 177, 180
White House (Washington, DC), 414-16
White Mountains (NH), 3-4, 8, 160-61,
  165, 169. *See also* Mt. Washington
White, John, 323
Whitehorse (Canada), 44, 64, 170
Whitehorse Ledge (NH), 214
Whittaker, Jim, 373, 414
Whymper, Edward, 28. *See also Scrambles
  in the Alps*
Wiessner, Fritz, 270; K2 Expedition
  (1939), 270-71
Wilkins, Sir Hubert, 208-9, 211
Willauer, Peter, 342
Williamson, Jed, 342
Wilson, Jumbo, 162
Wind River Range (WY), 310-11
Windamere Hotel, Darjeeling, 430
Windy Gap, 138, 140
Winnipeg (Canada), 209
Winter gear, development and testing of.
  See Military gear; Survival gear
Wolf Creek Glacier, 71, 77, 87, 89, 171;
  Wolf Creek, 174
Wolfe, Dudley: disappearance of (1939),
  273, 430; discovery of remains (1993),
  273
Wolfer, Col., 227
Wood Yukon Expedition (1941), 170

Wood, Foresta, 64, 71, 170, 172-74, 181, 245, 248, 250-51, 253 (ill.), 254; search for, 254-55
Wood, Peter, 248-49, 251, 290 (ill.)
Wood, Valerie, 248, 250-51, 254; search for, 254-55
Wood, Walter A., Jr., 64, 71, 77, 80, 82, 87-89, 167-71, 172 (ill.), 173, 177, 179-80, 189, 192-93, 197, 237-40, 245, 248-52, 253 (ill.), 254, 290 (ill.), 291
Woodbury, Bob, 208, 213-14
Woodruff, Maj. Gen., 167
Workman, Fanny Bullock, 121
Workman, William Hunter, 121
World War II, 170, 473; American readiness for, 189; prelude to, 161. *See also* Anzio; Battle of Britain; Fifth Army; Military gear; Mountain troops; Paris; Pearl Harbor; Poland; Survival gear; 10th Mountain Division
Woyil Bridge, 110
Wren, Christopher, 410
Wright, Bill, 230
Wu Qianxin, 461
Wu Yikang, 410
Wulsin, Fred, 208
Wylde, John, 301
Wylie, Barbara, 323
Wylie, Col., 319-20

X

Xaxaba, Chief's Island (Botswana), 406
Xian (China), 411-12
Xinjiang Institute of Geography (China), 412
Xinjiang Mountaineering Association, 465-66. *See also* Chinese Mountaineering Association

Xinjiang Province (China), 378, 411-13, 434, 436-39, 441, 449-51, 465-66, 468. *See also* Karakoram Road; Kashgar; Turfan; Ulugh Muztagh; Urumchi
Xinjiang Sports Federation, 437

Y

Yakutat (AK), 51-52, 60, 245, 248-49, 254-55; Yakutat Bay, 45, 51, 254
Yangtze River (China), 396
Yeager, Chuck, 414
Yerevan (Armenia), 366
Yoshizawa, Mr., 381
Yucatan (Mexico), 361-62; Mayan temples in, 361
Yugoslavia, 156, 363
Yukon River, 41
Yukon Territory (Canada), 23, 39, 41, 51. *See also* Bates Lake; Carcross; Mt. Logan; Saint Elias Mountains
Yukon White Pass Railroad, 170
Yunnan Province (China), 470-71
Yuno, 117-19

Z

Zaire, 354
Zermatt (Switzerland), 69, 335-36. *See also* Matterhorn centennial
Zhaks (inflatable rafts), 118-19, 140, 264-65, 289
Zhang Baohua, 461-62
Zhi Zhan Zhun, 394, 396, 398-401, 411, 422
Zhou Zheng, 438, 442, 454, 456-57, 459-60, 469-71
Zmutt Ridge (Matterhorn), 336
Zoji La (pass), 100, 108, 110, 112